The Legal Foundations of Public Administration

Third Edition

The Legal Foundations of Public Administration

Third Edition

**DONALD D. BARRY &
HOWARD R. WHITCOMB
Emeritus Professors of Political Science, Lehigh University**

ROWMAN & LITTLEFIELD PUBLISHERS, INC.
Lanham Boulder New York Toronto Oxford

ROWMAN & LITTLEFIELD PUBLISHERS, INC.

Published in the United States of America
by Rowman & Littlefield Publishers, Inc.
A wholly owned subsidiary of The Rowman & Littlefield Publishing Group, Inc.
4501 Forbes Boulevard, Suite 200, Lanham, Maryland 20706
www.rowmanlittlefield.com

PO Box 317
Oxford
OX2 9RU, UK

Copyright © 2005 by Rowman & Littlefield Publishers, Inc.

British Library Cataloging in Publication Information Available

Library of Congress Cataloging-in-Publication Data

Barry, Donald D., 1934–
   The legal foundations of public administration / Donald D. Barry &
Howard R. Whitcomb.
    p. cm.
Includes bibliographical references and index.
ISBN 0-7425-4380-3 (cloth : alk. paper)
1. Administrative law—United States. 2. Administrative
procedure—United States. 3. Public administration—United
States. 1. Whitcomb, Howard R. II. Title.
KF5402.B37 2005

                2004015161

Printed in the United States of America

♾ ™ The paper used in this publication meets the minimum of American National Standard for Information Sciences—Permanence of Paper for Printed Library Materials, ANSI/NISO Z39.48-1992.

This book is dedicated to Dianne and Annie.

Summary of Contents

Table of Cases   xv
Preface   xix
Acknowledgments   xxi

PART ONE   The Development of Administrative Law   *1*
  Chapter 1   Administrative Authority and Law   3
  Chapter 2   Origin and Development of the Administrative Process   21

PART TWO   Legislative and Judicial Controls over the Administrative Process   *49*
  Chapter 3   Delegation of Power   51
  Chapter 4   Judicial Review of Administrative Determinations   77

PART THREE   The Internal Administrative Process   *117*
  Chapter 5   Investigatory Power   119
  Chapter 6   Rules and Rule Making   145
  Chapter 7   The Right to Be Heard and Adjudicatory Policy Making   173
  Chapter 8   Informal Activity and the Exercise of Discretion   205

PART FOUR   Remedies   *231*
  Chapter 9   Remedies against Improper Administrative Acts   233
  Chapter 10   Open Government   261

APPENDIXES   *275*
  A.   Source Materials in Administrative Law, by Roseann Bowerman   277
  B.   Administrative Procedure Act   285
  C.   The Constitution of the United States of America   333

INDEX   351

Contents

Table of Cases   *xv*
Preface   *xix*
Acknowledgments   *xxi*

PART ONE
The Development of Administrative Law   *1*

Chapter 1
Administrative Authority and Law   *3*

Administrative Law as an Amalgam of Centrifugal Forces   *3*
   Types of Agencies Encompassed by Administrative Law   *4*
Administrative Law as a Unified Subject   *6*
The Administrative Process   *7*
   Delegation of Power   *7*
   Judicial Review   *7*
   Investigatory Power   *8*
   Rules and the Rule-Making Process   *8*
   The Right to Be Heard and Adjudicatory Policy Making   *8*
   Informal Activity and the Exercise of Discretion   *9*
   Remedies against Improper Administrative Acts   *9*
   Open Government   *9*
The Political Component of Administrative Law   *10*
   Dalton v. *Specter*   *10*
   Weiner v. *United States*   *13*
A Note on Analyzing Court Cases   *16*
   Briefing a Case   *17*

Chapter 2
Origin and Development of the Administrative Process   *21*

Historical Development of the American Administrative Process   *21*
   James O. Freedman, *Crisis and Legitimacy: The Administrative Process*
     and American Government   *23*
   The Administrative Procedure Act of 1946   *25*

The Administrative Procedure Act at a Half Century   *28*
 David H. Rosenbloom, *1946: Framing a Lasting Congressional Response
  to the Administrative State*   *29*
 Philip J. Harter, *The APA at Fifty: A Celebration, Not a
  Puzzlement*   *37*
 Philip K. Howard, *Keynote Address: Administrative Procedure and the
  Decline of Responsibility*   *39*
 Andrew F. Popper, *Administrative Law in the 21st Century*   *42*
A Century of Administrative Law Literature   *44*
 Emergence of Administrative Law as a Recognized Component of
  American Public Law   *44*
 Post–World War II Administrative Law Scholarship   *47*

PART TWO
Legislative and Judicial Controls over the Administrative Process   *49*

Chapter 3
Delegation of Power   *51*

Delegation by Congress   *51*
 The *Panama* Case   *52*
 The *Schechter* Case   *52*
Recent Judicial Views on Nondelegation   *55*
 Admonitions to Congress   *57*
Judicial Narrowing of Congressional Delegation   *58*
 Kent v. *Dulles*   *58*
 Whitman, Administrator of Environmental Protection Agency v.
  American Trucking Associations, Inc.   *62*
The Legislative Veto   *65*
 Immigration and Naturalization Service v. *Chadha*   *66*
Post-*Chadha* Delegation (Gramm-Rudman-Hollings)   *70*
 Constitutional Objections to Gramm-Rudman-Hollings   *70*
Congressional Delegation to the Judiciary   *72*
 Mistretta v. *United States*   *72*

Chapter 4
Judicial Review of Administrative Determinations   *77*

The Common Law of Judicial Review   *77*
 The Reviewability Question   *78*
 Case Law Concerning Reviewability   *78*
Preclusion of Judicial Review   *81*
 Bowen v. *Michigan Academy of Family Physicians*   *83*
Administrative Actions Committed by Law to Agency Discretion   *86*
 Citizens to Preserve Overton Park, Inc. v. *Volpe*   *87*
 Lincoln v. *Vigil*   *91*
A Sampling of Threshold Questions: Exhaustion and Standing   *93*
 Exhaustion of Administrative Remedies   *94*
 Porter v. *Nussle*   *95*

Standing   *98*
  Bennett v. *Spear*   *98*
Scope of Judicial Review   *103*
  Substantial Evidence   *105*
    Universal Camera Corp. v. *National Labor Relations Board*   *105*
  The Law-Fact Distinction   *109*
    National Labor Relations Board v. *Hearst Publications, Inc.*   *110*
  Scope of Judicial Review after the *Chevron* Case   *114*

PART THREE
The Internal Administrative Process   *117*

Chapter 5
Investigatory Power   *119*

Overview of the Internal Administrative Process   *119*
The Subpoena Power and Related Processes   *121*
  Federal Trade Commission v. *American Tobacco Co.*   *121*
  Oklahoma Press Pub. Co. v. *Walling*   *122*
Legality of Investigative Devices   *124*
  United States v. *Euge*   *125*
The Inspection of Premises   *128*
  Camara v. *Municipal Court of the City and County of San
    Francisco*   *129*
  Warrants in Administrative Investigations   *132*
  Marshall v. *Barlow's, Inc.*   *133*
Subpoenas and Inspections: Diverging Trends?   *136*
  New York v. *Burger*   *138*
  Donovan v. *Lone Steer, Inc.*   *142*

Chapter 6
Rules and Rule Making   *145*

The United States Quickly Amends a Rule   *145*
Rules in General   *147*
  Three Kinds of Rules   *148*
  United States v. *Picciotto*   *150*
Rule Making   *152*
  Notice and Comment   *153*
  Exemptions to Notice and Comment and Other Rule-Making
    Procedures   *154*
  Informal and Formal Rule Making   *155*
  United States v. *Florida East Coast Ry. Co.*   *157*
  Vermont Yankee Nuclear Power Corp. v. *Natural Resources Defense
    Council, Inc.*   *160*

Deregulation and Rule Making   *162*
   Motor Vehicle Manufacturers Association v. *State Farm Mutual*
     Automobile Insurance Company   *163*
Rule Making and Its Control   *166*
   The Role of Congress   *167*
   The Role of the President   *171*
   The Role of the Courts   *172*
Conclusion   *172*

Chapter 7
The Right to Be Heard and Adjudicatory Policy Making   *173*

The Right to Be Heard   *173*
   The Right-Privilege Distinction   *174*
   Goldberg v. *Kelly*   *175*
   Mathews v. *Eldridge*   *177*
   Application of the *Mathews* Doctrine   *181*
   Hodel v. *Virginia Surface Mining and Reclamation Association,*
     Inc.   *182*
Civil Forfeiture and Due Process   *184*
   United States v. *James Daniel Good Real Property*   *186*
Degree of Formality   *190*
   Goss v. *Lopez*   *191*
Adjudication and Policy Making   *195*
   Securities and Exchange Commission v. *Chenery Corporation*   *196*

Chapter 8
Informal Activity and the Exercise of Discretion   *205*

Advice from Governmental Officials: An Example of Informal
   Activity   *207*
   Estopping the Government   *207*
   Office of Personnel Management v. *Richmond*   *208*
   Barry I. Fredericks v. *Commissioner of Internal Revenue*   *213*
   Estoppel Remedies without Estoppel   *217*
Discretion and Its Control   *218*
   Securities and Exchange Commission v. *Sloan*   *220*
   Elian Gonzalez v. *Reno*   *223*
Informal Remedies: Ombudsmen and Others   *228*
Conclusion   *229*

PART FOUR
Remedies   *231*

Chapter 9
Remedies against Improper Administrative Acts   *233*

Declaratory and Injunctive Relief   *233*

Tort Suits against the Government   *234*
    Dalehite v. *United States*   *236*
    Effects of the *Dalehite* Case   *238*
State Tort Liability   *243*
The Liability of Individual Officers   *244*
    Liability of Judges   *245*
    Stump v. *Sparkman*   *245*
    Liability of Legislators   *250*
    Liability of Other Officials   *251*
    Richardson v. *McKnight*   *252*
    Bivins Actions   *254*
The Integration of Government and Officers' Liability   *255*
    Legislation Protecting Government Employees from Liability   *255*
    Liability under Section 1983   *255*
    Paying Judgments against Officials from Public Funds   *256*
Where Does Liability Go from Here?   *256*
    Private Legislation and Administrative Settlement of Claims   *258*

Chapter 10
Open Government   *261*

The Freedom of Information Act   *261*
    Environmental Protection Agency v. *Mink*   *262*
    Amendments to the Freedom of Information Act   *264*
The Privacy Act   *266*
    United States Department of Defense v. *Federal Labor Relations*
        Authority   *267*
Sunshine Acts   *271*
Executive Privilege   *272*
Conclusion   *273*

APPENDIXES   *275*
A   **Source Materials in Administrative Law, by Roseann**
    Bowerman   *277*
B   **Administrative Procedure Act**   *285*
C   **The Constitution of the United States of America**   *333*

INDEX   *351*

Table of Cases

Principal cases are in italic type. Cases cited or discussed are in roman type.
References are to pages.

Abbott Laboratories v. Gardner, 80

Alden v. Maine, 243

Allen v. United States, 242, 258

Allentown Mack Sales and Service v. National Labor Relations Board, 109

American School of Magnetic Healing v. Mc Annulty, 79–80

American Textile Manufacturers Institute v. Donovan, 55

Arizona v. California, 53

Baltimore Department of Social Services v. Bouknight, 138

Barry I. Fredericks v. Commissioner of Internal Revenue, 213

Bell Aerospace Co. v. National Labor Relations Board, 202–3

Bennett v. Spear, 98

Bi-Metallic Investment Co. v. State Board of Equalization, 152

Bivins v. Six Unknown Named Agents of the Fed. Bureau of Narcotics, 245, 254, 256

Block v. Community Nutrition Institute, 81

Board of Pardons v. Allen, 219

Board of Regents v. Roth, 177

Board of Trustees of the University of Alabama v. Garrett, 243

Bogan v. Scott-Harris, 251

Bowen v. Michigan Academy of Family Physicians, 82

Bowsher v. Synar, 115

Buckley v. Valeo, 33

California v. Ciraola, 138

Camara v. Municipal Court of the City and County of San Francisco, 129, 132, 136–38

Chevron U.S.A., Inc. v. Natural Resources Defense Council, Inc., 165–66, 114

Chevron, USA v. NRDC, Inc., 60

Chicago and Southern Air Lines v. Waterman Steamship Corp., 80

Citizens to Preserve Overton Park, Inc. v. Brinegar, 90

Citizens to Preserve Overton Park, Inc. v. Volpe, 87, 90

Clinton v. Jones, 251

Clinton v. New York, 71

Collonade Catering Corp. v. United States, 132, 137–38

Correctional Service Corporation v. Malesko, 254

Dalehite v. United States, 235, 239–42, 257–58

Dalten v. Specter, 10, 12, 91

Decatur v. Paulding, 79

Department of Justice v. Reporters Committee for Freedom of the Press, 267

Doe v. McMillan, 251

Dombrowski v. Eastland, 251

Donovan v. Dewey, 137

Donovan v. Lone Steer, Inc., 142

Elian Gonzalez v. Reno, 223

Environmental Protection Agency v. Mink, 262, 264

Federal Communications Commission v. ITT World Communications, 271–72
Federal Crop Insurance Corporation v. Merrill, 207–8, 218, 234
Federal Deposit Insurance Corp. v. Myer, 254
Federal Trade Commission v. American Tobacco Co., *121*, 124
Federal Trade Commission v. Ruberoid, 30
Feres v. United States, 239
Ferguson v. City of Charleston, 138
Field v. Clark, 51–52
Florida Prepaid v. College Savings Bank, 243
Food and Drug Administration v. Brown & Williamson Tobacco Corp., 60
Forrester v. White, 249–50
Frank v. Maryland, 128

Gaines v. Thompson, 79
Gegiow v. Uhl, 80
Gilbert v. Homar, 181
Gildea v. Ellershaw, 244
Glus v. Brooklyn Eastern Dist. Terminal, 207
Goldberg v. Kelly, *175*, 177, 190–91
Goss v. Lopez, *191*, 193–94

Harlow v. Fitzgerald, 244, 252
Heckler v. Chaney, 90–91
Hercules, Inc. v. United States, 258
Hirabayshi v. United States, 258
Hodel v. Virginia Surface Mining and Reclamation Association, Inc., *182*
Hohri v. United States, 259

Imbler v. Pachtman, 250
Immigration and Naturalization Service v. Chadha, 33, 65–66, *66*, 69, 71, 115
Indian Towing Co. v. United States, 238–40, 242
Industrial Union Department, AFL-CIO v. American Petroleum Institute, 55–56
Ingraham v. Wright, 194, 234

Jem Broadcasting v. Federal Communications Commission, 148
Johnson v. Robison, 82

Kalina v. Fletcher, 250
Kendall v. United States, 37
Kent v. Dulles, *58*, 60, 233–34
Kimel v. Florida Board of Regents, 243
Knuaff v. Shaughnessy, 174
Korematsu v. United States, 258

Laird v. Nelms, 257
Lane v. Hoglund, 80

Lawton v. Steele, 184
Lem Moon Sing v. United States, 79
Lichter v. United States, 53, 72
Lincoln v. Virgil, *91*
Londoner v. Denver, 152

Mackey v. Montrym, 181–82
Marshall v. Barlow's, *133*, 137–38, 233
Mathews v. Eldridge, *177*, 181, 185, 194
McAuliffe v. Mayor of New Bedford, 174
Miller v. Horton, 244
Mistretta v. United States, *60*, 72, 115
Model State Administrative Procedure Act, 147
Monell v. Department of Social Services of the City of New York, 256
Monroe v. Pape, 255–56
Morrison v. Olson, 15–16, 115
Morrissey v. Brewer, 176
Morton v. Ruiz, 154, 206
Moser v. United States, 217–18
Motor Vehicle Manufacturers Association v. State Farm Mutual Automobile Insurance Company, *163*, 166, 172
Muskopf v. Corning Hospital Dist., 257
Myers v. Bethlehem Shipbuilding Corporation, 94

National Labor Relations Board v. Hearst Publications, Inc., *110*
National Labor Relations Board v. Wyman-Gordon Co., 200–1, 203
National Treasury Employees Union v. Von Raab, 138
New York v. Burger, *138*
Nixon v. Fitzgerald, 251–52
North American Cold Storage Co. v. Chicago, 184

Office of Personnel Management v. Richmond, *208*
Office of the President v. Office of Independent Council, 273
Oklahoma Press Pub. Co. v. Walling, *122*, 124–25
Oliver v. United States, 137
One 1958 Plymouth Sedan v. Commonwealth of Pennsylvania, 185

Panama Refining Co. v. Ryan, 52–53
Pierson v. Ray, 245
Porter v. Nussle, *95*
Prescott v. United States, 258
Pulliam v. Allen, 249–50

Richardson v. McKnight, *252*
Rock Island Arkansas & Louisiana Railroad Co. v. United States, 208
Rosebush v. United States, 242
Russell v. Men of Devon, 257

Schechter Poultry Corp. v. United States, 52–53, 58

Securities and Exchange Commision v. Chenery, 195, *196*, 203

Securities and Exchange Commission v. Sloan, 220–23

See v. City of Seattle, 132, 137–38

Seminole Tribe of Florida v. Florida, 243

Service vs. Dulles, 148

Skidmore v. Swift Co., 149

Skinner v. Railway Labor Executives' Association, 138

Stark v. Wickard, 78, 80–81

Stork Restaurant, Inc. v. Boland, 105

Stump v. Sparkman, 245–49

Switchmen's Union v. National Mediation Board, 80

Tenney v. Brandhove, 251

Thomas Adams et al. v. United States, 258

Traynor v. Turnage, 83

United Scottish Insurance v. United States, 240

United States Department of Defense v. Federal Labor Relations Authority, *267*

United States v. Biswell, 133, 137–38

United States v. Euge, 60, *125*

United States v. Florida East Coast Ry. Co., 152–53, *157*, 159

United States v. Gaubert, 241–42

United States v. James Daniel Good Real Property, *186*

United States v. Muniz, 239

United States v. Nixon, 273

United States v. Picciotto, *149*

United States v. Reynolds, 273

United States v. Thompson, 235

United States v. Union Trust Co., 239

United States v. Varig Airlines, 240

United States v. Western Pacific Railroad Company, 94

Universal Camera Corp. v. National Labor Relations Board, *105*

Varig Airlines v. United States, 240

Vermont Yankee Nuclear Power Corp. v. Natural Resources Defense Council, Inc., 159, *160*

Wabash, St. Louis, and Pacific R.R. Co. v. Illinois, 21

Webster v. Doe, 91

Weiner v. United States, *13*

Westfall v. Irwin, 255

Whitman, Administrator of Environmental Protection Agency v. American Trucking Associations, Inc., 61, *62*

Wyman v. James, 132, 137

Yakus v. United States, 53

Preface

The major objective of this book is to introduce students of public administration to a selection of important issues in administrative law. While the book may be used with profit by others, including law school students, it is intended primarily for those who have had little or no prior experience with legal analysis or the use of the case method. The treatment here is briefer by a considerable margin than that found in the typical administrative law casebook-textbook. As indicated, only a *selection* of important issues in administrative law is included, although we consider these to be the issues of most importance to the present or future administrator. And these issues may not be treated as exhaustively as in the typical law school casebook: while a large number of recent cases and other up-to-date information will be found in the book, we do not consider it our primary function to set out for the reader "the law" as it has evolved in all of its particulars and in the most recent court opinions; rather, we are much more interested in making the administrator aware of the kinds of legal problems with which he or she is likely to be confronted. In a number of instances, therefore, we use one or two cases to illustrate the problem at hand rather than discussing numerous court decisions in order to sketch the broad contours of the present law. Moreover, the analysis that follows largely excludes questions involving the technicalities of legal procedure. These are matters better left to the attention of agency attorneys, on whom a public official with competence in other areas of administration will necessarily rely when it comes to legal problems.

The second edition of this book was in print for more than fifteen years. We were gratified by the reception it received from readers and pleasantly surprised that much of the material that it contained held up rather well over the years. Nevertheless, this third edition is a largely rewritten work that emphasizes a number of new and important developments in the field. Among the most noteworthy of these are the considerably expanded size of the Administrative Procedure Act (APA) through the addition of new statutory material (see appendix B for an edited text of the APA); the marking of fifty years since the adoption of the APA and evaluation of the act's continued importance (see chapter 2); the movement of administrative law more significantly into the arena of foreign affairs, as shown in numerous sections of this edition; the continued striving for administrative reform, led by successive presidential administrations; and the variety of governmental actions taken in response to the terrorist attacks on New York and Washington on September 11, 2001. The most important of these to date was the adoption in October 2001 of a wide-ranging statute known as the USA PATRIOT ACT, but other administrative moves taken in the wake of 9/11 are also discussed here.

Most of the developments so far mentioned relate to activities of the legislative and executive branches. But as always, the mark of the judiciary is strongly felt in administrative law. Many of the nearly forty cases set forth in the book are new to this edition. Some of the other cases, examined by us in the previous edition, have taken on new significance. For instance, it was simply impossible to anticipate in the middle 1980s the pervasive importance that *Chevron, USA v. Natural Resources Defense Council* (1984) would come to assume. It is without doubt one of the most important judicial decisions discussed in this book.

Finally, this edition has a new appendix, "Source Materials in Administrative Law," written by our colleague at Lehigh University, Roseann Bowerman. We hope that this work will help to guide students through the rich literature on the subject.

A number of people have provided us important help in writing this book. The staffs of the libraries at Lehigh University, Bowdoin College, and the University of Maine Law School aided in the location and acquisition of many of the sources we used. Roseann Bowerman, mentioned above, was particularly helpful in this regard. Sandra Edmiston, Senior Computing Consultant in Information Resources at Lehigh, solved a number of problems connected with formatting the manuscript. Andrew Coppola, a former graduate student at Lehigh, conducted research on a variety of subjects during the early stages of our work. Our colleagues in the Department of Political Science at Lehigh, as well as the departmental secretary, Dorothy Windish, supported our efforts throughout the work on the book. At Rowman & Littlefield we want particularly to acknowledge the help of our editor, Christopher Anzalone, and assistant managing editor, Stephen Driver. Our wives, to whom this book is dedicated, gave us unflagging support during the long period of this volume's creation.

Acknowledgments

We acknowledge the courtesy of the following publishers, publications, and authors who have permitted us to reprint excerpts from publications:

Cambridge University Press: James O. Freedman, *Crisis and Legitimacy: The Administrative Process and American Government*, 1978, excerpts from pp. 4–6. Reprinted with the permission of the author and Cambridge University Press.

Administrative Law Review: Philip J. Harter, "The APA at Fifty: A Celebration, Not a Puzzlement," 48 *Administrative Law Review* 309 (1996), excerpts from pp. 309–311; Philip K. Howard, "Keynote Address: Administrative Procedure and the Decline of Responsibility," 48 *Administrative Law Review* 312 (1996), excerpts from pp. 312–319; Andrew F. Popper, "Administrative Law in the 21st Century," 49 *Administrative Law Review* 187 (1997), excerpts from pp. 187–192; David H. Rosenbloom, "1946: Framing a Lasting Congressional Response to the Administrative State," 50 *Administrative Law Review* 173 (1998), excerpts from pp. 173–197. Reprinted by permission of the American Bar Association.

PART ONE

The Development of Administrative Law

CHAPTER 1

Administrative Authority and Law

CHAPTER 2

Origin and Development of the Administrative Process

Chapter 1

Administrative Authority and Law

The legal rules regarding an administrator's exercise of governmental authority on the one hand, and a private party's rights in relation to governmental authority on the other, constitute the basic subject matter of administrative law. As a separate area of study, administrative law is rather new in the United States, dating only from the late nineteenth century. It is also one of the broadest legal subjects since it embraces the activities of any and all government agencies other than courts and legislatures, at all levels of government. A study of the Environmental Protection Agency (EPA) could be considered an environmental law topic, but it might also fall within the broader field of administrative law. Many of the activities of the National Labor Relations Board (NLRB) are appropriate for analysis in both administrative law and labor law. An examination of the executive functions of departments in city or county governments might be narrowly called municipal law, but it fits within the broader context of administrative law as well. The same can be said for the myriad executive agencies at the state level.

ADMINISTRATIVE LAW AS AN AMALGAM OF CENTRIFUGAL FORCES

Considered from this perspective, administrative law should not be seen as a unified body of law but as a variety of administrative procedures and regulations whose content depends, to some extent, on the agencies and departments involved. As one scholar of the subject commented more than forty years ago:

> I am not sure that there is *an* administrative process. There are a series of . . . processes which, perhaps, bear more resemblance to one another than to anything else, but still not too much to one another. Those processes vary, and they

should vary, in accordance with the social problems and the practical needs which particular agencies were established to handle.[1]

Since this statement was made, the range and volume of administrative activity have grown significantly, leading several commentators to question whether "centrifugal forces" (separate bodies of labor law, tax law, public utility law, etc.) have made it unrealistic to maintain a disciplinary entity known as administrative law. Yet administrative law, as a course taught in law schools, political science departments, and public administration programs, continues to thrive, and the volume of writing on the subject is large. One journal exclusively devoted to administrative law, the *Administrative Law Review*, has been published for more than fifty years. The relevant material in the field (including not just legal literature but the output of legislatures, administrative agencies, and courts) challenges even the most diligent student of the subject. As one leading scholar put it recently: "[t]he subject is overwhelming. . . . Administrative law teachers . . . live nose barely above water, with a constant four-foot shelf of materials to read, with the constant question, what can I pare?"[2] In spite of such pressures, there are some who would expand the scope of administrative law even more. Kenneth Culp Davis has argued persuasively that certain aspects of criminal law, namely the activities of police and prosecutors, should be brought into the mainstream of the subject.[3] While not disagreeing with the logic of this proposal (police and prosecutors do, after all, perform a variety of administrative functions), we will limit the analysis in this book largely to activities of administrative agencies and officers traditionally covered in administrative law analyses.

Types of Agencies Encompassed by Administrative Law

Some of the earlier treatments of the subject tended to equate administrative law with the law of the independent regulatory commissions. These commissions played an important role in the development of the subject, and in many of the early landmark decisions, the Federal Communications Commission (FCC), Federal Trade Commission (FTC), Securities and Exchange Commission (SEC), or some other independent commission was one of the parties involved. As important as they continue to be, however, the independent commissions no longer play so dominant a role in the overall administrative process. Several of the older independent agencies have been abolished (the Federal Power Commission in 1977, the Civil Aeronautics Board in 1985, and the Interstate Commerce Commission in 1995, for instance), their functions absorbed by various executive-branch bodies. Those that remain (the FCC, FTC, SEC, and NLRB are the most well known) em-

---

[1] Paul M. Herzog, "Comment," in Monrad G. Paulsen, ed., *Legal Institutions Today and Tomorrow* 169 (1959).

[2] Peter L. Strauss, "Teaching Administrative Law: The Wonder of the Unknown," in Peter L. Strauss, Todd Rakoff, Roy A. Schotland, and Cynthia R. Farina, *Administrative Law: Cases and Comments* 33 (9th ed., 1995).

[3] Kenneth Culp Davis, 1 *Administrative Law Treatise* 2–3 (2nd ed., 1978).

ploy only a fraction of the number of people who work in the Department of Agriculture alone.

Regulatory commissions have a distinctive structure. They are multi-headed agencies consisting of several commissioners (typically five) rather than a single administrator. And they possess characteristics that give them a degree of independence. Commission members, although appointed by the president, serve terms longer than the president. The terms are staggered, and no more than a bare majority of members may be from one political party. Unlike appointees in the regular executive departments, commission members may not be removed at the pleasure of the president but only for grounds specified in the appropriate act of Congress.[4] An important body of case law involving the president's power to remove commissioners and other officials will be discussed later in this chapter.

In addition to the commission form, the federal bureaucracy has numerous other agencies designated as independent.[5] These bodies are headed by a single official, who is usually identified as an administrator or commissioner. Some such agencies perform purely staff functions, meaning that they render their services strictly for other government bodies or officials. An example is the General Services Administration (GSA), which manages government property and supplies. Our concern in this book is primarily with so-called line agencies, those that directly execute governmental policy.[6] Examples of independent agencies of this kind (i.e., non-commission-form line agencies) include the EPA and the Social Security Administration.

Not all administrative law functions are performed by independent agencies, however. A number of cabinet-level departments or bodies within such departments are charged with implementing governmental policies that directly affect private parties. Among many examples that might be mentioned, two of the most well-known agencies in this category are the Food and Drug Administration (FDA), within the Department of Health and Human Services, and the Occupational Safety and Health Administration, within the Department of Labor. Like the heads of some independent agencies, the chief officials of these bodies may be designated commissioner or administrator, or they may hold the rank of assistant secretary in the department to which they are attached.

Is there a logical explanation for Congress's choice of one form of regulatory agency rather than another? Hardly. The country has gone through phases of greater and lesser concern with presidential domination of administrative action. But the choice of a mechanism for the administration of one or another public policy initiative does not fit neatly into any historical pattern. As Richard J. Pierce Jr. and his associates have put it:

---

[4] But the independence of these commissions is by no means complete. One of the important areas of executive and legislative control is in budgetary matters. For further information see Strauss et al., above, note 2, 191.

[5] In 2001 a federal government source listed eighty-eight independent agencies. See United States Office of Personnel Management, "Federal Civilian Work Force Statistics: Employment Trends as of March 2001," http://www.opm.gov/feddata/etmar01.pdf.

[6] For an explanation and discussion of the line-staff distinction, see Jae Taik Kim, "Line and Staff Conflict," Jay M. Shafritz, ed., 1 *International Encyclopedia of Public Policy and Administration*, 1287 (1998).

Why some, and not other, agencies are designated independent is a question that admits of no easy answer. From a functional viewpoint, executive agencies have responsibilities that are similar to independent agencies. The FDA, for example, adjudicates, just as does the FTC. Both kinds of agencies make policy through rule making as well. The pattern is certainly uneven, if not inexplicable. Perhaps all it shows is that Congress has not succumbed to the hobgoblin of foolish consistency.[7]

To sum up, then, the administrative law functions under examination in this book may be performed by several kinds of bodies: independent commissions, other independent agencies, and cabinet-level departments or organizations under their jurisdiction.

Administrative agencies perform a wide variety of tasks. If, as suggested earlier, administrative law developed largely on the basis of economic regulation performed by independent commissions, it has long since moved beyond these narrow confines. In addition to functions in the economic sphere, large aspects of administrative activity are devoted to environmental, health, safety, and social equity matters, as well as to the awarding or denial of a broad range of benefits provided by the government. And, as just indicated, several types of agencies perform these functions. As these developments have proceeded, the term *regulation* appears to have broadened in meaning. Once "confined largely to economic concerns," as one recent source has put it, regulation now embraces the totality of public policy making and implementation by administrative agencies and officials.[8] This wide range of functions has given rise to a variety of arrangements for decision making, which may differ from each other considerably in their procedural requirements. One of the key tasks of this book is to provide an understanding of the basic forms of administrative action and the procedural arrangements that accompany them.

ADMINISTRATIVE LAW AS A UNIFIED SUBJECT

Several factors have contributed to the considerable measure of uniformity in administrative law and procedure. On the federal level there is the Administrative Procedure Act (APA), adopted in 1946 and applicable to most federal agencies, including the independent regulatory commissions. As provided in its first section (§ 551), the APA specifically excludes from coverage a number of bodies. The most important in this group are Congress, the judiciary, the government of the District of Columbia, courts martial, and military commissions. Developments leading up to the adoption of the APA will be reviewed in the next chapter. Many states have their own administrative procedure acts, administrative codes, or statutes contained in the general laws that cover administrative procedure, and a number of munici-

---

[7] Richard J. Pierce, Jr., Sidney A. Shapiro, and Paul R. Verkuil, *Administrative Law and Process* 94 (3rd ed., 1999).

[8] "Federal Regulation: An Introduction," *Congressional Quarterly's Federal Regulatory Directory* 2 (9th ed., 1999).

palities have ordinances covering the activities of numerous agencies. The National Conference of Commissioners of Uniform State Laws has drafted a model State Administrative Procedure Act. It has been put into effect, in whole or in part, in a number of states.

In addition to these legislative acts, the courts also contribute to the development of administrative law. The due process equal protection clauses of the Constitution, as well as other sections of that document, have served as the basis for significant litigation concerning the rights and powers of administrators and agencies. State constitutions also have provisions that courts apply in determining the propriety of administrative acts. And, of course, courts may also interpret the language of statutes covering administrative procedure when no constitutional issue is involved. When the United States Supreme Court makes a ruling on the constitutionality of a particular administrative action, especially if it is an action of a state or local body, it is contributing not just to the uniformity of administrative law but to the nationalization of that law as well. A significant amount of material in succeeding chapters is given over to selections from court opinions that are either landmark decisions or cases that illustrate important aspects of administrative law. For students without previous experience in studying judicial decisions, the final section of this chapter, "A Note on Analyzing Court Cases," will prove helpful.

THE ADMINISTRATIVE PROCESS

Consonant with the major objectives of this book and the primary audience for whom it is intended, little attention will be devoted to technical matters of legal procedure. We will concentrate, rather, on the major aspects of the administrative process and the important legal issues that arise under each of them. Although some attention will be paid to administrative law problems of states and localities, the national level will receive the major emphasis. The following is both a brief description of the major aspects of the administrative process and a rationale for the organization of the book.

Delegation of Power

After a chapter devoted to the historical development of administrative law, we will examine the basis for the exercise of administrative power, namely, the granting by the legislature to administrative agencies of the authority to act. The conditions under which this authority is granted, and the extent and nature of the grant, are crucial issues of administrative law that remain alive to this day. The basic questions of this chapter concern the appropriate level of legislative control over administrative action and the best means of achieving that control.

Judicial Review

Chapters 3 through 10 all concern judicial review, in the sense that all discuss cases in which courts have reviewed the propriety of administrative acts. But chapter 4 focuses on the rules that have been fashioned for judicial oversight of the work of agencies and officials. Just as the chapter on delegation of power deals with the proper role of the legislature regarding administrative action, this chapter examines the proper role of the courts in attempting to keep administrative power within appropriate bounds. The basic questions have to do with the kinds of administrative actions the courts can review, when review can take place, who can seek review, and the degree of scrutiny or deference the courts will give to the administrative actions in question.

Investigatory Power

An important element in the performance of administrative duties is information: administrators must have facts and data to carry out the functions assigned to their agency by the legislative body. But this need sometimes runs counter to the rights or interests of private parties. Legal rules that strike an appropriate balance in this area between governmental needs and private rights are still evolving.

Rules and the Rule-Making Process

Two major formal processes of administrative agencies are rule making and adjudication. Rules can be characterized as normally having general application and future effect. They are quasi-legislative in nature. The major issues connected with the subject involve the appropriate procedures to be used in the rule-making process and the question of whether an agency has the authority to adopt legislative-type rules.

The Right to Be Heard and Adjudicatory Policy Making

The right to a hearing implies an adjudicatory hearing, a quasi-judicial as opposed to quasi-legislative proceeding. Such hearings might involve the granting or revoking of a license, the suspension of a pupil from school, the termination of welfare benefits to an individual, or a myriad of other matters in which important legal interests are at stake. The most important questions with regard to hearings of this kind are, Who has the right to a hearing? If a hearing is required, at what stage in the process must it come? and, What procedural rules should apply in the hearing itself?

Can agency policy be developed through proceedings involving this kind of hearing, that is, through adjudicatory proceedings? The answer to this question is yes, but a conditional yes. The policy of an agency can be developed through orders adopted in quasi-judicial proceedings and through rules adopted via the rule-making process. Most observers hold that, where possible, rule making is superior to adjudication for the articulation of agency policy, but some agencies have not been granted clear rule-making power, and others, in spite of having such authority, prefer to develop policy on a case-by-case basis.

Informal Activity and the Exercise of Discretion

The informal administrative process refers to a wide range of administrative action that takes place outside of such formal proceedings as rule making and adjudication. Such action might involve advice from an administrator to a private party on, for example, the party's problem with a government pension, bank supervision by governmental authorities, the administration of driver's tests, or the accepting and processing of applications. The range of possible examples is endless. Such activity may have legal consequences, but it is not so commonly reviewed by courts as are formal administrative actions.

The exercise of discretion may take place in the context of the informal administrative process, but administrative discretion may also be treated as a somewhat distinct subject. Recent years have seen a revival of interest in studying administrative discretion, as students of administrative law have come to understand the enormous power that is placed in the hands of government officials. All commentators acknowledge that administrators need some discretion in order to carry out their functions in a reasonable and efficient manner. But excessive discretion can lead to the violation of the rights of private parties. Again, the problem is one of finding the proper balance. Recent efforts have been directed at devising mechanisms (both within the courts and in more informal complaint-handling systems) that will provide appropriate means for reviewing informal administrative activity and the exercise of discretion.

Remedies against Improper Administrative Acts

A private party who claims to have been the victim of an illegal administrative act has several options. If it is an act that is subject to judicial review, the party may seek an injunction and/or a declaration by the court that the act is illegal. If a governmental action has caused harm to an individual that cannot be corrected by a court's voiding the administrative act, a suit for damages might be instituted. A threshold question will involve the concept of sovereign immunity, that is, whether the governmental unit in question has consented to be sued. The history of the waiver of sovereign immunity in the United States is interesting and complex. A separate question is whether a plaintiff may sue a culpable official for damages. While sovereign immunity does not apply in these cases, a fairly high level of protection is available to many governmental officials who have acted in a reasonable manner and within the spheres of their duties, even if their acts have harmed private parties.

There are instances when neither the governmental unit nor the individual official will be held liable by a court, and yet it seems unjust for private parties to have to bear losses incurred through no fault of their own. Remedies that go beyond the bounds of the traditional law of damages are increasingly being proposed to cover such cases.

Open Government

No other area of administrative law has experienced such impressive development over the past three dozen years as this one. The direction of development has been strongly toward citizen access and participation in the administrative process. If information or participation is denied under the law in some concrete circumstances—and there are good reasons that government operations should not be open in certain cases—the presumption has definitely shifted in recent years in favor of public access wherever possible. As is the case with most controversial questions of administrative law, the basic issue involves finding an appropriate balance between citizen interests and governmental needs.

THE POLITICAL COMPONENT OF ADMINISTRATIVE LAW

Perhaps more than other branches of law, administrative law contains within it a large political element. Given that one side of an administrative law relationship is the government, this is understandable. Many aspects of administrative activity, from the appointment and dismissal of administrative personnel, through the budgetary process that funds administrative programs, to the policy framework within which administrators are expected to perform their functions, have clear political components. In the broadest sense, the problem of the political aspect of administrative law reduces itself to the following: How to maintain a reasonable check on the administration, by nonelected officials, of broad and often vague policies adopted by popularly elected officials, without unduly restricting the administrator's discretion or improperly influencing his or her decisions. This issue, which some commentators treat as a central problem of administrative law,[9] will receive considerable attention in this book.

To illustrate some of the political aspects of the field, the following pages will examine two political–legal problems that are well known to students of administrative law. The first deals with the sticky issue of military base closings and an attempt to create a mechanism for removing the task from political squabbling and obstruction. The second has to do with the president's power to remove officials.

Dalton v. *Specter*

Supreme Court of the United States, 1994.
511 U.S. 462, 114 S.Ct. 1719, 128 L.Ed.2d 497.

[Pennsylvania Senator Arlen Specter and others sued to enjoin the secretary of defense from closing the Philadelphia Navy Yard under the 1990 Defense Base Closure and Realignment Act. The act set forth a complex procedure for carrying out base closings, designed to insulate the process, to the extent possible, from influence brought on behalf of particular bases and localities. The scheme provided for a number of "gates" that had to be passed through before the base closing could take place. First, the secretary of defense prepared a base closure and re-

---

[9] See, for instance, Pierce, Shapiro, and Verkuil, above, note 7. The first chapter of this treatise is titled "The Political Nature of the Administrative Process."

alignment recommendation, which was sent to Congress and to the Defense Base Closure and Realignment Commission, an independent body of eight members appointed by the president. The commission, after public hearings, prepared a report that contained assessments of both the secretary's recommendations and the recommendations of the commission itself. This report was submitted to the president. The president could then either approve or disapprove the commission's recommendations as a whole. If he disapproved, the commission could prepare and submit a new report to the president. If the president again disapproved, the act provided that no bases could be closed that year. If he approved, he submitted the recommendations to Congress. Congress could, within forty-five days, adopt a joint resolution of disapproval. But if such a resolution was not adopted, the secretary was required to close all bases listed by the commission.

In 1991 the secretary recommended the closing of a number of bases. The commission did not agree with all of the secretary's recommendations, but it did agree that the Philadelphia Navy Yard, among other installations, should be closed. President Bush approved the commission's recommendations, and a joint resolution of disapproval was defeated by the House of Representatives. The stage was thus set for the closure of a number of bases, including the Philadelphia Navy Yard.

As this process was coming to an end, Senator Specter and others initiated their action in court. They alleged violations of the APA on two counts: the secretary violated certain substantive and procedural requirements of the act in recommending closure of the Philadelphia Navy Yard, and similar charges with regard to the commission's recommendations to the president. Of several issues that the courts considered in this case, the important one for our purposes was whether the acts of the secretary and the commission were subject to judicial review. The relevant provision of the APA on this point is 5 USC § 704, which provides for judicial review of "final agency action."

A U.S. District Court dismissed the suit, holding that the 1990 act itself precluded judicial review. But the Court of Appeals for the Third Circuit in relevant part reversed. Shortly thereafter, the U.S. Supreme Court issued its decision in *Franklin* v. *Massachusetts*, 505 US 788, 120 L.Ed.2d 636, 112 S.Ct 2767 (1992), which had a direct bearing on this case. *Franklin* held that a secretary of commerce report to the president was not "final agency action" and therefore was not appropriate for court review. It also asserted that the president was not an "agency" under the meaning of the APA, and therefore acts by the president could not be subject to judicial review (Article 702 of the APA reads in part: "A person suffering legal wrong because of agency action, or adversely affected or aggrieved by agency action . . . is entitled to judicial review thereof"). These and other points from the *Franklin* case were of crucial importance in the Supreme Court's opinion in this case.]

Chief Justice William Rehnquist delivered the opinion of the Court.

. . . In this case, respondents brought suit under the APA, alleging that the Secretary and the Commission did not follow the procedural mandates of the 1990 Act. But here, as in *Franklin*, the prerequisite to review under the APA—"final agency action"—is lacking. The reports submitted by the Secretary of Defense and the Commission, like the report of the Secretary of Commerce in *Franklin*, "carr[y] no direct consequences" for base closings. . . . The action that "will directly affect" the military bases . . . is taken by the President, when he submits his certification of approval to Congress. Accordingly, the Secretary's and Commission's reports serve "more like a tentative recommendation than a final and binding determina-tion." . . . The reports are like the ruling of a subordinate official, not final and therefore not subject to review." . . . The actions of the President, in turn, are not reviewable under the APA because, as we concluded in *Franklin*, the President is not an "agency." . . .

[In addition to the four justices who joined the chief justice in the opinion of the court, four other justices concurred in the judgment but expressed misgivings about the breadth of the majority opinion. Justice Harry Blackmun was concerned that the decision might be read as a blan-ket foreclosure on judicial review of presi-dential action. He asserted that if the president added a base to the commis-sion's list, in contravention of the statute, or if some other clear violation of the stat-ute's mandate were committed, judicial review would be in order. The other con-curring justices, in an opinion by Justice David Souter, emphasized that the "dis-tinctive statutory regime" used in the act, involving "a series of tight and rigid dead-lines on administrative review and Presi-dential action . . . with unbending dead-lines," made this procedure a highly unusual one that overcame "the strong presumption of judicial review."]

Two points of particular significance emerge from this case. First, Congress created an unusual statutory scheme in order to insulate the base-closing process from political pressure. As a result, judicial review was precluded. This matter has important implications addressed in other parts of this book, especially chapter 4, on judicial review. That chapter discusses a gen-eral presumption in favor of judicial review, and that presumption admits of very few exceptions. Obviously, the situation out of which *Dalton* v. *Spec-ter* arose constitutes one of those exceptions. The concurring justices in this case sought to emphasize how highly unusual the exception is. Second, *Dal-ton* v. *Specter* asserts that the president is not an agency within the meaning of the APA. Readers of this book will confront a number of examples of the president's being placed in a position under the law different from that of other governmental officials. It is worth pondering whether this unique status is always justified.

Our second example of political influence on the administrative process also involves the president, this time with regard to presidential power to remove various kinds of officials. While many officers in the executive branch serve at the president's pleasure, a great number of others are pro-tected by civil service status and can be dismissed only for specifically de-fined reasons and after certain procedural requirements have been met. Still other officials, although appointed by the president and not under civil service status, serve in agencies that contain some degree of insulation from presidential control. The rise of such independent agencies, created in part to protect the administrators in question from partisan influences, will be described in the next chapter. The power of the president to remove such officials has been the subject of continuing controversy over a number of decades. The following case is one example of this controversy. The excerpt reproduced below summarizes legal developments in this area prior to the case at hand.

Weiner v. *United States*

SUPREME COURT OF THE UNITED STATES, 1958.
357 U.S. 349, 78 S.Ct. 1275, 2 L.Ed.2d 1377.

[This case is based on a suit for back pay by a former member of the War Claims Commission, who asserted that he had been removed illegally. Weiner was appointed to the commission in 1950 by President Truman and was removed by President Eisenhower in 1953. In removing Weiner, Eisenhower stated that he wanted "personnel of my own selection" for the commission. Because of the commission's temporary nature (it went out of existence in 1954), Congress made no provision for the removal of a commissioner. The Court of Claims dismissed the suit, and it came to the U.S. Supreme Court. In his opinion for the court, Justice Felix Frankfurter discusses two earlier cases involving the president's removal power: *Myers* v. *United States*, 272 U.S. 52, 21, 71 L.Ed. 160, 47 S.Ct. 21 (1926) (opinion by a former president, Chief Justice William H. Taft); and *Humphrey's Executor* v. *United States*, 295 U.S. 602, 869, 79 L.Ed. 1611 55 S.Ct. (1935).]

Mr. Justice FRANKFURTER delivered the opinion of the Court . . .

We brought the case here . . . because it presents a variant of the constitutional issue decided in *Humphrey's Executor* v. *United States* . . .

Controversy pertaining to the scope and limits of the President's power of removal fills a thick chapter of our political and judicial history. The long stretches of its history, beginning with the very first Congress, with early echoes in the Reports of this Court, were laboriously traversed in *Myers* v. *United States*, . . . and need not be retraced. President Roosevelt's reliance upon the pronouncements of the Court in that case in removing a member of the Federal Trade Commission on the ground that "the aims and purposes of the Administration with respect to the work of the Commission can be carried out most effectively with personnel of my own selection" reflected contemporaneous professional opinion regarding the significance of the *Myers* decision. Speaking through a Chief Justice who himself had been President, the Court did not restrict itself to the immediate issue before it, the President's inherent power to remove a postmaster, obviously an executive official. As of set purpose and not by way of parenthetic casualness, the Court announced that the President had inherent constitutional power of removal also of officials who have "duties of a quasi-judicial character . . . whose decisions after hearing affect interests of individuals, the discharge of which the President can not in a particular case properly influence or control." . . . This view of presidential power was deemed to flow from his "constitutional duty of seeing that the laws be faithfully executed." . . .

The assumption was short-lived that the *Myers* case recognized the President's inherent constitutional power to remove officials, no matter what the relation of the executive to the discharge of their duties and no matter what restrictions Congress may have imposed regarding the nature of their tenure. The versatility of circumstances often mocks a natural desire for definitiveness. Within less than ten years a unanimous Court, in *Humphrey's Executor* v. *United States*, . . . narrowly confined the scope of the *Myers* decision to include only "all purely executive officers. . . ." The Court explicitly "disapproved" the expressions in *Myers* supporting the President's inherent constitutional power to remove members of quasi-judicial bodies. . . . Congress had given members of the Federal Trade Commission a seven-year term and also provided for the removal of a Commissioner by the President for inefficiency, neglect of duty or malfeasance in office. In the present case, Congress provided for a tenure defined by the relatively short period of time during which the War Claims Commission was to operate—that is, it was to wind up not later than three years after the expiration of the time for filing of claims. But nothing was said in the Act about removal.

This is another instance in which the most appropriate legal significance must be drawn from congressional failure of explicitness. Necessarily this is a problem in probabilities. We start with one certainty. The problem of the President's power to remove members of agencies entrusted with duties of the kind with which the War Claims Commission was charged was within the lively knowledge of Congress. Few contests between Congress and the President have so recurrently had the attention of Congress as that pertaining to the power of removal. Not the least significant aspect of the *Myers* case is that on the Court's special invitation Senator George Wharton Pepper, of Pennsylvania, presented the position of Congress at the bar of this Court.

Humphrey's case was a *cause cele-bre*—and not least in the halls of Congress. And what is the essence of the decision in Humphrey's case? It drew a sharp line of cleavage between officials who were part of the Executive establishment and were thus removable by virtue of the President's constitutional powers, and those who are members of a body "to exercise its judgment without the leave or hindrance of any other official or any department of the government" . . . as to whom a power of removal exists only if Congress may fairly be said to have conferred it. This sharp differentiation derives from the difference in functions between those who are part of the Executive establishment and those whose tasks require absolute freedom from Executive interference.

"For it is quite evident," again to quote *Humphrey's Executor*, "that one who holds his office only during the pleasure of another, cannot be depended upon to maintain an attitude of independence against the latter's will." . . .

Thus, the most reliable factor for drawing an inference regarding the President's power of removal in our case is the nature of the function that Congress vested in the War Claims Commission. What were the duties that Congress confided to this Commission? And can the inference fairly be drawn from the failure of Congress to provide for removal that these Commissioners were to remain in office at the will of the President? For such is the assertion of power on which petitioner's removal must rest. The ground of President Eisenhower's removal of petitioner was precisely the same as President Roosevelt's removal of Humphrey. Both Presidents desired to have Commissioners, one on the Federal Trade Commission, the other on the War Claims Commission, "of my own selection." They wanted these Commissioners to be their men. The terms of removal in the two cases are identical and express the assumption that the agencies of which the two Commissioners were members were subject in the discharge of their duties to the control of the Executive. An analysis of the Federal Trade Commission Act left this Court in no doubt that such was not the conception of Congress in creating the Federal Trade Commission. The terms of the War Claims Act of 1948 leave no doubt that such was not the conception of Congress regarding the War Claims Commission.

The history of this legislation emphatically underlines this fact. The short of it is that the origin of the Act was a bill . . . passed by the House that placed the administration of a very limited class of claims by Americans against Japan in the hands of the Federal Security Administrator and provided for a Commission to inquire into and report upon other types of claims. . . . The Federal Security Administrator was indubitably an arm of the President. When the House bill reached the Senate, it struck out all but the enacting clause, rewrote the bill, and established a Commission with "jurisdiction to receive and adjudicate according to law" three classes of claims. . . . The Commission was established as an adjudicating body with all the paraphernalia by which legal claims are put to the test of proof, with finality of determination "not subject to review by any other official of the United States or by any court by mandamus or otherwise." . . . Awards were to be paid out of a War Claims Fund in the hands of the Secretary of the Treasury, whereby such claims were given even more assured collectability than adheres to judgments rendered in the Court of Claims. . . .

Congress could, of course, have given jurisdiction over these claims to the District Courts or to the Court of Claims. The fact that it chose to establish a Commission to "adjudicate according to law" the classes of claims defined in the statute did not alter the intrinsic judicial character of the task with which the Commission was charged. The claims were to be "adjudicated according to law," that is, on the merits of each claim, supported by evidence and governing legal considerations, by a body that was "entirely free from the control or coercive influence, direct or indirect" . . . of either the Executive or the Congress. If, as one must take for granted, the War Claims Act precluded the President from influencing the Commission in passing on a particular claim, *a fortiori* must it be inferred that Congress did not wish to have hang over the Commission the Damocles' sword of removal by the President for no reason other than that he preferred to have on that Commission men of his own choosing.

For such is this case. We have not a removal for cause involving the rectitude of a member of an adjudicatory body, nor even a suspensory removal until the Senate could act upon it by confirming the appointment of a new Commissioner or otherwise dealing with the matter. Judging the matter in all the nakedness in which it is presented, namely, the claim that the President could remove a member of an adjudicatory body like the War Claims Commission merely because he wanted his own appointees on such a Commission, we are compelled to conclude that no such power is given to the President directly by the Constitution, and none is impliedly conferred upon him by statute simply because Congress said nothing about it. The philosophy of *Humphrey's Executor*, in its explicit language as well as its implications, precludes such a claim. The judgment is *Reversed*.

But the *Humphrey's* and *Weiner* cases did not settle all relevant issues regarding the president's removal power. Chief among several more recent cases on this point is *Morrison* v. *Olson*, 487 U.S. 564 (1988). At issue were the independent counsel provisions of the Ethics in Government Act of 1978. Under the act, an independent counsel could be appointed by a special court, upon the application of the attorney general, to investigate certain high-ranking government officials for violations of federal criminal law. Such an independent counsel could be removed only for "good cause." The independent counsel provisions of the act were challenged in court on several constitutional grounds, but the present discussion is limited to the issue of removability.

Asserting that prosecutorial activity was a "core executive function," those challenging the act argued that it was a violation of the separation of powers to limit the executive's control over that function in any way, even to the extent of conditioning removal on a showing of "good cause." But the majority of the Supreme Court rejected this view, denying that the "good cause" standard "unduly trammels on executive authority." The Court cited with approval the *Humphrey's* and *Weiner* cases, even while noting that these decisions emphasized the "quasi-legislative" and "quasi-judicial" nature of the functions that these officials performed. In the end it concluded that even with the statutory limitations on the executive's removal power, the president "retained ample authority to assure that the Counsel is competently performing his or her responsibilities in a manner that comports with the provisions of the Act."

By its reasoning in *Morrison*, the Court has moved from the "nature of the function" standard emphasized in *Weiner* to a less clearly articulated formulation, stated by Chief Justice Rehnquist as follows:

> We do not suggest that an analysis of the functions served by the officials at issue is irrelevant. But the real question is whether the removal restrictions are of such a nature that they impede the President's ability to perform his constitutional duty, and the functions of the officials in question must be analyzed in that light.

Justice Antonin Scalia wrote a long and passionate dissent. Citing the provision in Article II of the Constitution that "executive power shall be vested in a President of the United States," he asserted that "this does not mean *some* executive power, but *all* executive power." Thus, in Scalia's view, only officials whose functions fall outside of the purely executive category (as in *Humphrey's* and *Weiner*) should be subject to restrictions on the president's removal power.

The reason for the act's "good cause" provision, and for the Supreme Court's upholding of it, is clear enough: to provide independent prosecutors with sufficient autonomy to perform their functions effectively and to withstand potential executive branch interference. But some observers see in this independence the potential for the abuse of discretion. And a number of commentators share the view that the *Morrison* case has left the picture of the president's removal power confused and incomplete. As one source has put it, "the Court has not yet indicated the type of Executive Branch officers that must be subject to presidential power to remove 'at will,' or what constitutes adequate 'cause' for removal of officers to be removed only 'for cause.'"[10]

A NOTE ON ANALYZING COURT CASES

A good bit of the reading that follows involves court cases—either discussions of rules courts have made on certain issues or selections from actual court opinions. The person encountering court opinions for the first time

---

[10] Richard J. Pierce, Jr., 1 *Administrative Law Treatise* 71 (4th ed., 2002).

may have difficulty in understanding precisely what the court has decided, let alone seeing how the decision fits into the overall context of the subject being discussed. The facts of some cases are quite complex, and it is important to the understanding of any case to extract from the opinion the issues on which the court is being asked to rule. Even the most experienced analysts of court cases, therefore, often find it helpful to prepare an outline of the salient points of the case—usually called a "brief"—as an aid to understanding and discussion.

Briefing a Case

It is recommended that each of the approximately forty cases set forth in this book be briefed by the student. A brief typically uses an outline form and covers the following points:

1. Name and citation[11] of the case
2. Brief statement of the facts
3. Issue(s) the court must decide
4. Holding(s) of the court on these issues
5. Order of the court
6. Reasoning employed by the court to support the holding(s)
7. Major points of the concurring and/or dissenting opinions, if any

Since many of the cases presented below were decided by courts with more than one judge participating, it is also useful to indicate the voting lineup of the judges.

A brief need not be long. Most cases can be briefed on one side of an

---

[11] A uniform system of citation for case law reports (and many other legal citations) has long been used in the United States. It consists of three parts: volume number, name of the publication, and page number. Thus, for instance, the first set of numbers listed for *Weiner* v. *United States*, a case set forth earlier in this chapter, was 357 U.S. 349. This means that the case is found in volume 357 of the *United States Reports* and begins on page 349. Typically the year in which the case was decided is included in parentheses at the end of the citation. Three versions of U.S. Supreme Court cases are often cited: the official *U.S. Reports* ("U.S."), the *United States Supreme Court Reports, Lawyers' Edition* (L.Ed.), published by LEXIS Law Publishing, and the *Supreme Court Reporter* (S.Ct.), published by West Group. A few cases reproduced or discussed in this book are U.S. Court of Appeals or U.S. District Court opinions. These cases, published in unofficial editions by West Group, appeared originally in the *Federal Reporter* ("F."—for Court of Appeals cases) and the *Federal Supplement* ("F. Supp."—for District Court cases).

In many of the cases below, there will also be citations to legislative and administrative materials. The most common are (1) for statutes, the U.S. *Statutes at Large* (abbreviated as Stat.), a chronological publication arranged by sessions of Congress, and the *U.S. Code* (U.S.C.), in which the statutes in force are arranged by subject. There are also privately published, annotated versions of the *U.S. Code*, for instance, the *U.S. Code Annotated* (U.S.C.A.), published by West Group; (2) for administrative regulations, the *Federal Register* (F.R.), a daily publication, and the *Code of Federal Regulations* (C.F.R.), a compilation of federal regulations arranged by subject. Citations of statutes and regulations follow the same uniform format mentioned above, i.e., volume number (or "title" in the case of U.S.C. and C.F.R.), name of publication, and page number (or section number). Most of the states have equivalent publications for their statutes and administrative regulations.

In recent years, particularly with the advent of online publishing of legal materials, there has been a movement toward creating a citation system that does not employ volume and page numbers. At this point, however, no new system has gained uniform acceptance. On this point see the discussions in Morris L. Cohen and Kent C. Olson, *Legal Research in a Nutshell* 11–13 (7th ed., 2000) and Robert C. Berring and Elizabeth A. Edinger, *Finding the Law* 31–32 (11th ed., 1999). For more information on the matters discussed in this note, see Appendix A of this volume, "Source Materials in Administrative Law."

8½-by-11-inch sheet of paper. Many students err in the direction of writing briefs that are too long, often becoming bogged down in the facts. Remember that the brief is not a crutch but an aid to facilitate one's ability to understand and explain the case. And keep in mind above all that mastering a case means little in itself unless it serves to enhance understanding of the larger picture. The most important task in analyzing a case is to determine what it illustrates about the question of law being examined.

At this point the student will be asked to prepare a brief. Turn to page 13, where *Weiner* v. *United States* is found. Brief this case, and then compare your brief with the one prepared by the authors, which is printed below.

Weiner v. *United States*, 357 U.S. 349, 78 S.Ct. 1276, 2 L.Ed.2d 1377 (1958)

Facts:

Weiner, who was appointed to the War Claims Commission by President Truman, was dismissed by President Eisenhower because the president wanted "personnel of his own selection" on the commission. Weiner sued for back pay, claiming that his dismissal was illegal. The Court of Claims dismissed the petition and the Supreme Court took the case for review.

Issue:

Does the president have authority to remove Weiner for political reasons, namely, because he wanted his own appointee on the commission?

Holding:

No.

Order:

The judgment of the Court of Claims is reversed.

Reasoning:

(Opinion by Justice Frankfurter for a unanimous Court)

The most important factor in determining whether the president has removal power on the grounds stated is "the nature of the function" of the War Claims Commission. The commission's basic function is to adjudicate claims brought before it. Its task is of an "intrinsic judicial character." Such functions should be protected from outside interference both as to particular cases and as to the removal of a commissioner for the reasons stated: "no such power is given to the president directly by the Constitution, and none is impliedly conferred upon him by the statute simply because Congress said nothing on the matter." The Court suggested that it might be another matter if removal were based on reasons related to improper performance of official duties.

The Court relied heavily on the author of *Humphrey's Executor* v. *United States* (1935), where the Supreme Court rejected the president's assertion of authority to remove a member of the Federal Trade Commission, a body with an essentially adjudicatory function, for basically the same reasons. It distinguished the present case from *Myers* v. *United States* (1926), which upheld the president's power to remove an official from the purely executive position of postmaster.

Separate Concurring or Dissenting Opinions:

Frankfurter wrote for a unanimous Court. There were no concurring or dissenting opinions.

Chapter 2

Origin and Development of the Administrative Process

Many studies of the origin and development of the administrative process have focused on the creation of the Interstate Commerce Commission in 1887 as the point at which the United States embarked on a new pattern of unified, national regulation by independent administrative agencies.[1] This event was the classic example of Congress's creating an administrative agency to provide continuous expert supervision over matters of regulatory policy that were alien to the basic functions of either the courts or the legislatures. The history of the post–Civil War period had amply demonstrated that neither the individual states nor the federal courts were in a position to fashion remedies for the general public, which was suffering from a variety of unfair practices and the exorbitant rate structure of the railroad industry.[2] Congressional acknowledgment that national regulatory policy was needed to cope with problems such as unfair methods of competition and unfair labor practices led to the establishment of additional independent regulatory commissions in the twentieth century.[3]

HISTORICAL DEVELOPMENT OF THE AMERICAN ADMINISTRATIVE PROCESS

However, if we are to take a comprehensive look at the origin and development of the administrative process in the United States, we must go much

---

[1] For more information on the origins of the independent regulatory commissions, see Robert E. Cushman, *The Independent Regulatory Commissions* (1941), and Marver H. Bernstein, *Regulating Business by Independent Commission* (1955).

[2] For a discussion of the catalytic role of the Supreme Court's decision in *Wabash, St. Louis and Pacific R.R. Co.* v. *Illinois*, 118 U.S. 557 (1886) in the congressional decision to adopt the Interstate Commerce Act, see Cushman, above, note 1, 44.

[3] For an exhaustive compilation of articles and documents associated with twentieth century development of the administrative process, see Legislative Reference Service of the Library of Congress, *Separation of Powers and the Independent Agencies: Cases and Selected Readings*, S. Doc. No. 49, 91st Cong. 1st sess. (1969).

further back than 1887 and the creation of the first independent regulatory commission. One logical point would be the creation of the Republic, for in fact the forerunners of several of our administrative agencies date back to the 1790s. More appropriately, however, we need to go back still further, to the Anglo-American origins.

Professor R. John Tresolini[4] traced the origins of Anglo-American administrative law from the latter part of the twelfth century in England, when the first book on the common law was published.[5] In the process he examined the role of the sheriff in the centralization of royal authority, the judicial and administrative activities of itinerant justices, and most importantly, the justices of the peace, who by the eighteenth and early nineteenth centuries had become chief administrators. Only with the advent of the Industrial Revolution in the late eighteenth century did Britain evolve a more centralized system of administration, which gradually resulted in the diminution of the powers of the justice of the peace.

Tresolini also described the justices of the peace and magistrates as being the most important officers in the colonial period in America. The administration of many local laws and ordinances was entrusted to them. The agrarian nature of American society, coupled with the fear of centralized authority, obviated the need for complex administrative systems. Eventually, however, administrative power began to shift from local governmental units to those at the state or federal level. As in England, this gradual centralization of administrative power was accentuated by the onset of the Industrial Revolution, which required intervention by the national government in a variety of previously unregulated areas. As federal regulatory jurisdiction expanded, Congress increasingly delegated responsibility over technical matters to newly created administrative agencies. The enabling legislation creating these agencies authorized wide grants of discretionary authority to administrative officers. These grants of legislative and judicial authority were the forerunners of the rule-making and adjudicatory powers commonly exercised by independent regulatory bodies during the past century.

Tresolini also recounted the process whereby administrative law eventually received recognition as a legitimate component of public law.[6] With the exception of several enlightened scholars who perceived the need for the exploration of the workings of administrative law, the major thrust of the nineteenth and early twentieth century writings in both Great Britain and the United States sought either to condemn its growth or to deny its existence as a body of law. It was A. V. Dicey, the foremost scholar of English constitutional law, who was to exert the greatest influence in retarding the recognition of administrative law. He was eventually forced to capitulate in the face of court decisions upholding the exercise of administrative powers

---

[4] R. John Tresolini, "The Development of Administrative Law," 12 *University of Pittsburgh Law Review* 362 (1951).

[5] Ranulf Glanvil, *Tractatus de Legibus* (1187–1189).

[6] "That branch or department of law which is concerned with the state in its political or sovereign capacity, including constitutional and administrative law." *Black's Law Dictionary*, Revised 4th Edition (1968), p. 1394.

and, ultimately, the findings of the Committee on Ministers' Powers. Likewise, in the United States, administrative law was to receive belated recognition. The scholarly contributions of Frank J. Goodnow and Ernst Freund were to prove instrumental in that regard, as was the *Final Report of the Attorney General's Committee on Administrative Procedure.*[7]

The edited selections reproduced in this chapter constitute an overview of the historical development of the American administrative process. Collectively, they provide the student of the administrative process with a basis from which contemporary developments may be analyzed. They also demonstrate, to use Felix Frankfurter's words, that "administrative law has not come like a thief in the night."[8]

As noted earlier, the precursors of the Interstate Commerce Commission date back to the founding of the Republic. The following excerpt from James O. Freedman's book, *Crisis and Legitimacy: The Administrative Process and American Government*, traces the development of our modern regulatory systems from these modest beginnings.

Crisis and Legitimacy: The Administrative Process and American Government

James O. Freedman

Cambridge University Press, 1978, 4–6.
Reprinted by permission of the publisher and author. Footnotes omitted.

Roots of the Modern Administrative Process

The growth of the administrative process in the United States occurred gradually, as the original thirteen states matured into a continental nation, increasingly industrialized and urbanized, facing economic and social problems that required responses more technologically expert, more institutionally flexible, and more procedurally expeditious than either the Congress or the federal courts could provide. The creation of administrative agencies was designed to supply these institutional deficiencies in the formulation and administration of public policy.

Although the rise of the administrative process is often identified with the presidency of Franklin D. Roosevelt, in fact reliance upon administrative agencies to meet emerging national problems long antedates the New Deal. It is as old as the Republic itself. The First Congress of the United States, meeting in 1789, enacted legislation authorizing administrative officers to "estimate the duties payable" on imports and to adjudicate claims to military pensions for "invalids who were wounded and disabled during the late war." The forerunner of the Patent Office was created in 1790, the Office of Indian Affairs in 1796. The General Land Office was established in 1812. The administrative process thus has deep historical roots.

---

[7] Attorney General's Committee on Administrative Procedure, *Final Report of the Attorney General's Committee on Administrative Procedure*, S. Doc. No. 8, 77th Cong., 1st sess. (1941).

[8] Felix Frankfurter, "Foreword," 47 *Yale Law Journal* 515, 517 (1938).

Approximately one-third of the federal administrative agencies were created before 1900, notably the Civil Service Commission in 1883 and the Interstate Commerce Commission in 1887. By 1891, the Pension Office of the Department of the Interior, with six thousand employees and more than a half-million cases pending for adjudication, was, according to the commissioner, the "largest executive bureau in the world." Still another third of the federal agencies were created between 1900 and 1930, notably the Federal Reserve Board in 1913, the Federal Trade Commission in 1914, and the United States Tariff Commission in 1916. During these same decades, many state governments, responding to the influence of the Granger and Progressive movements, created administrative agencies to regulate banking, bridges, canals, ferries, grain elevators, insurance, railroad freight rates, and warehouses.

Reliance upon the administrative process was thus an established practice by the time that Roosevelt became president in 1933. But it nevertheless seems natural to associate the dominant position of the administrative process in modern government with President Roosevelt because the New Deal radiated a faith in the capacity of the administrative process perhaps exceeding that of any previous administration.

Faced with the devastating consequences of a major depression, the New Deal created a large number of administrative agencies to attack the nation's economic and social problems. These agencies, almost all of which eventually wrought major changes in American life, included the Federal Deposit Insurance Corporation (1933), the Tennessee Valley Authority (1933), the Federal Communications Commission (1934), the Securities and Exchange Commission (1934), the National Labor Relations Board (1935), and the Civil Aeronautics Board (1938).

In 1937, the President's Committee on Administrative Management reported critically to President Roosevelt that Congress had created more than a dozen major independent regulatory agencies since 1887, and went on to complain that "Congress is always tempted to turn each new responsibility over to a new independent commission. This is not only following the line of least resistance. It is also following a fifty-year-old tradition."

The tradition persists to this day. The demonstrated utility of the administrative process in meeting serious national problems during the New Deal years undoubtedly influenced the decision to create additional administrative agencies to meet the problems of controlling materials, manpower, prices, and production presented by World War II. In the decades since the war, the creation of new administrative agencies to deal with emerging national problems continued apace. Under Democrat and Republican presidents alike, Congress has regularly chosen to rely upon administrative regulation—rather than upon civil remedies, criminal penalties, subsidies to the private sector, or the free market, for example—to implement public policies in new and complex areas of federal concern. These areas have included atomic energy (the Atomic Energy Commission, 1946), military conscription (the Selective Service Commission, 1948), space exploration (the National Aeronautics and Space Administration, 1958), shipping (the Federal Maritime Commission, 1961), employment discrimination (the Equal Employment Opportunity Commission, 1965), environmental protection (the Environmental Protection Agency, 1970), occupational safety (the Occupational Safety and Health Review Commission, 1970), and consumer product safety (the Consumer Product Safety Commission, 1972).

The continuing growth in the administrative process has led to a corresponding increase in the prominence of administrative law in the decisions of the Supreme Court. The role of the Supreme Court in the shaping of American administrative law dates at least from the decision in *The Brig Aurora* [an early Supreme Court case upholding a congressional delegation of power to the president] in 1813. At one time, in 1957, decisions involving review of administrative action constituted the largest single category of cases decided by the Court on the merits, about one-third of the total. In the decades of the 1960s and 1970s, however, the Court considered proportionally fewer administrative law cases as other classes of litigation, particularly those involving criminal procedure and civil rights, assumed a heightened national importance and claimed a greater share of the Court's attention.

By the time of the nation's bicentennial in 1976, the federal administrative process had achieved considerable status. It embraced more than sixty independent regulatory agencies as well as perhaps several hundred administrative agencies located in the executive departments. Administrative agencies exercised regulatory responsibilities in scores of important and sensitive areas. The decisions rendered by the federal administrative agencies were many times the number rendered by the federal courts and probably affected the lives of more ordinary citizens more pervasively and intimately than the decisions of the federal courts. In virtually every relevant respect, the administrative process has become a fourth branch of government, comparable in the scope of its authority and the impact of its decision making to the three more familiar constitutional branches.

The United States thus has increasingly become an administrative state. Americans have sought to understand the implications of this fact for the character of American democracy, the nature of American justice, and the quality of American life. These implications have often been troubling— even though the administrative process had deep historical roots, even though its growth has been gradual and evolutionary, and even though that growth has occurred only by deliberative acts of democratic choice. If the United States is to realize the promise and respect the limitations of the administrative process, the quest for understanding its implications must be regularly renewed.

The Administrative Procedure Act of 1946

A major event in the evolution of administrative law was the adoption of the Administrative Procedure Act (APA) in 1946. But the APA was not conceived and brought into being overnight. It can be traced back at least as far as the early 1930s.

Concurrent with the de facto growth of federal regulatory agencies, described above by Freedman, a major debate raged in both governmental and nongovernmental circles over the structural relationships between these agencies and the courts. However, while the debate continued over the degree of judicial accountability of the administrative process, that process itself became more and more deeply entrenched in the everyday operations of American national government. The interaction of agencies and courts continued, giving rise to both an ever-expanding case law and an increasingly more mature administrative process. During the 1930s, proposals for the creation of a separate administrative court system were made by the American Bar Association's Special Committee on Administrative Law[9] and the President's Committee on Administrative Management;[10] however, the de facto growth and acceptance of the administrative process destined them to failure from the outset.

Acknowledging the failure of the administrative court proposals, the American Bar Association's Special Committee later shifted its focus to advocating greater judicialization of the then-existing administrative process. Its efforts culminated in the passage of the Walter-Logan bill; however, President Roosevelt vetoed the bill, and efforts to override the veto were unsuccessful.[11] The Walter-Logan bill emphasized structural reforms designed primarily to enlarge judicial controls, specifically involving the scope and subject matter of judicial review, over the agencies affected. James D. Landis described the impact the bill would have had on the administrative process:

> Only one thing can be certain and that is, that to apply the Procrustean formula suggested by the American Bar Association's pending proposals is to cut off here a foot and there a head, leaving broken and bleeding the process of administration itself.[12]

With the failure to override the president's veto, the high point of the movement for basic judicialization of the administrative process had been reached. Roughly simultaneously, a conviction was growing that judicial review itself would not solve the structural problems between agencies and courts. Virtually everyone agreed that some clarification of judicial review was necessary; however, it was no longer to be considered an end in itself. Carl McFarland captured the mood of the times quite accurately:

> Partly out of recognition of the real substance of the problem, partly to avoid undue expansion of judicial review through legislative action, and partly because of recent and rapid expansion in the realm of federal administration which has driven home bluntly the methods and operation of administrative agencies, attention has turned to the principles and details, the needs and inef-

---

[9] 59 *American Bar Association Report* 539–564 (1934) and 61 *American Bar Association Report* 720–793 (1936).

[10] *Report of the President's Committee on Administrative Management*, V, Part D., 39–42 (1937).

[11] Message of December 18, 1940, H. Doc. 986, 76th Cong., 3d sess. (1940); sustained by House of Representatives, 86 *Congressional Record*, Part 12, 76th Cong., 3d sess., 13953 (1940).

[12] James Landis, "Crucial Areas in Administrative Law," 53 *Harvard Law Review* 1077, 1102 (1940).

ficiencies, the virtues and injustices of the actual operation of the administrative system in the federal government.[13]

Although the legislative history of the APA has been traced back to the Seventy-third Congress (1933–1934),[14] its more direct source was two bills introduced during the second session of the Seventy-eighth Congress (1944) and revised and simplified during the early days of the first session of the Seventy-ninth Congress, in 1945. The act itself was finally adopted in 1946[15] by unanimous vote in both houses. According to Kenneth Culp Davis, "[t]he battle over fundamentals had ceased . . . [and] the federal administrative process seemed secure."[16]

Evaluations of the newly enacted legislation ran the full gamut, from claims that the APA was the "Magna Carta of Administrative Law" to the statement that the act constituted a "sabotage of the administrative process."[17] The intervening years have moderated the assessments, and scholar Bernard Schwartz's views are probably not unrepresentative today. Although Schwartz noted that the APA was not a comprehensive code of administrative procedure, he felt that it was a general framework of fundamental importance. In particular, he saw in the APA the initial "legislative attempt in the common-law world to state the essential principles of fair administrative procedure," a step that imposed on all federal agencies the best procedures developed up to that time.[18]

Another assessment of the APA was offered by Marver Bernstein in his classic, *Regulating Business by Independent Commissions*:

> Its significance seems . . . to be not so much in specific changes it has brought about in the procedure of adjudication as in the extent to which the Act represents an important stage in the unfolding of ideas and attitudes concerning the role of administrative discretion in modern government and the possibilities of achieving a fair measure of equity in the dispensing of administrative justice.
>
> It is more important for its political implications than for its specific procedural requirements and definitions.[19]

Thus, the enactment of the APA marked the maturation of the administrative process. In Professor Nathaniel Nathanson's words, "The turbulent administrative issues of the thirties have developed into a more or less peaceful maturity."[20]

---

[13] Carl McFarland, "The False Standard in Administrative Procedure," 27 *Cornell Law Quarterly* 433, 439 (1942).

[14] See *Legislative History of the Administrative Procedure Act*, S. Doc. No. 248, 79th Cong., 2d sess., 187–191 (1946), for a chronological table of main bills introduced dating back to the 73rd Congress.

[15] Administrative Procedure Act, 60 Stat. 237 (1946).

[16] Kenneth C. Davis, 1 *Administrative Law Treatise* 30 (1958).

[17] Frederick F. Blachly and Miriam E. Oatman, "Sabotage of the Administrative Process," 6 *Public Administration Review* 213 (1946).

[18] Bernard Schwartz, *Introduction to American Administrative Law* 134–135 (2nd ed., 1962).

[19] Bernstein, above, note 1, 194.

[20] Nathaniel Nathanson, "Central Issues in American Administrative Law," 45 *American Political Science Review* 348 (1951).

THE ADMINISTRATIVE PROCEDURE ACT AT A HALF CENTURY

The year 1996 marked the fiftieth anniversary of the adoption of the APA. A number of law reviews devoted attention to the development of the administrative process over the previous half century and to its future. Prominent among these were symposium issues of the *Administrative Law Review* on the "Fiftieth Anniversary of the Administrative Procedure Act"[21] and "The Future of the Administrative Process."[22] The four edited articles that appear below, selected from these symposia, provide a historical perspective on the APA, as well as insights into the further development of the American administrative process.[23] The first of the articles, by David H. Rosenbloom,[24] examines the APA in the context of the related initiatives of the 1946 congressional term, that is, the Federal Tort Claims Act, 60 Stat. 842, the Employment Act, 60 Stat. 23, and the Legislative Reorganization Act of 1946, 60 Stat. 812. While the excerpted portions of the article focus primarily on the APA, and to a lesser extent on the Legislative Reorganization Act, Congress viewed all four pieces of legislation as essential to providing for more effective control over the post–New Deal administrative state. Rosenbloom's introductory comments provide additional reinforcement to the discussion above concerning the situation the Roosevelt administration confronted in the mid-1930s with the burgeoning growth of the federal administrative apparatus. The principal outgrowth of those efforts was the creation of the Executive Office of the President,[25] which provided the executive branch with greater reorganization and budgetary authority. Consequently, Congress felt obligated to meet the executive's challenge with, in Rosenbloom's words, "a blueprint for redefining its relationships to the agencies and adjusting its position in the constitutional separation of powers."[26] Rosenbloom

---

[21] 48 *Administrative Law Review* 307 (1996).

[22] 49 *Administrative Law Review* 149 (1997).

[23] Space considerations prevent the inclusion in this volume of more than the four articles just mentioned. But the interested reader would profit from examining other parts of these symposia. For instance, Jeffery S. Lubbers provides an interesting assessment of issues that are likely to dominate in the field of administrative law in the future. He identifies seven issues: budgetary constraints triggering alternative approaches to regulation and enforcement; continuing tensions between the legislative and executive branches; regulatory reform; the information revolution; the devolution of federal responsibility on state and local government; the downsizing and retrenchment of the federal government; and issues pertaining to administrative adjudication. See Jeffrey S. Lubbers, "The Administrative Law Agenda for the Next Decade," 49 *Administrative Law Review* 159 (1997). Lubbers, a former director of research at the Administrative Conference of the United States (ACUS), concludes with a plea, now that the ACUS has been abolished, for the establishment of a center of research on administrative law in the federal government. To Lubbers, such a center could develop objective criteria for evaluating administrative reform initiatives advanced by both the president and Congress and help build consensus on reform issues. He argues that currently there is no locus of expertise on issues pertaining to administrative procedure and that the field of administrative law would benefit from its reestablishment. For background on the ACUS, see Jeffrey S. Lubbers, "Note about the Administrative Conference of the United States (1968–1995)," *A Guide to Federal Agency Rulemaking* xvii–xviii (3rd ed., 1998).

[24] David H. Rosenbloom, "1946: Framing a Lasting Congressional Response to the Administrative State," 50 *Administrative Law Review* 173 (1998).

[25] Reorganization Act of 1939, 55 Stat. 1.

[26] David H. Rosenbloom, above, note 24, 176.

concludes by providing an overview of efforts to secure administrative reform through the mid-1990s and the lessons that can be gained therefrom.

The *Administrative Law Review* symposium celebrating the fiftieth anniversary of the adoption of the APA included articles expressing widely divergent views of the APA. The next two excerpts illustrate that range of views. On the one hand, Philip J. Harter, chair of the American Bar Association's Section of Administrative Law and Regulatory Practice, presents an enthusiastic assessment. A dramatically different perspective is found in Philip K. Howard's frontal attack on administrative rule making.[27] In the selection below, Howard takes issue with the view that "more process means better decisions." He argues that responsibility is what makes things happen and that, in its absence, there can be no accountability. In his view the APA, with its emphasis on process, inhibits both accountability and responsibility. What is needed, according to Howard, is to accentuate those two concepts and let democracy work.[28]

The concluding excerpt of this section comes from the symposium issue examining "The Future of the American Administrative Process." Andrew F. Popper's article, entitled "Administrative Law in the 21st Century,"[29] provides a multidisciplinary perspective that challenges current administrative law paradigms. In this provocative piece, Popper decries the preservation of long-standing ritual in the field of administrative law and welcomes the contributions of anthropologists and political scientists, who are inclined to bring new perspectives to examining the regulatory state. According to Popper, "rather than trying to ask 'what is best?' when looking at a regulatory program, it may be more important to ask 'what has already happened?' and 'has the law caught up with the behavior?' "[30]

1946: Framing a Lasting Congressional Response to the Administrative State

David H. Rosenbloom

50 Administrative Law Review *173–197 (1998).*
Reprinted by permission of the American Bar Association. Footnotes omitted.

Introduction

Mention 1946 in a public administration or administrative law class and the Administrative Procedure Act of 1946 (APA) will quickly spring to mind. The APA is properly viewed as a basic law for regulating federal administration and structuring judicial review of agency decisions and other actions. It is a focal point of the study of administrative law, generates an immense

---

[27] Philip K. Howard, *The Death of Common Sense: How Law Is Suffocating America* (1994).

[28] Philip K. Howard, "Keynote Address: Administrative Procedure and the Decline of Responsibility," 48 *Administrative Law Review* 312 (1996).

[29] 49 *Administrative Law Review* 187 (1997).

[30] Ibid., 190.

amount of academic literature, and establishes the basis for a great deal of litigation. Little attention, however, has been paid to the APA as the core of a broader congressional effort in 1946 to reposition itself in order to exercise greater direction and control over the burgeoning post–New Deal federal administrative state. By drawing on the legislative debates, reports, other documents, and media coverage associated with the APA, the Legislative Reorganization Act of 1946, the Federal Tort Claims Act (FTCA), and the Employment Act, this Article reconstructs Congress's understanding in 1946 of its constitutional role and analyzes the blueprint it developed for supervising federal administration. This article demonstrates that the steps Congress took in 1946 created lasting political dynamics that have powerful, though somewhat misunderstood, consequences for federal public management and have frustrated contemporary administrative reforms.

I. 1946: Designing a Congressional Response to the New Administrative State

Congressional action in 1946 regarding federal administration was a direct, though delayed, response to the executive branch's growth in size and power during the New Deal and World War II. In the words of two leading Senators, William Fulbright (D-AR) and Robert La Follette, Jr. (Progressive-WI), Congress was searching for means to maintain "legislative supremacy" in the face of the growing strength of the Presidency "lest it lose its constitutional place in the Federal scheme." By the end of 1934 more than sixty new agencies were created. Approximately 250,000 new employees were hired during President Franklin D. Roosevelt's first term, eighty percent of whom were outside the traditional civil service system. As the Supreme Court stated in *FTC* v. *Ruberoid*, the resulting administrative state "deranged our three-branch legal theories," and prompted major institutional adjustment.

In 1937, Roosevelt created the President's Committee on Administrative Management (PCAM or Committee). Three leaders in the field of public administration, Louis Brownlow, Charles Merriam, and Luther Gulick, headed the PCAM. At that time, public administration was based on the premise that there was an apolitical science of public management and that "unity of command" typically yielded the greatest efficiency and economy. Given the composition of the PCAM and its relationship to the President, few doubted that it would favor greater executive power.

The Committee's famous Report claimed that the rapid governmental expansion of the early New Deal led to the breakdown of rational organizational arrangements and administrative systems. It complained that the establishment of more than 100 independent agencies created an unmanageable "headless 'fourth branch' of the government," and that the personnel system needed thorough reform. The PCAM proposed reorganizing and consolidating agencies, and making the President a true chief executive officer through a number of institutional and legal reforms. Anticipating opposition by those who feared enhanced executive power, the Committee chided that "[t]hose who waiver at the sight of needed power are false friends of modern democracy" and added that "[s]trong executive leadership is essential to democratic government today."

The Committee's Report prompted the creation of the Executive Office of the President. In addition, it was the stimulus for greater presidential reorganizational authority and a stronger role for the chief executive in budgeting. In the field of public administration, the PCAM Report has been hailed as a triumph in the application of scientific administrative design to government. Congress, however, rejected most of the Committee's recommendations because the Report did not specify an acceptable role for the legislature. Hostile critics, such as Representative Hamilton Fish (R-NY), viewed the Report as "a step to concentrate power in the hands of the President and set-up a species of fascism or Nazism or an American form of dictatorship." In a critique, a more moderate and ultimately successful Senator Frederick Hale (R-ME) urged that "[i]t is certainly up to a self-respecting Congress to see to it that this last vestige of congressional control is not taken away from us."

Leaders in the field of public administration offered few alternatives to legislative abdication. Legislatures were traditionally political and fragmented while public management was ideally apolitical, scientific, and unified. In 1945 Leonard White, a professor of political science at the University of Chicago and one-time Chairman of the United States Civil Service Commission, argued that '[t]he function of a legislative body . . . has changed as the character of our economy has evolved." To meet the challenge of maintaining its traditional role as a check on the Executive, Congress developed a blueprint for redefining its relationship to the agencies and adjusting its position in the constitutional separation of powers.

A. *Congress as Delegator*

As the scope and complexity of government increased during the New Deal, Congress tended to legislate relatively less and to delegate its authority to administrative agencies more often. In the 1930s and 1940s, the concept of delegation had not yet received the broad legitimacy it would later achieve. For some members of the legal community[,] delegation was per se suspect. Delegation was decried by several Congressmen during the legislative debates of the Walter-Logan Act of 1940, a precursor to the APA, which was successfully vetoed by President Franklin D. Roosevelt. Congressmen in both political parties criticized delegation. While not pandemic, the fear that delegation would lead to totalitarianism was frequently voiced and apparently real.

Several members shared a sense that the scope and complexity of demands on the federal government had outstripped Congress's legislative capacity. Once Congress fully accepted its role as delegator, it reconceptualized its relationship to the agencies now exercising more of its authority.

B. *Agencies as Extensions of Congress*

A second key feature of the congressional blueprint of 1946 was a subtle shift in a congressional view of administrative agencies. Previously, agencies might be considered agents or arms of Congress, but they were also viewed as somewhat independent and distinct from it. In 1946, the distinction was weakened and there was a greater tendency to view the agencies as immediate extensions of Congress. For instance, during hearings on the APA, David Simmons, President of the American Bar Association, urged Congress to "set up its own agencies" rather than separate bureaus and commissions to solve public policy problems. The APA and the Legislative Reorganization Act did not go as far as Simmons urged, but both treat federal agencies as legislative extensions.

The APA mandated that federal administration reflect the legislative values of participation in rulemaking and fair treatment of individuals—Congress's constituents—in adjudication and enforcement. One of Congressman Walter's arguments for the APA was that "[d]ay by day Congress takes account of the interests and desires of the people in framing legislation; and there is no reason why administrative agencies should not do so when they exercise legislative functions which Congress has delegated to them." Another supporter, Congressman John Gwynne (R-IA), noted that the bill "requires the agency to allow interested parties to appear and state their views and request that certain rules and regulations be adopted. That would be much like the hearings that we now have before our committees in the House." In Senator Homer Ferguson's (R-MI) view, treating agencies as extensions of Congress would enhance their legitimacy: "[i]n my opinion, there will be fewer complaints because of the activities of governmental agencies if they will attempt to live within the rules and regulations laid down by Congress. After all, the Congress is the policy-making body of the United States." Expressing the need for fairness, Senator Pat McCarran (D-NV), Chair of the Senate Judiciary Committee, called the APA "a bill of rights for the hundreds of thousands of Americans whose affairs are controlled or regulated in one way or another by agencies of the Federal Government. It is designed to provide guaranties of due process in administrative procedure." . . .

The Legislative Reorganization Act of 1946 was intended to enable congressional committees to "exercise continuous watchfulness of the execution [of law] by the administrative agencies." The Act reorganized the committee system and institutionalized the use of congressional staff for this purpose. Congressman La Follette, co-sponsor of the Act, conceptualized continuous watchfulness as "continuous review," which he also referred to as "supervising the administration of the laws" and as "consultation and collaboration between Congress and the Administration." . . .

Opponents of an administrative procedure act frequently objected to a one-size fits all approach. During the hearings on the Walter-Logan bill, several agency representatives indicated a strong desire to be exempt from comprehensive regulations. In 1945, Interstate Commerce Commission Commissioner Clyde Aichison called the APA bill a "retrograde step" because it would require the Commission to revamp its investigatory and reporting procedures. President Roosevelt's message vetoing the Walter-Logan Act approvingly quoted the New York City Bar Association's conclusion that the bill "would force administrative and departmental agencies having a wide variety of functions into a single mold which is so rigid, so needlessly interfering, as to bring about a widespread crippling of the administrative process."

Proponents of the APA thought individualized treatment of each agency was a losing strategy for effective control or supervision. In 1939, Congressman Walter contended that "there are approximately 100 agencies that have some legislative powers" and that the agencies "not only pay too little attention to the viewpoint of the public, but pay less attention to the clearly expressed intention of Congress." McCarran argued that "[d]iversity merely feeds confusion" and that when agencies are being created or empowered, "[i]t is utterly impractical to expect Congress . . . to enact a complete procedural law for one agency or one function. Under such circumstances, it is not surprising that procedural provisions respecting particular administrative agencies are often fragmentary, usually hastily improvised, and sometimes unwisely imitative."

Despite constitutional setbacks in cases such as *Buckley* v. *Valeo* and *Immigration and Naturalization Service* v. *Chadha*, the congressional tendency to view agencies as extensions persists. Perhaps strengthened by years of divided government, this trend intensified during the 1990s to the point that Congress, acting through its committees and subcommittees, is actively involved in establishing strategic plans for agencies and reviewing some agency rules prior to the time they can take effect.

The changing view of the relationship between Congress and agencies presented a major challenge to orthodox American public administrative thought in two respects. First, beginning with the civil service reform movement in the 1870s-1890s, leading American public administrative thinkers had insisted that administration was conceptually separate and should be institutionally independent from politics. In Woodrow Wilson's famous words, "administrative questions are not political questions." Once agencies have legislative functions and are viewed as extensions of legislatures, no dichotomy between administration and politics is possible. Under orthodox administration, a statute like the Federal Advisory Committee Act of 1972 is an impossibility. The Act's representation and participation provisions would not only be unnecessary, but actually undesirable. Gulick once complained that '[t]here are . . . highly inefficient arrangements like citizen boards and small local governments which *may* be necessary in a democracy." Wilson worried about public opinion becoming "meddlesome" in the science of public administration.

Second, American public administration had long been executive centered. Administration was execution and, therefore, appropriately the domain of the executive branch. In the words of the President's Committee on Administrative Management, "canons of efficiency require the establishment of a responsible and effective chief executive as the center of the energy, direction, and administrative management." John Rohr, a leading scholar of the constitutional aspects of American public administration noted that "[a]t the heart of the [Committee's] doctrine is a fundamental error that transforms the president from chief executive officer into sole executive officer." After the enactment of the APA and the legislative reorganization, it was difficult to avoid Rinehart Swenson's conclusion that "[c]ongressional control of administration is primary. Congress is the source of administration." . . .

II. Putting the Pieces Together

In 1946 Congress consciously readjusted its position in the constitutional scheme. Its new role emphasized delegation, regulation of administrative procedure, supervision of agencies, and detailed, systematic attention to public works projects and spending. As the hearings and debates on the APA, Legislative Reorganization Act, FTCA, and Employment Act collectively demonstrate, members of Congress recognized that control of federal administration was the key to maintaining a strong institutional position in the separation of powers. The 1946 blueprint successfully provided Congress with a variety of tools to influence federal agencies and draw them more firmly into its institutional sphere. Because these tools were also useful in members' bids for reelection, the 1946 blueprint proved highly durable and congressional involvement in federal administration flourished. . . .

The 1946 blueprint stimulated the growth in incumbency and decline in political competition. Fiorina noted that in the mid-1970s, "a lesser proportion of congressional effort is now going into programmatic activities and a greater proportion into pork barrel and casework activities. As a result, today's congressmen make relatively fewer enemies and relatively more friends among the people in their districts." . . .

After 1946, congressional incumbency not only benefitted from delegation, more efficient casework, a mandate for public works, and the ability to use committees and subcommittees to supervise agencies, it may also have been strengthened by the imposition of highly visible restrictions on federal administration. By the 1970s, "the bureaucracy serve[d] as a convenient lightning rod for public frustration and a convenient whipping boy for congressmen." Much of the whipping was for the sake of public relations, but some resulted in the strengthening of the APA. For example, the Freedom of Information Act of 1966 (FOIA), and amendments thereto in 1974, were strong congressional initiatives.

President Lyndon B. Johnson reluctantly signed FOIA, although he apparently thought the "goddam bill [would] screw [his] administration," and President Gerald Ford unsuccessfully vetoed the 1974 amendments. Other legislation, such as the Privacy Act and the Government in the Sunshine Act of 1976 demonstrates the use of administrative law to attempt to cure perceived bureaucratic ills.

III. 1946 in the 1990s

By the mid-1970s, the political and administrative problems with the 1946 blueprint were clear. The blueprint remained in place and was even augmented, but Congress began to feel the pressures of growing concern with budget deficits, prolonged and deepening distrust of government, and increased partisanship. The blueprint could no longer secure incumbency. Although the blueprint was originally developed with presidential support during the early days of Harry Truman's presidency, presidents had come to strongly oppose congressional relationships with federal agencies. Throughout the 1970s and 1980s, administrative reform was high on every president's agenda, although success was limited.

President Richard M. Nixon sought comprehensive reorganization of the executive branch, largely to gain greater executive control and coordination of federal administration. Although he succeeded in transforming the Bureau of the Budget into a stronger Office of Management and Budget (OMB) in 1970, he affected little else. Even this step was countered by Congress's creation of the Congressional Budget Office in 1974. Nixon and subsequent presidents also tried to gain greater centralized control over agency rulemaking with mixed success. President Jimmy Carter's Civil Service Reform Act of 1978 created a Senior Executive Service (SES) that promised to give political appointees greater control over the top of the career service. The original bill could have weakened the links between bureaus and subcommittees by permitting involuntary transfers of SES members among agencies. This provision was changed, however, while the bill was under consideration in Congress, and subsequent inter-agency mobility has been minuscule.

With the exception of the Department of Defense, President Reagan was probably more interested in getting agencies to do less rather than more. His strategy for dealing with them involved a mix of institutional controls, budget cuts, and reliance on loyal, ideologically compatible political appointees. Ironically, for all Reagan's bureaucracy bashing, the federal service actually had more departments and personnel at the end of his tenure than at its start. President George Bush carried some of the Reagan efforts forward but accomplished little, if any, lasting institutional change. It was not until the first Clinton-Gore administration that the Executive proposed a fundamentally different, executive-centered vision of federal administration.

The National Performance Review (NPR), headed by Vice President Albert Gore, Jr., has several goals. It seeks to "reinvent" government by making agencies act more like firms in a market economy: results-oriented, customer-driven, entrepreneurial, and "flatter" (less hierarchical). It challenges the 1946 blueprint by favoring deregulation of federal agencies. It seeks to free agencies from generic, across-the-board constraints by turning them into Performance Based Organizations or other formats that will operate largely outside of Title 5 of the United States Code. Among its stated objectives is "liberating agencies from congressional micromanagement." Overall, the NPR believes Congress's appropriate role is to establish policy objectives, empower and fund administrative units, and assess the results after a reasonable time has passed. . . .

With the possible exception of the line item veto, which was also part of the Republican "Contract with America" during the 1994 congressional election campaign, the NPR has not succeeded in reducing congressional involvement in federal administration. Its administrative vision draws heavily from experience in parliamentary systems and city manager cities in which there is no equivalent of the federal separation of powers. Major federal administrative reform requires congressional agreement, and, thus far, Congress has not been ready to abandon the 1946 blueprint. To the contrary, in the 1990s, Congress considerably strengthened its ability to supervise agencies and treat them as extensions.

The Government Performance and Results Act of 1993 (GPRA), enacted shortly before the NPR issued its first report, is a major congressional initiative with profound implications for the relationship between delegator and implementer. The bill had strong backing from reform-oriented segments of the public administration community and superficially appears to dovetail with the NPR because it seeks to make federal agencies result-oriented. The Act requires agencies to formulate five-year strategic plans with specific objectives, and to develop indicators, preferably quantitative, that will measure progress toward their goals. The GPRA specifically requires that agencies consult with Congress and interested parties, as well as OMB, in formulating their strategic plans.

From the perspective of 1946, GPRA offers a brilliant solution to the collective action problem that forces Congress to delegate broadly. It is often easier to form winning legislative coalitions on general objectives than on specifics. It is easy to vote "the public interest," but harder to say precisely what it is or how the burdens and benefits associated with achieving it should be distributed. Even where agreement is feasible, legislating detail can be time consuming, tedious work. But what stifles Congress as a whole may more readily be achieved by its working units. By requiring agencies to formulate specific objectives in consultation with it, Congress is, in effect, assigning the task of writing specifics into broad legislation to its subcommittees. Because these units are specialized, expert, and relatively small, majorities—or even consensus—among their members can often be readily formed. In contrast to 1946, Congress now believes it has the organizational strength to regulate or manage agencies individually, rather than generically. Post-GPRA, Congressional committees can establish precise program objectives for agencies. The Act is reminiscent of Kefauver's suggestion in 1945 that the various departments maintain offices adjacent to committee hearing rooms, and offers a mandate to micromanage. . . .

The Small Business Regulatory Enforcement Fairness Act of 1996 is another congressional initiative that strengthens the 1946 blueprint. Enacted as part of the Contract with American Advancement Act of 1996, it requires that every federal agency, including independent regulatory commissions, submit each final and interim rule for review by Congress and the General Accounting Office (GAO) before the rule can take effect. The Act empowers Congress to disapprove of a rule by joint resolution, which is subject to presidential veto (and legislative override). With some exceptions, major rules are subject to GAO analysis and a delay of at least sixty days while under congressional review. The Act strengthens Congress's ability to supervise the exercise of the authority it delegates. From a practical perspective, it pushes agencies to gain prior assurances from subcommittees that proposed rules are acceptable. Inevitably, it will increase congressional involvement in writing rules and will "blur the constitutional lines separating the branches of government."

Conclusion: Lessons for Administrative Reformers

The congressional blueprint of 1946 highlights the continuing importance of the separation of powers for federal administration. The President is charged with faithfully executing the laws, but the executive branch is also subordinate to Congress and the federal courts. First stated in 1838 with simple elegance by the Supreme Court in *Kendall* v. *United States*, the constitutional theory of congressional control of administration endures.

Despite its self-evident quality, this constitutional theory, as well as the political consequences that James Madison predicted would inevitably flow from it, have never been adequately appreciated by mainstream American public administrative thought. For more than a century, public administration has defined itself [as] a field of business or management. It sometimes claims, with Woodrow Wilson, that public administration "at most points stands apart even from the debatable ground of constitutional study." At other times, also with Wilson, it counsels the need to alter constitutional process for the sake of managerial efficiency, economy, and effectiveness—as though constitutional process, with its ramifications for institutional roles and power, does not present political questions.

Gore echoes Wilson in claiming that the NPR "is not about politics. . . . We want to make improving the way government does business a permanent part of how government works, regardless of which party is in power." And the NPR's perspective on Congress differs little, if at all, from Brownlow's view in 1949.

Until the plain lessons of institutional interest and power are integrated into administrative and reformist thought, history *will* repeat itself. Brownlow, and the President's Committee on Administrative Management that he chaired, were not successful in convincing Congress to empower, fund, and get out of the way. On the contrary, Congress responded to their quest for executive dominance by reengineering its constitutional position to supervise federal administration. Today, the NPR calls for deregulation of the executive branch and its liberation from legislative management. At the same time, Congress develops better tools to direct agencies. If the agencies are not already "owned" by Congress, the GPRA enables it to hijack them. It is far too late to treat congressional involvement in federal administration as haphazard or wayward. It follows the deliberate blueprint of 1946—a design that remains vibrant and shows no sign of obsolescence. Efforts at substantial administrative reform that fail to address it do not and will not succeed.

The APA at Fifty: A Celebration, Not a Puzzlement

Philip J. Harter

48 Administrative Law Review *309–311(1996)*.
Reprinted by permission of the American Bar Association.

Distilled from the best practices developed by agencies during the beginning of the administrative state—and rejecting the ABA's early calls for replicating court proceedings at virtually every turn—the Administrative Procedure Act developed the basic structure that has been followed since. As Justice Jackson wrote not long after its enactment: "The Act thus represents a long period of study and strife; it settles long-continued and hard-fought contentions, and enacts a formula upon which opposing social and political forces have come to rest. It contains many compromises and generalities and, no doubt, some ambiguities. Experience may reveal defects."

Here we are 50 years later. Many more hearings are conducted under its auspices by an administrative judiciary than by the Federal Courts. The basic arrangement by which judges fit within agencies was established in the APA and has endured; while there are currently debates over some changes—such as creating a centralized "corps" of administrative law judges—the notion of having judges be part of the executive branch is clearly accepted, something that was not before the APA. The overall machinery by which courts review agency action was also created by the Act. And so too was the process of rulemaking.

The rulemaking procedures of the APA are scant indeed. But their brevity contains several critically important political decisions. First, the entire notion of notice and comment rulemaking is fundamental. It provides a democratic means by which the people who will be affected—either by being regulated or as a beneficiary, or even as a "do-gooder"—can participate in the decision. While most of us simply take that right for granted, foreigners often express amazement: regulators at an intrusion on their "right" to simply issue the rule without having to go through the nuisance of any sort of consultation; the populace at our ability to have an agency actually consider our views when developing a rule. Second, it provides a means by which the agency can gain important information about the subject matter. Third[,] it is a means by which the discretion of an agency is held in check through judicial and political review. Fourth, the way the whole system works is to allow for the appropriate exercise of political discretion. The facts and the law define the range of political choice, but it is up to the agency to make the decision within that range. . . .

Congress is now engaged in a great deliberation on regulatory reform—an amendment of administrative procedure; a change in the APA. Does this signal a dissatisfaction with the APA, a need for fundamental change, a failure of the APA, a repudiation of the compromises struck so long ago? I think not.

Although it may be heretical to say in the current environment, the APA as it has evolved works pretty well; no, very well. If one listens carefully to the complaints over the regulatory process, the vast bulk of them fall within one or more of three categories: (1) The difficulty arose during the application of a rule—an enforcement case. Many war stories are funny or even absurd, but the problems lay in the exercise of discretion in the field, not with the Code of Federal Regulations. (2) The underlying statute forced the decision, so that any administrative process that was even remotely faithful to the will of Congress would have resulted in a decision subject to criticism. (3) The agency did not comply with the current requirements or at least with good practice. Very few of the complaints seem to center on the failure of the administrative process itself when notice and comment rulemaking, as it has evolved, has actually been followed. . . .

[Remarking on the controversies that continue to surround the administrative process in the United States, Harter concludes as follows:]

So what are we to do? To a degree we are just where we were 50 years ago—it is time to step back, survey good procedure, and capture it so that all may know and follow it while still allowing growth and experimentation. The basic structure of the APA is totally intact. Its political goals still live. Indeed, the gloss that has developed is largely the basis for the deliberations. We are, therefore, here to celebrate it!

Keynote Address: *Administrative Procedure and the Decline of Responsibility*

Philip K. Howard

48 Administrative Law Review *312–319 (1996)*.
Reprinted with permission of the American Bar Association.

One of the reasons why no one talks much about the Administrative Procedure Act is that it has almost nothing to do with administrative procedure in this town. The notice and comment procedures and the wide band of discretion that Congress provided in 1946 bear little relationship with the procedures that have been in effect in Washington for several decades. The APA nonetheless carries with it a legacy that is important in our lives. An important part of this legacy is its name, the Administrative Procedure Act. It has a portentive sound that makes everyone believe that somehow agencies are different than democracy, that process is superior to purpose and that, somehow, agencies will work in their own mysterious ways apart from the dirty functioning of democracy. This attitude, which I believe is pervasive among all those who deal with government, has, in my view, severely weakened our democracy.

My suggestion is that the APA, or the APA as modified by practice and judicial decision, should be substantially overhauled, perhaps repealed. The new statute should then be given a name that reflects what I believe its purpose ought to be, which is something like the Accountability in Government Act.

The problem that I perceive is not, of course, limited to the APA. It is fair to say that the administrative process suffers from the same infection that is afflicting public decisions all across America. This infection has purged responsibility from most public decisions, both individual responsibility and institutional responsibility.

I got into the project that became *The Death of Common Sense* not to look at administrative law . . . but to understand why things weren't working very well in government. I took a tour of basic institutions of our lives, which proved quite enlightening. For example, I went to schools and discovered that teachers could no longer kick a disruptive kid out of class without worrying about a thick book of procedures and a possible lawsuit; the effect was widespread disruption in our country's schools. In the workplace, I discovered that people were no longer candid to each other because there is a proper procedure that must be followed. Because of fear of legal liability for discrimination lawsuits and other claims, the country of the First Amendment, I discovered, no longer tolerates candor. My own firm, which only has a hundred employees and, I always thought, was a fairly close-knit organization, no longer gives recommendations, even to exemplary employees. Nor do most firms. Doctors are awash in forms and legally motivated procedures. They practice defensive medicine to a degree that hasn't been quantified, but talking to any doctor or hospital administrator, we know that substantial health care resources are devoted to unnecessary tests and procedures. And government, most Americans have concluded, doesn't seem to be able to do anything right. OSHA seemed particularly ineffective, starting with its violation citations for improper paperwork. The more studies I read, the more I became convinced that OSHA had had almost no effect on worker safety despite tens of billions of dollars spent by business over 25 years. . . .

As I walked through all of these institutions of our lives, what struck me was that they all had one thing in common: No one seemed to be using their judgment. There were procedures for everything but judgment nowhere. I mean, you don't have to be a rocket scientist to realize that if you warn against everything, the effect is, more or less, to warn against nothing. Most people understand that if you take authority away from teachers to run a classroom, some adolescents will be brilliant at exploiting the vacuum to the injury of everyone else who wants to learn.

As I looked into it a little deeper, what I found is that the reason it looked like no one was using their judgment is that we have reinvented our legal system, beginning in the 1960s, on the explicit premise that judgment should be banned from public decisions.

We developed this idea that law would be like an instruction manual telling everyone what to do. It would be extremely precise, and in furtherance of that, we've been writing rules at the speed of "fast forward" for about 35 years now. I had one of my research assistants try to count the number of words of federal law and regulations. A bad task. It turns out to be over 100 million words of law almost all written since the 1960s.

But rules, even millions of words of rules, can't substitute for certain kinds of choices. Where government has to make a decision—letting a contract, deciding which pesticides to ban, or the like—we invented, thanks to the legal process school, the primacy of process. There would be no irresponsible decisions, these inventors of the new legal system believed, if only we had enough procedures and enough judicial review at the end of the whole thing. What we accomplished in our quest to avoid irresponsible decisions was to eliminate the whole idea of responsibility. . . .

Why we invented this new legal system goes back to a period of the 1960s that most of us, as I look around the room, probably remember. This was a time of clashing values, and of rivers catching on fire from so much pollution, and the Vietnam War, and it's easy to see how we reached outside ourselves to find a system that would be value free.

One interesting political footnote about this new system is that both parties agreed that it was the way that government should work. Mutual distrust drove liberals and conservatives to manacle each other. Liberal reformers were so suspicious of business that they believed that they have to tell them exactly what to do or else they'll use their political influence to squirm out of every regulation. Therefore, liberal logic went, make law precise. Don't give business any leeway at all. Conservatives believe, of course, we should have as little government as possible. But in what government there is, they believe the bureaucrats are so abusive by nature that they have to be fitted with iron collars of rules and procedures. Only then, conservatives believe, could business be prevented from cutting off the knees of freedom-loving citizens. The one place where the right and left agreed is the reason we're in this mess. No one is allowed to use their judgment.

Now this legal system we've invented doesn't work very well. We all know that, which is probably the reason we're here. But the problem isn't regulation per se, because much of regulatory cost is probably worthwhile. Environmental regulation costs a lot and it *should* cost a lot. But it also happens to be inefficient, and this unnecessary cost probably runs into many billions. Our approach to regulation also impedes productivity. What does it do for our country, for example, when teachers can't run the classroom? What does it do for innovation when it takes practically 100 forms to start a deli in New York City?

But the worst of this rationalistic system is that it has changed our values. When you look outside yourself for the answer, you no longer value the sensible result. You become risk-adverse, because the complex shapes of every human decision never fit neatly in the square legal holes, even millions of them. And so what happens is that people start *not* making decisions. What one expert has called a "catastrophobia" has come across the land. We see it everywhere. Doctors practice defensive medicine. Warnings sprout up on the most mundane products. . . .

The attitude in administrative law today is that "more process means better decisions." In fact, more process means more defensiveness, it means distorted decisions. It means many fewer decisions. Conservatives tend to like the idea of procedural stalemates. But this also means that reform is almost impossible. As long as litigants have the resources, they can manipulate the process to slow everything down to a crawl. But what is worse is that when process is the supreme virtue, we've shut out any room for responsibility.

Responsibility, as we all know, is what makes things happen. That's how anything gets done. That's how you hold people accountable. Responsibility is all about values, it's about judgment, it's about risk taking, it's about timing. Process respects almost none of those things. So process has crowded out any room for leadership. . . .

Now the Constitution doesn't instruct us on the workings of agencies, which obviously don't fit neatly within one of the three branches of government. That's usually the excuse given in academic treatises for all of the procedures that are imposed upon agencies. But delegation is hardly an unusual concept. Our founders would have been surprised by modern government, but the idea of delegating responsibility to accomplish things is hardly unusual and would not, I believe, have shocked them.

But the trick to delegation is accountability. That's what happens when you send someone on an errand or run a business, that's what happens when you run an agency. The problem with our system today is that we've accomplished exactly the opposite. We have almost no accountability. . . .

Democracy as a system is all about accountability. But this system that we've built up in recent decades, under the banner of the Administrative

Procedure Act, almost perfectly accomplished exactly the opposite. Where no one has authority, no one is accountable. Who, we might ask, has the power?

But power is always captured somewhere. You all know the answer. The courts have the power. Secondarily, the power is held by interest groups and others who can afford the lawyers to play the process and go to the courts. . . .

Professor John Jefferies at the University of Virginia and I were recently talking about the epidemic of warnings. He suggested that we were probably at the point in America where one generic warning could apply to all products. His warning went something like, "Warning: This product should be used by a person exercising ordinary intelligence."

I would say that a similar admonition should be applied to the rules and administrative procedures that govern agencies. No system is ever going to create the right answer for us. No system is ever going to save us from our values, or the values of those that we disagree with. All it will do, and we should have learned it by now, is get in the way of sensible results and make it nearly impossible to hold anyone accountable. Our founders gave us a system. They called it "democracy." It contemplates delegation. I think the idea of agencies is not at all inconsistent with that. We need to go back to those time-honored tools—accountability and responsibility—and let democracy work.

Administrative Law in the 21st Century

Andrew F. Popper

49 Administrative Law Review *187–192 (1997).*
Reprinted by permission of the American Bar Association. Footnotes omitted.

These remarks are in response to the generous offer to look into the future of administrative law. It is tempting to respond in terms of the information revolution that in all likelihood will allow for a "virtual" administrative practice before an electronic agency. Computer-to-computer communication has become inexpensive and allows for parties to present advocacy statements in adjudication and comments in rulemaking without leaving their places of business. The technology explosion, symbolized by the Internet, creates the potential to assess public opinion, a phenomenon essential to effective governance. However, I would like to take a different approach, centered on a behavioral analysis, rather than on the Macintosh/Microsoft decade or century that lies ahead.

It is axiomatic that certain current administrative law paradigms will not be repeated in the 21st century. Although there has been some disagreement on form, there is no longer any doubt that alternative dispute resolution (ADR) in administrative practice is here to stay. Whether through refined settlement rules, negotiation, mediation, or other processes, these mechanisms are required because they are accepted by the polity. ADR exists in administrative law because command-and-control regulation costs too much, takes too long, and—if we are to believe political scientists—is no longer accepted by the polity. Similarly, economic regulation, controlling rates, routes, tariffs, entry and exit, the prime subjects of administrative action for 100 years, are no more. The world moved on, the rituals have changed, and acceptability by the public ended. Health and safety regulation based on a progressive vision of public safety is in resurgence because of the lack of public acceptance of environmental degradation.

These examples suggest that changes in administrative law and regulation are tied to broadly defined notions of public acceptability and perception. The legitimacy of agency behavior, in the end, is derived from sources that have an intensely political quality. This field, for better or worse, has the potential to be one of the more accurate mirrors or reflectors of public perception. That is bad news for non-majoritarian interests, interesting news for anthropologists and political scientists, and troubling news for APA purists.

I like the APA. Some of my best friends invest in the APA. Nevertheless, it is not now, nor has ever been, the APA that dictates private or public behaviors. Something more is involved.

Historically, a discourse on administrative law required separate discussions of its two gigantic subparts: process and substance. The study of how the regulatory state acts, a procedural inquiry, is captured in phrases that experience technical redefinition, such as control of discretion; deference; due process, fairness; efficiency and accountability; congressional oversight; separation of powers, functions and interests; and delegation. . . .

The second domain of administrative law involves the substance of what is regulated. This is the part of administrative law that is barely taught in the conventional course in administrative law (a mystery that has survived the last half-century) but is of fundamental public and political importance. In this area, a cultural anthropologist could spend years classifying the skeletal remains of regulation, deregulation, re-regulation, efficiency, the substance of cost-benefit analysis, the progressive state, the social welfare agenda, ruinous competition, public health and safety, property values, and the wonderful symbols (as in "the greens," "reds . . . or pink," eagles, chickens (sick and well), flags (burned or not), and an almost infinite variety of seals, spinning atoms to bundles of grains). Quite clearly, an anthropologist could structure an entire career interpreting the symbolic icons that form a shorthand for the target and consist of most activities, behaviors, and properties that are regulated. In my view, we would benefit from that study.

I am excited by the idea that other disciplines can be used to provide a perspective on the regulatory state. Rather than trying to ask "what is best?" when looking at a regulatory program, it may be more important to ask "what has already happened?" and "has the law caught up with the behavior?"

From a distance, it would seem that we do not create or disassemble regulatory programs because they are "best." Our administrative legal system instead is a rough approximation of continuously evolving ritual and custom that has been captured, codified, cleaned up for public viewing, and recorded for future study. Capturing and codifying constitute a vast investment and cause us to hold on to regulatory substance and process long after the ritual has changed. Too often, our section chiefs and tribal councils (of legislative, executive, and administrative affiliation and lineage) are consumed with preservation of outmoded rituals long after the masses or the polity have moved on.

This field suffers when it is dominated by those who mistakenly believe that their personal ideological perspective is the basis for creating or maintaining regulatory action. It is precisely that singular act of arrogance that has led to the discredited condition of the administrative state.

Perhaps in the 21st century, power will be possessed by those who comprehend the reflective nature of public regulation, as opposed to the proactive or reactive. It is by no means clear, however, that we will experience this sea change in leadership. In fact, for every case, decision, or practice that seeks to redefine law to capture the constantly changing rituals of our culture, there are counter forces seeking to hold fast to outlived practices. The consequence of this is public dissent and dissonance, followed by failed efforts at command-and-control regulation.

Resistance to this perspective, like resistance to change, is not hard to find. The Administrative Conference of the United States (ACUS) was seen as an organ of change or, in the parlance of this presentation, a group seeking to help agency practice reflect ritual. ACUS died a political, cruel death last fall.

A CENTURY OF ADMINISTRATIVE LAW LITERATURE

Students of the legal environment of public administration would be well served by familiarizing themselves with the rich literature of administrative law and process. This literature is voluminous and widely scattered in treatises, textbooks, monographs, journals, and governmental publications. However, there is a core body of reading that is readily accessible to those who desire to undertake further study. What follows is a brief introduction to this literature.[31]

Emergence of Administrative Law as a Recognized Component of American Public Law

Frank J. Goodnow was the first legal scholar to use *administrative law* as a descriptive term for law governing the administrative process. He argued that the failure to recognize administrative law in both England and the United States was due, not to its nonexistence, but rather to the failure of legal writers in those countries to classify the law. In 1893, he adopted a scheme of classification based on the relations that law governs and consequently defined administrative law as "that part of the law that governs the

---

[31] An alternative source introducing the literature of the field can be found in Marshall E. Dimock, *Law and Dynamic Administration* (1980), pp. 68–80. Dimock examines the tension among scholars who approached the field from the not always harmonious perspectives of administrative law and public administration.

relations of the executive and administrative authorities of government."[32] His recognition of a constitutional/administrative law dichotomy is illustrated by his statement that "administrative law is therefore that part of the public law that fixes the organization and determines the competence of the administrative authorities, and indicates to the individual remedies for violation of his rights."[33] Alternatively, he defined constitutional law as the general plan of state organization and action; however, he remarked that the distinction between the two was more of degree than of kind.

The following year, Ernst Freund used Goodnow's term *administrative law* and expressed the hope that it would become familiar to the public and the legal profession and that it would become one of the recognized branches of public law.[34] Administrative law, in Freund's own terminology, was the "body of law which is thus developed regulates and limits governmental action without involving constitutional questions."[35] Whereas constitutional law questions involved issues of liberty and sovereignty, those in administrative law dealt with issues such as the legality of official action, fiscal rights and liabilities of government, and questions of remedies against government. Ernst Freund's casebook, *Cases on Administrative Law* (1911), was the first of its kind in American administrative law and remained the only one until Felix Frankfurter and J. Forrester Davison published *Cases and Other Materials on Administrative Law* (1932). Freund was to further clarify his definition of administrative law in the second edition of his casebook by stating that "administrative law continues to be treated as law controlling the administration, and not as law produced by the administration."[36] This is an important distinction that continues to have wide support to this day.

Whereas Ernst Freund was to become the pioneer who influenced the scope of law school courses in administrative law, Frank Goodnow's influence was felt primarily in the political science and public administration curricula. Among the political scientists who wrote classics in Goodnow's footsteps were John Dickinson, *Administrative Justice and the Supremacy of Law in the United States* (1927), and J. Roland Pennock, *Administration and the Rule of Law* (1941).

Elihu Root's presidential address to the American Bar Association in 1916 stands out as one of the most accurate and prophetic statements ever made about the administrative process.[37] In the speech, Root asserted that the development of the field of administrative law was inevitable given the new methods of regulation in the increasingly complex society. He called for pragmatic experimentation to deal with the new social and industrial

---

[32] Frank J. Goodnow, *Comparative Administrative Law* 7 (1893).

[33] Ibid., 8–9.

[34] Ernst Freund, "The Law of the Constitution in America," 9 *Political Science Quarterly* 403, 404 (1894).

[35] Ibid.

[36] Ernst Freund, *Cases on Administrative Law* v (2nd rev. ed.,1928).

[37] 41 *American Bar Association Report* 355, 368–369 (1916).

conditions. Root also implored his profession to put aside the theoretical debate over the development of the administrative state.

The advice of these pioneer administrative law scholars was not heeded by the many in the legal profession who lamented the passing of simple government. Polemical outcries challenging both the desirability and the legality of administrative rule making and adjudicatory powers appeared in both England and the United States. Lord Hewart, Lord Chief Justice of England, published *The New Despotism* (1929), in which he maintained that administrative law did not exist in England and that what actually existed was "administrative lawlessness." Hewart's American counterpart was James M. Beck, a former solicitor general of the United States, who published *Our Wonderland of Bureaucracy* (1932), in which he drew an analogy between Uncle Sam and the fanciful dreams of Lewis Carroll's *Alice in Wonderland*:

> When Alice awoke from her dreams, as a sensible little girl she realized that the fancies of her mind in sleep were but the children of an idle brain. But Uncle Sam has not yet awakened from his dreams of government by bureaucracy, but even wanders further afield in crazy experiments in state socialism.[38]

However, more reasoned voices were being heard within the legal profession. Harlan Fiske Stone, later to become chief justice of the United States, stated that the rise of a system of administrative law was "perhaps the most striking change in the common law in this country."[39]

Stone contrasted the lack of receptivity by the legal profession and courts to the rise of administrative agencies under common law with that of the civil law. In continental Europe's civil law system, Stone argued, "The rise of administrative law, independently of the courts, came as a welcome formulation of principles for the guidance of official action, where no control had existed before."[40] Two years later, in a foreword to a symposium issue of the *Yale Law Journal,* Professor Felix Frankfurter asserted that "administrative law has not come like a thief in the night. It is not an innovation; its general recognition is."[41] A year later President Roosevelt appointed Frankfurter to the Supreme Court, making him the first academic scholar in the field of administrative law to be elevated to the high court.

Thus, for a period of almost a half century, there was a distinct time lag between the de facto existence of administrative law and its de jure recognition. As a consequence, several generations of lawyers and jurists were not, for the most part, beneficiaries of the systematized treatments of administrative law in law school curricula. The negativism of the legal profession, perhaps best illustrated by the American Bar Association's efforts during the 1930s, inhibited administrative procedure reform. The pragmatic growth of the administrative process and the de facto recognition of admin-

---

[38] James M. Beck, *Our Wonderland of Bureaucracy* vii–ix (1932).

[39] Harlan Fiske Stone, "The Common Law in the United States," 50 *Harvard Law Review* 4, 16 (1936).

[40] Ibid.

[41] Frankfurter, above, note 8, 517.

istrative law continued unabated without the benefit of a jurisprudential framework that one might expect as a new field of law evolves. However, in the post–World War II era, a whole new generation of scholars would rise to prominence in the field and provide such a framework.

Post–World War II Administrative Law Scholarship

The administrative law scholars who emerged in the post–World War II era were to have a profound impact on the field, one that is still in evidence today. For many of them, their scholarship was informed by extensive experience with federal administrative agencies, especially during the wartime emergency. The contributions of some of the most significant scholars are highlighted here. No discussion of the literature of administrative law over the past half century would be complete without acknowledgment of the prominent role Kenneth Culp Davis has played in American jurisprudence. The frequency of Supreme Court citations to his works is testament to his profound influence. He is best known for his definitive, multivolume *Administrative Law Treatise*, first published in 1958. The third edition of the *Treatise* (1994) was written jointly with Richard J. Pierce, Jr. The fourth edition, which appeared in 2002, identified Pierce as the sole author.[42] Davis was also the author of an influential monograph, *Discretionary Justice* (1969), which focused upon the little-examined portion of the administrative process that was not normally subject to either judicial review or trial-type adjudicatory hearings.

Walter Gellhorn was well known for his influential law school casebook, coedited with Clark Byse.[43] Also worthy of mention are Gellhorn's *Federal Administrative Proceedings* (1941), *When Americans Complain* (1966), and *Ombudsmen and Others* (1966). The latter two works, along with Davis's *Discretionary Justice*, provided further impetus to the drive to examine the vast area of administrative law outside the scope of the APA.

Louis Jaffe, the author with Nathaniel Nathanson of another highly regarded law school casebook of this era,[44] was best known for his exhaustive *Judicial Control of Administrative Action* (1965). In this work Jaffe examined all of the major aspects of the relationship between agencies and the courts. In its time it was considered to be a definitive work and was frequently cited in appellate court opinions.

The final legal scholar of the post–World War II era whom we want to highlight is Bernard Schwartz. Schwartz was a prolific scholar in both constitutional and administrative law. His passion, however, was the latter. He wrote treatises and textbooks on the subject and for many years wrote an annual survey of developments in the field of administrative law for leading

---

[42] Richard J. Pierce, Jr., is also the author, with Sidney A. Shapiro and Paul R. Verkuil, of *Administrative Law and Process* (3rd ed., 1999).

[43] The classic, multiple-edition text is now being published as Peter L. Strauss, Todd Rakoff, Roy A. Schotland, and Cynthia R. Farina, *Administrative Law: Cases and Comments* (9th ed., 1995).

[44] Louis L. Jaffe and Nathaniel Nathanson, *Administrative Law: Cases and Materials* (3rd ed., 1968).

law journals.[45] Also, in a somewhat unique early work, *The Professor and the Commission* (1959), Schwartz recounted his personal experience before a federal independent regulatory commission.

Scholars in political science and public administration during this era were also making significant contributions to the literature of administrative law and process. Marver H. Bernstein, in *Regulating Business by Independent Commission* (1955), presented a classic exposition of the "capture theory," whereby administrative agencies become captives of those interests that they are ostensibly regulating. Theodore Lowi's call for the revitalization of the delegation of powers doctrine first appeared in *The End of Liberalism* (1979) and then again in "Two Roads to Serfdom: Liberalism, Conservatism and Administrative Power."[46] Barbara H. Craig's *Chadha: The Story of an Epic Constitutional Struggle* (1988) is a highly readable account of the landmark legislative veto case, *Immigration and Naturalization Service* v. *Chadha*. Finally, A. Lee Fritschler, in his multiple-edition textbook *Smoking and Politics*, effectively used the case study method to introduce undergraduates to the regulatory process and the rudiments of administrative law.[47]

In the past several decades, the literature of administrative law has grown exponentially, and it simply isn't feasible to attempt to capture its essence here. It should be noted, however, that two of the most influential administrative law scholars of this period, Antonin Scalia and Stephen G. Breyer, were appointed associate justices of the Supreme Court by Presidents Reagan and Clinton, respectively.[48]

As administrative law courses became more commonplace in the curricula of political science and public administration, the traditional law school casebooks became increasingly ill suited for students without prior experience with legal analysis or the use of the case method.

Consequently, several textbooks aimed at this market have been published, including the present volume, which was published in two previous editions by the West Publishing Company.[49] Finally, there are several excellent interdisciplinary readers that provide excerpts of some of the best of the contemporary literature of the field.[50]

---

[45] From the 1950s to the 1970s these reviews appeared in the *Annual American Survey of Law*. More recently they were published in the *Administrative Law Review*.

[46] 36 *American University Law Review*, 295 (1987).

[47] A recent journalistic assessment of bureaucratic policies and processes is Cindy Skrzycki, *The Regulators: Anonymous Power Brokers in American Politics* (2003).

[48] Both individuals have published widely in law journals, and for a considerable period of time Scalia edited the ABA publication *Regulation*. Breyer is the author of *Regulation and Its Reform* (1982) and also collaborated with Richard B. Stewart on a multiple edition administrative law textbook, *Administrative Law and Regulatory Policy: Problems, Text, and Cases* (2nd ed., 1985).

[49] Among other multiple editions in this field are Kenneth F. Warren, *Administrative Law in the Political System* (3rd ed., 1996); Lief H. Carter and Christine Harrington, *Administrative Law and Politics: Cases and Comments* (2nd ed., 1991); and Daniel Hall, *Administrative Law: Bureaucracy in a Democracy* (2nd ed., 2002).

[50] See, in particular, Peter H. Schuck, *Foundations of Administrative Law* (1994), and Thomas O. Sargentich, *Administrative Law Anthology* (1994).

PART TWO

Legislative and Judicial Controls over the Administrative Process

CHAPTER 3

Delegation of Power

CHAPTER 4

Judicial Review of Administrative Determinations

Chapter 3

Delegation of Power

Under our system of separation of powers, the starting point for the analysis of administrative activity is the authority provided to the administrator by the legislature. "All legislative powers herein granted shall be vested in a Congress of the United States," reads Article I of the U.S. Constitution. Article I also provides Congress with the power to "collect taxes," "borrow money," "coin money," and perform many other specific functions, but it was clearly not contemplated that members of Congress would personally and directly take part in these activities. Article II states that the president "shall take care that the laws be faithfully executed" and mentions "executive departments" and "officers" under the president whose functions would involve administration of the legislation adopted by Congress.

DELEGATION BY CONGRESS

From the start, then, there was an expectation that participation by governmental departments and officials outside of Congress would be required to realize the objectives of legislation promulgated by Congress. Whether such activity involves "delegation" by Congress to the executive is open to question. The term *delegation* does not appear in the Constitution, and there is some disagreement as to its precise meaning. Justice John M. Harlan wrote for the Supreme Court in *Field* v. *Clark* in 1892, "That Congress cannot delegate legislative power . . . is a principle universally recognized as vital to the integrity and maintenance of the system of government ordained by the Constitution" (143 U.S. 649, 693). Most people would agree with this often-repeated statement if "legislative power" is used in a very narrow sense. But the concept of delegation is often employed more loosely. A writer has called it the "power to 'fill in the details' of legislative enactments."[1] In this sense, delegation is an activity that has been practiced at least since

---

[1] Sotirios A. Barber, *The Constitution and the Delegation of Congressional Power* 7 (1975).

the time of the adoption of the Constitution.[2] The inspiration for this definition is the well-known statement by Chief Justice John Marshall in 1825:
"The line has not been exactly drawn which separates those important subjects, which must be entirely regulated by the legislature itself, from those
of less interest, in which a general provision may be made, and power given
to those who are to act under such general provisions, to fill up the details"
[*Wayman* v. *Southard*, 23 U.S. (10 Wheat.) 1, 43]. Marshall's statement is
an acknowledgment, at an early point in American history, that some aspects of governmental policy, the details of broader frameworks set out by
Congress, would have to be left to administrative officials. And the fact that
"the line has not been exactly drawn" between what only Congress can do
and what may be left to other governmental officials is the nub of the
problem.

The Panama *Case*

It was not until the end of the nineteenth century that the so-called nondelegation doctrine began to be asserted. The statement quoted above from *Field*
v. *Clark* (1892), to the effect that "Congress cannot delegate legislative
power," was an important expression of the doctrine. In spite of such statements, however, the Supreme Court uniformly sustained delegations by
Congress until the 1930s. The year 1935 saw the only two Supreme Court
decisions invalidating congressional delegations to governmental authorities. In *Panama Refining Co.* v. *Ryan*, 293 U.S. 388 (1935), the Supreme
Court declared section 9(c) of the National Industrial Recovery Act of 1933
to be an improper delegation of power because of the absence in the statute
of a standard under which the president was to act. Section 9(c) gave the
president the power to prohibit the transportation in interstate commerce
of "hot oil" (oil produced in violation of state laws) but provided no guidelines
for the exercise of presidential power. As Justice Benjamin N. Cardozo
pointed out in the sole dissent, policy objectives stated elsewhere in the act
asserted that the legislation was designed "to eliminate unfair competitive
practices," and "to conserve natural resources," but these were not considered adequate by the majority of the Court.

The Schechter *Case*

The second delegation held invalid, in *Schechter Poultry Corp.* v. *United
States*, 295 U.S. 495 (1935), was much broader. Under section 3 of the National Industrial Recovery Act, the president was empowered to approve
"codes of fair competition" for various branches of industry and commerce to
regulate such matters as maximum hours, minimum wages, and collective
bargaining. When petitioners were convicted for violation of the "Live Poultry Code" adopted under section 3, they contended that the code had been
adopted pursuant to an unconstitutional delegation of power. The Supreme

---

[2] For examples see Justice Cardozo's dissenting opinion in *Panama Refining Co.* v. *Ryan*, 293
U.S. 388, 442 (1935).

Court unanimously supported this view. Said Chief Justice Charles E. Hughes for the Court:

> Section 3 of the Recovery Act is without precedent. It supplies no standards for any trade, industry or activity. It does not undertake to prescribe rules of conduct to be applied to particular states of fact determined by appropriate administrative procedure. . . . [T]he discretion of the President, in approving or prescribing codes, and thus enacting laws for the government of trade and industry throughout the country, is virtually unfettered. We think that the code-making authority thus conferred is an unconstitutional delegation of legislative power [295 U.S. 495, 541–542].

Justice Cardozo, who had dissented in the *Panama Refining* case, wrote a concurring opinion in *Schechter* in which he stated the following: "The delegated power . . . which has found expression in this code is not canalized within the banks that keep it from overflowing. It is unconfined and vagrant. . . . This is delegation running riot. No such plenitude of power is susceptible of transfer" (295 U.S. 495, 551–553).

Since *Panama* and *Schechter*, delegations by Congress have been uniformly upheld. Commentators appear to agree that "no delegation since has equaled the scope of the Recovery Act,"[3] but there have been numerous broad grants of power from Congress based on quite vague legislative standards, all of which have been sustained in constitutional challenges.[4] Writers are divided on the propriety and wisdom of this uncritical approach to delegation. Kenneth Culp Davis, in his important *Administrative Law Treatise* (1958), took the view that "the test of the validity of delegation ought to have more to do with [procedural] safeguards than with standards. . . . [T]he standards test is on the way out and the safeguards test in the ascendancy."[5] Davis has argued elsewhere that the objective of requiring every delegation to be accompanied by meaningful standards "had to fail, should have failed, and did fail."[6] But others regretted the reluctance of the courts to demand more of Congress. The political scientist Theodore Lowi stated that this "offers a jurisprudential carte blanche for poor legislative drafting and at the same time sweeps away all concern for the consequences." He favors a "revival of the still valid but universally disregarded rule in the *Schechter* case," adding that "[u]nder present conditions, when Congress delegates without a shred of guidance, the courts usually end up rewriting many of the statutes in the course of construction." Rather than such judicial activism, "a blanket invalidation under the *Schechter* rule is tantamount to a

---

[3] Barber, above, note 1, 95.

[4] Representative examples are *Yakus* v. *United States*, 321 U.S. 414 (1941); *Lichter* v. *United States*, 334 U.S. 742 (1948); and *Arizona* v. *California*, 373 U.S. 546 (1963). As Bernard Schwartz has put it in discussing delegation, "*Schechter* stands apart in any discussion of delegation. It involves the broadest delegation Congress ever made." Schwartz also noted that federal courts now sustain standards as broad as those condemned in *Panama*. *Administrative Law* 38 and 41 (1976).

[5] 1965 Pocket Part to Volume 1 §§ 2.17, 55.

[6] "A New Approach to Delegation," 36 *University of Chicago Law Review* 713, 719 (1969). Davis's later writings contain a more elaborate discussion of these matters, in which he tried to "alter the nondelegation doctrine to make it effective and useful." But he still rejects the standards test as workable. See his 1 *Administrative Law Treatise* 206 (2nd ed., 1978).

court order for Congress to do its own work. Therefore, the rule of law is a restraint upon rather than an expansion of judicial function."[7]

It is said that Congress is sometimes unable to provide clearer standards because the questions that it is dealing with are too complex or new[8] and that it is sometimes unwilling to do so because the issues in question are too controversial.[9] Whatever its motivation, it seems clear that Congress is disinclined to do much more than it has been doing in recent years to lay down precise standards for delegation.

Before we examine more recent delegation cases, it may be helpful to illustrate how statutory delegations have evolved historically. Peter Strauss has provided a fascinating example of the changes in statutory practice since the latter days of the nineteenth century by comparing the delegation provisions of two transportation safety measures.[10] In both instances Congress was responding to the perception that the then-dominant form of transportation was unsafe. In the first instance, the Federal Railway Safety Appliances Act of 1893, 27 Stat. 531, Congress acted "directly"[11] by specifying which of the new and safer technologies were to be used and left little discretion to the Interstate Commerce Commission (ICC), the administrative agency overseeing the implementation of the statute:

> It told the railroads just what technologies they were to employ (power brakes, automatic couplers, "grab bars" . . .), and declared the sanctions that were to apply in the event of failure. While the ICC was permitted to make certain interim decisions—whether to postpone the effective date of a standard, whether to recommend a prosecution to the Attorney General—Congress generally placed enforcement power in the hands of the prosecutors and the courts. . . . One reading the congressional debates is immediately gripped by a sense, not only of their seriousness of purpose and genuineness as debates, but also of their sharp focus on precise definition of the appropriate legal response to the problem at hand. That was Congress's business.[12]

---

[7] Theodore J. Lowi, *The End of Liberalism* 125, 300 (2nd ed., 1979). Other writings advocating a revival of the nondelegation doctrine include Judge J. Skelly Wright, "Beyond Discretionary Justice," 81 *Yale Law Journal* 575, 582 (1972), and John Hart Ely, *Democracy and Distrust: A Theory of Judicial Review* 131–134 (1980).

[8] Concerning the National Environmental Policy Act of 1969, Kenneth Culp Davis wrote: "The reason Congress refrained from stating meaningful guides as to whether or when environmental values should prevail is simply that no one knew how to write meaningful guides." 1 *Administrative Law Treatise* 153 (2nd ed., 1978).

[9] See, for example, Ely, above, note 7, 131–132: "How much more comfortable it must be simply to vote in favor of a bill calling for safe cars, clean air, or nondiscrimination, and to leave to others the chore of fleshing out what such a mandate might mean. How much safer, too—and here we get to the nub. For the fact seems to be that on most hard issues our representatives quite shrewdly prefer not to have to stand up and be counted but rather to let some executive-branch bureaucrat, or perhaps some independent regulatory commission, 'take the inevitable political heat.'"

[10] "Legislative Theory and the Rule of Law: Some Comments on Rubin," 89 *Columbia Law Review* 427, 428–430 (1989).

[11] Edward L. Rubin in his seminal article "Law and Legislation in the Administrative State," 89 *Columbia Law Review* 369, 380–385 (1989), uses the terms *direct* or *transitive* to describe the nineteenth-century model of statutes that left little discretion to the agency implementing congressional directives. Correspondingly, he uses *indirect* or *intransitive* to describe their twentieth-century counterparts, in which agencies are given wide latitude.

[12] Strauss, above, note 10, 429.

The equivalent legislative response in the mid-twentieth century was the National Traffic and Motor Vehicle Safety Act of 1966, 80 Stat. 718. This act, like its counterpart in 1893, sought the development and deployment of suitable technologies, such as seat belts, but Congress stopped short of identifying the measures that should be taken to make automobiles safer. Instead, it delegated the responsibility to the Department of Commerce (now the Department of Transportation) to decide what safety standards would be "reasonable, practicable and appropriate for the particular type of motor vehicle . . . for which it is prescribed," would "meet the need for motor vehicle safety," and could "be stated in objective terms."[13] The 1966 act is a classic illustration of what Edward L. Rubin described as an "indirect" statute.[14] According to Strauss, "Congress had neither time nor inclination to attend to legislative detail; there was no debate worthy of the name, just rhetoric about the seriousness of the problem and the need, at last, to see that something was done about it."[15]

RECENT JUDICIAL VIEWS ON NONDELEGATION

More recently, the voices of two Supreme Court justices—William Rehnquist, later to become chief justice, and Chief Justice Warren Burger—were added to those supporting a return to the nondelegation doctrine. Their views were expressed in two separate opinions (the first a concurrence and the second a dissent) in cases decided by the Supreme Court in the early 1980s. Rehnquist wrote both opinions, and Burger joined in the second. In both cases, *Industrial Union Department, AFL-CIO* v. *American Petroleum Institute*, 448 U.S. 607 (1980), and *American Textile Manufacturers Institute* v. *Donovan*, 452 U.S. 490 (1981), the nondelegation issue centered on section 6 (b)(5) of the Occupational Safety and Health Act of 1970, 84 Stat. 1594, 29 U.S.C. 655(b)(5). This part of the act provided that the secretary of labor, in establishing standards dealing with toxic materials or harmful physical agents, "shall set the standard which most adequately assures, to the extent feasible, on the basis of the best available evidence, that no employee will suffer material impairment of health or functional capacity" from exposure to such substances. In the first case, producers of benzene objected to the standard set by the Occupational Safety and Health Administration (OSHA, an agency within the department of labor) for exposure to benzene, and in the second, representatives of the cotton industry challenged OSHA's cotton dust standard. Suffice it to say here that in the first case, the Supreme Court affirmed a lower court decision, which held the benzene standard invalid, and in the second it agreed with a lower court that a cost-benefit analysis by OSHA was not required in establishing the cotton dust standard. What

---

[13] 15 U.S.C. §§ 1392(f)(3), 1391 (2), 1392 (a). Abbreviated use of U.S. Code provisions from Strauss, above, note 10, 429.

[14] Rubin, above, note 11.

[15] Strauss, above, note 10, 430.

concerns us here is Justice Rehnquist's attack, on delegation grounds, on the statutory language just quoted.

Two competing interpretations of the section 6(b)(5) of the Occupational Safety and Health Act of 1970 were at issue in the *Industrial Union Department, AFL-CIO* case (often called the *Benzene* case). By Rehnquist's account, the secretary of labor, one of the petitioners in the case, believed that a proposed standard is economically feasible so long as its impact "will not be such as to threaten the financial welfare of the affected firms or the general economy" [43 Fed. Reg. 5939 (1978)]. The secretary made no attempt to define what was meant by the concept of "bearable cost." On the other hand, the respondents argued that section 6(b)(5) must be read in light of section 3(8) of the same act, which defines an "occupational health and safety standard," and as a consequence, the secretary is required to justify any particular health standard on the basis of a balancing of costs and benefits. Justice Rehnquist attributed the difficulty that his colleagues were having in evaluating these opposing interpretations to the following dilemma: "[T]his litigation presents the Court with what has to be one of the most difficult issues that could confront a decisionmaker: whether the statistical possibility of future deaths should ever be disregarded in light of the economic costs of preventing those deaths" (448 U.S. 607, 672). He concluded by suggesting that the widely varying interpretations advanced by both parties to the case and by the justices themselves demonstrated that Congress had unlawfully delegated that choice to the secretary of labor and ultimately to the Supreme Court in its exercise of its judicial review function.

After engaging in a wide-ranging analysis of legislative power and its delegation, starting with John Locke's *Second Treatise on Civil Government* (1690), and an examination of the legislative history of the OSHA, Rehnquist returned to the nondelegation doctrine and its relevance to this case. The following excerpts from Rehnquist's concurring opinion represent the opening salvos of what continues to be a heated debate, both within the Court and among academic commentators,[16] over delegation-of-power questions:

> As formulated and enforced by this Court, the nondelegation doctrine serves three important functions. First, and most abstractly, it ensures to the extent consistent with orderly governmental administration that important choices of social policy are made by Congress, the branch of our Government most responsive to the popular will. . . . Second, the doctrine guarantees that, to the extent Congress finds it necessary to delegate authority, it provides the recipient of that authority with an "intelligible principle" to guide the exercise of the delegated discretion. . . . Third, and derivative of the second, the doctrine ensures that courts charged with reviewing the exercise of delegated legislative discretion will be able to test that exercise against ascertainable standards. . . .
>
> I believe the legislation at issue here fails on all three counts. The decision whether the law of diminishing returns should have any place in the regulation of toxic substances is quintessentially one of legislative policy. For Congress to pass that decision on to the Secretary in the manner it did violates, in my mind,

---

[16] A recent academic critique of the Supreme Court's delegation case law is David Schoenbrod, *Power without Responsibility: How Congress Abuses the People through Delegation* (1993).

John Locke's caveat—reflected in the cases cited earlier in this opinion—that legislatures are to make laws, not legislators. Nor, as I think the prior discussion amply demonstrates, do the provisions at issue or their legislative history provide the Secretary with any guidance that might lead him to his somewhat tentative conclusion that he must eliminate exposure to benzene as far as technologically and economically possible. Finally, I would suggest that the standard of "feasibility" renders meaningful judicial review impossible. . . .

If we are ever to reshoulder the burden of ensuring that Congress itself make the critical policy decisions, these are surely the cases in which to do it. It is difficult to imagine a more obvious example of Congress simply avoiding a choice which was both fundamental for purposes of the statute and yet politically so divisive that the necessary decision or compromise was difficult, if not impossible, to hammer out in the legislative forge. Far from detracting from the substantive authority of Congress, a declaration that the first sentence of § 6 (b)(5) . . . constitutes an invalid delegation to the Secretary of Labor would preserve the authority of Congress. If Congress wishes to legislate in an area which it has not previously sought to enter, it will in today's political world undoubtedly run into opposition no matter how the legislation is formulated. But that is the very essence of legislative authority under our system. It is the hard choices, and not the filling in of the blanks, which must be made by the elected representatives of the people. When fundamental policy decisions underlying important legislation about to be enacted are to be made, the buck stops with Congress and the President insofar as he exercises his constitutional role in the legislative process . . . [448 U.S. 607, 685–687].

Admonitions to Congress

In the so-called cotton dust case, Justice Rehnquist, now joined by Chief Justice Burger, continued his attempt to revive the nondelegation doctrine. He stated that Congress could have been more precise in addressing the issue of exposure levels (for instance, by requiring the secretary to engage in cost-benefit analysis) but that it had not been:

> Rather than make that choice and resolve the difficult policy issue, however, Congress passed. . . . The words "to the extent feasible" were used to mask a fundamental policy disagreement in Congress. I have no doubt that if Congress had been required to choose whether to mandate, permit, or prohibit the Secretary from engaging in cost-benefit analysis, there would have been no bill for the President to sign. . . . Congress simply left the crucial policy choices in the hands of the Secretary of Labor. As I stated at greater length last term, I believe that in so doing Congress unconstitutionally delegated its legislative responsibility to the Executive Branch [452 U.S. 545–548].

The addition of the voices of two Supreme Court justices to those calling for a return to the nondelegation doctrine undoubtedly adds authority to this development. It might be interpreted by members of Congress as an admonition to delegate more carefully. It remained doubtful, however, that support for the nondelegation doctrine would command a majority of the Supreme Court. The more likely scenario would be that of the Court's attempting to manage unwieldy delegations on a case-by-case basis.

A practical problem with legislation lacking clear standards is that courts are deprived of a reasonable basis for reviewing agency action. As

Justice Rehnquist put it in the excerpt from the *Benzene* case[17] quoted above, in his view "the standard of 'feasibility' renders meaningful judicial review impossible." Some observers, therefore, have looked to the courts, not for invalidation of delegation à la *Schechter*, but for other means of control of standardless delegations. The dominant measure employed by the courts to deal with standardless delegations has become the technique of interpreting broad delegations narrowly in order to avoid serious constitutional issues.

JUDICIAL NARROWING OF CONGRESSIONAL DELEGATION

In the case that follows, *Kent* v. *Dulles*, Rockwell Kent and Dr. Walter Briehl were denied passports under a regulation promulgated by the secretary of state providing that no passport would be issued for travel by Communists or others for purposes of furthering the Communist movement. The regulation was adopted under a statute which provided: "The Secretary of State may grant and issue passports . . . under such rules as the President shall designate and prescribe for and on behalf of the United States, and no other person shall grant, issue or verify such passports" (22 U.S.C. § 211a). Another statute made it unlawful to depart from or enter into the United States without a valid passport (8 U.S.C. § 1185). Both plaintiffs sued in U.S. district court for declaratory relief, but on that level and at the court of appeals their pleas were rejected. The case came to the U.S. Supreme Court on the discretionary writ of certiorari.[18] This case is a good example of judicial narrowing of congressional delegation.

Kent v. *Dulles*

SUPREME COURT OF THE UNITED STATES, 1958.
357 U.S. 116, 78 S.Ct. 1113, 2 L.Ed.2d 1204.

Mr. Justice DOUGLAS delivered the opinion of the Court. . . .

The right to travel is a part of the "liberty" of which the citizen cannot be deprived without due process of law under the Fifth. So much is conceded by the Solicitor General. . . . We need not decide the extent to which it can be curtailed. We are first concerned with the extent, if any, to which Congress has authorized its curtailment.

The difficulty is that while the power of the Secretary of State over the issuance of passports is expressed in broad terms, it was apparently long exercised quite narrowly. So far as material here, the cases of refusal of passports generally fell into two categories. First, questions perti-

---

[17] The *Industrial Union Department, AFL-CIO* v. *American Petroleum Institute* case is commonly referred to as the *Benzene* case for the chemical compound at issue.

[18] "It is most commonly used to refer to the Supreme Court of the United States, which uses the writ of certiorari as a discretionary device to choose the cases it wishes to hear." *Black's Law Dictionary, Abridged* (6th ed., 1991), p. 156.

nent to the citizenship of the applicant and his allegiance to the United States had to be resolved by the Secretary, for the command of Congress was that "No passport shall be granted or issued to or verified for any other persons than those owing allegiance, whether citizens or not, to the United States." 32 Stat. 386, 22 U.S.C. § 212, 22 U.S.C.A. § 212. Second, was the question whether the applicant was participating in illegal conduct, trying to escape the toils of the law, promoting passport frauds, or otherwise engaging in conduct which would violate the laws of the United States.

The grounds for refusal asserted here do not relate to citizenship or allegiance on the one hand or to criminal or unlawful conduct on the other. Yet, so far as relevant here, those two are the only ones which it could fairly be argued were adopted by Congress in light of prior administrative practice. One can find in the records of the State Department rulings of subordinates covering a wider range of activities than the two indicated. But as respects Communists these are scattered rulings and not consistently of one pattern. We can say with assurance that whatever may have been the practice after 1926, at the time the Act of July 3, 1926, was adopted, the administrative practice, so far as relevant here, had jelled only around the two categories mentioned. We, therefore, hesitate to impute to Congress, when in 1952 it made a passport necessary for foreign travel and left its issuance to the discretion of the Secretary of State, a purpose to give him unbridled discretion to grant or withhold a passport from a citizen for any substantive reason he may choose. . . .

Since we start with an exercise by an American citizen of an activity included in constitutional protection, we will not readily infer that Congress gave the Secretary of State unbridled discretion to grant or withhold it. If we were dealing with political questions entrusted to the Chief Executive by the Constitution we would have a different case. But there is more involved here. In part, of course, the issuance of the passport carries some implication of intention to extend the bearer diplomatic protection, though it does no more than "request all whom it may concern to permit safely and freely to pass, and in case of need to give all lawful aid and protection" to this citizen of the United States. But that function of the passport is subordinate. Its crucial function today is control over exit. And, as we have seen, the right of exit is a personal right included within the word "liberty" as used in the Fifth Amendment. If that "liberty" is to be regulated, it must be pursuant to the law-making functions of the Congress. And if that power is delegated, the standards must be adequate to pass scrutiny by the accepted tests. Where activities or enjoyment, natural and often necessary to the well-being of an American citizen, such as travel, are involved, we will construe narrowly all delegated powers that curtail or dilute them. We hesitate to find in this broad generalized power an authority to trench so heavily on the rights of the citizen.

Thus we do not reach the question of constitutionality. We only conclude that § 1185 and § 211a do not delegate to the Secretary the kind of authority exercised here. . . .

To repeat, we deal here with a constitutional right of the citizen, a right which we must assume Congress will be faithful to respect. We would be faced with important constitutional questions were we to hold that Congress by § 1185 and § 211a had given the Secretary authority to withhold passports to citizens because of their beliefs or associations. Congress has made no such provision in explicit terms; and absent one, the Secretary may not employ that standard to restrict the citizens' right of free movement.

Reversed.

[The dissenting opinion of Mr. Justice CLARK, with whom Mr. Justice BUR-TON, Mr. Justice HARLAN, and Mr. Justice WHITTAKER concur, is omitted.]

Professor Richard Stewart believes that a policy of judicial narrowing of broad statutory delegations might encourage Congress to write clear statements of legislative purpose to accompany their delegations.[19] But judicial narrowing is a device that the courts do not always choose to employ. For example, in the 1980 case *United States* v. *Euge*, which is discussed in chapter 5, Justice Rehnquist specifically rejected "a narrower interpretation of the duty imposed . . . by the actual language of the statute."[20] *Kent* v. *Dulles* thus stands as an illustration of the judicial narrowing technique, but it is not necessarily the last word on passport policy or freedom of travel.

Professor John F. Manning argues that judicial narrowing of congressional delegation, illustrated by *Kent* v. *Dulles,* is now the principle means whereby the Supreme Court disposes of administrative statutes that allegedly delegate legislative power in contravention of the Constitution.[21] This canon of interpretation was explicitly acknowledged in the Court's majority opinion in *Mistretta* v. *United States* (1989), a case that will be examined later in this chapter.[22] Judicial narrowing is seen by its defenders as a vehicle for advancing nondelegation interests, for example, promoting legislative responsibility and avoiding the excessive use of judicial review.[23] However, Manning argues that judicial narrowing can also have perverse effects, such as substituting "judicial discretion for agency discretion in defining the statute's meaning."[24] This can be dramatically illustrated by *Food and Drug Administration* v. *Brown & Williamson Tobacco Corp.*, 529 US 120 (2000), where the Court rejected the Food and Drug Administration's (FDA's) assertion of jurisdiction to regulate tobacco under the provisions of the Food, Drug, and Cosmetics Act (FDCA), 52 Stat. 120 (2000). The agency had concluded, after an extensive notice and comment period, that nicotine in tobacco was a "drug" subject to its regulatory jurisdiction. Despite the normal deference shown to an administrative agency's construction of statutes it administers,[25] the Court rejected the FDA's assumption of jurisdiction on the grounds that congressional intent, as expressed in no less than six post-FDCA tobacco statutes, precluded the FDA's jurisdiction to regulate to-

---

[19] Richard B. Stewart, "The Reformation of American Administrative Law," 88 *Harvard Law Review* 1667, 1697 (1975).

[20] 444 U.S. 707, 714 (1980).

[21] John F. Manning, "The Nondelegation Doctrine as a Canon of Avoidance," 2000 *Supreme Court Review* 223.

[22] 488 U.S. 361 (1989). Justice Blackmun, speaking for the majority in *Mistretta*, stated that "[I]n recent years, our application of the nondelegation doctrine principally has been limited to the interpretation of statutory texts, and, more particularly, to giving narrow constructions to statutory delegations that might otherwise be thought to be unconstitutional" (488 U.S. at 373, n 7).

[23] Manning, above, note 21, 223–224.

[24] Ibid., 247.

[25] See *Chevron, USA* v. *NRDC, Inc.*, 467 U.S. 837, 842–843 (1984).

bacco. This finding led Manning to remark that the narrowing "interpretative canon" can have an adverse impact on the proper allocation of power in the modern administrative state:

> If the nondelegation doctrine seeks to promote legislative responsibility for policy choices and to safeguard the process of bicameralism and presentment, it is odd for the judiciary to implement it through a technique that asserts the prerogative to alter a statute's conventional meaning and, in so doing, to disturb the apparent lines of compromise produced by the legislative process.[26]

Whitman, Administrator of Environmental Protection Agency v. *American Trucking Associations, Inc.*, 531 U.S. 457 (2001), presents yet another instance of the Court's majority avoiding the delegation-of-power question, which had been central to the findings of the court below. At issue were provisions of the Clean Air Act, 84 Stat. 1676 (1970), which required the administrator of the EPA to promulgate national ambient air quality standards (NAAQS) for air pollutants for which "air quality standards" had been issued. In 1997 the administrator revised the NAAQS for "particulate matter and ozone," and the American Trucking Associations, Inc., challenged the new standard. The statutory provision in question, Section 109(b)(1), instructed the EPA to set standards "the attainment and maintenance of which . . . are requisite to protect the public health" with "an adequate margin of safety." The Court of Appeals for the District of Columbia Circuit held that the EPA's interpretation of the statute constituted an unlawful delegation of legislative power on the grounds of the lack of an "intelligible principle" to guide the agency's exercise of authority. However, rather than declaring the section unconstitutional, the circuit court remanded the NAAQS to the agency for a more restrictive construction of Section 109(b)(1), thereby possibly avoiding the unconstitutional delegation. On appeal, the Supreme Court found the EPA's implementation policy to be unlawful, but not on the unlawful delegation grounds advanced by the court of appeals. Nevertheless, three justices—Scalia, Thomas, and Stevens—used this case as a vehicle for airing their respective views on delegation of powers.

Whitman, Administrator of EPA v. *American Trucking Associations, Inc.,* with its widely variant opinions, provides ample evidence to support Manning's assertion that "[f]ew doctrines have perplexed the Supreme Court more than the nondelegation doctrine."[27] Should the Court revive the nondelegation doctrine, as Justice Thomas argues, or simply acquiesce in its disuse? Are we really any closer to getting an answer to this question than we were in the early 1980s, when Justice Rehnquist, in the *Benzene* and cotton dust cases, made his clarion call for the revival of the nondelegation doctrine?

---

[26] Manning, above, note 21, 224.

[27] Ibid., 238.

Whitman, Administrator of Environmental Protection Agency v. American Trucking Associations, Inc.

SUPREME COURT OF THE UNITED STATES, 2001.
531 U.S. 457, 121 S.Ct. 903, 149 L.Ed. 2d 1.

Justice SCALIA delivered the opinion of the Court. . . .

These cases present the following questions: (1) Whether § 109(b)(1) of the Clean Air Act (CAA) delegates legislative power to the Administrator of the Environmental Protection Agency (EPA). . . .

Section 109(b)(1) of the CAA instructs the EPA to set "ambient air quality standards the attainment and maintenance of which in the judgment of the Administrator, based on [the] criteria [documents of § 108] and allowing an adequate margin of safety, are requisite to protect the public health." 42 U.S.C. § 7409(b)(1). The Court of Appeals held that this section as interpreted by the Administrator did not provide an "intelligible principle" to guide the EPA's exercise of authority in setting NAAQS. "[The] EPA," it said, "lacked any determinate criteria for drawing lines. It has failed to state intelligibly how much is too much." 175 F.3d at 1034. The court hence found that the EPA's interpretation (but not the statute itself) violated the nondelegation doctrine. . . . We disagree.

In a delegation challenge, the constitutional question is whether the statute has delegated legislative power to the agency. Article I, § 1, of the Constitution vests "all legislative Powers herein granted . . . in a Congress of the United States." This text permits no delegation of those powers . . . and so we repeatedly have said that when Congress confers decisionmaking authority upon agencies Congress must "lay down by legislative act an intelligible principle to which the person or body authorized to [act] is directed to conform." *J. W. Hampton, Jr., & Co.* v. *United States*, 276 U.S. 394, 409 (1928). We have never suggested that an agency can cure an unlawful delegation of legislative power by adopting in its discretion a limiting construction of the statute. . . . The idea that an agency can cure an unconstitutionally standardless delegation of power by declining to exercise some of that power seems to us internally contradictory. The very choice of which portion of the power to exercise—that is to say, the prescription of the standard that Congress had omitted—would itself be an exercise of the forbidden legislative authority. Whether the statute delegates legislative power is a question for the courts, and an agency's voluntary self-denial has no bearing upon the answer.

We agree with the Solicitor General that the text of § 109(b)(1) of the CAA at a minimum requires that "for a discrete set of pollutants and based on published air quality criteria that reflect the latest scientific knowledge, [the] EPA must establish uniform national standards at a level that is requisite to protect public health from the adverse effects of the pollutant in the ambient air." . . . Requisite, in turn, "means sufficient, but not more than necessary." . . . They . . . resemble the Occupational Safety and Health Act provision requiring the agency to "set the standard which most adequately assures, to the extent feasible, on the basis of the best available evidence, that no employee will suffer any impairment of health"— which the Court upheld in *Industrial Union Dept., AFL-CIO* v. *American Petroleum Institute*, 448 U.S. 607, 646 (1980), and which even then-Justice REHNQUIST, who alone in that case thought the statute violated the nondelegation doctrine, see id. at 671 (opinion concurring in judgment), would have upheld if, like the statute here, it did not permit economic costs to be considered. See

American Textile Mfrs. Institute, Inc. v. *Donovan*, 452 U.S. 490, 545 (1981) (REHNQUIST, J., dissenting).

The scope of discretion § 109(b)(1) allows is in fact well within the outer limits of our nondelegation precedents. In the history of the Court we have found the requisite "intelligible principle" lacking in only two statutes, one of which provided literally no guidance for the exercise of discretion, and the other of which conferred authority to regulate the entire economy on the basis of no more precise a standard than stimulating the economy by assuring "fair competition." See *Panama Refining Co.* v. *Ryan*, 293 U.S. 388, (1935); A. L. A. Schechter Poultry Corp. v. United States, 295 U.S. 495 (1935). . . . In short, we have "almost never felt qualified to second-guess Congress regarding the permissible degree of policy judgment that can be left to those executing or applying the law." *Mistretta* v. *United States*, 488 U.S. 361, 416 (1989) (SCALIA, J., dissenting); see id. at 373 (majority opinion).

It is true enough that the degree of agency discretion that is acceptable varies according to the scope of the power congressionally conferred. . . . It is therefore not conclusive for delegation purposes that, as respondents argue, ozone and particulate matter are "nonthreshold" pollutants that inflict a continuum of adverse health effects at any airborne concentration greater than zero, and hence require the EPA to make judgments of degree. "[A] certain degree of discretion, and thus of lawmaking, inheres in most executive or judicial action." *Mistretta* v. *United States*, supra, at 417 (SCALIA, J., dissenting) (emphasis deleted); see 488 U.S. at 378–379 (majority opinion). Section 109(b)(1) of the CAA, which to repeat we interpret as requiring the EPA to set air quality standards at the level that is "requisite"—that is, not lower or higher than is necessary—to protect the public health with an adequate mar-

gin of safety, fits comfortably within the scope of discretion permitted by our precedent.

We therefore reverse the judgment of the Court of Appeals remanding for reinterpretation that would avoid a supposed delegation of legislative power. It will remain for the Court of Appeals—on the remand that we direct for other reasons—to dispose of any other preserved challenge to the NAAQS under the judicial-review provisions contained in 42 U.S.C. § 7607(d)(9). . . .

To summarize our holdings in these unusually complex cases: . . . (2) Section 109(b)(1) does not delegate legislative power to the EPA in contravention of Art. I, § 1, of the Constitution. . . .

The judgment of the Court of Appeals is affirmed in part and reversed in part, and the cases are remanded for proceedings consistent with this opinion.

It is so ordered.

Justice THOMAS, concurring.

I agree with the majority that § 109's directive to the agency is no less an "intelligible principle" than a host of other directives that we have approved. . . . I also agree that the Court of Appeals' remand to the agency to make its own corrective interpretation does not accord with our understanding of the delegation issue. . . . I write separately, however, to express my concern that there may nevertheless be a genuine constitutional problem with § 109, a problem which the parties did not address.

The parties to this case who briefed the constitutional issue wrangled over constitutional doctrine with barely a nod to the text of the Constitution. Although this Court since 1928 has treated the "intelligible principle" requirement as the only constitutional limit on congressional grants of power to administrative agencies, see *J. W. Hampton, Jr., & Co.* v. *United States*, 276 U.S. 394, 409 (1928), the Constitution does not speak of "intelligible principles." Rather, it speaks in much simpler terms: "*All* legislative Powers herein granted shall be vested in a Congress." . . . I am not convinced that the intelligible principle doctrine serves to prevent all cessions of legislative power. I believe that there are cases in which the principle is intelligible and yet the significance of the delegated decision is simply too great for the decision to be called anything other than "legislative."

As it is, none of the parties to this case has examined the text of the Constitution or asked us to reconsider our precedents on cessions of legislative power. On a future day, however, I would be willing to address the question whether our delegation jurisprudence has strayed too far from our Founders' understanding of separation of powers.

Justice STEVENS, with whom Justice SOUTER joins, concurring in part and concurring in the judgment.

Section 109(b)(1) delegates to the Administrator of the Environmental Protection Agency (EPA) the authority to promulgate national ambient air quality standards (NAAQS). In Part III of its opinion . . . , the Court convincingly explains why the Court of Appeals erred when it concluded that § 109 effected "an unconstitutional delegation of legislative power." *American Trucking Assns., Inc.* v. *EPA*, 175 F.3d 1027, 1033 (CADC 1999) (per curiam). I wholeheartedly endorse the Court's result and endorse its explanation of its reasons, albeit with the following caveat.

The Court has two choices. We could choose to articulate our ultimate disposition of this issue by frankly acknowledging that the power delegated to the EPA is "legislative" but nevertheless conclude that the delegation is constitutional because adequately limited by the terms of the authorizing statute. Alternatively, we could pretend, as the Court does, that the authority delegated to the EPA is somehow not "legislative power." Despite the fact that there is language in our opinions that supports the Court's articulation of our holding, I am persuaded that it would be both wiser and more faithful to what we have actually done in delegation cases to admit that agency rulemaking authority is "legislative power."

The proper characterization of governmental power should generally depend on the nature of the power, not on the identity of the person exercising it. . . . If the NAAQS that the EPA promulgated had been prescribed by Congress, everyone would agree that those rules would be the product of an exercise of "legislative power." The same characterization is appropriate when an agency exercises rulemaking authority pursuant to a permissible delegation from Congress. . . .

It seems clear that an executive agency's exercise of rulemaking authority pursuant to a valid delegation from Congress is "legislative." As long as the delegation provides a sufficiently intelligible principle, there is nothing inherently unconstitutional about it. Accordingly, while I join Parts I, II, and IV of the Court's opinion, and agree with almost everything said in Part III, I would hold that when Congress enacted § 109, it effected a constitutional delegation of legislative power to the EPA.

[The separate opinion of Justice BREYER, concurring in part and concurring in the judgment, is omitted.]

In *American Trucking Associations, Inc.* v. *Environmental Protection Agency*, 283 F.3d 355 (D.C. Cir., 2002), the court of appeals, on remand,[28] ruled unanimously that the EPA could proceed with the regulations that in 1999 it had blocked on the grounds that the agency's interpretation of the statute constituted an unlawful delegation of legislative power.[29]

THE LEGISLATIVE VETO

In the previous section of this chapter, a device for judicial "correction" of broad legislative delegations has been discussed. A different approach, intended to provide a legislative check on the administrative implementation of a statute, has been referred to as "congressional reassertion of control via post-delegation review,"[30] or the "legislative veto."

The utility of this mechanism, which had been written into a significant number of statutes since the 1930s, was obviated in 1983 when the U.S. Supreme Court declared the legislative veto unconstitutional. The case was *Immigration and Naturalization Service* v. *Chadha,* 462 U.S. 919. Several considerations have made the *Chadha* decision particularly notable: its elimination of a potentially important device for controlling administration; the significant constitutional questions addressed by the case; and the broad sweep of Chief Justice Burger's majority opinion, which brought forth expressions of concern both from other members of the Supreme Court and from a number of commentators. As a consequence, *Chadha* has been one of the most-discussed Supreme Court cases in recent decades. The aspects of the decision relevant to the issue of delegation are examined below. Because the case also has significance with regard to rule-making powers of administrative agencies, it will be discussed again briefly in chapter 6.

In its generic form, the legislative veto involved a statutory stipulation by Congress that it reserves the right to disapprove of an action taken by an executive agency under the statute. Often the executive action in question is the adoption of an administrative regulation. But the executive act vetoed by Congress could also be an administrative decision of narrow application, which is the case in *Chadha*. Some of the statutes that contained legislative vetoes required that both houses of Congress participate in disapproving an administrative act, while others allowed a one-house veto. The one-house veto was authorized in the statute the Supreme Court reviewed in *Chadha*, which is the reason for the discussion of "bicameralism" in Chief Justice

---

[28] "To send back. The act of an appellate court when it sends a case back to the trial court and orders the trial court to conduct limited new hearings or an entirely new trial, or to take some further action." *Black's Law Dictionary, Abridged* (6th ed., 1991), p. 896.

[29] "The decision brought full circle a tortured legal struggle that wound through the Supreme Court and the full District of Columbia Circuit. It delighted clean-air advocates. And it imposes an obligation on Christie Whitman, the EPA administrator, to move aggressively to enforce regulations that have been in legal limbo for too long." Editorial from the *New York Times* as it appeared in the *International Herald Tribune*, March 30–31, 2002, 6.

[30] This phrase is from Judge Carl McGowan, "Congress, Court and Control of Delegated Power," 77 *Columbia Law Review* 1119, 1133 (1977).

Burger's majority opinion. Although bicameralism is a significant issue in the case, for our purposes the more important consideration is the relationship of the legislative veto to delegation. The question may be stated as follows: once Congress has delegated authority to an administrator or an agency, can it then, on its own and without resort to the full legislative process (in which the president has a role through signing or vetoing a bill), disapprove of action taken under that delegated power? This consideration is embraced in the discussion in *Chadha* involving separation of powers and the presentment clauses of the Constitution.

Immigration and Naturalization Service v. Chadha

SUPREME COURT OF THE UNITED STATES, 1983.
462 U.S. 919, 103 S.Ct. 2764, 77 L.Ed.2d 317.

[The Immigration and Nationality Act, § 244(a)(1), codified as 8 U.S.C. § 1254 (a)(1), granted the attorney general the discretion to suspend deportation proceedings and grant permanent resident status to certain aliens "whose deportation would in the opinion of the Attorney General, result in extreme hardship to the alien or to his spouse, parent, or child, who is a citizen of the United States or an alien lawfully admitted for permanent residence." The Immigration and Naturalization Service (INS), a division of the Department of Justice, discharges these responsibilities for the attorney general.

The act also provided, in § 244(c)(2), codified as 8 U.S.C. § 1254(c)(2), that one house of Congress, by resolution, could invalidate the attorney general's decision to allow a particular alien to remain in the United States.

Jagdish Rai Chadha was an East Indian born in Kenya and holding a British passport who spent a number of years in the United States on a student visa. After the visa expired, the INS began deportation proceedings against him. He petitioned for suspension of deportation, and after a hearing, an immigration judge ordered that the deportation be suspended. But in late 1975, a resolution was introduced in the House of Representatives opposing a grant of permanent residence to

Chadha and five other aliens on the grounds that they did not meet the statutory requirements, particularly a requirement relating to extreme hardship. The resolution passed without debate or recorded vote, and, as a resolution, it was not submitted to the Senate or presented to the president. The immigration judge then reopened the proceedings to implement the House resolution, and Chadha was ordered deported. Chadha appealed and, after exhausting his administrative remedies, filed for a review of the deportation order in the U.S. Court of Appeals for the Ninth Circuit. That court declared the legislative veto provision of the Immigration and Nationality Act unconstitutional, and the case came to the Supreme Court.

The Supreme Court was presented with numerous issues to resolve, several connected with whether the Supreme Court had the authority to decide the case at hand, as well as whether the legislative veto was "severable" from the rest of the statute. The severability issue involved the question of whether, if the legislative veto provision were struck down as unconstitutional, the rest of the Immigration and Nationality Act could still stand as valid law. These are interesting issues, but they are of only tangential importance to the subject matter of this chapter. The excerpts below, therefore, from

Chief Justice Burger's opinion for six members of the Court, will concentrate only on the part of the decision concerning separation of powers and bicameralism.]

Chief Justice BURGER delivered the opinion of the Court. . . .

We turn now to the question whether action of one House of Congress under § 244(c)(2) violates strictures of the Constitution. We begin, of course, with the presumption that the challenged statute is valid. Its wisdom is not the concern of the courts. . . .

By the same token, the fact that a given law or procedure is efficient, convenient, and useful in facilitating functions of government, standing alone, will not save it if it is contrary to the Constitution. Convenience and efficiency are not the primary objectives—or the hallmarks—of democratic government and our inquiry is sharpened rather than blunted by the fact that congressional veto provisions are appearing with increasing frequency in statutes which delegate authority to executive and independent agencies:

> Since 1932, when the first veto provision was enacted into law, 295 congressional veto-type procedures have been inserted in 196 different statutes as follows: from 1932 to 1939, five statutes were affected; from 1940–49, nineteen statutes; between 1950–59, thirty-four statutes; and from 1960–69, forty-nine. From the year 1970 through 1975, at least one hundred sixty-three such provisions visions were included in eighty-nine laws. Abourezk, The Congressional Veto: A Contemporary Response to Executive Encroachment on Legislative Prerogatives, 52 Ind. L. Rev. 323, 324 (1977).

But policy arguments supporting even useful "political inventions" are subject to the demands of the Constitution which defines powers and, with respect to this subject, sets out just how those powers are to be exercised.

Explicit and unambiguous provisions of the Constitution prescribe and define the respective functions of the Congress and of the Executive in the legislative process. Since the precise terms of those familiar provisions are critical to the resolution of these cases, we set them out verbatim. Article I provides:

> All legislative Powers herein granted shall be vested in a Congress of the United States, which shall consist of a Senate *and* House of Representatives. . . . (Emphasis added.)
>
> Every Bill which shall have passed the House of Representatives *and* the Senate, *shall,* before it becomes a law, be presented to the President of the United States; . . . (Emphasis added.)
>
> *Every* Order, Resolution, or Vote to which the Concurrence of the Senate and House of Representatives may be necessary (except on a question of Adjournment) *shall be* presented to the President of the United States; and before the Same shall take Effect, *shall be* approved by him, or being disapproved by him, *shall* be repassed by two thirds of the Senate and House of Representatives, according to the Rules and Limitations prescribed in the Case of a Bill. . . . (Emphasis added.)

These provisions of Art. I are integral parts of the constitutional design for the separation of powers. . . . The very structure of the articles delegating and separating powers under Arts. I, II, and III exemplifies the concept of separation of powers, and we now turn to Art I. . . .

The decision to provide the President with a limited and qualified power to nullify proposed legislation by veto was based on the profound conviction of the Framers that the powers conferred on Congress were the powers to be most carefully circumscribed. It is beyond doubt that lawmaking was a power to be shared by both Houses and the President. . . .

The President's role in the lawmaking process also reflects the Framers' careful efforts to check whatever propensity a particular Congress might have to enact oppressive, improvident or ill-considered measures. . . .

The bicameral requirement of Art. I, §§ 1, 7, was of scarcely less concern to the Framers than was the Presidential veto and indeed the two concepts are interdependent. By providing that no law could take effect without the concurrence of the prescribed majority of the Members of both Houses, the Framers reemphasized their belief . . . that legislation should not be enacted unless it has been carefully and fully considered by the Nation's elected officials. . . . [The chief justice then quotes from several authorities to support this view.]

We see therefore that the Framers were acutely conscious that the bicameral requirement and the Presentment Clauses would serve essential constitutional functions. The President's participation in the legislative process was to protect the Executive Branch from Congress and to protect the whole people from improvident laws. The division of the Congress into two distinctive bodies assures that the legislative power would be exercised only after opportunity for full study and debate in separate settings. The President's unilateral veto power, in turn, was limited by the power of two-thirds of both Houses of Congress to overrule a veto thereby precluding final arbitrary action of one person. . . . It emerges clearly that the prescription for legislative action in Art. I, §§ 1, 7, represents the Framers' decision that the legislative power of the Federal Government be exercised in accord with a single, finely wrought and exhaustively considered, procedure. . . .

Examination of the action taken here by one House pursuant to § 244(c)(2) reveals that it was essentially legislative in purpose and effect. In purporting to exercise power defined in Art. I, § 8, cl. 4, to "establish an uniform Rule of Naturalization," the House took action that had the purpose and effect of altering the legal rights, duties, and relations of persons, including the Attorney General, Executive Branch officials and Chadha, all outside the Legislative Branch. Section 244(c)(2) purports to authorize one House of Congress to require the Attorney General to deport an individual alien whose deportation otherwise would be canceled under § 244. The one-House veto operated in these cases to overrule the Attorney General and mandate Chadha's deportation; absent the House action, Chadha would remain in the United States. Congress has acted and its action has altered Chadha's status.

The legislative character of the one-House veto in these cases is confirmed by the character of the congressional action it supplants. Neither the House of Representatives nor the Senate contends that, absent the veto provision in § 244(c)(2), either of them, or both of them acting together, could effectively require the Attorney General to deport an alien once the Attorney General, in the exercise of legislatively delegated authority, had determined the alien should remain in the United States. Without the challenged provision in § 244(c)(2), this could have been achieved, if at all, only by legislation requiring deportation. Similarly, a veto by one House of Congress under § 244(c)(2) cannot be justified as an attempt at amending the standards set out in § 244(a)(1), or as a repeal of § 244 as applied to Chadha. Amendment and repeal of statutes, no less than enactment, must conform with Art. I.

The nature of the decision implemented by the one-House veto in these cases further manifests its legislative character. After long experience with the clumsy, time-consuming private bill procedure, Congress made a deliberate choice to delegate to the Executive Branch, and specifically to the Attorney General, the authority to allow deportable aliens to remain in this country in certain specified circumstances. It is not disputed that this choice to delegate authority is precisely the kind of decision that can be implemented only in accordance with the procedures set out in Art. I. Disagreement with the Attorney General's decision on Chadha's deportation—that is, Congress' decision to deport Chadha—no less than Congress' original choice to delegate to the Attorney General the authority to make that decision, involves determinations of policy that Congress can implement in only one way; bicameral passage followed by presentment to the President. Congress must abide by its delegation of authority until that delegation is legislatively altered or revoked. . . .

The bicameral requirement, the Presentment Clauses, the President's veto, and Congress' power to override a veto were intended to erect enduring checks on each Branch and to protect the people from the improvident exercise of power by mandating certain prescribed steps. To preserve those checks, and maintain the separation of powers, the carefully defined limits on the power of each Branch must not be eroded. To accomplish what has been attempted by one House of Congress in this case requires action in conformity with the express procedures of the Constitution's prescription for legislative action: passage by a majority of both Houses and presentment to the President. . . .

We hold that the congressional veto provision in § 244(c)(2) is severable from the Act and that it is unconstitutional. Accordingly, the judgment of the Court of Appeals is affirmed.

As the excerpt indicates, Chief Justice Burger was intent on showing that the House of Representatives' action regarding Chadha was a legislative act. Having determined that, he asserted that, because it was not accomplished through the regular legislative process, it was unconstitutional. Justice Powell concurred in the result, but he justified his decision on narrower grounds. He felt that the use of the legislative veto in the *Chadha* case was not an exercise of legislative power, but "clearly adjudicatory," "a function ordinarily entrusted to the federal courts." He would have invalidated the legislative veto used in the *Chadha* case on that basis, not reaching "the broader question whether legislative vetoes are invalid under the Presentment Clauses" (462 U.S. 964, 965, 967). Justice White in his comprehensive dissenting opinion saw the legislative veto as an indispensable innovation that helps Congress ensure the accountability of executive and independent agencies. He, not unlike Justice Powell, was particularly troubled by the breadth of the majority's ruling, especially given its potential impact on administrative rule making, by far the most common context in which the Congress had incorporated legislative veto provisions into statutory law. The crux of his argument is illustrated by the following passage from his dissent:

> Absent the veto, the agencies receiving delegations of legislative or quasi-legislative power may issue regulations having the force of law without bicameral approval and without the President's signature. It is thus not apparent why the reservation of a veto over the exercise of that legislative power must be subject to a more exacting test [462 U.S. 986–987].

As Louis Fisher of the Library of Congress was to point out several years later, the legislative veto was not completely eliminated by *Chadha*. It would reappear in several alternative forms.[31] One such mechanism for se-

---

[31] Louis Fisher, "Judicial Misjudgments about the Lawmaking Process: The Legislative Veto Case," 45 *Public Administration Review* 705 (1985).

curing administrative accountability in rule making would be the "joint resolution of disapproval," which will be examined in chapter 6.

POST-CHADHA *DELEGATION (GRAMM-RUDMAN-HOLLINGS)*

The adoption of Gramm-Rudman-Hollings (G-R-H), formally known as the Balanced Budget and Emergency Deficit Control Act of 1985,[32] provided yet another opportunity for the federal courts to rule on a major delegation of congressional power. G-R-H mandated annual reductions in the federal deficit so as to produce a balanced budget in 1991. The key provision was a determination, to be made by the comptroller general of the United States, that the automatic deficit reduction provisions of the act were to be implemented. The comptroller general, the head of the General Accounting Office (GAO), was to make this determination on the basis of data provided by the Office of Management and Budget (OMB) and the Congressional Budget Office (CBO). The president, in turn, would prepare the sequestration order, which would result in the budget cuts necessary to achieve the deficit reduction specified in the comptroller general's report.[33]

Both proponents and detractors foresaw the likelihood of constitutional challenges to the bill, and consequently, provisions were incorporated in it so as to ensure expedited judicial review. The legislature also provided a fallback procedure in the event that the OMB/CBO/GAO reporting procedures were declared unconstitutional. If that were the case, the OMB/CBO report would be transmitted to a temporary joint House and Senate committee on deficit reduction, which would be empowered to report a joint resolution that could trigger sequestration if it were passed by both houses and signed by the president. This fallback procedure was obviously sensitive to the principle of "bicameralism" and to "the presentment clauses," which had been the focus of the Supreme Court's deliberations in *Chadha*, the "legislative veto" case discussed earlier in this chapter.

Constitutional Objections to Gramm-Rudman-Hollings

The principal suit challenging the law's delegation of power to unelected officials (i.e., officials in the OMB, the CBO, and the GAO) was brought by Representative Michael Synar on behalf of fellow members of Congress. The Justice Department's brief on the merits of the case asserted that the comptroller general's role violated the principle of separation of powers.

The case was decided by the Supreme Court in 1986. By a seven-to-two margin, the Court affirmed a lower court ruling that the comptroller general's role in the deficit reduction process violated the doctrine of separation of powers [*Bowsher* v. *Synar*, 478 U.S. 714 (1986)]. More specifically, by virtue of the congressional retention of the removal power over the official re-

---

[32] 99 Stat. 1038 (1985). See summary of conference agreement in the *Congressional Record*, vol. 131, no. 172, pp. H 11876–77 (Proceedings of December 11, 1985).

[33] Ibid.

sponsible for the execution of the Deficit Control Act, Congress had in effect intruded into the executive function. Chief Justice Burger's majority opinion included an explicit refusal to consider Congressman Synar's principal challenge to the act, which was that the assignment of the automatic budget-cutting powers to the comptroller general violated the delegation of powers.[34]

The Supreme Court's ruling left intact the aforementioned fallback provision, which called for using the ordinary legislative process to enact the mandated cuts; however, it left unresolved the question as to whether the Deficit Control Act might have been modified so as to avoid the constitutional infirmity. For example, the budget-cutting power might have been assigned to an officer of the executive branch, such as the director of the OMB. Had that solution been exercised, it would have raised anew the delegation-of-power question that the Court had chosen so far to avoid.

The deficit reduction debate would take several turns before President Clinton was able to present a balanced budget for fiscal year 1999, the first in three decades. Two legislative initiatives are worth noting here, although neither would be responsible for the achievement of the balanced budget and significant reduction of national debt over the next several years. Despite repeated efforts, the Balanced Budget Amendment proposals never received the requisite two-thirds vote in the House and Senate necessary for submission to the states for ratification. Secondly, the Line-Item Veto Act [110 Stat. 1120 (1996)], which became effective on January 1, 1997, was declared unconstitutional by the Supreme Court in *Clinton* v. *New York* (524 U.S. 417) in 1998 on grounds that the cancellation procedures set forth in the act violated the presentment clause of the Constitution. President Clinton had exercised his authority to cancel provisions of the Balanced Budget Act of 1997 and the Taxpayer Relief Act of 1997 that would have had adverse effects on the budget deficit and on Medicare costs (111 Stat. 251, 515, and 111 Stat. 788, 895–896, 990–993, respectively). According to Justice John Paul Stevens, speaking for the majority, the president, by repealing a portion of each statute, had, in effect, amended both acts of Congress. Such an action was prohibited, as had been noted in *Chadha*: "[R]epeal of statutes, no less than enactment, must conform with Art. I" [462 U.S. 919, 954 (1983), as quoted in 524 U.S. 417, 438].

---

[34] *Bowsher* v. *Synar*, 478 U.S. 714, 738, note 10. Bernard Schwartz's article, "An Administrative Law 'Might Have Been'—Chief Justice Burger's *Bowsher* v. *Synar* Draft," 42 *Administrative Law Review* 221 (1990), provides a fascinating insight into the Court's internal decision-making process. Schwartz argues that had Burger's original draft become the *Bowsher* opinion, "it could have had a drastic effect upon administrative agencies, since it virtually would have placed the Supreme Court imprimatur upon the claim that independent agencies are unconstitutional" (p. 221). This view, which cast doubt on the *Humphrey's Executor* precedent (see discussion thereof in chapter 1), was in vogue in the Reagan Justice Department, as evidenced by a widely reported speech of then Attorney General Edwin Meese, in which he stated, "[w]e should abandon the idea that there are such things as 'quasi-legislative' or 'quasi-judicial' functions that can be properly delegated to independent agencies" (*Washington Post*, January 4, 1986, A20, as cited in Schwartz, p. 223). This point of view did not die with the Reagan administration. In the midst of the crisis of confidence regarding corporate leadership in 2002, Securities and Exchange Commission (SEC) Chairman Harvey L. Pitt recommended that the SEC be made a cabinet-level department. Critics from both parties were quick to point out that the SEC would lose its status as an independent agency if this were to take place (*New York Times*, July 25, 2002, C9).

CONGRESSIONAL DELEGATION TO THE JUDICIARY

Up to this point in the chapter, we have focused exclusively on congressional delegations to agencies of the executive branch. By way of conclusion, we examine an unusual kind of delegation to personnel associated with the judicial branch.

Mistretta v. *United States*, 488 U.S. 361 (1989), is something of an anomaly in the contemporary delegation-of-power case law. It was decided in the midst of the period discussed earlier in this chapter, when the Supreme Court was generally predisposed to construe delegations narrowly so as to avoid constitutional questions. One commentator asserts that one has to go back to 1948 (to *Lichter* v. *United States*, 334 U.S. 742) to find a case in which the Court had endorsed a generally permissive approach to delegation.[35] In *Mistretta* the Court decisively rejected the petitioner's argument that Congress had granted the U.S. Sentencing Commission excessive legislative discretion in violation of the nondelegation doctrine. Justice Scalia, the lone dissenter, concluded that there had been an unlawful delegation of rulemaking authority to the Sentencing Commission. Can the permissiveness of the majority opinion be explained, in part, by the fact that the recipient of the delegation is an independent commission within the judicial branch of the federal government?

Mistretta v. United States

SUPREME COURT OF THE UNITED STATES, 1989.
488 U.S. 361, 109 S.Ct. 647, 102 L.Ed. 2d 714.

[The Sentencing Reform Act of 1984 (SRA) abolished the system of indeterminate sentencing that had been used in federal criminal cases for almost a century. This system had given federal judges wide discretion in all phases of the sentencing process. Criticism of this "outmoded rehabilitation model" focused on both the variations in sentencing of similarly situated offenders and the uncertainty as to the time an offender would spend in prison.[36]

The SRA modified the old sentencing process in five principal ways: (1) it replaced the "rehabilitative model" with one designed to serve the goals of retribution, education, deterrence, and incapacitation; (2) it established the U.S. Sentenc-

ing Commission and authorized it to promulgate sentencing guidelines; (3) it made all sentences determinate with only "good behavior" reductions; (4) the commission's guidelines were to be binding, although judges were given discretion to deviate therefrom as long as they provided specific reasons for doing so; and (5) it permitted appellate review of sentences that deviated from the guidelines.

Mistretta, who had been convicted on cocaine-related charges and sentenced in accordance with the guidelines, sought to have the act declared unconstitutional on both unlawful delegation of power and separation of power grounds. The Supreme Court granted his petition for certiorari before judgment in the court of

---

[35] Schoenbrod, above, note 16, p. 44.

[36] See Senate Report No. 98-225 (1983).

appeals so as to consider the constitutionality of the guidelines.]

Justice BLACKMUN delivered the opinion of the Court. . . .

Delegation of Power

Petitioner argues that in delegating the power to promulgate sentencing guidelines for every federal criminal offense to an independent Sentencing Commission, Congress has granted the Commission excessive legislative discretion in violation of the constitutionally based nondelegation doctrine. We do not agree.

The nondelegation doctrine is rooted in the principle of separation of powers that underlies our tripartite system of Government. The Constitution provides that "[a]ll legislative Powers herein granted shall be vested in a Congress of the United States," . . . and we long have insisted that "the integrity and maintenance of the system of government ordained by the Constitution" mandate that Congress generally cannot delegate its legislative power to another Branch. *Field v. Clark*, 143 U.S. 649, 692 (1892). We also have recognized, however, that the separation-of-powers principle, and the nondelegation doctrine in particular, do not prevent Congress from obtaining the assistance of its coordinate Branches. In a passage now enshrined in our jurisprudence, Chief Justice Taft, writing for the Court, explained our approach to such cooperative ventures: "In determining what [Congress] may do in seeking assistance from another branch, the extent and character of that assistance must be fixed according to common sense and the inherent necessities of the government coordination." *J. W. Hampton, Jr., & Co.* v. *United States*, 276 U.S. 394, 406 (1928). So long as Congress "shall lay down by legislative act an intelligible principle to which the person or body authorized to [exercise the delegated authority] is directed to conform, such legislative action

is not a forbidden delegation of legislative power." Id., at 409.

Applying this "intelligible principle" test to congressional delegations, our jurisprudence has been driven by a practical understanding that in our increasingly complex society, replete with ever changing and more technical problems, Congress simply cannot do its job absent an ability to delegate power under broad general directives. . . .

In light of our approval of these broad delegations, we harbor no doubt that Congress' delegation of authority to the Sentencing Commission is sufficiently specific and detailed to meet constitutional requirements. Congress charged the Commission with three goals: to "assure the meeting of the purposes of sentencing as set forth" in the Act; to "provide certainty and fairness in meeting the purposes of sentencing, avoiding unwarranted sentencing disparities among defendants with similar records . . . while maintaining sufficient flexibility to permit individualized sentences," where appropriate; and to "reflect, to the extent practicable, advancement in knowledge of human behavior as it relates to the criminal justice process." 28 U. S. C. § 991(b)(1). Congress further specified four "purposes" of sentencing that the Commission must pursue in carrying out its mandate: "to reflect the seriousness of the offense, to promote respect for the law, and to provide just punishment for the offense"; "to afford adequate deterrence to criminal conduct"; "to protect the public from further crimes of the defendant"; and "to provide the defendant with needed . . . correctional treatment." 18 U. S. C. § 3553(a)(2). . . .

[Justice Blackmun then described the constraints that Congress imposed on the Commission in its development of a system of "sentencing ranges," as well as the factors that should be taken into consideration as it formulated categories of offenses *and* defendants.]

Congress has met that standard here. The Act sets forth more than merely an "intelligible principle" or minimal standards. One court has aptly put it: "The statute outlines the policies which prompted establishment of the Commission, explains what the Commission should do and how it should do it, and sets out specific directives to govern particular situations." *United States* v. *Chambless*, 680 F. Supp. 793, 796 (ED La. 1988).

Developing proportionate penalties for hundreds of different crimes by a virtually limitless array of offenders is precisely the sort of intricate, labor-intensive task for which delegation to an expert body is especially appropriate. Although Congress has delegated significant discretion to the Commission to draw judgments from its analysis of existing sentencing practice and alternative sentencing models, "Congress is not confined to that method of executing its policy which involves the least possible delegation of discretion to administrative officers." *Yakus* v. *United States*, 321 U.S., at 425–426. We have no doubt that in the hands of the Commission "the criteria which Congress has supplied are wholly adequate for carrying out the general policy and purpose" of the Act. *Sunshine Coal Co.* v. *Adkins*, 310 U.S. 381, 398 (1940).

Separation of Powers

Having determined that Congress has set forth sufficient standards for the exercise of the Commission's delegated authority, we turn to Mistretta's claim that the Act violates the constitutional principle of separation of powers. . . .

"When this Court is asked to invalidate a statutory provision that has been approved by both Houses of the Congress and signed by the President, particularly an Act of Congress that confronts a deeply vexing national problem, it should only do so for the most compelling constitutional reasons." *Bowsher* v. *Synar*, 478 U.S., at 736 (opinion concurring in judgment). Although the unique composition and responsibilities of the Sentencing Commission give rise to serious concerns about a disruption of the appropriate balance of governmental power among the coordinate Branches, we conclude, upon close inspection, that petitioner's fears for the fundamental structural protections of the Constitution prove, at least in this case, to be "more smoke than fire," and do not compel us to invalidate Congress' considered scheme for resolving the seemingly intractable dilemma of excessive disparity in criminal sentencing. . . .

We conclude that in creating the Sentencing Commission—an unusual hybrid in structure and authority—Congress neither delegated excessive legislative power nor upset the constitutionally mandated balance of powers among the coordinate Branches. The Constitution's structural protections do not prohibit Congress from delegating to an expert body located within the Judicial Branch the intricate task of formulating sentencing guidelines consistent with such significant statutory direction as is present here. Nor does our system of checked and balanced authority prohibit Congress from calling upon the accumulated wisdom and experience of the Judicial Branch in creating policy on a matter uniquely within the ken of judges. Accordingly, we hold that the Act is constitutional.

The judgment of United States District Court for the Western District of Missouri is affirmed.

It is so ordered.

Justice SCALIA, dissenting. . . .

Precisely because the scope of delegation is largely uncontrollable by the courts, we must be particularly rigorous in preserving the Constitution's structural restrictions that deter excessive delegation. The major one, it seems to me, is that the power to make law cannot be exercised by anyone other than Congress, except in conjunction with the lawful exercise of executive or judicial power.

The whole theory of *lawful* congressional "delegation" is not that Congress is sometimes too busy or too divided and can therefore assign its responsibility of making law to someone else; but rather that a certain degree of discretion, and thus of lawmaking, inheres in most executive or judicial action, and it is up to Congress, by the relative specificity or generality of its statutory commands, to determine—up to a point—how small or how large that degree shall be. . . .

I think the Court errs, in other words, not so much because it mistakes the degree of commingling, but because it fails to recognize that this case is not about commingling, but about the creation of a new Branch altogether, a sort of junior-varsity Congress. It may well be that in some circumstances such a Branch would be desirable; perhaps the agency before us here will prove to be so. But there are many desirable dispositions that do not accord with the constitutional structure we live under. And in the long run the improvisation of a constitutional structure on the basis of currently perceived utility will be disastrous.

I respectfully dissent from the Court's decision, and would reverse the judgment of the District Court.

Chapter 4

Judicial Review of Administrative Determinations

As indicated in chapter 1, since the judicial check is one of the foremost mechanisms for control of improper administrative activity, much of this book deals with court scrutiny of administrative action. In this chapter attention is given to the ground rules of judicial review. We consider such basic issues as what administrative actions are reviewable, who can seek review, when in the process judicial review is permitted, and what the scope of the court's reviewing power is.

THE COMMON LAW OF JUDICIAL REVIEW

The authority for judicial review to scrutinize allegedly illegal administrative action is derived from both statutory and nonstatutory sources.[1] In the former case one looks to the statute books, and in the latter case, to the continuously evolving common law. The statutory authority for judicial review can be either of a "general" variety, such as sections 701 and the following of the Administrative Procedure Act (APA), or a more "specific" variety, in which regulatory statutes explicitly authorize review of certain agency actions. The principle bases of nonstatutory judicial review of administrative actions are the prerogative writs, such as certiorari and mandamus, and their simplified contemporary counterparts, injunctions and declaratory relief.[2]

---

[1] For a discussion of the constitutional bases of judicial review in both federal and state jurisdictions, see Louis L. Jaffe, *Judicial Control of Administrative Action* 376 et seq. (1965).

[2] Injunction: "A court order prohibiting someone from doing some specified act or commanding someone to undo some wrong or injury." *Black's Law Dictionary*, Abridged (6th ed., 1991), p. 540. Declaratory Relief or Declaratory Judgment: "Statutory remedy for the determination of a justiciable controversy where the plaintiff is in doubt as to his legal rights." *Black's Law Dictionary*, Abridged (6th ed., 1991), pp. 283–284. See Walter Gellhorn, Clark Byse, and Peter L. Strauss, *Administrative Law: Cases and Comments* (7th ed., 1979), for an excellent discussion of injunctive and declaratory relief (919 et seq.) and the prerogative writs (923 et seq.).

The Reviewability Question

A leading authority, Louis L. Jaffe, argued that "[i]n most cases statutes or common-law decisions make clear the reviewability of an administrative action at the suit of at least one or more classes of potential plaintiff."[3] However, the more difficult question, and one that needs to be explored here, is whether, in cases of statutory silence or ambiguity, there is a common-law reviewability.

The mixed interpretations of the complex case law on the reviewability/unreviewability question can be illustrated by juxtaposing the views of Justice Frankfurter with those of the attorney general's committee. Frankfurter's dissent, in *Stark* v. *Wickard* (1944), stated in part that "[a]part from the text and texture of a particular law in relation to which judicial review is sought, 'judicial review' is a mischievous abstraction. There is no such thing as a common law of judicial review in the federal courts" [321 U.S. 228, 312 (1944)]. However, the attorney general's committee expressed a different view: "Legislation has played little part in defining the area of reviewable administrative action. Such limits as there are to that area have been marked out largely by the gradual judicial process of inclusion and exclusion, aided at times by the courts' judgment as to the probable legislative intent derived from the spirit of the statutory scheme."[4]

One can further complicate the situation by again citing Jaffe, who asserted that "in our system of remedies, an individual whose interest is acutely and immediately affected by an administrative action presumptively has a right to secure at some point a judicial determination of its validity."[5] Although thorough analysis of these mixes of prescription and description is not possible here, a brief recounting of the historical development of the presumption of reviewability is in order. As this survey will make clear, the evolution toward a presumption of judicial review has not been a straight-line development. Nor should such a presumption be taken to mean that judicial review of administrative acts will be available to all persons at all times.

Case Law Concerning Reviewability

An examination of the nineteenth-century case law on the question of presumption of reviewability/unreviewability reveals a clear disposition against reviewability. The classic precedent of this period is *Decatur* v. *Paulding*, 39 U.S. (14 Pet.) 497 (1840), which involved a mandamus action brought by Mrs. Stephen Decatur, the naval hero's widow, against the secretary of the U.S. Navy, James K. Paulding, to pay her two pensions, one a general naval pension and the other granted her by private legislation. The

---

[3] Jaffe, above, note 1, 336.

[4] *Final Report of the Attorney General's Committee on Administrative Procedure*, S. Doc. No. 8, 77th Cong., 1st sess. (1941).

[5] Jaffe, above, note 1, 336.

secretary had ruled that she might have either one, but not both. The Supreme Court, in denying mandamus, held that "[t]he interference of the Courts with the performance of the ordinary duties of the executive departments of the government, would be productive of nothing but mischief; and we are quite satisfied that such a power was never intended to be given to them" [397 U.S. (14 Pet.) 516].

In the latter part of the nineteenth century, the question of the propriety of judicial control of executive action arose again in cases involving public land grants[6] and the exclusion or deportation of aliens,[7] and not surprisingly, the reasoning and dispositions in these cases were similar to those in *Decatur* v. *Paulding*. Davis gave the following explanation for the judicial preference for unreviewability:

> The probable explanation for the early judicial attitude is that the judges had not yet developed a clear vision of the possibility of a limited review. If the choice was between something approaching a judicial assumption of administrative tasks and a refusal of all review, a preference for unreviewability was easy. But the courts gradually developed systems of limited review. As soon as the judges clearly perceived that they could restrict their review to questions of jurisdiction, statutory interpretation, fair procedure, and substantial evidence, it is hardly surprising that the presumption gradually shifted to the side of reviewability.[8]

Although this common-law attitude of unreviewability persisted into the twentieth century, unless Congress had made an affirmative effort to make administrative determinations reviewable, a 1902 decision signaled the shift toward the presumption of reviewability. *American School of Magnetic Healing* v. *McAnnulty,* 187 U.S. 94 (1902), involved review of the postmaster general's fraud order barring use of the mails for conducting the plaintiff's business. The question brought before the court in this bill of equity was "as to the power of the court to grant relief where the Postmaster has assumed and exercised jurisdiction in a case not covered by the statutes, and where he has ordered the detention of mail matter when the statutes have not granted him power so to order" (187 U.S. 107–108). The Court answered:

> That the conduct of the Post Office is a part of the administrative department of the government is entirely true, but that does not necessarily and always oust the courts of jurisdiction to grant relief to a party aggrieved in any action by the head or one of the subordinate officials of the department which is unauthorized by the statue under which he assumes to act. . . . Otherwise, the individual is left to the absolutely uncontrolled and arbitrary action of a public and administrative officer, whose action is unauthorized by any law and is in violation of the rights of the individual [187 U.S. 108–110].

---

[6] *Gaines* v. *Thompson*, 74 U.S. (7 Wall.) 347 (1869).

[7] *Lem Moon Sing* v. *United States*, 158 U.S. 538 (1895).

[8] Kenneth C. Davis, 4 *Administrative Law Treatise* 31 (1958).

The Court in the next decade moved on to reverse the presumption in immigration[9] and land grant cases,[10] which had been bastions of the nineteenth-century presumption against reviewability. Although the presumption of reviewability was temporarily sidetracked in *Switchmen's Union* v. *National Mediation Board,* 320 U.S. 297 (1943), which has been described as "an expression of the mood of judicial self-deprecation and abdication,"[11] the Supreme Court quickly reverted back to the presumption in *Stark* v. *Wickard* (1944). In that case, Justice Stanley F. Reed, in spite of Justice Frankfurter's protestations in dissent, held as follows:

> The responsibility of determining the limits of statutory grants of authority . . . is a judicial function entrusted to the courts by congress by the statutes establishing the courts and marking their jurisdiction. . . . [U]nder Article 3, Congress established courts to adjudicate cases and controversies as to claims of infringement of individual rights whether by unlawful action of private persons or by the exertions of unauthorized administrative power.[12]

Summing up the situation in 1965, on the basis of *Stark,* Professor Jaffe wrote,

> [I]t can safely be said that the prevailing and the correct view is that of Mr. Justice Reed. . . . Congress, barring constitutional impediments, may indeed exclude judicial review. But judicial review is the rule. It rests on the congressional grant of general jurisdiction to the article III courts. It is a basic right; it is a traditional power and the intention to exclude it must be made specifically manifest.[13]

Professor Jaffe's view has been confirmed by subsequent case law. In the important case of *Abbott Laboratories* v. *Gardner,* 387 U.S. 136 (1967), the Supreme Court stated that "only upon a showing of 'clear and convincing evidence' of a contrary legislative intent should the courts restrict access to judicial review" (387 U.S. 141). Elsewhere in the same opinion, the Court described the general legislative intent at the federal level (as manifested in the APA): "the Administrative Procedure Act . . . embodies the basic presumption of judicial review . . . so long as no statute precludes such relief or the action is not one committed by law to agency discretion . . . " (387 U.S. 140).

The pertinent provisions of the APA are §§ 704 and 701. Section 704 provides: "Agency action made reviewable by statute and final agency action for which there is no adequate remedy in a court are subject to judicial re-

---

[9] *Gegiow* v. *Uhl,* 239 U.S. 3 (1915).

[10] *Lane* v. *Hoglund,* 244 U.S. 174 (1917).

[11] Jaffe, above, note 1, 344.

[12] *Stark* v. *Wickard,* 321 U.S. 288, 310. Although *American School of Magnetic Healing* v. *McAnnulty, Gegiow* v. *Uhl, Lane* v. *Hoglund,* and *Stark* support the conclusion that generally there is a right to judicial review, one must be aware of the exceptions. In this regard, see either Davis, above, note 8, 25–30, or Jaffe, above, note 1, 348–353.

[13] Jaffe, above, note 1, 346.

view." This general provision is conditioned, however, by § 701: "This chapter applies, according to the provisions thereof, except to the extent that—(1) statutes preclude judicial review; or (2) agency action is committed to agency discretion by law."

PRECLUSION OF JUDICIAL REVIEW

Under the APA, then, the two bases for denying review are statutory preclusion and cases involving agency discretion.[14] More than fifty years after the adoption of the APA, the federal courts still struggle to resolve cases and controversies in which claims of preclusion have been advanced by administrative agencies. The resulting case law can be subdivided into those situations in which the claims of statutory preclusion are implied and those in which they are express.[15] In either event, to use Professor Jaffe's view as quoted above, the congressional intention to preclude "must be made specifically manifest."

The classic precedent rejecting an implied preclusion is the aforementioned case of *Stark* v. *Wickard* (1944), in which the secretary of agriculture attempted to foreclose federal court review of an alleged error of law in an agency milk marketing order. However, one can find an exception to this general rule in *Block* v. *Community Nutrition Institute,* 467 U.S. 340 (1984), which also involved the Agriculture Marketing Agreement Act of 1937, 50 Stat. 246, as amended, 7 U.S.C. § 601 et seq. The court of appeals, relying on *Stark*, supported the presumption favoring judicial review; however, the Supreme Court concluded that

> [t]he presumption favoring judicial review of administrative action is just that—a presumption. This presumption, like all presumptions used in interpreting statutes, may be overcome by specific language or specific legislative history that is a reliable indicator of congressional intent [467 U.S. 349].

Consequently, upon finding such indicators, the unanimous Court ruled to preclude consumer challenges to the secretary of agriculture's marketing orders.

Although instances of statutory provisions specifically barring judicial review are not common, a few congressional enactments have contained such statements. Perhaps the best illustration of such language was found in the enabling legislation of the Veterans' Administration (VA), which for much of the agency's history absolutely precluded review of its actions.[16] In

---

[14] A thoughtful comment on this general subject, "A Brief Concluding Note on the Constitutionality of Precluding Review," may be found in Peter L. Strauss, Todd Rakoff, Roy A. Schotland, and Cynthia R. Farina, *Administrative Law: Cases and Comments* 1220–1225 (9th ed., 1995).

[15] Ibid., 1192–1209, for discussion of preclusion cases. But courts have shown some reluctance to permit judicial review of functions that fall within the area of foreign affairs and international diplomacy, even where the statute appears to confer review. See *Chicago and Southern Air Lines* v. *Waterman Steamship Corp.*, 333 U.S. 103 (1948).

[16] See both Alfred C. Aman, Jr., and William T. Mayton, *Administrative Law* (2nd ed., 2001), 361–362, and Strauss, et al., above, note 14, for additional background on the historical development

1970 Congress amended § 211(a) of Title 38 of the U.S. Code, regarding the VA's authority in the area of veterans' benefits, to read as follows: "the decisions of the Administrator on any question of law or fact under any law administered by the Veterans' Administration providing benefits for veterans . . . shall be final and conclusive and no . . . court of the United States shall have the power or jurisdiction to review such decision." This provision was litigated in the celebrated case of *Johnson* v. *Robison,* 415 U.S. 361 (1974).

Robison, a conscientious objector who had satisfactorily completed two years of alternative service, was denied educational assistance benefits by the VA on the ground that he did not qualify as an "eligible veteran" under 38 U.S.C.A. § 1661(a). Robison filed a class-action suit in the U.S. district court in Massachusetts seeking a declaratory judgment that this and related provisions violated the First Amendment's guarantee of religious freedom and the Fifth Amendment's guarantee of equal protection of the laws. Johnson, the administrator of Veterans Affairs, moved to dismiss the action on the ground that on the basis of 38 U.S.C.A. § 211(a) (quoted above), judicial review of decisions of the administrator is prohibited. The district court ruled that judicial review was available, rejected Robison's First Amendment claim, but upheld his equal protection claim. The Supreme Court, one justice dissenting, rejected both Robison's First Amendment and equal protection claims. Justice William J. Brennan, writing for the court majority, stated:

> We consider first appellants' contention that § 211 (a) bars federal courts from deciding the constitutionality of veterans' benefits legislation. Such a construction would, of course, raise serious questions concerning the constitutionality of § 211 (a), and in such case "it is a cardinal principle that this Court will first ascertain whether a construction of the statute is fairly possible by which the [constitutional] question[s] may be avoided." *United States* v. *Thirty-seven Photographs*, 402 U.S. 363, 369 (1971). . . .
>
> Plainly, no explicit provision of § 211 (a) bars judicial consideration of appellee's constitutional claims. That section provides that "the *decisions* of the Administrator on any question of law or fact *under* any law administered by the Veterans' Administration providing benefits for veterans . . . shall be final and conclusive and no . . . court of the United States shall have power or jurisdiction to review any such decision. . . ." (Emphasis added.) The prohibitions would appear to be aimed at review only of those decisions of law or fact that arise in the *administration* by the Veterans' Administration of a *statute* providing benefits for veterans. A decision of law or fact "under" a statute is made by the Administrator in the interpretation or application of a particular provision of the statute to a particular set of facts. Appellee's constitutional challenge is not to any such decision of the *Administrator*, but rather to a decision of Congress to create a statutory class entitled to benefits that does not include I-O conscientious objectors who performed alternative civilian service. Thus, as the District Court stated: "The questions of law presented in these proceedings arise under the Constitution, not under the statute whose validity is challenged." 352 F.Supp., at 853. . . .

---

of these preclusion provisions up to the 1988 legislation (102 Stat. 4105) creating a new Article I court, the Court of Veterans Appeals, to review VA benefit decisions.

[The Court majority opinion proceeded to examine VA administrative practice and the legislative history of the 1970 congressional amendment.]

Thus, the 1970 amendment was enacted to overrule the interpretation of the Court of Appeals for the District of Columbia Circuit and thereby restore vitality to the two primary purposes [editors' note—i.e., avoidance of expensive and time-consuming litigation and assurance of uniformity in VA decision-making] to be served by the no-review clause. Nothing whatever in the legislative history of the 1970 amendment, or predecessor no-review clauses, suggests any congressional intent to preclude judicial cognizance of constitutional challenges to veterans' benefits legislation. Such challenges obviously do not contravene the purposes of the no-review clause, for they cannot be expected to burden the courts by their volume, nor do they involve technical considerations of Veterans' Administration policy. We therefore conclude, in agreement with the District Court, that a construction of § 211 (a) that does not extend the prohibitions of that section to actions challenging the constitutionality of laws providing benefits for veterans is not only "fairly possible" but is the most reasonable construction, for neither the text nor the scant legislative history of § 211 (a) provides the "clear and convincing" evidence of congressional intent required by this Court before a statute will be construed to restrict access to judicial review. See *Abbott Laboratories* v. *Gardner*, 387 U.S. 136, 141 (1967). 415 U.S. 366–367, 373–374.

Further court action extending judicial review over veterans benefits[17] led Congress in 1988 to pass the Veterans' Judicial Review Act (102 Stat. 4105). The law created a new Article I Court of Veteran Appeals to review the VA's benefit decisions. Judgments of this body were reviewable by the Court of Appeals for the Federal Circuit. Thus, the long-standing express preclusion provisions of the VA were finally abolished.

The following Medicare case, which is illustrative of the contemporary preclusion case law, contains analyses of both the implied and express preclusion claims advanced by the secretary of health and human services.

Bowen v. *Michigan Academy of Family Physicians*

Supreme Court of the United States, 1986.
476 U.S. 667, 106 S.Ct. 2133, 90 L.Ed. 2d 623.

Mr. Justice STEVENS delivered the opinion of the Court.

The question presented in this case is whether Congress, in either § 1395ff or § 1395ii of Title 42 of the United States Code, barred judicial review of regulations promulgated under Part B of the Medicare program.

Respondents, who include an association of family physicians and several individual doctors, filed suit to challenge the validity of 42 CFR 405.504(b) (1985),

which authorizes the payment of benefits in different amounts for similar physicians' services. The District Court held that the regulation contravened several provisions of the statute governing the Medicare program:

There is no basis to justify the segregation of allopathic family physicians from all other types of physicians. Such segregation is not rationally related to any legitimate purpose of the Medicare statute. To lump MDs who are family physicians, but who

---

[17] See, e.g., *Traynor* v. *Turnage*, 485 U.S. 535 (1988).

have chosen not to become board certified family physicians for whatever motive, with chiropractors, dentists, and podiatrists for the purpose of determining Medicare reimbursement defies all reason. *Michigan Academy of Family Physicians* v. *Blue Cross and Blue Shield of Michigan*, 502 F. Supp. 751, 755 (ED Mich. 1980).

Because it ruled in favor of respondents on statutory grounds, the District Court did not reach their constitutional claims. . . . The Court of Appeals agreed with the District Court that the Secretary's regulation was "obvious[ly] inconsisten[t] with the plain language of the Medicare statute" and held that "this regulation is irrational and is invalid." *Michigan Academy of Family Physicians* v. *Blue Cross and Blue Shield of Michigan*, 728 F.2d 326, 332 (CA6 1984). Like the District Court, it too declined to reach respondents' constitutional claims. . . .

The Secretary of Health and Human Services has not sought review of the decision on the merits invalidating the regulation. Instead, he renews the contention, rejected by both the District Court and the Court of Appeals, that Congress has forbidden judicial review of all questions affecting the amount of benefits payable under Part B of the Medicare program. Because the question is important and has divided the Courts of Appeals, we granted the petition for a writ of certiorari. We now affirm. . . .

We begin with the strong presumption that Congress intends judicial review of administrative action. From the beginning "our cases [have established] that judicial review of a final agency action by an aggrieved person will not be cut off unless there is persuasive reason to believe that such was the purpose of Congress." *Abbott Laboratories* v. *Gardner*, 387 U.S. 136, 140 (1967) (citing cases). See generally L. Jaffe, *Judicial Control of Administrative Action* 339–353 (1965). . . . In undertaking the comprehensive rethinking of the place of administrative agencies in a regime of separate and divided powers that culminated in the passage of the Administrative Procedure Act (APA) . . . the Senate Committee on the Judiciary remarked:

> Very rarely do statutes withhold judicial review. It has never been the policy of Congress to prevent the administration of its own statutes from being judicially confined to the scope of authority granted or to the objectives specified. Its policy could not be otherwise, for in such a case statutes would in effect be blank checks drawn to the credit of some administrative officer or board. S. Rep. No. 752, 79th Cong., 1st Sess., 26 (1945).

Subject to constitutional constraints, Congress can, of course, make exceptions to the historic practice whereby courts review agency action. The presumption of judicial review is, after all, a presumption, and "like all presumptions used in interpreting statutes, may be overcome by," inter alia, "specific language or specific legislative history that is a reliable indicator of congressional intent," or a specific congressional intent to preclude judicial review that is "'fairly discernible' in the detail of the legislative scheme." *Block* v. *Community Nutrition Institute*, 467 U.S. 340, 349, 351 (1984).

In this case, the Government asserts that two statutory provisions remove the Secretary's regulation from review under the grant of general federal-question jurisdiction found in 28 U.S.C. § 1331. First, the Government contends that 42 U.S.C. § 1395ff(b) . . . , which authorizes "Appeal by individuals," impliedly forecloses administrative or judicial review of any action taken under Part B of the Medicare program by failing to authorize such review while simultaneously authorizing administrative and judicial review of "any determination . . . as to . . . the amount of benefits under part A." . . . Second, the Government asserts that 42 U.S.C. § 1395ii . . . which makes applicable 42 U.S.C. § 405(h) . . . of the Social Security Act to the Medicare program, expressly precludes all administrative or judicial review not otherwise provided in that statute. We find neither argument persuasive.

Section 1395ff on its face is an explicit authorization of judicial review, not a bar. As a general matter, "'[the] mere fact that some acts are made reviewable should not suffice to support an implication of exclusion as to others. The right to review is too important to be excluded on such slender and indeterminate evidence of legislative intent.'" *Abbott Laboratories* v. *Gardner*, 387 U.S., at 141 (quoting L. Jaffe, *Judicial Control of Administrative Action* 357 (1965)). . . .

[The Court then examined the methods by which Medicare Part B benefit awards were to be computed.]

Careful analysis of the governing statutory provisions and their legislative history thus reveals that Congress intended to bar judicial review only of determinations of the amount of benefits to be awarded under Part B. Congress delegated this task to carriers who would finally determine such matters in conformity with the regulations and instructions of the Secretary. We conclude, therefore, that those matters which Congress did not leave to be determined in a "fair hearing" conducted by the carrier—including challenges to the validity of the Secretary's instructions and regulations—are not impliedly insulated from judicial review by 42 U.S.C. § 1395ff. . . .

In light of Congress' express provision for carrier review of millions of what it characterized as "trivial" claims, it is implausible to think it intended that there be no forum to adjudicate statutory and constitutional challenges to regulations promulgated by the Secretary. The Government nevertheless maintains that this is precisely what Congress intended to accomplish in 42 U.S.C. § 1395ii. . . . That section states that 42 U.S.C. § 405(h) . . . along with a string citation of 10 other provisions of Title II of the Social Security Act, "shall also apply with respect to this

subchapter to the same extent as they are applicable with respect to subchapter II of this chapter." Section 405(h), in turn, reads in full as follows:

(h) Finality of Secretary's decision

The findings and decision of the Secretary after a hearing shall be binding upon all individuals who were parties to such hearing. No findings of fact or decision of the Secretary shall be reviewed by any person, tribunal, or governmental agency except as herein provided. No action against the United States, the Secretary, or any officer or employee thereof shall be brought under section 1331 or 1346 of title 28 to recover on any claim arising under this subchapter.

The Government contends that the third sentence of § 405(h) by its terms prevents any resort to the grant of general federal-question jurisdiction contained in 28 U.S.C. § 1331. It finds support for this construction in *Weinberger* v. *Salfi*, 422 U.S. 749, 756–762 (1975), and *Heckler* v. *Ringer*, 466 U.S. 602, 614–616, 620–626 (1984). Respondents counter that the dispositions in these two cases are consistent with the view that Congress' purpose was to make clear that whatever specific procedures it provided for judicial review of final action by the Secretary were exclusive, and could not be circumvented by resort to the general jurisdiction of the federal courts. Cf. *Weinberger* v. *Salfi*, 422 U.S., at 764–765; *Heckler* v. *Ringer*, 466 U.S., at 621–622.

Whichever may be the better reading of *Salfi* and *Ringer*, we need not pass on the meaning of § 405(h) in the abstract to resolve this case. Section 405(h) does not apply on its own terms to Part B of the Medicare program, but is instead incorporated mutatis mutandis by § 1395ii. The legislative history of both the statute establishing the Medicare program and the 1972 amendments thereto provides specific evidence of Congress' intent to foreclose review only of "amount determinations"—i. e., those "quite minor matters," 118 Cong. Rec. 33992 (1972) (remarks of Sen. Bennett), remitted finally and exclusively to adjudication by private insurance carriers in a "fair hearing." By the same token, matters which Congress did not delegate to private carriers, such as challenges to the validity of the Secretary's instructions and regulations, are cognizable in courts of law. In the face of this persuasive evidence of legislative intent, we will not indulge the Government's assumption that Congress contemplated review by carriers of "trivial" monetary claims, ibid., but intended no review at all of substantial statutory and constitutional challenges to the Secretary's administration of Part B of the Medicare program. This is an extreme position, and one we would be most reluctant to adopt without "a showing of 'clear and convincing evidence,'" *Abbott Laboratories* v. *Gardner*, 387 U.S., at 141, to overcome the "strong presumption that Congress did not mean to prohibit all judicial review" of executive action, *Dunlop* v. *Bachowski*, 421 U.S., at 567. We ordinarily presume that Congress intends the executive to obey its statutory commands and, accordingly, that it expects the courts to grant relief when an executive agency violates such a command. That presumption has not been surmounted here.

The judgment of the Court of Appeals is affirmed.

Justice REHNQUIST took no part in the consideration or decision of this case.

ADMINISTRATIVE ACTIONS COMMITTED BY LAW TO AGENCY DISCRETION

Most commentators agree that this is a "tricky problem."[18] Section 706 of the APA provides that the court shall vacate agency action found to be "arbitrary, capricious, an abuse of discretion, or otherwise not in accordance with the law." But § 701 stated: "this chapter applies . . . except to the extent that . . . agency action is committed to agency discretion by law." Numerous analysts have wrestled with these seemingly contradictory provisions and have reached varying conclusions. Most, however, appear to minimize the importance of the "committed to agency discretion by law" provision of § 706. Davis stated: "When legislative intent is unexpressed or unclear, the best generalization may be that courts limit themselves to issues appropriate for judicial determination."[19] Schwartz concluded that "the exception for agency discretion [is limited] to situations where the statute shows some positive intention to eliminate review. . . . The exception . . . accordingly adds little or nothing to that of cases where 'statutes preclude judicial review.'"[20] Jaffe stated: "presumptively, an exercise of discretion is reviewable for legal error, procedural defect, or 'abuse.'"[21] *Overton Park* is an important Supreme Court case that deals with the issue.

---

[18] Jaffe, above, note 1, 359. See also Kenneth Culp Davis, *Administrative Law: Cases—Text—Problems* 63 (6th ed., 1977).

[19] Davis, above, note 18, 64.

[20] Bernard Schwartz, *Administrative Law* 454 (1976).

[21] Jaffe, above, note 1, 363.

Citizens to Preserve Overton Park, Inc. v. *Volpe*

SUPREME COURT OF THE UNITED STATES, 1971.
401 U.S. 402, 91 S.Ct. 814, 28 L.Ed. 2d 136.

Opinion of the Court by Mr. Justice MAR-SHALL, announced by Mr. Justice STEWART.

The growing public concern about the quality of our natural environment has prompted Congress in recent years to enact legislation designed to curb the accelerating destruction of our country's natural beauty. We are concerned in this case with § 4 (f) of the Department of Transportation Act of 1966, as amended, and § 18 (a) of the Federal-Aid Highway Act of 1968, 82 Stat. 823, 23 U.S.C. § 138 (1964 ed., Supp. V) (hereafter § 138). These statutes prohibit the Secretary of Transportation from authorizing the use of federal funds to finance the construction of highways through public parks if a "feasible and prudent" alternative route exists. If no such route is available, the statutes allow him to approve construction through parks only if there has been "all possible planning to minimize harm" to the park.

Petitioners, private citizens as well as local and national conservation organizations, contend that the Secretary has violated these statutes by authorizing the expenditure of federal funds for the construction of a six-lane interstate highway through a public park in Memphis, Tennessee. Their claim was rejected by the District Court, which granted the Secretary's motion for summary judgment, and the Court of Appeals for the Sixth Circuit affirmed. After oral argument, this Court granted a stay that halted construction and, treating the application for the stay as a petition for certiorari, granted review. . . . We now reverse the judgment below and remand for further proceedings in the District Court.

Overton Park is a 342-acre city park located near the center of Memphis. The park contains a zoo, a nine-hole municipal golf course, an outdoor theater, nature trails, a bridle path, an art academy, picnic areas, and 170 acres of forest. The proposed highway, which is to be a six-lane, high-speed, expressway, will sever the zoo from the rest of the park. Although the roadway will be depressed below ground level except where it crosses a small creek, 26 acres of the park will be destroyed. The highway is to be a segment of Interstate Highway I-40, part of the National System of Interstate and Defense Highways. I-40 will provide Memphis with a major east-west expressway which will allow easier access to downtown Memphis from the residential areas on the eastern edge of the city.

Although the route through the park was approved by the Bureau of Public Roads in 1956 and by the Federal Highway Administrator in 1966, the enactment of § 4 (f) of the Department of Transportation Act prevented distribution of federal funds for the section of the highway designated to go through Overton Park until the Secretary of Transportation determined whether the requirements of § 4 (f) had been met. Federal funding for the rest of the project was, however, available; and the state acquired a right-of-way on both sides of the park. In April 1968, the Secretary announced that he concurred in the judgment of local officials that I-40 should be built through the park. And in September 1969 the State acquired the right-of-way inside Overton Park from the city. Final approval for the project—the route as well as the design—was not announced until November 1969, after Congress had reiterated in § 138 of the Federal–Aid Highway Act that highway construction through public parks was to be restricted.

Neither announcement approving the route and design of I-40 was accompanied by a statement of the Secretary's factual findings. He did not indicate why he believed there were no feasible and prudent alternative routes or why design changes could not be made to reduce the harm to the park.

Petitioners contend that the Secretary's action is invalid without such formal findings and that the Secretary did not make an independent determination but merely relied on the judgment of the Memphis City Council. They also contend that it would be "feasible and prudent" to route I-40 around Overton Park either to the north or to the south. And they argue that if these alternative routes are not "feasible and prudent," the present plan does not include "all possible" methods for reducing harm to the park. Petitioners claim that I-40 could be built under the park by using either of two possible tunneling methods, and they claim that, at a minimum, by using advanced drainage techniques the expressway could be depressed below ground level along the entire route through the park including the section that crosses the small creek.

Respondents argue that it was unnecessary for the Secretary to make formal findings, and that he did, in fact, exercise his own independent judgment which was supported by the facts. In the District Court, respondents introduced affidavits, prepared specifically for this litigation, which indicated that the Secretary had made the decision and that the decision was supportable. These affidavits were contradicted by affidavits introduced by petitioners, who also sought to take the deposition of a former Federal Highway Administrator who had participated in the decision to route I-40 through Overton Park.

The District Court and the Court of Appeals found that formal findings by the Secretary were not necessary and refused to order the deposition of the former Federal Highway Administrator because those courts believed that probing of the mental processes of an administrative decisionmaker was prohibited. And, believing that the Secretary's authority was wide and reviewing courts' authority narrow in the approval of highway routes, the lower courts held that the affidavits contained no basis for a determination that the Secretary had exceeded his authority.

We agree that formal findings were not required. But we do not believe that in this case judicial review based solely on litigation affidavits was adequate.

A threshold question—whether petitioners are entitled to any judicial review—is easily answered. Section 701 of the Administrative Procedure Act . . . provides that the action of "each authority of the Government of the United States," which includes the Department of Transportation, is subject to judicial review except where there is a statutory prohibition on review or where "agency action is committed to agency discretion by law." In this case, there is no indication that Congress sought to prohibit judicial review and there is most certainly no "showing of 'clear and convincing evidence' of a . . . legislative intent" to restrict access to judicial review. *Abbott Laboratories* v. *Gardner*, 387 U.S. 136, 141 (1967); *Brownell* v. *We Shung*, 352 U.S., 180, 185 (1956).

Similarly, the Secretary's decision here does not fall within the exception for action "committed to agency discretion." This is a very narrow exception. . . . The legislative history of the Administrative Procedure Act indicates that it is applicable in those rare instances where "statutes are drawn in such broad terms that in a given case there is no law to apply." S. Rep. No. 752, 79th Cong., 1st Sess., 26 (1945).

Section 4 (f) of the Department of Transportation Act and § 138 of the Federal-Aid Highway Act are clear and specific directives. Both the Department of Transportation Act and the Federal-Aid Highway Act provide that the Secretary "shall not approve any program or project" that requires the use of any public parkland "unless (1) there is no feasible and prudent alternative to the use of such land, and (2) such program includes all possible planning to minimize harm to such park. . . ." 23 U.S.C. § 138 (1964 ed., Supp. V); 49 U.S.C. § 1653 (f) (1964 ed., Supp. V). This language is a plain and explicit bar to the use of federal funds for construction of highways through parks— only the most unusual situations are exempted.

Despite the clarity of the statutory language, respondents argue that the Secretary has wide discretion. They recognize that the requirement that there be no "feasible" alternative route admits of little administrative discretion. For this exemption to apply the Secretary must find that as a matter of sound engineering it would not be feasible to build the highway along any other route. Respondents argue, however, that the requirement that there be no other "prudent" route requires the Secretary to engage in a wide-ranging balancing of competing interests. They contend that the Secretary should weigh the detriment resulting from the destruction of parkland against the cost of other routes, safety considerations, and other factors, and determine on the basis of the importance that he attaches to these other factors whether, on balance, alternative feasible routes would be "prudent."

But no such wide-ranging endeavor was intended. It is obvious that in most cases considerations of cost, directness of route, and community disruption will indicate that parkland should be used for highway construction whenever possible. Although it may be necessary to transfer funds from one jurisdiction to another, there will always be a smaller outlay required from the public purse when parkland is used since the public already owns the land and there will be no need to pay for right-of-way. . . .

Congress clearly did not intend that cost and disruption of the community were to be ignored by the Secretary. But the very existence of the statutes indicates that protection of parkland was to be given paramount importance. The few green havens that are public parks were not to be lost unless there were truly unusual factors present in a particular case or the cost or community disruption resulting from alternative routes reached extraordinary magnitudes. If the statutes are to have any meaning, the Secretary cannot approve the destruction of parkland unless he finds that alternative routes present unique problems.

Plainly, there is "law to apply" and thus the exemption for action "committed to agency discretion" is inapplicable. But the existence of judicial review is only the start: the standard for review must also be determined. . . .

[There follows a discussion of the scope of judicial review to be applied in the case, in which the petitioners' alternative pleas for review under the substantial evidence test and *de novo* review of whether the secretary's decision was "unwarranted by the facts" are rejected by the Court.]

The lower courts based their review on the litigation affidavits that were presented. These affidavits were merely "post hoc" rationalizations, Burlington *Truck Lines* v. *United States*, 371 U.S. 156, 168–169 (1962), which have traditionally been found to be an inadequate basis for review. . . . And they clearly do not constitute the "whole record" compiled by the agency: the basis for review required by § 706 of the Administrative Procedure Act.

Thus it is necessary to remand this case to the District Court for plenary review of the Secretary's decision. That review is to be based on the full administrative record that was before the Secretary at the time he made his decision. But since the bare record may not disclose the factors that were considered or the Secretary's construction of the evidence it may be necessary for the District Court to require some explanation in order to determine if the Secretary acted within the scope of his authority and if the Secretary's action was justifiable under the applicable standard.

The court may require the administrative officials who participated in the decision to give testimony explaining their action. Of course, such inquiry into the mental processes of administrative decisionmakers is usually to be avoided. . . . And where there are administrative findings that were made at the same time as the decision, as was the case in *Morgan*, there must be a strong showing of bad faith or improper behavior before such inquiry may be made. But here there are no such formal findings and it may be

that the only way there can be effective judicial review is by examining the decisionmakers themselves.

The District Court is not, however, required to make such an inquiry. It may be that the Secretary can prepare formal findings including the information required by DOT Order 5610.1 that will provide an adequate explanation for his action. Such an explanation will, to some extent, be a "post hoc rationalization" and thus must be viewed critically. If the District Court decides that additional explanation is necessary, that court should consider which method will prove the most expeditious so that full review may be had as soon as possible.

Reversed and remanded.

Mr. Justice DOUGLAS took no part in the consideration or decision of this case.

[The separate opinions of Mr. Justice BLACK, with whom Mr. Justice BRENNAN joins, and of Mr. Justice BLACKMUN are omitted.]

In a fascinating analysis of the impact of *Overton Park* on the law of judicial review,[22] Strauss and colleagues have pointed out that the highway was never built. The coup de grâce came when the secretary of transportation was directed by the district court to make a route determination in accordance with the applicable law, and in his decision in January 1973 he stated:

> On the basis of the record before me and in light of guidance provided by the Supreme Court, I find that an Interstate highway as proposed by the State through Overton Park cannot be approved. . . . I cannot find . . . that there are no prudent and feasible alternatives to the use of parkland nor that the broader environmental protection objectives of the NEPA and the Federal-Aid Highway Act have been met, nor that the existing proposal would comply with FHWA standards on noise.[23]

Subsequent efforts by the state of Tennessee to revive the project died with an adverse Court of Appeals decision in *Citizens to Preserve Overton Park, Inc.* v. *Brinegar,* 494 F. 2d 1212 (6th Cir., 1974), and a subsequent denial of a writ of certiorari by the Supreme Court, 421 U.S. 991 (1975).

In two cases decided in the 1980s, the Supreme Court retreated from the breadth of the *Overton Park* ruling. These cases, *Heckler* v. *Chaney,* 470

---

[22] Strauss, et al., above, note 14, 577–584.

[23] As quoted in Strauss, et al., above, note 14, 578.

U.S. 821 (1985), and *Webster* v. *Doe*, 486 U.S. 592 (1988), had the effect of broadening the interpretation of the "committed to agency discretion" exception of the APA's § 701(a)(2) and weakening the presumption of reviewability.[24] The following case involving the termination of a clinical health program for handicapped Indian children relies heavily of the *Heckler* and *Webster* precedents.

Lincoln v. Vigil

SUPREME COURT OF THE UNITED STATES, 1993.
508 U.S. 182, 113 S.Ct. 2024, 124 L.Ed. 2d 101.

Justice SOUTER delivered the opinion for a unanimous Court.

[In 1985 the Indian Health Service, a federal agency, discontinued a clinical program for handicapped Indian children and reassigned the program staff to consultancy roles with other nationwide Indian Health Service programs. Respondents, handicapped Indian children eligible to receive benefits under the Indian Children's Program, sought both declaratory and injunctive relief against Lincoln, the acting director of the Indian Health Service. They argued that the service's discontinuance of the clinical services violated the federal trust responsibility to Indians, the enabling legislation authorizing expenditures for Indian health, the APA, various agency regulations, and the due process clause of the Fifth Amendment. The district court ordered the service to reinstate the program, and the Court of Appeals for the Tenth Circuit affirmed. The excerpts below do not include that portion of the opinion in which the Court concluded that the APA's notice-and-comment provisions had not been violated by the agency's decision to terminate the program.]

For several years in the late 1970s and early 1980s, the Indian Health Service provided diagnostic and treatment services, referred to collectively as the Indian Children's Program (Program), to handicapped Indian children in the Southwest. In 1985, the Service decided to reallocate the Program's resources to a nationwide effort to assist such children. We hold that the Service's decision to discontinue the Program was "committed to agency discretion by law" and therefore not subject to judicial review under the Administrative Procedure Act, 5 U.S.C. § 701(a)(2), and that the Service's exercise of that discretion was not subject to the notice-and-comment rulemaking requirements imposed by § 553. . . .

First is the question whether it was error for the Court of Appeals to hold the substance of the Service's decision to terminate the Program reviewable under the APA. The APA provides that "[a] person suffering legal wrong because of agency action, or adversely affected or aggrieved by agency action within the meaning of a relevant statute, is entitled to judicial review thereof," . . . and we have read the APA as embodying a "basic presumption of judicial review," *Abbott Laboratories* v. *Gardner*, 387 U.S. 136, 140 (1967). This is "just" a presumption, however, *Block* v. *Community Nutrition Institute*, 467 U.S. 340, 349 (1984), and under § 701(a)(2) agency action is not subject to judicial review "to the extent that" such action "is committed to agency discretion by law." As we explained in *Heckler* v. *Chaney*, 470 U.S. 821, 830 (1985), § 701(a)(2) makes it

---

[24] See also *Dalton* v. *Specter*, 511 U.S. 462 (1994), which was discussed in chapter 1.

clear that "review is not to be had" in those rare circumstances where the relevant statute "is drawn so that a court would have no meaningful standard against which to judge the agency's exercise of discretion." . . . "In such a case, the statute ('law') can be taken to have 'committed' the decisionmaking to the agency's judgment absolutely." *Heckler*, supra, at 830.

Over the years, we have read § 701(a)(2) to preclude judicial review of certain categories of administrative decisions that courts traditionally have regarded as "committed to agency discretion." . . . In *Heckler* itself, we held an agency's decision not to institute enforcement proceedings to be presumptively unreviewable under § 701(a)(2). 470 U.S. at 831. An agency's "decision not to enforce often involves a complicated balancing of a number of factors which are peculiarly within its expertise," ibid., and for this and other good reasons, we concluded, "such a decision has traditionally been 'committed to agency discretion,'" id., at 832. Similarly, in *ICC* v. *Locomotive Engineers*, 482 U.S. 270, 282 (1987), we held that § 701(a)(2) precludes judicial review of another type of administrative decision traditionally left to agency discretion, an agency's refusal to grant reconsideration of an action because of material error. In so holding, we emphasized "the impossibility of devising an adequate standard of review for such agency action." Ibid. . . .

The allocation of funds from a lump-sum appropriation is another administrative decision traditionally regarded as committed to agency discretion. After all, the very point of a lump-sum appropriation is to give an agency the capacity to adapt to changing circumstances and meet its statutory responsibilities in what it sees as the most effective or desirable way. . . . For this reason, a fundamental principle of appropriations law is that where "Congress merely appropriates lump-sum amounts without statutorily restricting what can be done with those funds, a clear inference arises that it does not intend to impose legally binding restrictions, and indicia in committee reports and other legislative history as to how the funds should or are expected to be spent do not establish any legal requirements on" the agency. . . . Put another way, a lump-sum appropriation reflects a congressional recognition that an agency must be allowed "flexibility to shift . . . funds within a particular . . . appropriation account so that" the agency "can make necessary adjustments for 'unforeseen developments'" and "'changing requirements.'" *LTV Aerospace Corp.*, 55 Comp. General, 307, at 318.

Like the decision against instituting enforcement proceedings, then, an agency's allocation of funds from a lump-sum appropriation requires "a complicated balancing of a number of factors which are peculiarly within its expertise": whether its "resources are best spent" on one program or another; whether it "is likely to succeed" in fulfilling its statutory mandate; whether a particular program "best fits the agency's overall policies"; and, "indeed, whether the agency has enough resources" to fund a program "at all." *Heckler*, 470 U.S. at 831. As in *Heckler*, so here, the "agency is far better equipped than the courts to deal with the many variables involved in the proper ordering of its priorities." *Heckler*, 470 U.S. at 831–832. Of course, an agency is not free simply to disregard statutory responsibilities: Congress may always circumscribe agency discretion to allocate resources by putting restrictions in the operative statutes (though not, as we have seen, just in the legislative history) . . . . And, of course, we hardly need to note that an agency's decision to ignore congressional expectations may expose it to grave political consequences. But as long as the agency allocates funds from a lump-sum appropriation to meet permissible statutory objectives, § 701(a)(2) gives the courts no leave to intrude. "To [that] extent," the decision to allocate funds "is committed to agency discretion by law." . . .

The Service's decision to discontinue the Program is accordingly unreviewable under § 701(a)(2). As the Court of Appeals recognized, the appropriations Acts for the relevant period do not so much as mention the Program, and both the Snyder Act and the Improvement Act likewise speak about Indian health only in general terms. It is true that the Service repeatedly apprised Congress of the Program's continued operation, but, as we have explained, these representations do not translate through the medium of legislative history into legally binding obligations. The reallocation of agency resources to assist handicapped Indian children nationwide clearly falls within the Service's statutory mandate to provide health care to Indian people . . . and

respondents, indeed, do not seriously contend otherwise. The decision to terminate the Program was committed to the Service's discretion. . . .

One final note: although respondents claimed in the District Court that the Service's termination of the Program violated their rights under the Fifth Amendment's Due Process Clause, see supra, at 189, that court expressly declined to address respondents' constitutional arguments. . . . Thus, while the APA contemplates, in the absence of a clear expression of contrary congressional intent, that judicial review will be available for colorable constitutional claims . . . the record at this stage does not allow mature consideration of constitutional issues, which we leave for the Court of Appeals on remand. . . .

The judgment of the Court of Appeals is reversed, and the case is remanded for further proceedings consistent with this opinion.

It is so ordered.

A SAMPLING OF THRESHOLD QUESTIONS: EXHAUSTION AND STANDING

Assuming that judicial review is not precluded, the person petitioning a court for review of administrative action may face other barriers, including such "threshold questions" as standing, ripeness, exhaustion, and primary jurisdiction. These are rather technical matters that are of more significance to the legal practitioner than the public administrator, and all are treated extensively in the standard law school texts. The discussion that follows will only sketch the broad outlines of these four issues, giving greater attention to the first and third of these.

To state these issues in their most brief form, *standing* involves the question of whether a party has sufficient interest in a controversy to bring an action in court; *ripeness* concerns the issue of whether a problem has matured to the point where it is real and imminent, as opposed to abstract and remote, and thus is appropriate for court review; *exhaustion* (exhaustion of administrative remedies) raises the question of whether a party should be required to pursue further administrative appeal before bringing the matter to court; and *primary jurisdiction* involves the somewhat similar but distinct question of whether a court or an administrative body is the appropriate organ to decide the issue in question. On all of these matters, the relevant statutory law may provide some answers, but the present law on each of these issues is based on a substantial body of case law as well.

Exhaustion of Administrative Remedies

The doctrine of exhaustion of administrative remedies is frequently confused with the doctrine of primary jurisdiction. The exhaustion doctrine concerns timing of judicial review and consequently is distinguishable from the doctrine of primary jurisdiction, which determines whether the agency or court should make the initial determination. The Supreme Court differentiated between the two in *United States* v. *Western Pacific Railroad Company* (1956):

> "Exhaustion" applies where a claim is cognizable in the first instance by an administrative agency alone; judicial interference is held until the administrative process has run its course. "Primary jurisdiction," on the other hand, applies where a claim is originally cognizable in the courts, and comes into play whenever enforcement of the claim requires the resolution of issues which, under a regulatory scheme, have been placed within the special competence of an administrative body; in such a case the judicial process is suspended pending referral of such issues to the administrative body for its view [352 U.S. 59, 63–64 (1956)].

Whereas exhaustion of administrative remedies may be clearly distinguished from primary jurisdiction, it is not nearly as easily distinguished from the requirement of ripeness, which also concerns the timing of judicial review. According to Kenneth C. Davis, "[w]hen a court determines at what stage of administrative action judicial review may be sought, the court is either applying the requirement of ripeness, the broad doctrine that governs the kinds of functions that courts may perform, or the relatively narrow doctrine of exhaustion, which focuses not upon the functions of courts but merely upon the completion or lack of completion of the administrative action."[25]

The exhaustion doctrine's most famous application was in *Myers* v. *Bethlehem Shipbuilding Corporation*, in which Justice Louis D. Brandeis referred to "the long settled rule of judicial administration that no one is entitled to judicial relief for a supposed or threatened injury until the prescribed administrative remedy has been exhausted" [303 U.S. 41, 50–51 (1938)]. The case itself involved the question of "whether a federal district court has equity jurisdiction to enjoin the National Labor Relations Board (NLRB) from holding a hearing upon complaint filed by it against an employer alleged to be engaged in unfair labor practices" (303 U.S. 43). Bethlehem Shipbuilding, the plaintiff in the district court, had asserted that its activities did not "affect interstate commerce," and consequently the NLRB was without jurisdiction to render a constitutionally valid order. Bethlehem further alleged irreparable injury if the hearing were held, in terms of both loss of time for its officers and employees and the unsettling effect on employer-employee relations (303 U.S. 47–48). Under the rule enunciated by

---

[25] Davis, 3 *Administrative Law Treatise* 57 (1958).

the Supreme Court, the agency concerned in the first instance is required to pass on its own jurisdiction. If the agency erred, the error theoretically could be corrected on judicial review. This decision took on added importance for the entire system of regulation since "[i]t came at a moment when the New Deal and administrative law appeared to be battling for their legal lives. The law suit was an avowed part of the frontal attack on the nascent system of regulation. And so the Government's victory became an August dogma of the new dispensation."[26] The recent unanimous Supreme Court decision set forth below provides an illustration of the application of this long-standing doctrine.

Porter v. *Nussle*

SUPREME COURT OF THE UNITED STATES, 2002.
534 U.S. 516, 122 S.Ct. 983, 152 L.Ed. 2d 12.

[Ronald Nussle, a Connecticut prison inmate, brought an action challenging prison conditions without first having exhausted the state-sanctioned administrative remedies as required by a provision of the federal Prison Litigation Reform Act of 1995 (PLRA), as amended (42 USC § 1997e(a)). In his 42 U.S.C. § 1983[27] action, Nussle alleged cruel and unusual punishment in violation of the Eighth Amendment, as made applicable to the states by the Fourteenth Amendment. More specifically, he claimed that he had been subjected to a pattern of harassment and intimidation, and that on one occasion he had been beaten severely. The district court, relying on § 1997e(a), dismissed the suit for failure to exhaust administrative remedies. However, on appeal the Court of Appeals for the Second Circuit reversed on the grounds that the terminology *prison conditions* in § 1997e(a) governs only conditions affecting prisoners generally and not single incidents, such as those alleged here, that affect particular prisoners. In its judgment, actions seeking relief from "excessive force" were to be disaggregated from those challenging "conditions of confinement." The Supreme Court granted certiorari to resolve intercircuit conflict on the issue of whether prisoners alleging excessive force by prison guards must meet the statutory exhaustion requirements before commencing a civil rights action. The excerpts below from Justice Ruth Bader Ginsburg's opinion, speaking for a unanimous Supreme Court, focus on the meaning of the key words *prison conditions* in § 1997e(a) and the relevant prior decisions relating to "suits by prisoners."]

Justice GINSBURG delivered the opinion of the Court. . . .

Ordinarily, plaintiffs pursuing civil rights claims under 42 U.S.C. § 1983 need not exhaust administrative remedies be-

---

[26] Jaffe, above, note 1, 433.

[27] So-called Section 1983 suits are brought in federal courts against officials who operate under state law. The Civil Rights Act of 1871 provides in part: "Every person who, under color of any statute, ordinance, regulation, custom, or usage, of any State or Territory, subjects or causes to be subjected, any citizen of the United States or other person within the jurisdiction thereof to the deprivation of any rights, privileges, or immunities secured by the Constitution and laws, shall be liable to the party injured in an action at law, suit in equity, or other proper proceeding for redress" (42 U.S.C. Section 1983).

fore filing suit in court. . . . Prisoner suits alleging constitutional deprivations while incarcerated once fell within this general rule. . . .

In 1980, however, Congress introduced an exhaustion prescription for suits initiated by state prisoners. . . . This measure authorized district courts to stay a state prisoner's § 1983 action "for a period not to exceed 180 days" while the prisoner exhausted available "plain, speedy, and effective administrative remedies." . . . Exhaustion under the 1980 prescription was in large part discretionary; it could be ordered only if the State's prison grievance system met specified federal standards, and even then, only if, in the particular case, the court believed the requirement "appropriate and in the interests of justice." . . . We described this provision as a "limited exhaustion requirement" in *McCarthy* v. *Madigan*, 503 U.S. 140, 150–151 (1992), and thought it inapplicable to prisoner suits for damages when monetary relief was unavailable through the prison grievance system.

In 1995, as part of the PLRA, Congress invigorated the exhaustion prescription. The revised exhaustion provision, titled "Suits by prisoners," states: "No action shall be brought with respect to prison conditions under section 1983 of this title, or any other Federal law, by a prisoner confined in any jail, prison, or other correctional facility until such administrative remedies as are available are exhausted." . . .

The current exhaustion provision differs markedly from its predecessor. Once within the discretion of the district court, exhaustion in cases covered by § 1997e(a) is now mandatory. . . . All "available" remedies must now be exhausted; those remedies need not meet federal standards, nor must they be "plain, speedy, and effective." . . . Even when the prisoner seeks relief not available in grievance proceed-

ings, notably money damages, exhaustion is a prerequisite to suit. [*Booth* v. *Churner*, 532 U.S. 731, 740–741] And unlike the previous provision, which encompassed only § 1983 suits, exhaustion is now required for all "actions . . . brought with respect to prison conditions," whether under § 1983 or "any other Federal law." . . . Thus federal prisoners suing under *Bivens* v. *Six Unknown Fed. Narcotics Agents* . . . (1971), must first exhaust inmate grievance procedures just as state prisoners must exhaust administrative processes prior to instituting a § 1983 suit.

Beyond doubt, Congress enacted § 1997e(a) to reduce the quantity and improve the quality of prisoner suits; to this purpose, Congress afforded corrections officials time and opportunity to address complaints internally before allowing the initiation of a federal case. In some instances, corrective action taken in response to an inmate's grievance might improve prison administration and satisfy the inmate, thereby obviating the need for litigation. In other instances, the internal review might "filter out some frivolous claims." And for cases ultimately brought to court, adjudication could be facilitated by an administrative record that clarifies the contours of the controversy. [*Booth*, 532 U.S. at 737.]

Congress described the cases covered by § 1997e(a)'s exhaustion requirement as "actions . . . brought with respect to prison conditions." Nussle's case requires us to determine what the § 1997e(a) term "prison conditions" means, given Congress' failure to define the term in the text of the exhaustion provision. We are guided in this endeavor by the PLRA's text and context, and by our prior decisions relating to "suits by prisoners." . . .

As to precedent, the pathmarking opinion is *McCarthy* v. *Bronson* . . . (1991), which construed 28 U.S.C. § 636(b)(1)(B) (1988 ed.), a Judicial Code provision authorizing district judges to refer to magistrate judges, inter alia, "prisoner petitions challenging conditions of confinement." The petitioning prisoner in *McCarthy* argued that § 636(b)(1)(B) allowed nonconsensual referrals "only when a prisoner challenges ongoing prison conditions." . . . The complaint in *McCarthy* targeted no "ongoing prison conditions"; it homed in on "an isolated incident" of excessive force. . . . For that reason, according to the *McCarthy* petitioner, nonconsensual referral of his case was impermissible. . . .

We did not "quarrel with" the prisoner's assertion in *McCarthy* that "the most natural reading of the phrase 'challenging conditions of confinement,' when viewed in isolation, would not include suits seeking relief from isolated episodes of unconstitutional conduct." . . . We nonetheless concluded that the petitioner's argument failed upon reading the phrase "in its proper context." . . . We found no suggestion in § 636(b)(1)(B) that Congress meant to divide prisoner petitions "into subcategories." . . . "On the contrary," we observed, "when the relevant section is read in its entirety, it suggests that Congress intended to authorize the nonconsensual reference of all prisoner petitions to a magistrate." . . . The Federal Magistrates Act, we noted, covers actions of two kinds: challenges to "conditions of confinement"; and "applications for habeas corpus relief." . . . Congress, we concluded, "intended to include in their entirety those two primary categories of suits brought by prisoners." [*McCarthy v. Bronson*, 500 U.S. 136, 138–140.]

"Just three years before [§ 636(b) (1)(B)] was drafted," we explained in *McCarthy*, "our opinion in *Preiser v. Rodriguez* . . . (1973), had described [the] two broad categories of prisoner petitions: (1) those challenging the fact or duration of confinement itself; and (2) those challenging the conditions of confinement." . . .

Preiser v. *Rodriguez* . . . left no doubt, we further stated in *McCarthy*, that "the latter category unambiguously embraced the kind of single episode cases that petitioner's construction would exclude." . . . We found it telling that Congress, in composing the Magistrates Act, chose language "that so clearly paralleled our *Preiser* opinion." . . . We considered it significant as well that the purpose of the Magistrates Act—to lighten the caseload of overworked district judges—would be thwarted by opening the door to satellite litigation over "the precise contours of [the] suggested exception for single episode cases." . . .

As in *McCarthy*, we here read the term "prison conditions" not in isolation, but "in its proper context." . . . The PLRA exhaustion provision is captioned "Suits by prisoners" . . . ; this unqualified heading scarcely aids the argument that Congress meant to bisect the universe of prisoner suits. [*McCarthy*, 500 U.S. at 139–143.]

This Court generally "presumes that Congress expects its statutes to be read in conformity with the Court's precedents." *United States* v. *Wells*, 519 U.S. 482, 495 (1997). That presumption, and the PLRA's dominant concern to promote administrative redress, filter out groundless claims, and foster better prepared litigation of claims aired in court, . . . persuade us that § 1997e(a)'s key words "prison conditions" are properly read through the lens of *McCarthy* and *Preiser*. Those decisions tug strongly away from classifying suits about prison guards' use of excessive force, one or many times, as anything other than actions "with respect to prison conditions." . . .

For the reasons stated, we hold that the PLRA's exhaustion requirement applies to all inmate suits about prison life, whether they involve general circumstances or particular episodes, and whether they allege excessive force or some other wrong. . . . Accordingly, the judgment of the Court of Appeals is reversed, and the case is remanded for further proceedings consistent with this opinion.

It is so ordered.

Standing

Standing, an analysis suggests, "is part of the law of judicial jurisdiction, that law which defines the role of the courts in society and is, of all law, the most judge-made. Standing in particular determines whom a court may hear make arguments about the legality of an official action."[28] Barriers to gaining standing were relaxed substantially during the 1960s and 1970s. As an important 1962 Supreme Court case put it, one must demonstrate a "personal stake in the outcome" in order to have standing in a controversy [*Baker* v. *Carr*, 369 U.S. 186, 204 (1962)]. Many of the more recent standing decisions have amounted to assessments of the presence or absence of such a personal stake. The Supreme Court, for example, accorded standing in one important case when it was able to answer affirmatively "the question whether the interest to be protected by the complainant is arguably within the zone of interests to be protected by the statute or constitutional guarantee in question" [*Association of Data Processing Service Organizations, Inc.* v. *Camp*, 397 U.S. 150, 153 (1970)]. However, it denied standing in another significant case in which it found "a mere interest in a problem" rather than "injury in fact" [*Sierra Club* v. *Morton*, 405 U.S. 727 (1972)].

Bennett v. Spear

SUPREME COURT OF THE UNITED STATES, 1997.
520 U.S. 154, 117 S.Ct. 1154, 137 L.Ed. 2d 281.

[This case illustrates some of the complexities of present-day standing law. In presenting its views before the Supreme Court, the government argued that petitioners lacked standing on three grounds: that they failed to meet the standing requirements of Article III of the Constitution; that judicial review under the statute's citizen-suit provision did not extend to petitioners' types of claims; and that the "Biological Opinion" that served as the basis for petitioners' complaint did not constitute "final agency action" under the APA. The third of these issues, which was discussed in chapter 1, in *Dalton* v. *Specter*, 114 U.S. 1719 (1994), is not included in the excerpt from the case set forth below.]

Justice SCALIA delivered the opinion for a unanimous Court.

This is a challenge to a biological opinion issued by the Fish and Wildlife Service in accordance with the Endangered Species Act of 1973 (ESA) . . . concerning the operation of the Klamath Irrigation Project by the Bureau of Reclamation, and the project's impact on two varieties of endangered fish. The question for decision is whether the petitioners, who have competing economic

---

[28] Joseph Vining, *Legal Identity* 1 (1978). The author also noted that in this area of judge-made law, it is difficult to find a common thread in judicial decisions. Judicial behavior, he says, is "erratic, even bizarre." Ibid.

and other interests in Klamath Project water, have standing to seek judicial review of the biological opinion under the citizen-suit provision of the ESA, § 1540(g)(1), and the Administrative Procedure Act (APA). . . .

The ESA requires the Secretary of the Interior to promulgate regulations listing those species of animals that are "threatened" or "endangered" under specified criteria, and to designate their "critical habitat." . . . The ESA further requires each federal agency to "insure that any action authorized, funded, or carried out by such agency . . . is not likely to jeopardize the continued existence of any endangered species or threatened species or result in the destruction or adverse modification of habitat of such species which is determined by the Secretary . . . to be critical." . . . If an agency determines that action it proposes to take may adversely affect a listed species, it must engage in formal consultation with the Fish and Wildlife Service, as delegate of the Secretary . . . after which the Service must provide the agency with a written statement (the Biological Opinion) explaining how the proposed action will affect the species or its habitat. . . . If the Service concludes that the proposed action will "jeopardize the continued existence of any [listed] species or result in the destruction or adverse modification of [critical habitat]" . . . the Biological Opinion must outline any "reasonable and prudent alternatives" that the Service believes will avoid that consequence. . . . Additionally, if the Biological Opinion concludes that the agency action will not result in jeopardy or adverse habitat modification, or if it offers reasonable and prudent alternatives to avoid that consequence, the Service must provide the agency with a written statement (known as the "Incidental Take Statement") specifying the "impact of such incidental taking on the species," any "reasonable and prudent measures that the [Service] considers necessary or

appropriate to minimize such impact," and setting forth "the terms and conditions . . . that must be complied with by the Federal agency . . . to implement [those measures]." . . .

The Klamath Project, one of the oldest federal reclamation schemes, is a series of lakes, rivers, dams and irrigation canals in northern California and southern Oregon. The project was undertaken by the Secretary of the Interior pursuant to the Reclamation Act of 1902 . . . and the Act of Feb. 9, 1905 . . . and is administered by the Bureau of Reclamation, which is under the Secretary's jurisdiction. In 1992, the Bureau notified the Service that operation of the project might affect the Lost River Sucker (Deltistes luxatus) and Shortnose Sucker (Chasmistes brevirostris), species of fish that were listed as endangered in 1988. . . . After formal consultation with the Bureau in accordance with 50 CFR § 402.14 (1995), the Service issued a Biological Opinion which concluded that the "'long-term operation of the Klamath Project was likely to jeopardize the continued existence of the Lost River and shortnose suckers.'" . . . The Biological Opinion identified "reasonable and prudent alternatives" the Service believed would avoid jeopardy, which included the maintenance of minimum water levels on Clear Lake and Gerber reservoirs. The Bureau later notified the Service that it intended to operate the project in compliance with the Biological Opinion.

Petitioners, two Oregon irrigation districts that receive Klamath Project water and the operators of two ranches within those districts, filed the present action against the director and regional director of the Service and the Secretary of the Interior. . . .

The complaint asserts that petitioners' use of the reservoirs and related waterways for "recreational, aesthetic and commercial purposes, as well as for their primary sources of irrigation" will be "irreparably damaged" by the actions complained of . . . and that the restrictions on water delivery "recommended" by the Biological Opinion "adversely affect plaintiffs by substantially reducing the quantity of available irrigation water." . . . In essence, petitioners claim a competing interest in the water the Biological Opinion declares necessary for the preservation of the suckers.

The District Court dismissed the complaint for lack of jurisdiction. It concluded that petitioners did not have standing because their "recreational, aesthetic, and commercial interests . . . do not fall within the zone of interests sought to be protected by ESA." . . . The Court of Appeals for the Ninth Circuit affirmed. *Bennett* v. *Plenert*, 63 F.3d 915 (1995). It held that the "zone of interests" test limits the class of persons who may obtain judicial review not only under the APA, but also under the citizen-suit provision of the ESA . . . and that "only plaintiffs who allege an interest in the *preservation* of endangered species fall within the zone of interests protected by the ESA" 63 F.3d at 919 (emphasis in original). We granted certiorari. . . .

In this Court, petitioners raise two questions: first, whether the prudential standing rule known as the "zone of interests" test applies to claims brought under the citizen-suit provision of the ESA; and second, if so, whether petitioners have standing under that test notwithstanding that the interests they seek to vindicate are economic rather than environmental. . . .

We first turn to the question the Court of Appeals found dispositive: whether petitioners lack standing by virtue of the zone-of-interests test. Although petitioners contend that their claims lie both under the ESA and the APA, we look first at the ESA because it may permit petitioners to recover their litigation costs . . . and because the APA by its terms independently authorizes review only when

"there is no other adequate remedy in a court." . . .

The "zone of interests" formulation was first employed in Association of *Data Processing Service Organizations, Inc.* v. *Camp*, 397 U.S. 150 (1970). There, certain data processors sought to invalidate a ruling by the Comptroller of the Currency authorizing national banks to sell data processing services on the ground that it violated, inter alia, § 4 of the Bank Service Corporation Act of 1962 . . . , which prohibited bank service corporations from engaging in "any activity other than the performance of bank services for banks." The Court of Appeals had held that the banks' data-processing competitors were without standing to challenge the alleged violation of § 4. In reversing, we stated the applicable prudential standing requirement to be "whether the interest sought to be protected by the complainant is arguably within the zone of interests to be protected or regulated by the statute or constitutional guarantee in question." *Data Processing*, supra, at 153. . . . We have made clear, however, that the breadth of the zone of interests varies according to the provisions of law at issue, so that what comes within the zone of interests of a statute for purposes of obtaining judicial review of administrative action under the "'generous review provisions'" of the APA may not do so for other purposes, *Clarke* v. *Securities Industry Assn.*, 479 U.S. 388, 400, n. 16 (1987) (quoting *Data Processing*, supra, at 156). . . .

The first operative portion of the [ESA's citizen suit] provision says that "any person may commence a civil suit"—an authorization of remarkable breadth when compared with the language Congress ordinarily uses. Even in some other environmental statutes, Congress has used more restrictive formulations, such as "[any person] having an interest which is or may be adversely affected," . . ."any person suffering legal wrong," . . . or "any person having a valid legal interest which is or may be adversely affected . . . whenever such action constitutes a case or controversy." . . . And in contexts other than the environment, Congress has often been even more restrictive. In statutes concerning unfair trade practices and other commercial matters, for example, it has authorized suit only by "any person injured in his business or property," . . . or only by "competitors, customers, or subsequent purchasers." . . .

Our readiness to take the term "any person" at face value is greatly augmented by two interrelated considerations: that the overall subject matter of this legislation is the environment (a matter in which it is common to think all persons have an interest) and that the obvious purpose of the particular provision in question is to encourage enforcement by so-called "private attorneys general"— evidenced by its elimination of the usual amount-in-controversy and diversity-of-citizenship requirements, its provision for recovery of the costs of litigation (including even expert witness fees), and its reservation to the Government of a right of first refusal to pursue the action initially and a right to intervene later. Given these factors, we think the conclusion of expanded standing follows a fortiori from our decision in *Trafficante* v. *Metropolitan Life Ins. Co.*, 409 U.S. 205 (1972), which held that standing was expanded to the full extent permitted under Article III by a provision of the Civil Rights Act of 1968 that authorized "any person who claims to have been injured by a discriminatory housing practice" to sue for violations of the Act. There also we relied on textual evidence of a statutory scheme to rely on private litigation to ensure compliance with the Act. . . . The statutory language here is even clearer, and the subject of the legislation makes the intent to permit enforcement by everyman even more plausible.

It is true that the plaintiffs here are seeking to prevent application of environmental restrictions rather than to implement them. But the "any person" formulation applies to all the causes of action authorized by § 1540(g)—not only to actions against private violators of environmental restrictions, and not only to actions against the Secretary asserting underenforcement under § 1533, but also to actions against the Secretary asserting overenforcement under § 1533. As we shall discuss below, the citizen-suit provision does favor environmentalists in that it covers all private violations of the Act but not all failures of the Secretary to meet his administrative responsibilities; but there is no textual basis for saying that its expansion of standing requirements applies to environmentalists alone. The Court of Appeals therefore erred in concluding that petitioners lacked standing under the zone-of-interests test to bring their claims under the ESA's citizen-suit provision. . . .

The Government's . . . contention is that petitioners' complaint fails to satisfy the standing requirements imposed by the "case" or "controversy" provision of Article III. This "irreducible constitutional minimum" of standing requires: (1) that the plaintiff have suffered an "injury in fact"—an invasion of a judicially cognizable interest which is (a) concrete and particularized and (b) actual or imminent, not conjectural or hypothetical; (2) that there be a causal connection between the injury and the conduct complained of— the injury must be fairly traceable to the challenged action of the defendant, and not the result of the independent action of some third party not before the court; and (3) that it be likely, as opposed to merely speculative, that the injury will be redressed by a favorable decision. . . .

Petitioners allege, among other things, that they currently receive irrigation water from Clear Lake, that the Bureau "will abide by the restrictions imposed by the Biological Opinion," . . . and that "the restrictions on lake levels imposed in the Biological Opinion adversely affect [petitioners] by substantially reducing the quantity of available irrigation water." . . . Given petitioners' allegation that the amount of available water will be reduced and that they will be adversely affected thereby, it is easy to presume specific facts under which petitioners will be injured—for example, the Bureau's distribution of the reduction pro rata among its customers. The complaint alleges the requisite injury in fact.

The Government also contests compliance with the second and third Article III standing requirements, contending that any injury suffered by petitioners is neither "fairly traceable" to the Service's Biological Opinion, nor "redressable" by a favorable judicial ruling, because the "action agency" (the Bureau) retains ultimate responsibility for determining whether and how a proposed action shall go forward. . . .

The Service itself is, to put it mildly, keenly aware of the virtually determinative effect of its biological opinions. The Incidental Take Statement at issue in the present case begins by instructing the reader that any taking of a listed species is prohibited unless "such taking is in compliance with this incidental take statement," and warning that "the measures described below are nondiscretionary, and must be taken by [the Bureau]." . . . Given all of this, and given petitioners' allegation that the Bureau had, until issuance of the Biological Opinion, operated the Klamath Project in the same manner throughout the twentieth century, it is not difficult to conclude that petitioners have met their burden—which is relatively modest at this stage of the litigation—of alleging that their injury is "fairly traceable" to the Service's Biological Opinion and that it will "likely" be redressed—i.e., the Bureau will not impose such water level restrictions—if the Biological Opinion is set aside. . . .

The Court of Appeals erred in affirming the District Court's dismissal of petitioners' claims for lack of jurisdiction. Petitioners' complaint alleges facts sufficient to meet the requirements of Article III standing, and none of their ESA claims is precluded by the zone-of-interests test. . . .

The judgment of the Court of Appeals is reversed, and the case is remanded for further proceedings consistent with this opinion.

It is so ordered.

On remand, the District Court for the District of Oregon granted the plaintiffs' motion for summary judgment challenging the Biological Opinions issued by the Fish and Wildlife Service, 5 F. Supp. 2d 882 (1998). In a followup proceeding the plaintiffs were awarded $348,000 in attorney fees and costs [*Bennett* v. *Spear*, 1998 U.S. Dist. LEXIS 16087 (1998)].

For those wishing to explore the law of standing further, an extremely provocative article, "Is Standing Law or Politics?"[29] by Richard J. Pierce, is highly recommended. In this article Professor Pierce, building on the research of Frank B. Cross,[30] examines a series of five Supreme Court standing decisions from the 1990s and finds a "strong convergence between the

---

[29] 77 *North Carolina Law Review* 1741 (1999).

[30] "Political Science and the New Regal Realism: A Case of Unfortunate Interdisciplinary Ignorance," 92 *Northwestern University Law Review* 251 (1997).

ideological preferences of the Justices and their voting patterns."[31] On that basis he asserts that judicial decisions involving the law of standing can be predicted by his students largely on considerations of ideology:

> They can predict judicial decisions in this area with much greater accuracy if they ignore doctrine and rely entirely on a simple description of the law of standing that is rooted in political science: judges provide access to the court to individuals who seek to further the political and ideological agendas of judges.[32]

The Supreme Court's two "line item veto" cases of the late 1990s dealt with one of the most politically significant issues of recent years. They were also important cases involving standing. In 1996 the Line Item Veto Act was adopted (Public Law 104-30, 110 Stat. 1200). The statute gave the president the authority to cancel certain tax benefit and spending measures in acts that he had already signed into law. In the first case, six members of Congress (four senators and two congressmen) who had voted against the act brought suit to have the line item veto declared in violation of Article I of the Constitution. The Supreme Court ruled five to four that the members of Congress lacked standing. The majority held that as plaintiffs they had neither sufficient personal injury nor sufficient personal stake in the outcome to qualify as parties to such a suit [*Raines* v. *Byrd*, 521 U.S. 811 (1997)].

The next year the Court heard another case involving the Line Item Veto Act. This time the plaintiffs comprised a diverse number of parties, including the City of New York, two hospital associations, a hospital, two labor unions, and a farmers' cooperative, all of whom claimed injury because of President Clinton's use of the line item veto. All of the justices agreed that at least some of the parties had standing, and six members ruled that the act violated the presentment clause of Article I of the Constitution [*Clinton* v. *New York*, 524 U.S. 417 (1998)].

The lineup of Court members in the two cases may not give particularly strong support to Pierce's thesis about the ideological preferences of the justices. But both decisions certainly do demonstrate how standing can figure in the resolution of politically important matters.

SCOPE OF JUDICIAL REVIEW

Assuming that none of the barriers to judicial review discussed above exist, the next relevant matter is the scope of review. Scope of review has to do with the degree or extent of judicial scrutiny of agency action. The extent of review achieved should strike an appropriate balance: a judicial posture that treats agency action with too much deference, or too cursorily, tends toward making review meaningless; review that probes too deeply can result in decisions being made, in effect, by the courts rather than by the agencies charged with such functions.

It is generally said that administrators are charged with making find-

---

[31] Pierce, above note 29, at 1754, including, in particular, note 90.

[32] Ibid, at 1742–1743.

ings of fact while courts decide questions of law. The distinction is stated more fully by Professor Jaffe:

> The distinction between fact and law is vital to a correct appreciation of the respective roles of the administrative and the judiciary. The administrative is the sole fact finder. The judiciary may set aside a finding of fact not adequately supported by the record, but, with certain exceptions its function is at that point exhausted. It has, as it were, a veto but no positive power of determination. On the other hand, the administrative and the judiciary share the role of law pronouncing and law making. They are in partnership. The court may supersede the administrative and itself determine the question of law; it is the senior partner.[33]

On review, therefore, the general function of the court is to assure that the law has been applied correctly and that the administrative decision has a basis in fact. While these principles have evolved over time through court articulation, they have to some extent been codified in the statutory law as well. A good example is the APA. As noted earlier in this chapter, § 701 provides for judicial review except to the extent that it is precluded by statute or committed to agency discretion. Section 706, on scope of review, reads as follows:

> To the extent necessary to decision and when presented, the reviewing court shall decide all relevant questions of law, interpret constitutional and statutory provisions, and determine the meaning or applicability of the terms of an agency action. The reviewing court shall—

(1) compel agency action unlawfully withheld or unreasonably delayed; and

(2) hold unlawful and set aside agency action, findings, and conclusions found to be—

   (A) arbitrary, capricious, an abuse of discretion, or otherwise not in accordance with law;

   (B) contrary to constitutional right, power, privilege, or immunity;

   (C) in excess of statutory jurisdiction, authority, or limitations, or short of statutory right;

   (D) without observance of procedure required by law;

   (E) unsupported by substantial evidence in a case subject to sections 556 and 557 of this title or otherwise reviewed on the record of an agency hearing provided by statute; or

   (F) unwarranted by the facts to the extent that the facts are subject to trial de novo by the reviewing court. In making the foregoing determinations, the court shall review the whole record or those parts of it cited by a party, and due account shall be taken of the rule of prejudicial error.

As the numerous provisions of § 706 suggest, a variety of issues might be treated in this part of the chapter. We will concentrate on a broad examination of just two: *the substantial evidence rule* and *the law-fact distinction*. In addition, we will conclude with a preliminary discussion of § 706 (2)(C) in

---

[33] Jaffe, above, note 1, p. 546.

the aftermath of the Supreme Court decision in *Chevron, U.S.A.* v. *Natural Resources Defense Council,* 467 U.S. 837 (1984). This case will also be examined in chapters 6 and 8.

Substantial Evidence

Section 706 (2) (E) of the APA, just quoted, indicates that agency action must be based on substantial evidence. But the substantial evidence test far predates the APA.[34] The precise meaning of the term is not readily apparent. An oft-quoted statement by Chief Justice Hughes is that substantial evidence "is more than a mere scintilla. It means such relevant evidence as a reasonable mind might accept as adequate to support a conclusion" [*Consolidated Edison Co.* v. *NLRB*, 305 U.S. 197, 229 (1938)]. And others have suggested that substantial evidence represents a compromise between the "clearly erroneous" test, which allows broad judicial review, and a narrower standard that requires agency findings to be upheld when supported by any evidence on the record.[35] Still, there is "often greater difficulty in applying the test than in formulating it."[36] A leading case on the meaning of substantial evidence, decided just a few years after the adoption of the APA, is the *Universal Camera* case.

Universal Camera Corp. v. National Labor Relations Board

Supreme Court of the United States, 1951.
340 U.S. 474, 71 S.Ct. 456, 95 L.Ed. 456.

Justice FRANKFURTER delivered the opinion of the Court.

The essential issue raised by this case . . . is the effect of the Administrative Procedure Act and the legislation colloquially known as the Taft-Hartley Act on the duty of Courts of Appeals when called upon to review orders of the National Labor Relations Board.

The Court of Appeals for the Second Circuit granted enforcement of an order directing, in the main, that petitioner reinstate with back pay an employee found to have been discharged because he gave testimony under the Wagner Act and cease and desist from discriminating against any employee who files charges or gives testimony under that Act. The court below, Judge Swan dissenting, decreed full enforcement of the order. . . . Because the views of that court regarding the effect of the new legislation on the relation between the Board and the Courts of Appeals in the enforcement of the Board's orders conflicted with those of the Court of Appeals for the Sixth Circuit we brought both cases here. . . . The clash of opinion obviously required settlement by this Court.

Want of certainty in judicial review of Labor Board decisions partly reflects the intractability of any formula to furnish

---

[34] Schwartz, above, note 20, 592, writes that the principle of substantial evidence "was first developed in connection with review of the Interstate Commerce Commission." He cites a 1912 ICC case in which the term was used.

[35] Ernest Gellhorn, *Administrative Law and Process* 265 (1972).

[36] *Stork Restaurant, Inc.* v. *Boland*, 282 N.Y. 256, 274, 26 N.E. 2d 247, 255 (1940), as quoted in Schwartz, above, note 20, at 592.

definiteness of content for all the impalpable factors involved in judicial review. But in part doubts as to the nature of the reviewing power and uncertainties in its application derive from history, and to that extent an elucidation of this history may clear them away.

The Wagner Act provided: "The findings of the Board as to the facts, if supported by evidence, shall be conclusive." Act of July 5, 1935, § 10 (e), 49 Stat. 449, 454, 29 U.S.C. § 160 (e). This Court read "evidence" to mean "substantial evidence," *Washington, V. & M. Coach Co.* v. *Labor Board*, 301 U.S. 142, and we said that "substantial evidence is more than a mere scintilla. It means such relevant evidence as a reasonable mind might accept as adequate to support a conclusion." *Consolidated Edison Co.* v. *Labor Board*, 305 U.S. 197, 229. Accordingly, it "must do more than create a suspicion of the existence of the fact to be established. . . . [I]t must be enough to justify, if the trial were to a jury, a refusal to direct a verdict when the conclusion sought to be drawn from it is one of fact for the jury." *Labor Board* v. *Columbian Enameling & Stamping Co.*, 306 U.S. 292, 300.

The very smoothness of the "substantial evidence" formula as the standard for reviewing the evidentiary validity of the Board's findings established its currency. But the inevitably variant applications of the standard to conflicting evidence soon brought contrariety of views and in due course bred criticism. Even though the whole record may have been canvassed in order to determine whether the evidentiary foundation of a determination by the Board was "substantial," the phrasing of this Court's process of review readily lent itself to the notion that it was enough that the evidence supporting the Board's result was "substantial" when considered by itself. It is fair to say that by imperceptible steps regard for the fact-finding function of the Board led to the assumption that the requirements of the Wagner

Act were met when the reviewing court could find in the record evidence which, when viewed in isolation, substantiated the Board's findings. . . . This is not to say that every member of this Court was consciously guided by this view or that the Court ever explicitly avowed this practice as doctrine. What matters is that the belief justifiably arose that the Court had so construed the obligation to review. . . .

The final report of the Attorney General's Committee was submitted in January, 1941. The majority concluded that "[d]issatisfaction with the existing standards as to the scope of judicial review derives largely from dissatisfaction with the fact-finding procedures now employed by the administrative bodies." Departure from the "substantial evidence" test, it thought, would either create unnecessary uncertainty or transfer to courts the responsibility for ascertaining and assaying matters the significance of which lies outside judicial competence. Accordingly, it recommended against legislation embodying a general scheme of judicial review.

Three members of the Committee registered a dissent. Their view was that the "present system or lack of system of judicial review" led to inconsistency and uncertainty. They reported that under a "prevalent" interpretation of the "substantial evidence" rule "if what is called 'substantial evidence' is found anywhere in the record to support conclusions of fact, the courts are said to be obliged to sustain the decision, without reference to how heavily the countervailing evidence may preponderate—unless indeed the stage of arbitrary decision is reached. Under this interpretation, the courts need to read only one side of the case and, if they find any evidence there, the administrative action is to be sustained and the record to the contrary is to be ignored." Their view led them to recommend that Congress enact principles of review applicable to all agencies not excepted by unique characteristics. One of these principles was expressed by the formula that judicial review could extend to "findings, inferences, or conclusions of fact unsupported, upon the whole record, by substantial evidence." So far as the history of this movement for enlarged review reveals, the phrase "upon the whole record" makes its first appearance in this recommendation of the minority of the Attorney General's Committee. This evidence of the close relationship between the phrase and the criticism out of which it arose is important, for the substance of this formula for judicial review found its way into the statute books when Congress with unquestioning—we might even say uncritical—unanimity enacted the Administrative Procedure Act. . . .

Similar dissatisfaction with too restricted application of the "substantial evidence" test is reflected in the legislative history of the Taft-Hartley Act. The bill as reported to the House provided that the "findings of the Board as to the facts shall be conclusive unless it is made to appear to the satisfaction of the court either (1) that the findings of fact are against the manifest weight of the evidence, or (2) that the findings of fact are not supported by substantial evidence." The bill left the House with this provision. Early committee prints in the Senate provided for review by "weight of the evidence" or "clearly erroneous" standards. But, as the Senate Committee Report relates, "it was finally decided to conform the statute to the corresponding section of the Administrative Procedure Act where the substantial evidence test prevails. In order to clarify any ambiguity in that statute, however, the committee inserted the words 'questions of fact, if supported by substantial evidence on the record considered as a whole. . . . '"

This phraseology was adopted by the Senate. The House conferees agreed. They reported to the House: "It is believed that the provisions of the conference agreement relating to the courts' review-

ing power will be adequate to preclude such decisions as those in *N. L. R. B.* v. *Nevada Consol. Copper Corp.* . . . and in the *Wilson, Columbia Products, Union Pacific Stages, Hearst, Republic Aviation,* and *Le Tournai,* etc. cases . . . without unduly burdening the courts." The Senate version became the law.

It is fair to say that in all this Congress expressed a mood. And it expressed its mood not merely by oratory but by legislation. As legislation that mood must be respected, even though it can only serve as a standard for judgment and not as a body of rigid rules assuring sameness of application. Enforcement of such broad standards implies subtlety of mind and solidity of judgment. But it is not for us to question that Congress may assume such qualities in the federal judiciary.

From the legislative story we have summarized, two concrete conclusions do emerge. One is the identity of aim of the Administrative Procedure Act and the Taft-Hartley Act regarding the proof with which the Labor Board must support a decision. The other is that now Congress has left no room for doubt as to the kind of scrutiny which a Court of Appeals must give the record before the Board to satisfy itself that the Board's order rests on adequate proof.

It would be mischievous word-playing to find that the scope of review under the Taft-Hartley Act is any different from that under the Administrative Procedure Act. The Senate Committee which reported the review clause of the Taft-Hartley Act expressly indicated that the two standards were to conform in this regard, and the wording of the two Acts is for purposes of judicial administration identical. And so we hold that the standard of proof specifically required of the Labor Board by the Taft-Hartley Act is the same as that to be exacted by courts reviewing every administrative action subject to the Administrative Procedure Act.

Whether or not it was ever permissible for courts to determine the substantiality of evidence supporting a Labor Board decision merely on the basis of evidence which in and of itself justified it, without taking into account contradictory evidence or evidence from which conflicting inferences could be drawn, the new legislation definitively precludes such a theory of review and bars its practice. The substantiality of evidence must take into account whatever in the record fairly detracts from its weight. This is clearly the significance of the requirement in both statutes that courts consider the whole record. Committee reports and the adoption in the Administrative Procedure Act of the minority views of the Attorney General's Committee demonstrate that to enjoin such a duty on the reviewing court was one of the important purposes of the movement which eventuated in that enactment. . . .

We conclude, therefore, that the Administrative Procedure Act and the Taft-Hartley Act direct that courts must now assume more responsibility for the reasonableness and fairness of Labor Board decisions than some courts have shown in the past. Reviewing courts must be influenced by a feeling that they are not to abdicate the conventional judicial function. Congress has imposed on them responsibility for assuring that the Board keeps within reasonable grounds. . . .

The decision of the Court of Appeals is assailed on two grounds. It is said (1) that the court erred in holding that it was barred from taking into account the report of the examiner on questions of fact insofar as that report was rejected by the Board, and (2) that the Board's order was not supported by substantial evidence on the record considered as a whole, even apart from the validity of the court's refusal to consider the rejected portions of the examiner's report.

The latter contention is easily met. It is true that two of the earlier decisions of the court below were among those disapproved by Congress. But this disapproval, we have seen, may well have been caused by unintended intimations of judicial phrasing. And in any event, it is clear from the court's opinion in this case that it in fact did consider the "record as a whole," and did not deem itself merely the judicial echo of the Board's conclusion. . . .

The first contention, however, raises serious questions to which we now turn. . . .

We do not require that the examiner's findings be given more weight than in reason and in light of judicial experience they deserve. The "substantial evidence" standard is not modified in any way when the Board and its examiner disagree. We intend only to recognize that evidence supporting a conclusion may be less substantial when an impartial, experienced examiner who has observed the witnesses and lived with the case had drawn conclusions different from the Board's than when he has reached the same conclusion. The findings of the examiner are to be considered along with the consistency and inherent probability of testimony. The significance of his report, of course, depends largely on the importance of credibility in the particular case. To give it this significance does not seem to us materially more difficult than to heed the other factors which in sum determine whether evidence is "substantial." . . .

This Court has refused to accept assumptions of fact which are demonstrably false, . . . even when agreed to by the parties. . . . Machinery for discovery of evidence has been strengthened; the boundaries of judicial notice have been slowly but perceptibly enlarged. It would reverse this process for courts to deny examiners' findings the probative force they would have in the conduct of affairs outside a courtroom.

We therefore remand the cause to the Court of Appeals. On reconsideration of the record it should accord the findings of the trial examiner the relevance that they reasonably command in answering the comprehensive question whether the evidence supporting the Board's order is substantial. But the court need not limit its reexamination of the case to the effect of that report on its decision. We leave it free to grant or deny enforcement as it thinks the principles expressed in this opinion dictate.

Judgment vacated and cause remanded.

A more contemporary application of the substantial evidence rule can be found in *Allentown Mack Sales and Service* v. *National Labor Relations Board*, 522 U.S. 354 (1998), a withdrawal of union recognition case, in which a decision of the NLRB was overturned on the grounds that its fact-finding was not supported by substantial evidence. The NLRB had held that Allentown Mack had been guilty of an unfair labor practice by conducting an independent poll, because it "had not demonstrated that it held a reasonable doubt, based on objective considerations, that the Union continued to enjoy the support of a majority of the bargaining unit employees" (316 N.L.R.B. 1199). Consequently, the Board ordered the petitioner, Allentown Mack, to recognize and bargain with the union. The Court of Appeals for the District of Columbia ordered enforcement of the order, and the Supreme Court granted certiorari. The Supreme Court held with differing five-member majorities that the NLRB's "good-faith reasonable doubt" test was rational and consistent with the enabling statute. More importantly for our purposes, it concluded that the Board's factual finding that the petitioner lacked such a "doubt" was not supported by substantial evidence on the record as a whole. The Supreme Court's narrow majority was, in effect, responding negatively to the question "whether on this record it would have been possible for a reasonable jury to reach the Board's conclusion." In a strong rebuke of the NLRB, Justice Scalia, who spoke for the five-member majorities on both questions, concluded by noting:

> When the Board purports to be engaged in simple fact-finding, unconstrained by substantive presumptions or evidentiary rules of exclusion, it is not free to prescribe what inferences from the evidence it will accept and reject, but must draw those inferences that the evidence fairly demands. "Substantial evidence" review exists precisely to ensure that the Board achieves minimal compliance with this obligation, which is the foundation of all honest and legitimate adjudication [522 U.S. 359, 378–379].

Consequently, the court of appeals' judgment was reversed, and the case was remanded with instructions to deny enforcement of the order to recognize and bargain with the union.

The Law-Fact Distinction

As suggested above, the general rule is that the agency is charged with making findings of fact while courts, on review, decide questions of law. Thus, "a court is theoretically free to determine for itself the correctness of the agency's legal judgments. However, even then the agency's interpretations are often entitled to great weight."[37] In addition to such judicial deference to agency interpretation, another factor sometimes favoring the agency position is that there is "surprisingly little agreement on how questions of fact and law can be distinguished."[38] A leading case on this question is the following.

National Labor Relations Board v. Hearst Publications, Inc.

SUPREME COURT OF THE UNITED STATES, 1944.
322 U.S. 111, 64 S.Ct. 851, 88 L.Ed. 1170.

[The respondents refused to bargain collectively with a union representing newsboys, contending that the latter were not "employees" within the meaning of the term under the National Labor Relations Act, 49 Stat. 450, 29 U.S.C.A. § 152. Proceedings were instituted before the NLRB, which found that the respondents had violated sections of the Act, and ordered them to cease and desist from such violations and to bargain collectively with the union upon request.

The court of appeals, on review, set aside the NLRB order. It concluded that the Act imported common-law standards for determining the employee question and held that the newsboys were not employees. The case came to the Supreme Court on certiorari.]

Mr. Justice RUTLEDGE delivered the opinion of the Court. . . .

The papers are distributed to the ultimate consumer through a variety of channels, including independent dealers and newsstands often attached to drug, grocery or confectionery stores, carriers who make home deliveries, and newsboys who sell on the streets of the city and its suburbs. Only the last of these are involved in this case.

The newsboys work under varying terms and conditions. They may be "bootjackers," selling to the general public at places other than established corners, or they may sell at fixed "spots." They may sell only casually or part-time, or full-time; and they may be employed regularly and continuously or only temporarily. The units which the Board determined to be appropriate are composed of those who sell full-time at established spots. Those vendors, misnamed boys, are generally mature men, dependent upon the proceeds of their sales for their sustenance, and frequently supporters of families. Working thus as news vendors on a regular basis, often for a number of years, they form a stable group with relatively little turnover, in contrast to schoolboys and others who sell as bootjackers, temporary and casual distributors.

Over-all circulation and distribution of the papers are under the general supervision of circulation managers. But for purposes of street distribution each paper has divided metropolitan Los Angeles into geographic districts. Each district is under the direct and close supervision of a district manager. His function in the mechanics of distribution is to supply the newsboys in his district with papers which he obtains from the publisher and to turn over to the publisher the receipts which he collects from their sales, either directly or with the assistance of "checkmen" or "main spot" boys. The latter, stationed at the important corners or "spots" in the district, are newsboys who, among

---

[37] Gellhorn, above, note 35, 263.

[38] Ibid., 264.

other things, receive delivery of the papers, redistribute them to other newsboys stationed at less important corners, and collect receipts from their sales. For that service, which occupies a minor portion of their working day, the checkmen receive a small salary from the publisher. The bulk of their day, however, they spend in hawking papers at their "spots" like other full-time newsboys. A large part of the appropriate units selected by the Board for the News and the Herald are checkmen who, in that capacity, clearly are employees of those papers.

The newsboys' compensation consists in the difference between the prices at which they sell the papers and the prices they pay for them. The former are fixed by the publishers and the latter are fixed either by the publishers or, in the case of the News, by the district manager. In practice the newsboys receive their papers on credit. They pay for those sold either sometime during or after the close of their selling day, returning for credit all unsold papers. Lost or otherwise unreturned papers, however, must be paid for as though sold. Not only is the "profit" per paper thus effectively fixed by the publisher, but substantial control of the newsboys' total "take home" can be effected through the ability to designate their sales areas and the power to determine the number of papers allocated to each. While as a practical matter this power is not exercised fully, the newsboys' "right" to decide how many papers they will take is also not absolute. In practice, the Board found, they cannot determine the size of their established order without the cooperation of the district manager. And often the number of papers they must take is determined unilaterally by the district managers.

In addition to effectively fixing the compensation, respondents in a variety of ways prescribe, if not the minutiae of daily activities, at least the broad terms and conditions of work. This is accom-

plished largely through the supervisory efforts of the district managers, who serve as the nexus between the publishers and the newsboys. The district managers assign "spots" or corners to which the newsboys are expected to confine their selling activities. Transfers from one "spot" to another may be ordered by the district manager for reasons of discipline or efficiency or other cause. Transportation to the spots from the newspaper building is offered by each of respondents. Hours of work on the spots are determined not simply by the impersonal pressures of the market, but to a real extent by explicit instructions from the district managers. Adherence to the prescribed hours is observed closely by the district managers or other supervisory agents of the publishers. Sanctions, varying in severity from reprimand to dismissal, are visited on the tardy and the delinquent. By similar supervisory controls minimum standards of diligence and good conduct while at work are sought to be enforced. However wide may be the latitude for individual initiative beyond those standards, district managers' instructions in what the publishers apparently regard as helpful sales technique are expected to be followed. Such varied items as the manner of displaying the paper, of emphasizing current features and headlines, and of placing advertising placards, or the advantages of soliciting customers at specific stores or in the traffic lanes are among the subjects of this instruction. Moreover, newsboys are furnished with sales equipment, such as racks, boxes and change aprons, and advertising placards by the publishers. In this pattern of employment the Board found that the newsboys are an integral part of the publishers' distribution system and circulation organization. And the record discloses that the newsboys and checkmen feel they are employees of the papers; and respondents' supervisory employees, if not respondents themselves, regard them as such.

In addition to questioning the sufficiency of the evidence to sustain these findings, respondents point to a number of other attributes characterizing their relationship with the newsboys and urge that on the entire record the latter cannot be considered their employees. They base this conclusion on the argument that by common-law standards the extent of their control and direction of the newsboys' working activities creates no more than an "independent contractor" relationship and that common-law standards determine the "employee" relationship under the Act. . . .

The principal question is whether the newsboys are "employees." Because Congress did not explicitly define the term, respondents say its meaning must be determined by reference to common-law standards. In their view "common-law standards" are those the courts have applied in distinguishing between "employees" and "independent contractors" when working out various problems unrelated to the Wagner Act's purposes and provisions.

The argument assumes that there is some simple, uniform and easily applicable test which the courts have used, in dealing with such problems, to determine whether persons doing work for others fall in one class or the other. Unfortunately this is not true. . . . Few problems in the law have given greater variety of application and conflict in results than the cases arising in the borderland between what is clearly an employer-employee relationship and what is clearly one of independent, entrepreneurial dealing. . . .

Two possible consequences could follow. One would be to refer the decision of who are employees to local state law. The alternative would be to make it turn on a sort of pervading general essence distilled from state law. Congress obviously did not intend the former result. It would introduce variations into the statute's oper-

ation as wide as the differences the forty-eight states and other local jurisdictions make in applying the distinction for wholly different purposes. Persons who might be "employees" in one state would be "independent contractors" in another. They would be within or without the statute's protection depending not on whether their situation falls factually within the ambit Congress had in mind, but upon the accidents of the location of their work and the attitude of the particular local jurisdiction in casting doubtful cases one way or the other. Persons working across state lines might fall in one class or the other, possibly both, depending on whether the Board and the courts would be required to give effect to the law of one state or of the adjoining one, or to that of each in relation to the portion of the work done within its borders.

Both the terms and the purposes of the statute, as well as the legislative history, show that Congress had in mind no such patchwork plan for securing freedom of employees' organization and of collective bargaining. The Wagner Act is federal legislation, administered by a national agency, intended to solve a national problem on a national scale. Cf. e. g., Sen. Rep. No. 573, 74th Cong., 1st Sess. 2-4. . . . It is an Act, therefore, in reference to which it is not only proper but necessary for us to assume, "in the absence of a plain indication to the contrary, that Congress . . . is not making the application of the federal act dependent on state law." . . .

Whether, given the intended national uniformity, the term "employee" includes such workers as these newsboys must be answered primarily from the history, terms and purposes of the legislation. . . .

It will not do, for deciding this question as one of uniform national application, to import wholesale the traditional common-law conceptions or some distilled essence of their local variations as exclusively controlling limitations upon the scope of the statute's effectiveness. To do this would be merely to select some of the local, hairline variations for nation-wide application and thus to reject others for coverage under the Act. That result hardly would be consistent with the statute's broad terms and purposes. . . .

Unless the common-law tests are to be imported and made exclusively controlling, without regard to the statute's purposes, it cannot be irrelevant that the particular workers in these cases are subject, as a matter of economic fact, to the evils the statute was designed to eradicate and that the remedies it affords are appropriate for preventing them or curing their harmful effects in the special situation. . . .

It is not necessary in this case to make a completely definitive limitation around the term "employee." That task has been assigned primarily to the agency created by Congress to administer the Act. . . .

In making that body's determinations as to the facts in these matters conclusive, if supported by evidence, Congress entrusted to it primarily the decision whether the evidence establishes the material facts. Hence in reviewing the Board's ultimate conclusions, it is not the court's function to substitute its own inferences of fact for the Board's, when the latter have support in the record. . . . Undoubtedly questions of statutory interpretation, especially when arising in the first instance in judicial proceedings, are for the courts to resolve, giving appropriate weight to the judgment of those whose special duty is to administer the questioned statute. . . . But where the question is one of specific application of a broad statutory term in a proceeding in which the agency administering the statute must determine it initially, the reviewing court's function is limited. Like the commissioner's determination under the Longshoremen's & Harbor Workers' Act, that a man is not a "member of a crew"

(*South Chicago Coal & Dock Co.* v. *Bassett*, 309 U.S. 251) or that he was injured "in the course of employment" (*Parker* v. *Motor Boat Sales*314 U.S. 244) and the Federal Communications Commission's determination that one company is under the "control" of another (*Rochester Telephone Corp.* v. *United States*, 307 U.S. 125), the Board's determination that specified persons are "employees" under this Act is to be accepted if it has "warrant in the record" and a reasonable basis in law.

In this case the Board found that the designated newsboys work continuously and regularly, rely upon their earnings for the support of themselves and their families, and have their total wages influenced in large measure by the publishers, who dictate their buying and selling prices, fix their markets and control their supply of papers. Their hours of work and their efforts on the job are supervised and to some extent prescribed by the publishers or their agents. Much of their sales equipment and advertising materials is furnished by the publishers with the intention that it be used for the publisher's benefit. Stating that "the primary consideration in the determination of the applicability of the statutory definition is whether effectuation of the declared policy and purposes of the Act comprehend securing to the individual the rights guaranteed and protection afforded by the Act," the Board concluded that the newsboys are employees. The record sustains the Board's findings and there is ample basis in the law for its conclusion. . . .

The judgments are reversed and the causes are remanded for further proceedings not inconsistent with this opinion.

Reversed.

Mr. Justice REED concurs in the result. . . .

Dissent: Mr. Justice ROBERTS:

I think the judgment of the Circuit Court of Appeals should be affirmed. . . .

I think it plain that newsboys are not "employees" of the respondents within the meaning and intent of the National Labor Relations Act. When Congress, in § 2 (3), said "The term 'employee' shall include any employee . . . ," it stated as clearly as language could do it that the provisions of the Act were to extend to those who, as a result of decades of tradition which had become part of the common understanding of our people, bear the named relationship. Clearly also Congress did not delegate to the National Labor Relations Board the function of defining the relationship of employment so as to promote what the Board understood to be the underlying purpose of the statute. The question who is an employee, so as to make the statute applicable to him, is a question of the meaning of the Act and, therefore, is a judicial and not an administrative question. . . .

Scope of Judicial Review after the Chevron Case

APA § 706(2)(C) specifies that a reviewing court shall "hold unlawful or set aside agency action, findings, and conclusions found to be—in excess of statutory jurisdiction, authority, or limitations, or short of statutory right. . . ." The judiciary's construction of this provision, that is, the amount of deference due agency statutory constructions, has been the source of heightened controversy ever since *Chevron, U.S.A., Inc.* v. *Natural Resources Defense Council, Inc.* 467 U.S. 837 (1984). In that case Justice Stevens, speaking for a unanimous Supreme Court, announced a highly deferential attitude toward an agency's construction of the statutes that it is responsible for administering. Richard J. Pierce has characterized *Chevron* as "one of the most important decisions in the history of administrative law." According to Pierce, *Chevron* "has been cited and applied in more cases than any other Supreme Court decision in history" and, therefore, "deserves careful analysis."[39] Since this book gives further consideration to *Chevron* in chapter 6, "Rules and Rule Making," and chapter 8, "Informal Activity and the Exercise of Discretion," only a brief examination of the case is warranted here, in the context of our discussion of judicial review.

At issue in *Chevron* was the interpretation of the term *stationary source* as it had been used in the 1977 amendments to the Clean Air Act, 91 Stat. 685. In 1981 the Environmental Protection Agency (EPA), in a reversal of the policy of the previous administration, concluded that a plantwide definition of *source*, commonly known as the "bubble concept," was appropriate. Under this definition, a company installing new pollution-control devices could avoid a new source review process by the EPA if the proposed changes did not increase emissions above the previously specified threshold. In other words, if pollution were increased by an addition to a plant, these new pollutants could be offset by corresponding decreases elsewhere in the facility,

---

[39] Richard J. Pierce, Jr., 1 *Administrative Law Treatise* 140 (4th ed., 2002). Pierce's positive view of the *Chevron* precedent is evidenced by his statement that the "Court's reconceptualization of the process of statutory construction is an enormous improvement over the inconsistent and wooden characterizations of the process that dominated judicial decisionmaking in the pre-*Chevron* era" (Ibid., 142). More critical assessments of *Chevron* may be found in Cass R. Sunstein, "Law and Administration after *Chevron*," 90 *Columbia Law Review* 2071 (1990), and Cynthia Farina, "Statutory Interpretation and the Balance of Power in the Administrative State," 89 *Columbia Law Review* 452 (1989).

thereby avoiding the necessity of a new review. The Natural Resources Defense Council successfully challenged the new interpretation of *source* in the Court of Appeals for the District of Columbia, which concluded that the EPA had not documented the impact that acceptance of the bubble concept would have on air quality.

On review, the six participating members of the Supreme Court unanimously reversed, thereby upholding the EPA's new interpretation of *source*. In doing so, the Court established a two-step approach to agency construction of statutes:

> When a court reviews an agency's construction of the statute it administers, it is confronted with two questions. First, always, is the question of whether Congress has directly spoken to the precise question at issue. If the intent of Congress is clear, that is the end of the matter; for the court, as well as the agency, must give effect to the unambiguously expressed intent of Congress. If, however, the court determines Congress has not directly addressed the precise question at issue, the court does not simply impose its own construction on the statute, as would be necessary in the absence of an administrative interpretation. Rather, if the statute is silent or ambiguous with respect to the specific issue, the question for the court is whether the agency's answer is based on a permissible construction of the statute [467 U.S. 842–843].

The Court went on to admonish the circuit court for attempting to substitute its interpretation for that of the administrative agency. In Justice Stevens's words:

> While agencies are not directly accountable to the people, the Chief Executive is, and it is entirely appropriate for this political branch of Government to make such policy choices—resolving the competing interests which Congress itself either inadvertently did not resolve, or intentionally left to be resolved by the agency charged with the administration of the statute in light of everyday realities [476 U.S. 865–866].

One commentator argued that this decision, with its reallocation of governmental authority, "far exceeds that of the Supreme Court's more celebrated constitutional writings on the subject of separation of powers in the 1980s."[40]

---

[40] Su. stein, above, note 39, 2075. The celebrated rulings that Sunstein alluded to include *Mistretta* v. *Unit d States*, 488 U.S. 361 (1989), *Morrison* v. *Olson*, 487 U.S. 654 (1988), *Bowsher* v. *Synar*, 478 U.S. 714 (1986), and *Immigration and Naturalization Service* v. *Chadha*, 462 U.S. 919 (1983), all of which have been discussed in previous chapters.

PART THREE

The Internal Administrative Process

CHAPTER 5

Investigatory Power

CHAPTER 6

Rules and Rule Making

CHAPTER 7

The Right to Be Heard and Adjudicatory Policy Making

CHAPTER 8

Informal Activity and the Exercise of Discretion

Investigatory Power

OVERVIEW OF THE INTERNAL ADMINISTRATIVE PROCESS

Part III of this book concerns the activity of administrators in carrying out the functions they are charged with by law. We have divided the subject into four categories. In discharging their duties, administrators often need to make factual determinations: whether a party is entitled to a governmental benefit or is covered by a regulatory statute or is engaging in an allegedly illegal activity or a myriad of other matters of this kind. This chapter deals with the legal issues associated with efforts by administrators to gather information in situations such as these.

One of the ways in which governmental agencies attempt to spell out in more detail the sometimes vague statements of legislative intent found in their statutes is through the adoption of substatutory pronouncements of their own. These statements are usually called *rules* or *regulations* (the terms are normally considered equivalents), and the process of adoption is called *rule making*. This is the subject of chapter 6.

Rule making normally affects a whole group of private parties, such as all taxpayers or property owners in a city or all airlines or television licensees. But administrators also interact with individuals and smaller groups. They may have to make individual decisions, such as whether an advertiser is engaged in deceptive advertising, whether a welfare recipient is entitled to continue to receive benefits, or whether a petitioner is entitled to a zoning variance. If sufficiently important interests are at stake, a proceeding with some degree of formality, sometimes approaching that of a court proceeding, must be held. This kind of procedure goes under a number of names, including *adjudication* and *quasi-judicial proceedings*. The most formal of these are called *trial-type* hearings. A recurring question, which is continually being addressed by courts, legislatures, and commentators on administrative procedure, is whether the interests at stake in a particular administrative proceeding are sufficiently important to require "some kind of hearing."[1]

---

[1] Henry J. Friendly, "Some Kind of Hearing," 123 *University of Pennsylvania Law Review* 1267 (1975).

It takes little reflection to realize that rule making often amounts to "administrative policy making" or at least supplementation of legislative policy. What may not be so immediately apparent is that an administrative agency can also create policy by adjudication as well. In chapter 7 we will address these aspects of administrative adjudication.

Finally, a great deal of the activity of administrative agencies in their dealings with private parties involves neither rule making nor adjudication. Advice given to a citizen by a governmental employee; the refusal by immigration authorities to allow an alien to enter the country; a telephone call from a regulatory commission lawyer to a company official indicating that, in the lawyer's opinion, the company may be doing something illegal—these and many other administrative activities can be placed in the categories *informal activity* and *the exercise of discretion*—categories which, until several decades ago, were rather neglected areas of administrative law. Chapter 8 examines this extremely important area.

Administrative investigations generally take one of two broad forms: (1) the examination of papers, records, or other documents (as well as testimony by individuals), and (2) the inspection of premises and other objects. Administrators derive their investigatory authority from legislation describing the functions and duties of their agencies.[2] Legal controversies typically arise over the alleged clash between statutory investigatory authority and constitutional guarantees protecting private parties, most often the Fourth Amendment's protection against unreasonable search and seizure and the Fifth Amendment's guarantee against self-incrimination. Although both amendments are brief and rather directly stated,[3] a great number of disputes over the years have involved the precise meaning of their terms. Moreover, it is clear that the judicial interpretation of these provisions has evolved somewhat over time.

As indicated in the introduction to this volume, administrative law and criminal law are separate subjects with some degree of overlap, in the sense that those engaged in criminal law enforcement often perform functions analogous to those performed by other administrators. Investigatory activity is an area in which this overlap is particularly evident. The enormous body of law concerning criminal investigatory authority is of tangential importance to the present discussion, which will concentrate on more traditional examples of administrative investigations.

---

[2] Such authority may also be provided in general legislation such as the Administrative Procedure Act. In the case of the APA, the relevant provisions are derivative. Section 555(c) provides: "Process, requirement of a report, inspection, or other investigative act or demand may not be issued, made, or enforced except as authorized by law. . . ." Section 555 (d) provides: "Agency subpoenas authorized by law shall be issued to a party on request and, when required by rules of procedures, on a statement or showing of general relevance and reasonable scope of the evidence sought. On contest, the court shall sustain the subpoena or similar process or demand to the extent that it is found to be in accordance with law."

[3] The Fourth Amendment reads: "The right of the people to be secure in their persons, houses, papers, and effects, against unreasonable searches and seizures, shall not be violated, and no warrants shall issue, but upon probable cause, supported by oath and affirmation, and particularly describing the place to be searched, and the persons or things to be seized."

The Fifth Amendment reads, in part: "No person . . . shall be compelled in any criminal case to be a witness against himself. . . ."

THE SUBPOENA POWER AND RELATED PROCESSES

Records and other data may be required to be kept by private parties and filed with governmental agencies. Thus, for instance, taxpayers are required to submit income tax statements by April 15 of each year, and governmental contractors are required to provide various kinds of information to governmental agencies, such as data on their affirmative action programs. Records and other documents not required to be routinely filed with government agencies may also be within the reach of the government, through what is broadly referred to as compulsory process.[4] This is one of the areas in which the interpretation of the law has evolved considerably over the years.

A case often cited as indicative of the early position of the courts on the matter is *Federal Trade Commission* v. *American Tobacco Company* (1924).

Federal Trade Commission v. *American Tobacco Co.*

SUPREME COURT OF THE UNITED States, 1924.
264 U.S. 298, 44 S.Ct. 336, 68 L.Ed. 696.

[The Federal Trade Commission (FTC), under a broad statutory subpoena power, undertook an investigation of charges that two tobacco companies had engaged in unfair competition by controlling prices. It ordered the companies to produce "all letters and telegrams received by the Company from, or sent by it to, all of its jobber customers between January 1, 1921, to December 31, 1921, inclusive." The companies refused, on constitutional grounds, to provide the information. The district court upheld the position of the companies, and the Supreme Court affirmed in a unanimous opinion by Justice Holmes.]

Mr. Justice HOLMES delivered the opinion of the Court. . . .

The mere facts of carrying on a commerce not confined within state lines, and of being organized as a corporation, do not make men's affairs public. . . . Anyone who respects the spirit as well as the letter of the Fourth Amendment would be loath to believe that Congress intended to authorize one of its subordinate agencies to sweep all our traditions into the fire . . . and to direct fishing expeditions into private papers on the possibility that they may disclose evidence of crime. We do not discuss the question whether it could do so if it tried, as nothing short of the most explicit language would induce us to attribute to Congress that intent. The interruption of business, the possible revelation of trade secrets, and the expense that compliance with the Commission's wholesale demand would cause, are the least considerations. It is contrary to the first principles of justice to allow a search through all the respondents' records, relevant or irrelevant, in the hope that something will turn up. . . .

---

[4] One needs to be aware of a recent limitation placed on agency power to require record keeping and reporting. The Paperwork Reduction Act of 1980, as amended in 1995 (44 USC §§ 3501–3520), has multiple purposes; however, its principal objective is to minimize the paperwork burden on the private sector. The act established an Office of Information and Regulatory Affairs within OMB to monitor new demands for information on the private sector. Such agency requests are to be shown to be "necessary for the proper performance of the agency, . . . and [having] practical utility" [44 U.S.C. § 3506 (c) (3)]. For additional background of the statute as originally enacted, see William F. Funk, "The Paperwork Reduction Act: Paperwork Reduction Meets Administrative Law," 24 *Harvard Journal of Legislation* 1 (1987).

The right of access given by the statute is to documentary evidence—not to all documents, but to such documents as are evidence. The analogies of the law do not allow the party wanting evidence to call for all documents in order to see if they do not contain it. Some ground must be shown for supposing that the documents called for do contain it. . . . A general subpoena in the form of these petitions would be bad. Some evidence of the materiality of the papers demanded must be produced. . . .

We have considered this case on the general claim of authority put forward by the Commission. The argument for the Government attaches some force to the investigations and proceedings upon which the Commission had entered. The investigations and complaints seem to have been only on hearsay or suspicion; but, even if they were induced by substantial evidence under oath, the rudimentary principles of justice that we have laid down would apply. We cannot attribute to Congress an intent to defy the Fourth Amendment or even to come so near to doing so as to raise a serious question of constitutional law.

Judgments affirmed.

But the hand of the government was strengthened by later interpretations of the Supreme Court. A particularly significant case in this evolution was the 1946 *Oklahoma Press* decision. The reader will note that Justice Wiley B. Rutledge uses the term *figurative* or *constructive search* in his opinion. The following definitions have been offered for the term *constructive*: "true legally even if not factually," "inferred," "presumed from circumstances," and "tantamount to."[5]

Oklahoma Press Pub. Co. v. *Walling*

SUPREME COURT OF THE UNITED STATES, 1946.
327 U.S. 186, 66 S.Ct. 494, 90 L.Ed. 614.

[A grant of subpoena power similar to that in the *American Tobacco* case was the basis for a request by the administrator of the Fair Labor Standards Act for records from certain employers. Appellants objected that it had not even been shown that they were covered by the act, and therefore resisted complying with the subpoena, a position that was rejected at the court of appeals level.]

Mr. Justice RUTLEDGE delivered the opinion of the Court.

These cases bring for decision important questions concerning the Administrator's right to judicial enforcement of subpoenas duces tecum issued by him in the course of investigations conducted pursuant to § 11 (a) of the Fair Labor Standards Act. 52 Stat. 1060. . . . The subpoenas sought the production of specified records to determine whether petitioners were violating the Fair Labor Standards Act, including records relating to coverage. Petitioners, newspaper publishing corporations, maintain that the Act is not applicable to them, for constitutional and other reasons, and insist that the question of coverage must be adjudicated before the subpoenas may be enforced. . . .

Other questions pertain to whether enforcement of the subpoenas as directed by the circuit courts of appeals will violate

---

[5] William P. Statsky, *West's Legal Thesaurus/Dictionary* 178 (1985).

any of petitioners' rights secured by the Fourth Amendment and related issues concerning Congress' intent. It is claimed that enforcement would permit the Administrator to conduct general fishing expeditions into petitioners' books, records and papers, in order to secure evidence that they have violated the Act, without a prior charge or complaint and simply to secure information upon which to base one, all allegedly in violation of the Amendment's search and seizure provisions. . . .

The short answer to the Fourth Amendment objections is that the records in these cases present no question of actual search and seizure, but raise only the question whether orders of court for the production of specified records have been validly made; and no sufficient showing appears to justify setting them aside. No officer or other person has sought to enter petitioners' premises against their will, to search them, or to seize or examine their books, records or papers without their assent, otherwise than pursuant to orders of court authorized by law and made after adequate opportunity to present objections, which in fact were made. Nor has any objection been taken to the breadth of the subpoenas or to any other specific defect which would invalidate them. . . .

The very purpose of the subpoena and of the order, as of the authorized investigation, is to discover and procure evidence, not to prove a pending charge or complaint, but upon which to make one if, in the Administrator's judgment, the facts thus discovered should justify doing so. . . .

The primary source of misconception concerning the Fourth Amendment's function lies perhaps in the identification of cases involving so-called "figurative" or "constructive" search with cases of actual search and seizure. . . .

The confusion, obscuring the basic distinction between actual and so-called "constructive" search has been accentu-ated where the records and papers sought are of corporate character, as in these cases. Historically private corporations have been subject to broad visitorial power, both in England and in this country. And it long has been established that Congress may exercise wide investigative power over them, analogous to the visitorial power of the incorporating state, when their activities take place within or affect interstate commerce. Correspondingly, it has been settled that corporations are not entitled to all of the constitutional protections which private individuals have in these and related matters. As has been noted, they are not at all within the privilege against self-incrimination. . . .

Without attempt to summarize or accurately distinguish all of the cases, the fair distillation, in so far as they apply merely to the production of corporate records and papers in response to a subpoena or order authorized by law and safeguarded by judicial sanction, seems to be that the Fifth Amendment affords no protection by virtue of the self-incrimination provision, whether for the corporation or for its officers; and the Fourth, if applicable, at the most guards against abuse only by way of too much indefiniteness or breadth in the things required to be "particularly described," if also the inquiry is one the demanding agency is authorized by law to make and the materials specified are relevant. The gist of the protection is in the requirement, expressed in terms, that the disclosure sought shall not be unreasonable. . . .

[I]t is impossible to conceive how a violation of petitioners' rights could have been involved. Both were corporations. The only records or documents sought were corporate ones. No possible element of self-incrimination was therefore presented or in fact claimed. All the records sought were relevant to the authorized inquiry, the purpose of which was to determine two issues, whether petitioners were subject to the Act and, if so, whether they were violating it. These were subjects of investigation authorized by § 11 (a), the latter expressly, the former by necessary implication. It is not to be doubted that Congress could authorize investigation of these matters. In all these respects, the specifications more than meet the requirements long established by many precedents. . . .

What has been said disposes of petitioners' principal contention upon the sufficiency of the showing. Other assignments, however, present the further questions whether any showing is required beyond the Administrator's allegations of coverage and relevance of the required materials to that question; and, if so, of what character. Stated otherwise, they are whether the court may order enforcement only upon a finding of "proba-

ble cause," that is, probability in fact, of coverage. . . .

Congress has made no requirement in terms of any showing of "probable cause"; and, in view of what has already been said, any possible constitutional requirement of that sort was satisfied by the Administrator's showing in this case, including not only the allegations concerning coverage, but also that he was proceeding with his investigation in accordance with the mandate of Congress and that the records sought were relevant to that purpose. . . .

Accordingly the judgments in both causes . . . are affirmed.

Affirmed.

[The dissenting opinion of Justice MURPHY is omitted. Justice JACKSON took no part in the consideration or decision of these cases.]

LEGALITY OF INVESTIGATIVE DEVICES

Four years after *Oklahoma Press*, the Supreme Court suggested how outmoded the thrust of the *American Tobacco* case was by referring to "the colorful and nostalgic slogan 'no fishing expeditions.'" In the same opinion, the Court brought out an important distinction between the judicial and administrative processes, which, impliedly at least, had not received recognition at the time of *American Tobacco*:

> Because judicial power is reluctant if not unable to summon evidence until it is shown to be relevant to issues in litigation, it does not follow that an administrative agency charged with seeing that the laws are enforced may not have and exercise powers of original inquiry. It has a power of inquisition, if one chooses to call it that, which is not derived from the judicial function. It is more analogous to the Grand Jury, which does not depend on a case or controversy for power to get evidence but can investigate merely on suspicion that the law is being violated, or even just because it wants assurances that it is not [*United States* v. *Morton Salt Co.* 338 U.S. 632, 642–643 (1950)].

In addition to the holding in the *Oklahoma Press,* which sanctioned the use of wide-ranging subpoena power by administrators, two other important points in the opinion should be noted. The first is the distinction between constructive search of papers and documents and actual search and seizure. As Justice Rutledge pointed out, the latter is based on probable cause, an element not required in a constructive search. This will be an important consideration in the cases on inspection of premises covered below. Second,

Oklahoma Press makes it clear that corporations and their officers have long been excluded from the protection of the Fifth Amendment's self-incrimination provisions. By a series of judicial decisions, this exclusion has been extended to other organizations such as trade unions and even small partnerships. The self-incrimination clause may also be bypassed in several other ways as well. For instance, a grant of immunity from prosecution may be used to require a person to testify. And the courts have ruled that if one person's records are in the custody of another person, the Fifth Amendment provides no protection for such papers.[6]

The following case is an illustration of the broad reach of government investigatory power in more recent times. Justice Rehnquist's majority opinion clearly states the facts and issues. Although his opinion, as well as Justice Thurgood Marshall's dissent, mentions the constitutional implications of the case, the reasoning of all the opinions (including a dissent by Justice Brennan) largely turns on *statutory construction*, namely, the determination as to whether the statute permitted the investigative device used in this case.

United States v. Euge

Supreme Court of the United States, 1980.
444 U.S. 707, 100 S.Ct. 874, 63 L.Ed. 2d 141.

Justice REHNQUIST delivered the opinion of the Court.

The United States sued in the District Court seeking enforcement of an Internal Revenue Service summons requiring respondent to appear and provide handwriting exemplars. Enforcement was denied by the Court of Appeals for the Eighth Circuit . . . and we granted certiorari. . . . We now hold that Congress has empowered the IRS to compel handwriting exemplars under its summons authority conferred by 26 U. S. C. § 7602.

I

The facts are not in dispute. In October 1977, an agent in the Intelligence Division of the Internal Revenue Service was assigned to investigate respondent's income tax liability for the years 1973 through 1976. Respondent had not filed any tax returns for those years. The Service sought to employ the "bank deposits method" of reconstructing respondent's income for those years, as a means of calculating his tax liability. Under this method of proof, the sums deposited in the taxpayer's bank accounts are scrutinized to determine whether they represent taxable income.

During the course of the investigation, the agent found only two bank accounts registered in respondent's name. Twenty other bank accounts were discovered, however, which the agent had reason to believe were being maintained by respondent under aliases to conceal taxable income. The statements for these accounts were sent to post office boxes held in respondent's name; the signature cards for the accounts listed addresses of properties owned by respondent; and the agent had documented frequent transfers of funds between the accounts.

---

[6] On these and other ways around the self-incrimination provision, see Richard J. Pierce, Jr., 1 *Administrative Law Treatise* 229–249 (4th ed., 2002).

In an effort to determine whether the sums deposited in these accounts represented income attributable to respondent, the agent issued a summons on October 7, 1977, requiring respondent to appear and execute handwriting exemplars of the various signatures appearing on the bank signature cards. Respondent declined to comply with the summons.

The United States commenced this action under 26 U. S. C. § 7604 (a). The District Court held that the summons should be enforced, ordering respondent to provide 10 handwriting exemplars of 8 different signatures. The Court of Appeals reversed, ruling that the summons authority vested in the Internal Revenue Service under 26 U. S. C. § 7602 does not authorize the IRS to compel the execution of handwriting exemplars.

II

The structure and history of the statutory authority of the Internal Revenue Service to summon witnesses to produce evidence necessary for tax investigations has been repeatedly reviewed by this Court in recent years. Under § 7602, the Secretary of the Treasury, and therefore the IRS as his designate, is authorized to summon individuals to "appear before the Secretary . . . and to produce such books, papers, records, or other data, and to give such testimony, under oath, as may be relevant or material to such inquiry. . . ." The question presented here is whether this power to compel a witness to "appear," to produce "other data," and to "give testimony," includes the power to compel the execution of handwriting exemplars. We conclude that it does, for several reasons. While the language may not be explicit in its authorization of handwriting exemplars, the duty to appear and give testimony, a duty imposed by § 7602, has traditionally encompassed a duty to provide some forms of nontestimonial, physical evidence, including handwriting exem-

plars. Further, this Court has consistently construed congressional intent to require that if the summons authority claimed is necessary for the effective performance of congressionally imposed responsibilities to enforce the tax code, that authority should be upheld absent express statutory prohibition or substantial countervailing policies. The authority claimed here is necessary for the effective exercise of the Service's enforcement responsibilities; it is entirely consistent with the statutory language; and it is not in derogation of any constitutional rights or countervailing policies enunciated by Congress. . . .

Through § 7602, Congress has imposed a duty on persons possessing information "relevant or material" to an investigation of federal tax liability to produce that information at the request of the Secretary or his delegate. That duty to provide relevant information expressly obligates the person summoned to produce documentary evidence and to "appear" and "give testimony." Imposition of such an evidentiary obligation is, of course, not a novel innovation attributable to § 7602. The common law has been the source of a comparable evidentiary obligation for centuries. In determining the scope of the obligation Congress intended to impose by use of this language, we have previously analogized, as an interpretive guide, to the common-law duties attaching to the issuance of a testimonial summons. Congress, through legislation, may expand or contract the duty imposed, but absent some contrary expression, there is a wealth of history helpful in defining the duties imposed by the issuance of a summons.

The scope of the "testimonial" or evidentiary duty imposed by common law or statute has traditionally been interpreted as an expansive duty limited principally by relevance and privilege. . . .

This broad duty to provide most relevant, nonprivileged evidence has not been considered to exist only in the common law. The Court has recognized that by statute "Congress may provide for the performance of this duty." *Blackmer* v. *United States*, 284 U.S. 421, 438 (1932). By imposing an obligation to produce documents as well as to appear and give testimony, we believe the language of § 7602 suggests an intention to codify a broad testimonial obligation, including an obligation to provide some physical evidence relevant and material to a tax investigation, subject to the traditional privileges and limitations. This conclusion seems inherent in the imposition of an obligation to "appear," since an obligation to appear necessarily entails an obligation to display physical features to the summoning authority. Congress thereby authorized the Service to compel the production of some physical evidence, and it is certainly possible to conclude that this authorization extended to the execution of handwriting exemplars, one variety of relevant physical evidence. This construction of the language conforms with the historical notions of the testimonial duty attaching to the issuance of a summons. . . .

Section 7602 does not, by its terms, compel the production of handwriting exemplars, and therefore, a narrower interpretation of the duty imposed is not precluded by the actual language of the statute. A narrower interpretation *is* precluded, however, by the precedents of this Court construing that statute. As early as 1911, this Court established the benchmarks for interpreting the authority of the Internal Revenue Service to enforce tax obligations in holding that "the administration of the statute may well be taken to embrace all appropriate measures for its enforcement, [unless] there is . . . substantial reason for assigning to the [phrases] . . . a narrower interpretation." *United States* v. *Chamberlin*, 219 U.S. 250, 269. This precise mode of construction has consistently been applied by this Court in construing the breadth of the

summons authority Congress intended to confer in § 7602. . . . There is thus a formidable line of precedent construing congressional intent to uphold the claimed enforcement authority of the Service if authority is necessary for the effective enforcement of the revenue laws and is not undercut by contrary legislative purposes.

Applying these principles, we conclude that Congress empowered the Service to seek, and obliged the witness to provide, handwriting exemplars relevant to the investigation. . . .

There is certainly nothing in the statutory language, or in the legislative history, precluding the interpretation asserted by the Service. Nor is there any constitutional privilege of the taxpayer or other parties that is violated by this construction. Compulsion of handwriting exemplars is neither a search or seizure subject to Fourth Amendment protections, *United States* v. *Mara*, 410 U.S. 19 (1973), nor testimonial evidence protected by the Fifth Amendment privilege against self-incrimination. *Gilbert* v. *California*, 388 U.S. 263 (1967). The compulsion of handwriting exemplars has been the subject of far less protection than the compulsion of testimony and documents. Since Congress has explicitly established an obligation to provide the more protected forms of evidence, it would seem curious had it chosen not to impose an obligation to produce a form of evidence tradition has found it less important to protect.

As we have emphasized in other cases dealing with § 7602 proceedings, the summoned party is entitled to challenge the issuance of the summons in an adversary proceeding in federal court prior to enforcement, and may assert appropriate defenses. The Service must also establish compliance with the good-faith requirements recognized by this Court, *United States* v. *LaSalle National Bank*, 437 U.S. 298, 318, and with the requirement of § 7605 (b) that "[no] taxpayer shall be subjected to unnecessary examination or investigation. . . ." These protections are quite sufficient to lead us to refuse to strain to imply additional ones from the neutral language Congress has used in § 7602.

We accordingly reverse the judgment of the Court of Appeals refusing enforcement of the summons.

Reversed.

[The dissenting opinion of Justice BRENNAN, with whom Justice MARSHALL and Justice STEVENS join, is omitted].

Justice MARSHALL, dissenting.

In my view, the Fifth Amendment's privilege against compulsory self-incrimination prohibits the Government from requiring a person to provide handwriting exemplars. As I stated in my dissenting opinion in *United States* v. *Mara*, 410 U.S. 19, 33 . . . (1973), "I cannot accept the notion that the Government can compel a man to cooperate affirmatively in securing incriminating evidence when that evidence could not be obtained without the cooperation of the suspect." The Fifth Amendment privilege is rooted in "the basic stream of religious and political principle[,] . . . reflects the limits of the individual's attornment to the state," *In re Gault*, 387 U.S. 1, 47 (1967), and embodies the "respect a government—state or federal—must accord to the dignity and integrity of its citizens," *Miranda* v. *Arizona*, 384 U.S. 436, 460 (1966). I continue to believe, then, that "[it] is only by prohibiting the Government from compelling an individual to cooperate affirmatively in securing incriminating evidence which could not be obtained without his active assistance, that 'the inviolability of the human personality' is assured." *United States* v. *Mara*, supra, at 34–35 (dissenting opinion) (quoting *Miranda* v. *Arizona*, supra, at 460).

In order to avoid this constitutional problem, I agree with my Brother BRENNAN . . . that 26 U. S. C. § 7602 should be construed not to permit Internal Revenue Service personnel to compel the production of handwriting exemplars. Accordingly, I dissent.

THE INSPECTION OF PREMISES

The line of development traced through the preceding cases is strongly in the direction of increasing governmental investigatory power. At first glance, the direction with regard to administrative inspection of premises appears to be otherwise. Let us look at the relevant cases.

The Supreme Court did not take up constitutional questions of administrative inspections until 1959. Then, in *Frank* v. *Maryland*, 359 U.S. 360, the Court upheld by a five-to-four vote a provision of the Baltimore City Code allowing warrantless inspections of private dwellings by a health inspector based on suspicion that a nuisance existed. The *Frank* decision remained controlling until the *Camara* case of 1967.

Camara v. Municipal Court of the City and County of San Francisco

Supreme Court of the United States, 1967.
387 U.S. 523, 87 S.Ct. 1727, 18 L.Ed. 2d 930.

Mr. Justice WHITE delivered the opinion of the Court. . . .

In *Frank* v. *Maryland*, 359 U.S. 360, this Court upheld, by a five-to-four vote, a state court conviction of a homeowner who refused to permit a municipal health inspector to enter and inspect his premises without a search warrant. In *Eaton* v. *Price*, 364 U.S. 263, a similar conviction was affirmed by an equally divided Court. Since those closely divided decisions, more intensive efforts at all levels of government to contain and eliminate urban blight have led to increasing use of such inspection techniques, while numerous decisions of this Court have more fully defined the Fourth Amendment's effect on state and municipal action. . . .

Appellant brought this action in a California Superior Court alleging that he was awaiting trial on a criminal charge of violating the San Francisco Housing Code by refusing to permit a warrantless inspection of his residence, and that a writ of prohibition should issue to the criminal court because the ordinance authorizing such inspections is unconstitutional on its face. The Superior Court denied the writ, the District Court of Appeals affirmed, and the Supreme Court of California denied a petition for hearing. Appellant properly raised and had considered by the California courts the federal constitutional questions he now presents to this Court.

Though there were no judicial findings of fact in this prohibition proceeding, we shall set forth the parties' factual allegations. On November 6, 1963, an inspector of the Division of Housing Inspection of the San Francisco Department of Public Health entered an apartment building to make a routine annual inspection for possible violations of the city's Housing Code. The building's manager informed the inspector that appellant, lessee of the ground floor, was using the rear of his leasehold as a personal residence. Claiming that the building's occupancy permit did not allow residential use of the ground floor, the inspector confronted appellant and demanded that he permit an inspection of the premises. Appellant refused to allow the inspection because the inspector lacked a search warrant.

The inspector returned on November 8, again without a warrant, and appellant again refused to allow an inspection. A citation was then mailed ordering appellant to appear at the district attorney's office. When appellant failed to appear, two inspectors returned to his apartment on November 22. They informed appellant that he was required by law to permit an inspection under § 503 of the Housing Code:

> Sec. 503 RIGHT TO ENTER BUILDING. Authorized employees of the City departments or City agencies, so far as may be necessary for the performance of their duties, shall, upon presentation of proper credentials, have the right to enter, at reasonable times, any building, structure, or premises in the City to perform any duty imposed upon them by the Municipal Code.

Appellant nevertheless refused the inspectors access to his apartment without a search warrant. Thereafter, a complaint was filed charging him with refusing to permit a lawful inspection in violation of § 507 of the Code. Appellant was arrested on December 2 and released on bail. When his demurrer to the criminal complaint was denied, appellant filed this petition for a writ of prohibition.

Appellant has argued throughout this litigation that § 503 is contrary to the Fourth and Fourteenth Amendments in that it authorizes municipal officials to enter a private dwelling without a search warrant and without probable cause to believe that a violation of the Housing Code exists therein. Consequently, appellant contends, he may not be prosecuted under § 507 for refusing to permit an inspection unconstitutionally authorized by § 503. Relying on *Frank* v. *Maryland*, *Eaton* v. *Price*, and decisions in other States, the District Court of Appeal held that § 503 does not violate Fourth Amendment rights because it "is part of a regulatory scheme which is essentially civil rather than criminal in nature, inasmuch as that section creates a right of inspection which is limited in scope and may not be exercised under unreasonable conditions." Having concluded that *Frank* v. *Maryland*, to the extent that it sanctioned such warrantless inspections, must be overruled, we reverse. . . .

[W]e hold that administrative searches of the kind at issue here are significant intrusions upon the interests protected by the Fourth Amendment, that such searches when authorized and conducted without a warrant procedure lack the traditional safeguards which the Fourth Amendment guarantees to the individual, and that the reasons put forth in *Frank* v. *Maryland* and in other cases for upholding these warrantless searches are insufficient to justify so substantial a weakening of the Fourth Amendment's protections. Because of the nature of the municipal programs under consideration, however, these conclusions must be the beginning, not the end, of our inquiry. The *Frank* majority gave recognition to the unique character of these inspection programs by refusing to require search warrants; to reject that disposition does not justify ignoring the question whether some other accommodation between public need and individual rights is essential. . . .

The Fourth Amendment provides that, "no Warrants shall issue, but upon

probable cause." Borrowing from more typical Fourth Amendment cases, appellant argues not only that code enforcement inspection programs must be circumscribed by a warrant procedure, but also that warrants should issue only when the inspector possesses probable cause to believe that a particular dwelling contains violations of the minimum standards prescribed by the code being enforced. We disagree.

In cases in which the Fourth Amendment requires that a warrant to search be obtained, "probable cause" is the standard by which a particular decision to search is tested against the constitutional mandate of reasonableness. To apply this standard, it is obviously necessary first to focus upon the governmental interest which allegedly justifies official intrusion upon the constitutionally protected interests of the private citizen. For example, in a criminal investigation, the police may undertake to recover specific stolen or contraband goods. But that public interest would hardly justify a sweeping search of an entire city conducted in the hope that these goods might be found. Consequently, a search for these goods, even with a warrant, is "reasonable" only when there is "probable cause" to believe that they will be uncovered in a particular dwelling.

Unlike the search pursuant to a criminal investigation, the inspection programs at issue here are aimed at securing city-wide compliance with minimum physical standards for private property. The primary governmental interest at stake is to prevent even the unintentional development of conditions which are hazardous to public health and safety. . . .

There is unanimous agreement among those most familiar with this field that the only effective way to seek universal compliance with the minimum standards required by municipal codes is through routine periodic inspections of all structures. It is here that the probable cause debate is focused, for the agency's decision to conduct an area inspection is unavoidably based on its appraisal of conditions in the area as a whole, not on its knowledge of conditions in each particular building. . . . [W]e think that a number of persuasive factors combine to support the reasonableness of area code-enforcement inspections. First, such programs have a long history of judicial and public acceptance. . . . Second, the public interest demands that all dangerous conditions be prevented or abated, yet it is doubtful that any other canvassing technique would achieve acceptable results. Many such conditions—faulty wiring is an obvious example—are not observable from outside the building and indeed may not be apparent to the inexpert occupant himself. Finally, because the inspections are neither personal in nature nor aimed at the discovery of evidence of crime, they involve a relatively limited invasion of the urban citizen's privacy. . . .

Having concluded that the area inspection is a "reasonable" search of private property within the meaning of the Fourth Amendment, it is obvious that "probable cause" to issue a warrant to inspect must exist if reasonable legislative or administrative standards for conducting an area inspection are satisfied with respect to a particular dwelling. Such standards, which will vary with the municipal program being enforced, may be based upon the passage of time, the nature of the building (e. g., a multi-family apartment house), or the condition of the entire area, but they will not necessarily depend upon specific knowledge of the condition of the particular dwelling. It has been suggested that so to vary the probable cause test from the standard applied in criminal cases would be to authorize a "synthetic search warrant" and thereby to lessen the overall protections of the Fourth Amendment. *Frank* v. *Maryland*, 359 U.S., at 373. But we do not agree. The warrant procedure is designed to guaran-

tee that a decision to search private property is justified by a reasonable governmental interest. But reasonableness is still the ultimate standard. If a valid public interest justifies the intrusion contemplated, then there is probable cause to issue a suitably restricted search warrant. Cf. *Oklahoma Press Pub. Co.* v. *Walling*, 327 U.S. 186. . . .

Since our holding emphasizes the controlling standard of reasonableness, nothing we say today is intended to foreclose prompt inspections, even without a warrant, that the law has traditionally upheld in emergency situations. See *North American Cold Storage Co.* v. *City of Chicago*, 211 U.S. 306 (seizure of unwholesome food); *Jacobson* v. *Massachusetts*, 197 U.S. 11 (compulsory smallpox vaccination); *Compagnie Francaise* v. *Board of Health*, 186 U.S. 380 (health quarantine); *Kroplin* v. *Truax*, 119 Ohio St. 610, 165 N. E. 498 (summary destruction of tubercular cattle). On the other hand, in the case of most routine area inspections, there is no compelling urgency to inspect at a particular time or on a particular day. Moreover, most citizens allow inspections of their property without a warrant. Thus, as a practical matter and in light of the Fourth Amendment's requirement that a warrant specify the property to be searched, it seems likely that warrants should normally be sought only after entry is refused unless there has been a citizen complaint or there is other satisfactory reason for securing immediate entry. Similarly, the requirement of a warrant procedure does not suggest any change in what seems to be the prevailing local policy, in most situations, of authorizing entry, but not entry by force, to inspect. . . .

The judgment is vacated and the case is remanded for further proceedings not inconsistent with this opinion.

It is so ordered.

[The dissenting opinion of Justice

Clark, with whom Justice Harlan and
Justice Stewart join, is omitted.]

Warrants in Administrative Investigations

Looking back at the *Camara* holding from a perspective of three dozen
years, it is clear that the decision was just the first in a series of cases questioning the need for a warrant in a wide range of administrative investigations. In *Wyman* v. *James*, 400 U.S. 309 (1971), a welfare recipient sought
to prevent a periodic home visit by a welfare caseworker on the grounds that
such a visit constituted a search and thus a warrant was required. But the
Supreme Court ruled that the home visit was a reasonable administrative
tool and need not be based on a warrant. It contrasted the home visit with
the situation in *Camara* in these terms: "Mrs. James is not being prosecuted
for her refusal to permit a home visit and is not about to be so prosecuted.
. . . If a statute made her refusal a criminal offense, and if this case were
one concerning her prosecution under the statute, *Camara* . . . would have
conceivable pertinency" (400 U.S. 325).

A companion to the *Camara* case, decided on the same day, was *See* v.
City of Seattle, 387 U.S. 541 (1967). The case was based on an action by the
city against a warehouse owner who refused to submit to fire inspections.
The lower courts ruled for the city, but the Supreme Court, with the same
voting lineup as in *Camara*, reversed, holding that "warrants are a necessary and a tolerable limitation on the right to enter upon and inspect commercial enterprises" and that there is "no justification for so relaxing the
Fourth Amendment safeguards when the official inspection is intended to
aid enforcement of laws prescribing minimal physical standards for commercial enterprises" (387 U.S. 543–544). Some commentators wondered
whether *See* implied a warrant requirement for all administrative entries
into business establishments, although the majority in *See* did note that
they were not questioning "such accepted regulatory techniques as licensing
programs" (387 U.S. 546). The Supreme Court soon had occasion to consider
cases falling into this category.

In *Colonnade Catering Corp.* v. *United States,* 397 U.S. 72 (1970), Internal Revenue Service (IRS) agents, suspecting a violation of federal excise
tax laws, visited petitioner's establishment, which was licensed to serve al-
coholic beverages. They requested to inspect the locked liquor storeroom,
and when refused entry they broke in and removed bottles of liquor that
they suspected of being refilled, which would have been a violation of a federal statute. Pertinent articles of the U.S. Code gave the secretary of the
treasury or his agents broad power to enter and inspect the premises of
retail dealers in liquor. In case of refusal to permit entry, the code provided
for forfeiture of a $500 fine. In a proceeding on the question of suppression
of the seized liquor as evidence, the Supreme Court found that while "Congress has broad power to design such powers of inspection under the liquor
laws as it deems necessary to meet the evils at hand" (397 U.S. 72, 76), the
statutory scheme did not provide for using force when entry was refused,
but only for the assessing of a fine. In other words, while the government

lost the case, the principle of warrantless inspection in this case was left undisturbed.

United States v. *Biswell*, 406 U.S. 311 (1972), involved the inspection by a treasury agent of a locked gun storeroom of a pawn shop operator who was federally licensed to deal in sporting weapons. Such warrantless inspections were authorized under the Gun Control Act of 1968, 82 Stat. 1213. The operator asked the agent if he had a warrant, and when told that warrantless inspections were authorized under the statute, he permitted entry. When the pawn shop operator was convicted of possessing illegal weapons found in the search, he moved to overturn the conviction by charging that the search violated the Fourth Amendment.

The Supreme Court, with only one justice dissenting, ruled that a warrantless inspection in this case was justified:

> When a dealer chooses to engage in this pervasively regulated business and to accept a federal license, he does so with the knowledge that his business records, firearms, and ammunition will be subject to effective inspection. . . . We have little difficulty in concluding that where, as here, regulatory inspections further urgent federal interest and the possibility of abuse and the threat to privacy are not of impressive dimensions, the inspection may proceed without a warrant where specifically authorized by statute [406 U.S. 316–317].

A capstone case in the area of inspection of commercial establishments is *Marshall* v. *Barlow's*. It amounted to a showdown of sorts between the line of cases requiring warrants and those condoning warrantless inspections.

Marshall v. Barlow's, Inc.

Supreme Court of the United States, 1978.
436 U.S. 307, 98 S.Ct. 1816, 56 L.Ed. 2d 305.

[The Occupational Safety and Health Act of 1970 (OSHA) empowered the secretary of labor to search the work area of facilities covered by the act for purposes of uncovering safety hazards and violations of OSHA regulations. The act provided no requirement of a search warrant. An OSHA inspector was denied admission to the employee area of Barlow's Inc., an electrical and plumbing installation business in Pocatello, Idaho. The secretary of labor, Ray Marshall, obtained a court order compelling Ferrol G. Barlow to admit the inspector, and Barlow again refused. Barlow then sought injunctive relief against the warrantless search OSHA claimed it had the authority to conduct, asserting that such searches violated the Fourth Amendment. A federal district court ruled in Barlow's favor, holding that *Camara* and *See* controlled this case. The secretary appealed, and the case came to the Supreme Court.]

Justice WHITE delivered the opinion of the Court. . . .

The Secretary urges that warrantless inspections to enforce OSHA are reasonable within the meaning of the Fourth Amendment. Among other things, he relies on § 8 (a) of the Act, 29 U. S. C. § 657 (a), which authorizes inspection of business premises without a warrant and which the Secretary urges represents a congressional construction of the Fourth Amendment that the courts should not reject. Regrettably, we are unable to agree. . . .

This Court has already held that warrantless searches are generally unreasonable, and that this rule applies to commercial premises as well as homes. In *Camara* v. *Municipal Court*, 387 U.S. 523, 528–529 (1967) we held:

> [E]xcept in certain carefully defined classes of cases, a search of private property without proper consent is "unreasonable" unless it has been authorized by a valid search warrant.

On the same day, we also ruled:

> As we explained in *Camara*, a search of private houses is presumptively unreasonable if conducted without a warrant. The businessman, like the occupant of a residence, has a constitutional right to go about his business free from unreasonable official entries upon his private commercial property. The businessman, too, has that right placed in jeopardy if the decision to enter and inspect for violation of regulatory laws can be made and enforced by the inspector in the field without official authority evidenced by a warrant. *See* v. *Seattle*, 387 U.S. 541, 543 (1967).

These same cases also held that the Fourth Amendment prohibition against unreasonable searches protects against warrantless intrusions during civil as well as criminal investigations. *See* v. *City of Seattle*, supra, at 543. The reason is found in the "basic purpose of this Amendment . . . [which] is to safeguard the privacy and security of individuals against arbitrary invasions by governmental officials." *Camara*, supra, at 528. If the government intrudes on a person's property, the privacy interest suffers whether the government's motivation is to investigate violations of criminal laws or breaches of other statutory or regulatory standards. It therefore appears that unless some recognized exception to the warrant requirement applies, *See* v. *Seattle* would require a warrant to conduct the inspection sought in this case.

The Secretary urges that an exception from the search warrant requirement has been recognized for "pervasively regulated [businesses]," *United States* v. *Biswell*, 406 U.S. 311, 316 (1972), and for "closely regulated" industries "long subject to close supervision and inspection." *Colonnade Catering Corp.* v. *United States*, 397 U.S. 72, 74, 77 (1970). These cases are indeed exceptions, but they represent responses to relatively unique circumstances. Certain industries have such a history of government oversight that no reasonable expectation of privacy . . . could exist for a proprietor over the stock of such an enterprise. Liquor *(Colonnade [Catering Corp.* v. *United States* (1970)]) and firearms ([*United States* v.] *Biswell* [1972]) are industries of this type; when an entrepreneur embarks upon such a business, he has voluntarily chosen to subject himself to a full arsenal of governmental regulation. . . .

The clear import of our cases is that the closely regulated industry of the type involved in *Colonnade* and *Biswell* is the exception. The Secretary would make it the rule. . . .

The Secretary submits that warrantless inspections are essential to the proper enforcement of OSHA because they afford the opportunity to inspect without prior notice and hence to preserve the advantages of surprise. While the dangerous conditions outlawed by the Act include structural defects that cannot be quickly hidden or remedied, the Act also regulates a myriad of safety details that may be amenable to speedy alteration or disguise. The risk is that during the interval between an inspector's initial request to search a plant and his procuring a warrant following the owner's refusal of permission, violations of this latter type could be corrected and thus escape the inspector's notice. To the suggestion that warrants may be issued ex parte and executed without delay and without prior notice, thereby preserving the element of surprise, the Secretary expresses concern for the administrative strain that would be experienced by the inspection system, and by the courts, should ex parte warrants issued in advance become standard practice.

We are unconvinced, however, that requiring warrants to inspect will impose serious burdens on the inspection system or the courts, will prevent inspections necessary to enforce the statute, or will make them less effective. In the first place, the great majority of businessmen can be expected in normal course to consent to inspection without warrant; the Secretary has not brought to this Court's attention any widespread pattern of refusal. . . .

Whether the Secretary proceeds to secure a warrant or other process, with or without prior notice, his entitlement to inspect will not depend on his demonstrating probable cause to believe that conditions in violation of OSHA exist on the premises. Probable cause in the criminal law sense is not required. For purposes of an administrative search such as this, probable cause justifying the issuance of a warrant may be based not only on specific evidence of an existing violation but also on a showing that "reasonable legislative or administrative standards for conducting an . . . inspection are satisfied with respect to a particular [establishment]." *Camara* v. *Municipal Court*, 387 U.S., at 538. A warrant showing that a specific business has been chosen for an OSHA search on the basis of a general administrative plan for the enforcement of the Act derived from neutral sources such as, for example, dispersion of employees in various types of industries across a given area, and the desired frequency of searches in any of the lesser divisions of the area, would protect an employer's Fourth Amendment rights. We doubt that the consumption of enforcement energies in the obtaining of such warrants will exceed manageable proportions.

Finally, the Secretary urges that re-

quiring a warrant for OSHA inspectors will mean that, as a practical matter, warrantless-search provisions in other regulatory statutes are also constitutionally infirm. The reasonableness of a warrantless search, however, will depend upon the specific enforcement needs and privacy guarantees of each statute. Some of the statutes cited apply only to a single industry, where regulations might already be so pervasive that a *Colonnade-Biswell* exception to the warrant requirement could apply. Some statutes already envision resort to federal-court enforcement when entry is refused, employing specific language in some cases and general language in others. In short, we base today's opinion on the facts and law concerned with OSHA and do not retreat from a holding appropriate to that statute because of its real or imagined effect on other, different administrative schemes. . . .

We hold that Barlow's was entitled to a declaratory judgment that the Act is unconstitutional insofar as it purports to authorize inspections without warrant or its equivalent and to an injunction enjoining the Act's enforcement to that extent. The judgment of the District Court is therefore affirmed.

So ordered.

Justice BRENNAN took no part in the consideration or decision of this case.

Justice STEVENS, with whom Justice BLACKMUN and Justice REHNQUIST join, dissenting. . . .

The Fourth Amendment contains two separate Clauses, each flatly prohibiting a category of governmental conduct. The first Clause states that the right to be free from unreasonable searches "shall not be violated"; the second unequivocally prohibits the issuance of warrants except "upon probable cause." In this case the ultimate question is whether the category of warrantless searches authorized by the statute is "unreasonable" within the meaning of the first Clause.

In cases involving the investigation of criminal activity, the Court has held that the reasonableness of a search generally depends upon whether it was conducted pursuant to a valid warrant. . . . There is, however, also a category of searches which are reasonable within the meaning of the first Clause even though the probable-cause requirement of the Warrant Clause cannot be satisfied. The regulatory inspection program challenged in this case, in my judgment, falls within this category. . . .

The warrant requirement is linked "textually . . . to the probable-cause concept" in the Warrant Clause. *South Dakota* v. *Opperman* [428 U.S. at 370]. The routine OSHA inspections are, by definition, not based on cause to believe there is a violation on the premises to be inspected. Hence, if the inspections were measured against the requirements of the Warrant Clause, they would be automatically and unequivocally unreasonable.

Because of the acknowledged importance and reasonableness of routine inspections in the enforcement of federal regulatory statutes such as OSHA, the Court recognizes that requiring full compliance with the Warrant Clause would invalidate all such inspection programs.

Yet, rather than simply analyzing such programs under the "Reasonableness" Clause of the Fourth Amendment, the Court holds the OSHA program invalid under the Warrant Clause and then avoids a blanket prohibition on all routine, regulatory inspections by relying on the notion that the "probable cause" requirement in the Warrant Clause may be relaxed whenever the Court believes that the governmental need to conduct a category of "searches" outweighs the intrusion on interests protected by the Fourth Amendment. . . .

Fidelity to the original understanding of the Fourth Amendment, therefore, leads to the conclusion that the Warrant Clause has no application to routine, regulatory inspections of commercial premises. If such inspections are valid, it is because they comport with the ultimate reasonableness standard of the Fourth Amendment. If the Court were correct in its view that such inspections, if undertaken without a warrant, are unreasonable in the constitutional sense, the issuance of a "new-fangled warrant"—to use Mr. Justice Clark's characteristically expressive term—without any true showing of particularized probable cause would not be sufficient to validate them. . . .

SUBPOENAS AND INSPECTIONS: DIVERGING TRENDS?

As suggested earlier, the trend of the inspection cases, at least as represented in *Camara*, *See*, and *Barlow's*, which required warrants prior to entry onto premises, seems to diverge from that of the constructive search cases covered at the beginning of the chapter, which have allowed an ever wider use of the subpoena power by government agencies. For two reasons, however, the differences between these two categories of cases may not be as great as they initially appear. The first reason is the court-developed relaxation of the warrant requirement in inspection cases, and the second reason is the number of exceptions to the warrant requirement that have surfaced over the years.

Regarding the relaxation of the warrant requirement, in *Camara* the Court said that probable cause could be satisfied on an area basis, without reference to "the condition of the particular building," while in *Barlow's*, the Court indicated approval of a "warrant showing that a specific business has been chosen for an OSHA search on the basis of a general administrative plan for the enforcement of the Act. . . ." In other words, a warrant in such cases would appear to be quite easy to obtain. To quote the *Barlow's* majority again, a warrant "with or without prior notice . . . will not depend on [the Secretary's] demonstrating probable cause. . . ." The relaxation of the warrant requirement in *Camara* and *Barlow's* led one commentator to conclude that "[t]he practical difference between what the Court requires and what could be done through warrantless inspections may be so slight as to be almost non-existent."[7]

Regarding the second point mentioned above, exceptions to the warrant requirement in inspection cases, *Wyman* (1971), *Colonnade* (1970), and *Biswell* (1972), have already been mentioned. In the first of these, it was concluded that the home visit to a welfare recipient was not subject to the warrant requirement. The other two cases established the principle that warrantless inspections would be permitted in pervasively regulated businesses such as selling liquor and firearms. Subsequently, the Supreme Court condoned warrantless administrative inspections in another line of cases. In 1981 the right of inspectors to conduct a warrantless inspection of a stone quarry under provisions of the Federal Mine Safety and Health Act of 1977 was upheld (91 Stat. 1290). Writing for the majority, Justice Marshall distinguished the situation from that in *Marshall* v. *Barlow's* and justified the warrantless search on the ground that "the Mine Safety and Health Act applies to industrial activity with a notorious history of serious accidents and unhealthful working conditions" [*Donovan* v. *Dewey*, 452 U.S. 594, 603 (1981)].

Justice Rehnquist concurred in the judgment in *Donovan* v. *Dewey* because he concluded that the stone quarry being inspected "was largely visible to the naked eye" and there was no need to enter the buildings or enclosed property of the defendant. He went on to invoke the "open fields exception" in support of his view. When public officials enter outdoor premises belonging to a firm or individual for investigative purposes, a somewhat different situation obtains. The Supreme Court held in 1974 that a health inspector did not violate the Fourth Amendment when he went onto the land of a corporation without its knowledge or consent to make observations of smoke being emitted from the plant's chimneys. These observations were "well within the 'open fields' exception to the Fourth Amendment" and were not controlled by the rulings in *Camara* or *See* [*Air Pollution Variance Board of the State of Colorado* v. *Western Alfalfa Corp.*, 416 U.S. 861, 865 (1974)]. In 1984 the Supreme Court indicated (in two cases covered in a single decision) that the "open fields exception" could apply to warrantless inspections of farmlands and woodlands where marijuana was being grown [*Oliver* v. *United States*, 466 U.S. 170 (1984)]. And, in a pair of five-to-four decisions rendered on the same day in 1986, the Court ruled that the "open fields exception" covered aerial surveillance where the evidence in question, al-

---

[7] Kenneth Culp Davis, 1 *Administrative Law Treatise* 258 (2nd ed., 1978).

though not within buildings, was behind walls or fences. One case involved monitoring pollution from an industrial plant, and the other concerned aerial surveillance of a marijuana garden in the fenced-in yard of a private home.[8]

More recently, the Supreme Court has continued to hand down rulings regarding subpoenas and physical inspections. In the former category, the Supreme Court in *Baltimore Department of Social Services* v. *Bouknight*, 493 U.S. 549 (1990), rejected a claim of Fifth Amendment privilege by a mother who had refused to comply with a juvenile court order to turn over a child in her custody. And, in two 1989 cases involving searches of individuals, *Skinner* v. *Railway Labor Executives' Association,* 489 U.S. 602, and *National Treasury Employees Union* v. *Von Raab*, 489 U.S. 656, the Court upheld the use of warrantless blood and urine testing for railroad crews after major accidents and for employees of the Customs Service seeking transfer or promotion to sensitive positions involving drug interdiction or the use of firearms, respectively.[9]

A roughly contemporaneous case to those noted immediately above, *New York* v. *Burger* (1987), provides an illustration of just how far the Supreme Court has been leaning toward the *Colonnade-Biswell* line of cases as opposed to that of *Camara, See*, and *Barlow's*. In dissent, Justice Brennan argues that the Court has rendered meaningless the "general rule that a warrant is required for administrative searches of commercial property" and that "*See* has been constructively overruled."

New York v. Burger

Supreme Court of the United States, 1987.
482 U.S. 691, 107 S.Ct. 2636, 96 L.Ed. 2d 601.

[At issue in this case was a New York statute that authorized warrantless inspections of junkyards. After the police officers ascertained that the owner had neither a license nor the "police book," a required record of the automobile and vehicle parts in his possession, they announced their intention to inspect the property, and the owner did not object. In the ensuing inspection, stolen automobiles and vehicle parts were discovered, and Burger was charged with multiple counts of possession of stolen property and one count of operating as a vehicle dismantler without a license. The state trial court rejected the owner's motion to suppress the evidence obtained as a result of the investigation and upheld the statute. After an unsuccessful reargument, the intermediate appellate court affirmed; however, the New York Court of Appeals reversed on the grounds that Section 415-a5 of the statute, authorizing the warrantless inspection, was in violation of the Fourth Amendment's unreasonable search and seizure provision. Because of

---

[8] *Dow Chemical* v. *United States*, 476 U.S. 227 (1986), and *California* v. *Ciraola*, 476 U.S. 207 (1986), respectively.

[9] The Supreme Court held in 2001 in *Ferguson* v. *City of Charleston*, 532 U.S. 67, that an involuntary urine test designed to obtain evidence of state hospital maternity patients' cocaine use is an unreasonable search in violation of the Fourth Amendment.

the important state interest in administrative schemes regulating the junkyard industry, the Court granted certiorari.]

Justice BLACKMUN delivered the opinion of the Court.

This case presents the question whether the warrantless search of an automobile junkyard, conducted pursuant to a statute authorizing such a search, falls within the exception to the warrant requirement for administrative inspections of pervasively regulated industries. The case also presents the question whether an otherwise proper administrative inspection is unconstitutional because the ultimate purpose of the regulatory statute pursuant to which the search is done— the deterrence of criminal behavior—is the same as that of penal laws, with the result that the inspection may disclose violations not only of the regulatory statute but also of the penal statutes. . . .

An expectation of privacy in commercial premises . . . is different from, and indeed less than, a similar expectation in an individual's home. See *Donovan* v. *Dewey*, 452 U.S. 594, 598–599 (1981). This expectation is particularly attenuated in commercial property employed in "closely regulated" industries. The Court observed in *Marshall* v. *Barlow's, Inc.*: "Certain industries have such a history of government oversight that no reasonable expectation of privacy could exist for a proprietor over the stock of such an enterprise." 436 U.S. 313. . . .

Because the owner or operator of commercial premises in a "closely regulated" industry has a reduced expectation of privacy, the warrant and probable-cause requirements, which fulfill the traditional Fourth Amendment standard of reasonableness for a government search . . . have lessened application in this context. Rather, we conclude that, as in other situations of "special need," . . . where the privacy interests of the owner are weakened and the government interests in regulating particular businesses are concomitantly heightened, a warrantless inspection of commercial premises may well be reasonable within the meaning of the Fourth Amendment.

This warrantless inspection, however, even in the context of a pervasively regulated business, will be deemed to be reasonable only so long as three criteria are met. First, there must be a "substantial" government interest that informs the regulatory scheme pursuant to which the inspection is made. See *Donovan* v. *Dewey*, 452 U.S., at 602 ("substantial federal interest in improving the health and safety conditions in the Nation's underground and surface mines"); *United States* v. *Biswell*, 406 U.S. 315 (regulation of firearms is "of central importance to federal efforts to prevent violent crime and to assist States in regulating the firearms traffic within their borders"); *Colonnade Corp.* v. *United States*, 397 U.S. 75 (federal interest in "protecting the revenue against various types of fraud").

Second, the warrantless inspections must be "necessary to further [the] regulatory scheme." . . . For example, in Dewey we recognized that forcing mine inspectors to obtain a warrant before every inspection might alert mine owners or operators to the impending inspection, thereby frustrating the purposes of the Mine Safety and Health Act—to detect and thus to deter safety and health violations. . . .

Finally, "the statute's inspection program, in terms of the certainty and regularity of its application, [must] provid[e] a constitutionally adequate substitute for a warrant." . . . In other words, the regulatory statute must perform the two basic functions of a warrant: it must advise the owner of the commercial premises that the search is being made pursuant to the law and has a properly defined scope, and it must limit the discretion of the inspecting officers. . . . To perform this first function, the statute must be "sufficiently comprehensive and defined that the owner of commercial property cannot help but be aware that his property will be subject to periodic inspections undertaken for specific purposes." [*Donovan* v. *Dewey*, 452 U.S. at 600]. In addition, in defining how a statute limits the discretion of the inspectors, we have observed that it must be "carefully limited in time, place, and scope." *United States* v. *Biswell*, 406 U.S., at 315. . . .

Searches made pursuant to § 415-a5, in our view, clearly fall within this established exception to the warrant requirement for administrative inspections in "closely regulated" businesses. First, the nature of the regulatory statute reveals that the operation of a junkyard, part of which is devoted to vehicle dismantling, is a "closely regulated" business in the State of New York. The provisions regulating the activity of vehicle dismantling are extensive. An operator cannot engage in this industry without first obtaining a license, which means that he must meet the registration requirements and must pay a fee. Under § 415-a5(a), the operator must maintain a police book recording the acquisition and disposition of motor vehicles and vehicle parts, and make such records and inventory available for inspection by the police or any agent of the Department of Motor Vehicles. The operator also must display his registration number prominently at his place of business, on business documentation, and on vehicles and parts that pass through his business. . . . Moreover, the person engaged in this activity is subject to criminal penalties, as well as to loss of license or civil fines, for failure to comply with these provisions. . . .

Accordingly, in light of the regulatory framework governing his business and the history of regulation of related industries, an operator of a junkyard engaging

in vehicle dismantling has a reduced expectation of privacy in this "closely regulated" business. . . .

The New York regulatory scheme satisfies the three criteria necessary to make reasonable warrantless inspections pursuant to § 415-a5. . . .

A search conducted pursuant to § 415-a5, therefore, clearly falls within the well-established exception to the warrant requirement for administrative inspections of "closely regulated" businesses. The Court of Appeals, nevertheless, struck down the statute as violative of the Fourth Amendment because, in its view, the statute had no truly administrative purpose but was "designed simply to give the police an expedient means of enforcing penal sanctions for possession of stolen property." . . . The court rested its conclusion that the administrative goal of the statute was pretextual and that § 415-a5 really "authorize[d] searches undertaken solely to uncover evidence of criminality" particularly on the fact that, even if an operator failed to produce his police book, the inspecting officers could continue their inspection for stolen vehicles and parts. . . . The court also suggested that the identity of the inspectors—police officers—was significant in revealing the true nature of the statutory scheme. [67 N.Y. 2d 338 at 344–345, 493 N.E. 2d 926, at 929–930.]

In arriving at this conclusion, the Court of Appeals failed to recognize that a State can address a major social problem *both by* way of an administrative scheme and through penal sanctions. . . .

In *United States* v. *Biswell*, we recognized this fact that both administrative and penal schemes can serve the same purposes by observing that the ultimate purposes of the Gun Control Act were "to prevent violent crime and to assist the States in regulating the firearms traffic within their borders." . . .

This case, too, reveals that an administrative scheme may have the same ultimate purpose as penal laws, even if its regulatory goals are narrower. As we have explained above, New York, like many States, faces a serious social problem in automobile theft and has a substantial interest in regulating the vehicle-dismantling industry because of this problem. The New York penal laws address automobile theft by punishing it or the possession of stolen property, including possession by individuals in the business of buying and selling property. . . . In accordance with its interest in regulating the automobile-junkyard industry, the State also has devised a regulatory manner of dealing with this problem. Section 415-a, as a whole, serves the regulatory goals of seeking to ensure that vehicle dismantlers are legitimate businesspersons and that stolen vehicles and vehicle parts passing through automobile junkyards can be identified. . . .

Finally, we fail to see any constitutional significance in the fact that police officers, rather than "administrative" agents, are permitted to conduct the § 415-a5 inspection. The significance respondent alleges lies in the role of police officers as enforcers of the penal laws and in the officers' power to arrest for offenses other than violations of the administrative scheme. It is, however, important to note that state police officers, like those in New York, have numerous duties in addition to those associated with traditional police work. . . . As a practical matter, many States do not have the resources to assign the enforcement of a particular administrative scheme to a specialized agency. So long as a regulatory scheme is properly administrative, it is not rendered illegal by the fact that the inspecting officer has the power to arrest individuals for violations other than those created by the scheme itself. In sum, we decline to impose upon the States the burden of requiring the enforcement of their regulatory statutes to be carried out by specialized agents. . . .

Accordingly, the judgment of the New York Court of Appeals is reversed, and the case is remanded to that court for further proceedings not inconsistent with this opinion.

It is so ordered.

Justice BRENNAN, with whom Justice MARSHALL joins, and with whom Justice O'CONNOR joins as to all but Part III, dissenting.

Warrantless inspections of pervasively regulated businesses are valid if necessary to further an urgent state interest, and if authorized by a statute that carefully limits their time, place, and scope. I have no objection to this general rule. Today, however, the Court finds pervasive regulation in the barest of administrative schemes. Burger's vehicle-dismantling business is not closely regulated (unless most New York City businesses are), and an administrative warrant therefore was required to search it. The Court also perceives careful guidance and control of police discretion in a statute that is patently insufficient to eliminate the need for a warrant. Finally, the Court characterizes as administrative a search for evidence of only criminal wrongdoing. As a result, the Court renders virtually meaningless the general rule that a warrant is required for administrative searches of commercial property. . . .

In sum, if New York City's administrative scheme renders the vehicle-dismantling business closely regulated, few businesses will escape such a finding. Under these circumstances, the warrant requirement is the exception not the rule, and *See* has been constructively overruled. . . .

The implications of the Court's opinion, if realized, will virtually eliminate Fourth Amendment protection of commercial entities in the context of administrative searches. No State may require, as a condition of doing business, a blanket submission to warrantless searches for any purpose. I respectfully dissent.

Finally, we examine a 1984 case that combines some of the features of the two major subjects of this chapter, the use of the subpoena power and the administrative entry onto private premises. Justice Rehnquist's short opinion for a unanimous Court cites and discusses several of the important precedents covered previously in this chapter. Thus, *Donovan* v. *Lone Steer, Inc.* provides a fitting conclusion to the chapter's broader issues.

Donovan v. *Lone Steer, Inc.*

SUPREME COURT OF THE UNITED STATES, 1984.
464 U.S. 408, 104 S.Ct. 769, 78 L.Ed. 2d 567.

Justice REHNQUIST delivered the opinion of the Court.

Section 11(a) of the Fair Labor Standards Act of 1938 (FLSA or Act) . . . authorizes the Secretary of Labor to investigate and gather data regarding wages, hours, and other conditions of employment to determine whether an employer is violating the Act. Section 9 of the FLSA . . . empowers the Secretary of Labor to subpoena witnesses and documentary evidence relating to any matter under investigation. Pursuant to those provisions, an official of the Department of Labor served an administrative subpoena duces tecum on an employee of appellee Lone Steer, Inc., a motel and restaurant located in Steele, N. D. The subpoena directed an officer or agent of appellee with personal knowledge of appellee's records to appear at the Wage and Hour Division of the United States Department of Labor in Bismarck, N. D., and to produce certain payroll and sales records. In an action filed by appellee to challenge the validity of the subpoena, the District Court for the District of North Dakota held that, although the Secretary of Labor had complied with the applicable provisions of the FLSA in issuing the subpoena, enforcement of the subpoena would violate the Fourth Amendment of the United States Constitution because the Secretary had not previously obtained a judicial warrant. We noted probable jurisdiction of the Secretary's appeal . . . and we now reverse the judgment of the District Court.

On January 6, 1982, Al Godes, a Compliance Officer with the Wage and Hour Division of the Department of Labor, telephoned Susann White, appellee's manager, to inform her that he intended to begin an investigation of appellee the following morning and to request that she have available for inspection payroll records for all employees for the past two years. White telephoned Godes later that day to inform him that it would not be convenient to conduct the inspection on the following morning. After some preliminary skirmishing between the parties, during which appellee inquired about the scope and reason for the proposed investigation and appellants declined to provide specific information, Godes and Gerald Hill, Assistant Area Director from the Wage and Hour Division in Denver, arrived at appellee's premises on February 2, 1982, for the purpose of conducting the investigation. After waiting for White, Godes served the administrative subpoena at issue here on one of appellee's other employees. The subpoena was directed to any employee of appellee having custody and personal knowledge of the records specifically described therein, records which appellee was required by law to maintain. . . . The subpoena directed the employee to appear with those records at the Wage and Hour Division of the Department of Labor in Bismarck, N. D.

Appellee refused to comply with the subpoena and sought declaratory and injunctive relief in the District Court, claiming that the subpoena constituted an unlawful search and seizure in violation of the Fourth Amendment. . . . Relying on our decision in *Marshall* v. *Barlow's, Inc.* . . . (1978) . . . the District Court held that the applicable provisions of the FLSA violate the Fourth Amendment insofar as they authorize the Secretary of Labor to issue an administrative subpoena without previously having obtained a judicial warrant. In *Barlow's* this Court declared unconstitutional the provisions of the Occupational Safety and Health Act of 1970 (OSHA) which authorized inspectors to enter an employer's premises without a warrant to conduct inspections of work areas. The District Court rejected appellants' arguments that *Barlow's* is not dispositive of the issue here by stating:

> . . . The reasoning of the Supreme Court in *Barlow's* applies with equal—if not greater—force in the instant situation.
>
> In sum, I hold that the Secretary of Labor may not proceed to enter upon the premises of Lone Steer, Inc., for the purpose of inspecting its records under SECTION 11 of the Fair Labor Standards Act without first having obtained a valid warrant. . . .

We think that the District Court undertook to decide a case not before it when it held that appellants may not "enter upon the premises" of appellee to inspect its records without first having obtained a warrant. The only "entry" upon appellee's premises by appellants, so far as the record discloses, is that of Godes on February 2, 1982, when he and Gerald Hill entered the motel and restaurant to attempt to conduct an investigation. The stipulation of facts entered into by the parties, . . . and incorporated into the opinion of the District Court. . . . Statement 2a-8a, describe what happened next:

> They asked for Ms. White and were told she was not available but expected shortly. They were offered some coffee, and waited in the lobby area. After 20–30 minutes, when Ms. White had not appeared, Mr. Godes served an Administrative Subpoena Duces Tecum on employee Karen Arnold. . . .

An entry into the public lobby of a motel and restaurant for the purpose of serving an administrative subpoena is scarcely the sort of governmental act which is forbidden by the Fourth Amendment. The administrative subpoena itself did not authorize either entry or inspection of appellee's premises; it merely directed appellee to produce relevant wage and hour records at appellants' regional office some 25 miles away.

The governmental actions which required antecedent administrative warrants in *Marshall* v. *Barlow's, Inc.* . . . and *Camara* v. *Municipal Court* . . . (1967), are quite different from th governmental action in this case. In *Barlow's* an OSHA inspector sought to conduct a search of nonpublic working areas of an electrical and plumbing installation business. In *Camara* a San Francisco housing inspector sought to inspect the premises of an apartment building in that city. See also *See* v. *City of Seattle*, 387 U.S. 541 (1967) (involving a similar search by a fire inspector of commercial premises). In each case, this Court held that an administrative warrant was required before such a search could be conducted without the consent of the owner of the premises.

It is plain to us that those cases turned upon the effort of the government inspectors to make nonconsensual entries into areas not open to the public. As we have indicated, no such entry was made by appellants in this case. Thus the enforceability of the administrative subpoena duces tecum at issue here is governed, not by our decision in *Barlow's* as the District Court concluded, but rather by our decision in *Oklahoma Press Publishing Co.* v. *Walling*, 327 U.S. 186 (1946). In *Oklahoma Press* the Court rejected an employer's claim that the subpoena power conferred upon the Secretary of Labor by the FLSA violates the Fourth Amendment.

> The short answer to the Fourth Amendment objections is that the records in these cases present no question of actual search and seizure, but raise only the question whether orders of court for the production of specified records have been validly made; and no sufficient showing appears to justify setting them aside. No officer or other person has sought to enter petitioners' premises against their will, to search them, or to seize or examine their books, records or papers without their assent, otherwise than pursuant to orders of court authorized by law and made after adequate opportunity to present objections. . . . 327 U.S. 195 (footnotes omitted).

We cited *Oklahoma Press* with approval in *See* v. *City of Seattle*, . . . a companion case to *Camara*, and described the constitutional requirements for administrative subpoenas as follows:

> It is now settled that, when an administrative agency subpoenas corporate books or records, the Fourth Amendment requires that the subpoena be sufficiently limited in scope, relevant in purpose, and specific in

directive so that compliance will not be unreasonably burdensome. . . . *See* v. *City of Seattle*, 387 U.S. at 544 (footnote omitted).

See also *United States* v. *Morton Salt Co.*, 338 U.S. 632, 652-653 (1950).

Thus although our cases make it clear that the Secretary of Labor may issue an administrative subpoena without a warrant, they nonetheless provide protection for a subpoenaed employer by allowing him to question the reasonableness of the subpoena, before suffering any penalties for refusing to comply with it, by raising objections in an action in district court. *See* v. *City of Seattle*, supra, at 544-545; *Oklahoma Press*, supra, at 208-209. . . . Our holding here, which simply reaffirms our holding in *Oklahoma Press*, in no way leaves an employer defenseless against an unreasonably burdensome administrative subpoena requiring the production of documents. We hold only that the defenses available to an employer do not include the right to insist upon a judicial warrant as a condition precedent to a valid administrative subpoena.

Appellee insists that "[the] official inspection procedure used by the appellants [reveals] that the use of the administrative subpoena is inextricably intertwined with the entry process," . . . and states that it is appellants' established policy to seek entry inspections by expressly relying on its inspection authority under § 11 of the FLSA. . . . We need only observe that no nonconsensual entry into protected premises was involved in this case.

The judgment of the District Court is accordingly reversed.

Chapter 6

Rules and Rule Making

THE UNITED STATES QUICKLY AMENDS A RULE

Six days after the terrorist attacks on the World Trade Center and the Pentagon on September 11, 2001, the Immigration and Naturalization Service (INS) moved to tighten its control over certain noncitizens. This was the first in a series of moves by the Bush administration aimed at rewriting immigration and surveillance laws in the wake of the tragedy. The INS's specific action was to adopt an "interim rule" relating to the custody of aliens arrested by the agency. Below, set forth side by side, are the old rule on this subject (on the left) and the new provision, adopted on September 17, 2001 (on the right). The crucial addition in the new rule is printed in italics. The original version of the rule was published in Title 8 of the *Code of Federal Regulations* (CFR), Part 287.3, and the revision appeared in the *Federal Register* (FR) on September 20, 2001 (Volume 66, number 183, pages 48334–48335).

Code of Federal Regulations *Title 8—Aliens and Nationality* *[Version in effect until* *September 17, 2001]*	*Code of Federal Regulations* *Title 8—Aliens and Nationality* *[Version in effect from* *September 17, 2001]*
§287.3 Disposition of cases of aliens arrested without warrant . . . (d) Custody Procedures. Unless voluntary departure has been granted pursuant to subpart C of 8 CFR part 240, a determination will be made within 24 hours of the arrest whether the alien will be continued in custody or released on bond or recognizance	§287.3 Disposition of cases of aliens arrested without warrant . . . (d) Custody Procedures. Unless voluntary departure has been granted pursuant to subpart C of 8 CFR part 240, a determination will be made within *48 hours of the arrest, except in the event of an emergency or other extraordinary circumstance in which case*

and whether a notice to appear and warrant of arrest . . . will be issued.	*a determination will be made within an additional reasonable period of time,* whether the alien will be continued in custody or released on bond or recognizance and whether a notice to appear and warrant of arrest . . . will be issued.

As noted, the document just quoted from (in its earlier and later versions) is a *rule*. It was adopted not by the popularly elected Congress but by an administrative agency headed by an appointed official. Yet the rule has the force of law, and its effect on persons to whom it applies could be significant. Rules (or *regulations*—the terms are used interchangeably in this context) constitute an important part of the corpus of American law. Regulations (and in fact all actions of administrative agencies) rest on grants of authority from the legislature. We already know from chapter 3 that the legislative language giving an administrative agency the authority to act (the delegation) may be fairly detailed and specific, or it may be rather vague and open ended.

Regarding arresting and holding aliens, §1357 of Title 8 of the U.S. Code is the relevant provision. It gives officials of the INS the power to maintain custody over aliens for a number of reasons, such as suspicion of illegal entry into the United States or belief that an alien has committed a felony. According to the statute, this authority is to be exercised "under regulations prescribed by the Attorney General." Accordingly, a regulation has been adopted allowing the attorney general to delegate certain powers to the commissioner of the INS. Under this regulation, the "Commissioner may issue regulations as deemed necessary or appropriate for the exercise of any authority delegated to him by the Attorney General, and may redelegate any such authority to any other officer or employee of the Service."[1]

What we see here, then, is an example not only of delegation but also of subdelegation. Congress delegated authority to the attorney general, who redelegated it to the commissioner of immigration and naturalization, who in turn passed it on to subordinate officers and employees. There was a time when subdelegations of this kind were considered constitutionally suspect. But in recent years both the courts and commentators have come to accept subdelegation more readily, understanding that not all important functions of an agency can be performed by its head. As a leading commentator on the subject has observed, "subdelegation has become a mainstay of government operation."[2]

This is not to suggest, however, that the new rule described in this section will not be subject to challenge. A careful reading of the September 17, 2001, revision indicates that the period of custody of aliens arrested under this provision has not been raised just from twenty-four to forty-eight hours. It may extend for a longer time "in the event of an emergency or other extraordinary circumstance." This part of the rule was brought into effect by

---

[1] 8 CFR 2.1.

[2] Richard J. Pierce, Jr., 1 *Administrative Law Treatise* 112 (4th ed., 2002).

President Bush's emergency and major disaster declarations with regard to parts of Virginia and New York almost immediately after the attacks.[3]

But courts have been wary about granting the government too much power under the statutory provision on which the rule is based. And a number of commentators, including some within Congress, have expressed the view that holding an alien for an indefinite period without bringing charges exceeds the bounds of what the statute intended.

Another notable point regarding this regulation is that it is designated as interim. This means that the rule takes immediate effect rather than going through the usual procedure of notice and public comment before promulgation. In adopting the rule, the commissioner of the INS cited the foreign affairs and good cause exceptions of Section 553 of the APA to justify this designation.[4] These provisions allow expedited rule-making procedures that forgo the steps normally prescribed in the law. In a statement accompanying the rule, the commissioner called for an after-the-fact public comment period of two months from the time of the rule's effective date. The adoption of interim rules and the use of other types of rule making that depart from the basic provisions of § 553 of the APA will be discussed below.

Interim regulation

RULES IN GENERAL

For most purposes an administrative rule can be distinguished from an administrative adjudicatory decision in two ways. First, a rule generally has future effect while a decision applies to a factual situation. And second, a rule is a statement of general applicability while a decision applies to an individual or a small number of parties. These distinctions operate satisfactorily in most cases and reflect the general understanding of the differences between the two terms. Some administrative activities confound this basic classification, however. For instance, a licensing proceeding or the issuing of an injunction typically applies to individual parties but can be said to have future effect. Yet both clearly fall into the category of adjudicatory proceedings.

Rule

The most well-known statutory definitions of rules only partially embrace the two characteristics mentioned above. The Model State Administrative Procedure Act emphasizes the general nature of a rule by stating that the term "means the whole or part of an agency statement of *general* applicability that implements, interprets, or prescribes (i) law or policy, or (ii) the organization, procedure, or practice requirements of an agency [emphasis added]."[5] The federal APA stresses the prospective nature of a rule by defining it as "the whole or a part of an agency statement of *general or particular applicability and future effect* designed to implement, interpret

Def. Rule.

---

[3] 66 FR 48683 (September 21, 2001).

[4] See §§ 553 (a) 1, (b) (B), and (d) of the APA in Appendix B.

[5] 14 *Uniform Laws Annotated* § 1–102 (10). *1985 Cumulative Annual Pocket Part* (emphasis added). The Uniform Law Commissioners' Model State Administrative Procedure Act (1981) is also available online at http://www2.law.cornell.edu/cgi-bin/foliocgi.exe/stateapa/query=/doc/{t1}.

[handwritten margin note: Rules vs. decisions]

or prescribe policy [emphasis added]. . . ."[6] In spite of these definitional inconsistencies, however, it is clear that most administrative regulations are designed to have both prospective effect and general applicability.

The distinction between rules and decisions is not unimportant. Significant procedural differences have traditionally been associated with the processes by which these two kinds of acts are adopted. We will take up that matter in the discussion of rule making.

Three Kinds of Rules

[handwritten margin note: 3 kinds rules 1) procedural 2) interpretive 3) legislative]

It is generally said that there are three kinds of rules: procedural, interpretive, and legislative (or substantive). Procedural rules have caused little difficulty for analysts. They are internal "housekeeping" types of rules adopted by the agency to guide it in the procedures it will follow in carrying out its duties. If an agency fails to follow one of its procedural rules (even if it was not required to adopt such rules), its decision based on that faulty action may be reversed by a court. Thus, for instance, when the secretary of state discharged a foreign service officer without following the state department's regulation that such decisions "shall be reached after consideration of the complete file, arguments, briefs, and testimony presented," a unanimous Supreme Court reversed the secretary's action [*Service* v. *Dulles* 354 U.S. 363 (1957)].

[handwritten margin note: Procedural – Housekeeping rules to guide its procedures]

Procedural rules may be contested by parties regulated by administrative agencies, as a 1994 case involving the Federal Communications Commission (FCC) illustrates. Section 553 of the APA provides that "rules of organization, procedure or practice" are exempt from notice and comment requirements. The FCC adopted stringent rules regarding applications for FM station licenses; the rules established a fixed filing period and required "substantial completeness" for all applications. The rules were published in the *Federal Register* but without prior notice or the opportunity for comment. After Jem Broadcasting Company's application was rejected as incomplete, Jem sued the FCC, asserting that the rule should have been adopted only after notice and comment. The Court of Appeals rejected Jem's contention, holding that the FCC rule "fall[s] comfortably within the realm of the procedural" [*Jem Broadcasting* v. *Federal Communications Commission*, 22 F.3d 320 (1994)].

More difficult to deal with are legislative and interpretive rules. Distinguishing these two types of rules is not always easy, but important legal consequences depend on which category rules are seen to fall into. The recognition of a difference between the two types of rules has been traced back to the 1920s. The early view was that legislative rules were only "those promulgated pursuant to a *specific* delegation of rule-making power."[7] More recently, commentators have been divided on the issue, some holding that

---

[6] Section 551 (4), emphasis added. See Appendix B of this book. The original draft of the APA limited the definition of rules to "statements of general applicability." The change of language was made to assure that rule making could, when necessary, be addressed to named persons. See Bernard Schwartz, *Administrative Law* 166 (3rd ed., 1991).

[7] Michael Asimow, "Public Participation in the Adoption of Interpretive Rules and Policy Statements," 75 *Michigan Law Review* 520, 561 (1977), emphasis in the original.

legislative permission to adopt legislative-type rules can be implicit,[8] while others insist that at least a general grant of rule-making authority must be found in the statute.[9] In any case, legislative rules are akin to statutes in their legal effect; they "receive statutory force upon going into effect," as the Attorney General's Committee's *Final Report* put it.[10] They are said to have the force of law, and courts are not supposed to substitute their judgment on the wisdom of such rules.

Interpretive rules, on the other hand, are considered merely the agency's interpretation of the statute. They do not supplement the statute or prescribe conduct under a grant from the legislature. While such rules do not bind a court, they are entitled to some weight. As the important case of *Skidmore* v. *Swift Co.* put it, they "do constitute a body of experience and informed judgment to which courts and litigants may properly resort for guidance" [323 U.S. 134 L.Ed. 124 (1944)].

Another distinction between interpretive and legislative rules involves the procedures by which they are adopted. The notice and comment provisions of §553 of the APA do not apply to interpretative rules (most commentators now use the term *interpretive rules*), although both substantive and interpretive rules of general applicability must be published in the *Federal Register*.

One of the problems with the legislative-interpretive dichotomy has been the difficulty, in concrete cases, of distinguishing the two, a problem that is heightened by the increase in rule making at the federal level in recent years. Rules are not always labeled legislative or interpretive by the issuing agency, and even when they are, some courts have found that the labels given are not reliable.

In connection with this point, a number of guidelines have been offered regarding the matter of categorizing rules. The so-called legal effect standard either accepts the agency's label for its rules or attempts otherwise to determine whether the agency has a clear legislative mandate to adopt such rules. The "substantial impact" test pays less attention to the labels attached to rules, including those provided by the agency. Rather, it considers whether the regulation in question will have a substantial impact on the persons who will be affected by it. If it will, then § 553 of the APA, requiring notice and comment, must be applied. Those courts using the substantial impact test are saying, in effect, "If the regulation will have a substantial impact, it is a substantive rule, no matter what it is called by the agency." It should be said, however, that neither of these tests has proved fully satisfactory in practice. They both present problems in their application to specific fact situations, and their merit continues to be debated by scholars.[11]

---

[8] William F. West, *Administrative Rulemaking: Politics and Processes* 43 (1985); Alfred C. Aman, Jr., and William T. Mayton, *Administrative Law* 83 (2nd ed., 2001).

[9] Pierce 1, above, note 2, 327.

[10] As quoted in Manning Gilbert Warren III, "The Notice Requirement in Administrative Rulemaking: An Analysis of Legislative and Interpretive Rules," 29 *Administrative Law Review* 367, 372 (1977).

[11] See Michael Asimow, "Nonlegislative Rulemaking and Regulatory Reform," 1985 *Duke Law Journal* 381 (1985); Robert A. Anthony, "'Interpretive' Rules, 'Legislative' Rules and 'Spurious' Rules:

The following case, decided at the court of appeals level, involves what the U.S. Park Service designated an interpretive rule. In its decision the court avoided both the substantial impact and the legal effect language. Rather, it asked whether the rule in question created law or merely clarified existing law. In looking at the issue in this way, the court gave little deference to the agency's categorization of the rule. Note also that the rule in question in this case supplemented a bona fide legislative regulation, adopted pursuant to the notice and comment provisions of § 553 of the APA.

United States v. Picciotto

UNITED STATES COURT OF APPEALS FOR THE DISTRICT OF COLUMBIA, 1989.
875 F.2d 345.

[Concepcion Picciotto engaged in an around-the-clock vigil on the sidewalk adjacent to Lafayette Park, across the street from the White House in Washington, D.C., in order to publicize the dangers of nuclear war. She was arrested for storing what was considered an excessive amount of property at the demonstration site. After being found guilty and sentenced to a suspended ten-day jail term and probation, she appealed. At issue in the case was a Park Service regulation regarding the storing of property in the park.]

OPINION BY: MIKVA . . . The Park Service has promulgated regulations governing activity in all national capital region parks, which include parks in the District of Columbia and parts of Virginia and Maryland. . . . Subsection (g) imposes certain restrictions on demonstrations and special events. Some of the restrictions apply to all parks in this area; some to specific parks. Lafayette Park is one of the sites for which specific restrictions have been adopted.

Subsection (g) also contains, in addition to defined regulations, an open-ended provision, as follows:

A permit may contain additional reasonable conditions and additional time limitations, consistent with this section, in the interest of protecting park resources, the use of nearby areas by other persons, and other legitimate park value concerns.

. . . This provision, along with the rest of § 7.96, was properly adopted pursuant to the APA's notice and comment requirements. . . .

The Regional Director of National Capital Parks adopted . . . a number of "additional conditions" that were made generally applicable to all demonstrators in Lafayette Park. Appellant was convicted for violating the first of these:

Property may not be stored in the Park, including, but not limited to construction materials, lumber, paint, tools, household items, food, tarps, bedding, luggage, and other personal property. (In this regard, certain personal property that is reasonably required by a demonstration participant during any one 24-hour period will not be considered to violate this permit condition. Such property may include items such as a coat, a thermos, and a small quantity of literature. However, the quantity of these items may not exceed that which is reasonably necessary in a 24-hour period.)

Appellant received a copy of these "additional conditions" from Supervisory Park Ranger Philip Walsh, but the Park Service did not publish a general notice of

Lifting the Smog," 8 *American University Administrative Law Journal* 1, esp. 16–20 (1994); Keith Werhan, "Delegalizing Administrative Law," 1996 *University of Illinois Law Review* 423, esp. 444–445 (1996).

proposed rulemaking in the Federal Register and neither appellant nor the general public was given an opportunity to comment.

The Park Service, like any other government agency, must conform to the APA's notice and comment requirements when engaging in any informal agency rulemaking procedures, unless properly relying on an exception. A rule which is subject to the APA's procedural requirements, but was adopted without them, is invalid. . . . Certainly, a criminal prosecution founded on an agency rule should be held to the strict letter of the APA.

The Park Service interprets clause 13 as granting it the authority to impose new substantive restrictions uniformly on all demonstrators in any national capital region park, without engaging in notice and comment procedures. It claims that since clause 13 went through notice and comment, the new restrictions do not need to. In essence, the Park Service is claiming that an agency can grant itself a valid exemption to the APA for all future regulations, and be free of APA's troublesome rulemaking procedures forever after, simply by announcing its independence in a general rule. That is not the law. Such agency-generated exemptions would frustrate Congress' underlying policy in enacting the APA by rendering compliance optional. The statute's direct mandate requires notice and comment procedures for any rule that does not fall within certain express exceptions. . . . The Park Service cannot construct its own veto of Congressional directions. . . .

Furthermore, the Park Service's reading of clause 13 is implausible as well as unlawful. The provision specifies that "a permit" may contain additional conditions and time limitations. By its own terms, the language allows the Park Service only to attach specific limitations to individual permits as part of its permit-granting procedure, not to adopt rules applicable to the general public. Since the APA does not specify procedures for informal agency decisions such as whether or not to permit a particular demonstration, the Park Service would not be acting inconsistently with the APA by announcing its procedures for approving permits on individualized terms. Thus the regulation, read as written, would not be inconsistent with the APA: the Park Service could adjust permits to the specific circumstances of individual demonstrations, but the limitations attached to any given permit would be reviewable under the APA's arbitrary and capricious standard. . . .

We need not, however, decipher the correct reading of clause 13. The agency is entitled ordinarily to construe its own regulation. . . . The issue before this court is whether a conviction based on a violation of the Lafayette Park storage rule, adopted pursuant to clause 13 but without notice and comment, can stand. We find that clause 13 does not provide a basis for upholding the conviction, because clause 13 either does not authorize the imposition of general rules such as the Lafayette Park storage restriction, or it attempts to and is therefore invalid.

The APA does provide for exemptions from its notice and comment requirements. But we note at the outset that the APA's notice and comment exemptions must be narrowly construed. . . .

The Park Service argues that the "additional conditions" are exempt as "interpretive," rather than "substantive" rules. . . . The task of differentiating between substantive and interpretive rules is not always an easy one; in general, substantive rules create law, whereas interpretive rules clarify existing law. This court has previously found agency rules explaining ambiguous terms in statutes and regulations to be interpretive. . . . We have also held rules that merely restate existing duties, rather than creating new duties, to be interpretive. . . . In contrast, we have found rules that grant rights and impose obligations to be substantive. . . .

[The Park Service's] publication of the rule calls it an "additional condition," and describes it and other additional conditions as adopted pursuant to both clause 13 and a rule permitting the regional director to limit sound amplification equipment. In contrast, an interpretive rule explains an existing requirement; it does not impose an "additional" one. . . . When the Park Service adopted a similarly site-specific, albeit stricter, regulation prohibiting storage of property on the sidewalks surrounding the White House, the Park Service adopted it as a substantive rule requiring notice and comment, not as an interpretive rule. . . .

We find this evidence persuasive that the Park Service intended the Lafayette Park storage rule as an independent substantive rule. A reviewing court need not classify a rule as interpretive just because the agency says that it is. . . . The fact that this rule establishes a criminal offense entailing possible imprisonment for the violator is even more reason for this court to be wary of the agency's last minute justifications.

The Park Service also argues that it did not include the storage rule when it engaged in notice and comment because it wanted to vary rules according to site. There is an exemption to the APA that permits an agency to promulgate a rule without notice and comment when the agency finds for "good cause" that the procedures are impracticable, unnecessary, or contrary to the public interest. . . . To come within that exemption, the agency must incorporate, in the rule issued, a statement explaining why it found good cause to omit those procedures. . . . Because the Park Service did not incorporate any such statement in the "additional conditions" that contained the Lafayette Park storage rule, we need not decide whether the Park Service had good cause to disregard APA procedures. We do note, however, that the Park Service's previous adoption of extensive and detailed site-specific regulations after notice and comment erects a high burden of persuasion. . . .

The rule that appellant was convicted of violating is a substantive regulation, subject to the APA's procedural requirements but adopted in their absence. Before a person is threatened with jail for such a violation, the government must ensure that the rule itself is not in violation of the law. The government cannot meet that burden in this case. Appellant's conviction is

Reversed.

RULE MAKING

As suggested above, different procedural requirements are associated with the adoption of rules on the one hand and adjudicatory decisions on the other. These differences have their roots in interpretations of the constitutional provisions guaranteeing due process of law made in the early part of the last century, specifically the two Supreme Court cases of *Londoner* v. *Denver*, 210 U.S. 373 (1908), and *Bi-Metallic Investment Co.* v. *State Board of Equalization*, 239 U.S. 441 (1915). The important 1973 case of *United States* v. *Florida East Coast Ry. Co.*, 410 U.S. 224, which will be discussed below, explains the significance of these two cases well. As Justice Rehnquist said for the majority:

The basic distinction between rulemaking and adjudication is illustrated by this court's treatment of two related cases under the Due Process Clause of the Fourteenth Amendment. In *Londoner* v. *Denver*, . . . the Court held that due process had not been accorded a landowner who objected to the amount assessed against his land as its share of the benefit resulting from the paving of a street. Local procedure had accorded him the right to file a written complaint and objection, but not to be heard orally. This Court held that due process of law required that he "have the right to support his allegations by argument, however brief; and, if need be, by proof, however informal." But in the later case of *Bi-Metallic Investment Co.* v. *State Board of Equalization* . . . , the Court held that no hearing at all was constitutionally required prior to a decision by state tax officers in Colorado to increase the valuation of all taxable property in Denver by a substantial percentage. The Court distinguished *Londoner* by stating that there a small number of persons "were exceptionally affected, in each case upon individual grounds."

Later decisions have continued to observe the distinction adverted to in *Bi-Metallic Investment Co.* . . .

The importance of these two old cases can hardly be exaggerated. They are said to have "introduced the modern era of administrative law."[12] And their basic thrust, that a hearing with oral participation will be required in adjudication but not in rule making, is the orthodox view on the matter to this day. Thus, for instance, the APA provides that rules may be adopted without oral participation by interested parties.[13]

Particularly in recent years, however, this simple distinction between rule making and adjudication has been increasingly challenged. A number of statutes applying to particular agencies provide for oral participation in rule making. And for a time lower courts sought to provide more than the minimum requirements of § 553. Moreover, some commentators believe that the distinction is no longer a satisfactory one in contemporary administrative law. We will return to this matter below.

Notice and Comment

Section 553 of the APA describes a general procedure for rule making. It also provides several exceptions to this procedure. The conventional method is typically referred to as notice and comment rule making and is found in parts b and c of § 553. The relevant passage of part b reads:

> (b) General notice of proposed rule making shall be published in the Federal Register, unless persons subject thereto are named and either personally served or otherwise have actual notice thereof in accordance with law. The notice shall include—
>
> (1) a statement of the time, place, and nature of public rule making proceedings;
>
> (2) reference to the legal authority under which the rule is proposed; and
>
> (3) either the terms or substance of the proposed rule or a description of the subjects and issues involved.

---

[12] Paul R. Verkuil, "The Emerging Concept of Administrative Procedure," 78 *Columbia Law Review* 258, 264 (1978).

[13] § 553(c).

After notice, the agency is required (under part c) to "give interested persons an opportunity to participate in the rule making through submission of written data, views or arguments with or without opportunity for oral participation." This period is followed by the adoption of the rule, with publication no less than thirty days before its effective date. Official notice is provided through publication in the *Federal Register*. This "legal newspaper," as it is called by its publisher, the National Archives and Records Administration, is published every business day. It has been in existence since 1936. Regulations of "general and permanent" importance are codified by subject in the *Code of Federal Regulations*, a publication containing fifty titles that is updated annually.[14] The *Federal Register* system was created by an act of Congress in 1935 when problems arose as a result of the absence of an official notice publication for administrative rules. Almost all states now have publications analogous to the *Federal Register* and *Code of Federal Regulations*.[15]

An unpublished regulation may be ruled by a court to have no legal effect. A relevant case is *Morton* v. *Ruiz* (1974).[16] The appellees, husband and wife, were members of an Indian tribe who lived off, but near, a reservation. The Bureau of Indian Affairs (BIA) denied them relief benefits, basing its decision on a BIA manual, in effect since 1952, that limited such assistance to Indians living on reservations. But the manual had never been published in the *Federal Register*, and the BIA in congressional appropriation hearings had made numerous representations to the effect that Native Americans living near reservations were eligible for BIA services. The unanimous decision of the Supreme Court was based on a number of considerations, but one of its reasons for ruling against the BIA was that a rule of this importance, affecting "substantial individual rights and obligations," should have been published in the *Federal Register*.

Exemptions to Notice and Comment and Other Rule-Making Procedures

As noted, § 553 contains several exemptions. The section opens by stating that it does not apply to:

(1) a military or foreign affairs function of the United States; or
    (2) a matter relating to agency management or personnel or to public property, loans, grants, benefits, or contracts.

Later the section indicates that the notice and comment provisions do not apply to "interpretative rules, general statements of policy, or rules of agency organization, procedure, or practice." In addition, § 553 allows agencies to dispense with notice for "good cause." To invoke this exemption, the agency must make a finding that regular procedures are "impracticable, unnecessary, or contrary to the public interest." As noted above, the Commis-

---

[14] "The Federal Register," http://www.nara.gov/fedreg/.

[15] "The Universal Legal Citation Project: A Draft User Guide to the AALL Universal Regulatory Citation," 90 *Law Library Journal* 509, 520 (1998). This source lists one state without a CFR equivalent and four states without an FR equivalent.

[16] 415 U.S. 199 (1974).

sioner of the INS invoked both the foreign affairs and the good cause exemptions in adopting the rule that increased the agency's authority with regard to holding arrested aliens. This was an interim rule, which allows for comment after the rule's promulgation. In situations of this kind, the interim rule can be seen as a practical compromise that allows quick action while also providing some level of public participation.[17]

Another species of expedited rule making is known as *direct final rule making*. Under this procedure, noncontroversial regulations, which would be likely to produce little or no critical comment, can be adopted without notice or comment under the good cause exemption. If significant adverse comment were to ensue after the rule's adoption, it could be withdrawn and the regular notice and comment procedure employed.[18]

Another innovation intended to streamline the administrative process is known as *negotiated rule making*. Under this procedure, issues in dispute in a rule-making proposal are subjected to negotiation by interested parties. In 1990 Congress enacted two statutes[19] that support this procedure, which has come to be called *Reg-Neg*: The Negotiated Rulemaking Act of 1990[20] and the Administrative Dispute Resolution Act.[21] These statutes are codified as part of the APA, §§ 561–583. Judgments as to the effectiveness of Reg-Neg vary. The process appears to be more effective when a rule will have "only modest effects on a few interests," as one source put it,[22] but will be less likely to prove useful with a major rule, when many interests have a stake in the outcome. On the other hand, participants in Reg-Neg have generally reported high satisfaction with the process.[23] There is broad agreement that rules for which Reg-Neg is employed are likely to constitute only a small percentage of the total number of regulations adopted at the federal level.

Informal and Formal Rule Making

As noted, the procedure discussed above for adopting regulations under § 553 of the APA is often called notice and comment rule making because of the provision that allows exclusion of oral participation in the process. This procedure is also termed *informal rule making*, to distinguish it from more formal rule-making arrangements envisaged in another part of § 553:

---

[17] Michael Asimow, "Interim-Final Rules: Making Haste Slowly," 51 *Administrative Law Review* 703 (1999); Pierce 1, above, note 2, 509.

[18] Ronald M. Levin, "Direct Final Rulemaking, 64 *George Washington Law Review* 1 (1995); Lars Noah, "Doubts about Direct Final Rulemaking," 51 *Administrative Law Review* 401 (1999); Ronald M. Levin, "More on Direct Final Rulemaking: Streamlining, Not Corner-Cutting," 51 *Administrative Law Review* 757 (1999).

[19] Codified as part of the APA, §§ 561–583.

[20] 104 Stat. 4969.

[21] 104 Stat. 2736.

[22] Richard J. Pierce, Jr., Sidney A. Shapiro, and Paul R. Verkuil, *Administrative Law and Process* 335 (3rd ed., 1999).

[23] Cornelius M. Kerwin, *Rulemaking: How Government Agencies Write Law and Make Policy* 200–202 (3rd ed., 2003).

"When rules are required by statute to be made on the record after opportunity for agency hearing," this passage states, then §§ 556 and 557 of the APA will apply. These sections, which cover what are normally called adjudicatory hearings, provide for a good deal of formality in proceedings, including oral arguments, the right to submit rebuttal evidence, and the right to cross-examination.

A small number of federal statutes provide for on-the-record proceedings in rule making, but they are very much the exception rather than the rule. While it might be argued that these more formal proceedings provide interested parties a greater opportunity to present their views, the costs, both in person-hours of agency time and in slowness of policy making, can be considerable. Professor Robert W. Hamilton's study of on-the-record rule making makes this point well. Although published three decades ago, it is still widely cited by commentators for the accuracy of its observations. Hamilton succinctly summarizes the results of sixteen on-the-record hearings held by the Food and Drug Administration in the 1960s. He says they varied from "unnecessarily drawn out proceedings to virtual disasters":

> In not one instance did the agency complete a rulemaking proceeding involving a hearing in less than two years, and in two instances more than ten years elapsed between the first proposal and the final order. The *average* time lapse was roughly four years. The hearings themselves tended to be drawn out, repetitious and unproductive. The *Foods for Special Dietary Uses* hearing consumed over 200 days of testimony and amassed a transcript of more than 32,000 pages. Most of the hearing was devoted to cross examination of expert government witnesses. Another proceeding involving the standard identity for peanut butter developed a transcript of over 7,700 pages, largely directed to the question of whether the product peanut butter should consist of 90 percent or 89½ percent peanuts.[24]

As might be expected, formal rule making of this kind is widely condemned by commentators.[25] In recent years there has been some support for a middle ground between the basic notice and comment provisions of § 553 (informal rule making) and the trial-type procedures just discussed (formal rule making). What has been referred to as *hybrid* or *553-plus* rule making allows some level of oral participation to interested parties. Occasionally agencies themselves will provide further procedural steps, such as limited cross-examination. And for a time some courts imposed rule-making procedures beyond those required by § 553. As will be shown below, however, judicial action of this kind has been specifically rejected by the Supreme Court in the *Vermont Yankee* case. Congress may authorize additional rule-making procedures for individual agencies, and has done so on a number of occasions. Assessments of the utility of such hybrid procedures have so far not been very positive.[26]

---

[24] Robert W. Hamilton, "Procedures for the Adoption of Rules of General Applicability: The Need for Procedural Innovations in Administrative Rule-making," 60 *California Law Review* 1278, 1287–88 (1972).

[25] See, for instance, Pierce 1, above, note 2, 416, who asserts that the procedure "simply does not work."

[26] See, e.g., Pierce, Shapiro, and Verkuil, above, note 22, 342.

The Supreme Court's attitude with regard to rule making was clarified to a considerable extent in the last decades of the twentieth century. The Court made several important decisions supporting the adequacy of notice and comment rule making under § 553 and rejected efforts by lower courts to require, in the absence of specific statutory provisions, more-formal rule making proceedings. The following two cases illustrate this point.

United States v. Florida East Coast Ry. Co.

SUPREME COURT OF THE UNITED STATES, 1973.
410 U.S. 224, 93 S.Ct. 810, 35 L.Ed. 2d 223.

[The Interstate Commerce Act empowered the Interstate Commerce Commission (ICC) "after hearing" to establish "rules, regulations and practices" with regard to freight car service.[27] Traditionally the commission had accorded full trial-type hearings under this provision, but recently it had begun to use the less formal notice and comment proceedings. Acting under specific authority provided by a 1966 amendment to the ICC Act to cope with the shortage of rail cars, the commission had adopted "incentive per diem rates" for use by one railroad of freight cars owned by another. Two railroad companies moved to set aside the rates on the ground that the APA and the hearing provision of the Interstate Commerce Act required opportunity for greater participation than they had been accorded. The district court sustained the railroads' position and the case came to the Supreme Court.]

Mr. Justice REHNQUIST delivered the opinion of the Court. . . .

In *United States* v. *Allegheny-Ludlum Steel Corp.* [406 U.S. 742 (1972)], we held that the language of § 1 (14)(a) of the Interstate Commerce Act authorizing the Commission to act "after hearing" was not the equivalent of a requirement that a rule be made "on the record after opportunity for an agency hearing" as the latter term is used in § 553 (c) of the Administrative Procedure Act. Since the 1966 amendment to § 1 (14)(a), under which the Commission was here proceeding, does not by its terms add to the hearing requirement contained in the earlier language, the same result should obtain here unless that amendment contains language that is tantamount to such a requirement. Appellees contend that such language is found in the provisions of that Act requiring that:

> The Commission shall give consideration to the national level of ownership of such type of freight car and to other factors affecting the adequacy of the national freight car supply, and shall, on the basis of such consideration, determine whether compensation should be computed. . . .

While this language is undoubtedly a mandate to the Commission to consider the factors there set forth in reaching any conclusion as to imposition of per diem incentive charges, it adds to the hearing requirements of the section neither expressly nor by implication. We know of no reason to think that an administrative agency in reaching a decision cannot accord consideration to factors such as those set forth in the 1966 amendment by means other than a trial-type hearing or the presentation of oral argument by the affected parties. Congress by that amendment specified necessary components of the ultimate decision, but it did not spec-

[27] Section 1(14)(a).

ify the method by which the Commission should acquire information about those components. . . .

The term "hearing" in its legal context undoubtedly has a host of meanings. Its meaning undoubtedly will vary, depending on whether it is used in the context of a rulemaking-type proceeding or in the context of a proceeding devoted to the adjudication of particular disputed facts. It is by no means apparent what the drafters of the Esch Car Service Act of 1917 . . . which became the first part of § 1 (14)(a) of the Interstate Commerce Act, meant by the term. Such an intent would surely be an ephemeral one if, indeed, Congress in 1917 had in mind anything more specific than the language it actually used, for none of the parties refer to any legislative history that would shed light on the intended meaning of the words "after hearing." What is apparent, though, is that the term was used in granting authority to the Commission to make rules and regulations of a prospective nature. . . .

[C]onfronted with a grant of substantive authority made after the Administrative Procedure Act was enacted, we think that reference to that Act, in which Congress devoted itself exclusively to questions such as the nature and scope of hearings, is a satisfactory basis for determining what is meant by the term "hearing" used in another statute. Turning to that Act, we are convinced that the term "hearing" as used therein does not necessarily embrace either the right to present evidence orally and to cross-examine opposing witnesses, or the right to present oral argument to the agency's decisionmaker.

Section 553 excepts from its requirements rulemaking devoted to "interpretative rules, general statements of policy, or rules of agency organization, procedure, or practice," and rulemaking "when the agency for good cause finds . . . that notice and public procedure thereon are impracticable, unnecessary, or contrary to the public interest." This exception does not apply, however, "when notice or hearing is required by statute"; in those cases, even though interpretative rulemaking be involved, the requirements of § 553 apply. But since these requirements themselves do not mandate any oral presentation, . . . it cannot be doubted that a statute that requires a "hearing" prior to rulemaking may in some circumstances be satisfied by procedures that meet only the standards of § 553. The Court's opinion in *FPC* v. *Texaco Inc.*, 377 U.S. 33 (1964), supports such a broad definition of the term "hearing."

Similarly, even where the statute requires that the rulemaking procedure take place "on the record after opportunity for an agency hearing," thus triggering the applicability of § 556, subsection (d) provides that the agency may proceed by the submission of all or part of the evidence in written form if a party will not be "prejudiced thereby." Again, the Act makes it plain that a specific statutory mandate that the proceedings take place on the record after hearing may be satisfied in some circumstances by evidentiary submission in written form only.

We think this treatment of the term "hearing" in the Administrative Procedure Act affords a sufficient basis for concluding that the requirement of a "hearing" contained in § 1 (14)(a), in a situation where the Commission was acting under the 1966 statutory rulemaking authority that Congress had conferred upon it, did not by its own force require the Commission either to hear oral testimony, to permit cross-examination of Commission witnesses, or to hear oral argument. Here, the Commission promulgated a tentative draft of an order, and accorded all interested parties 60 days in which to file statements of position, submissions of evidence, and other relevant observations. The parties had fair notice of exactly what the Commission proposed to do, and were given an opportunity to comment, to object, or to make some other form of written submission. The final order of the Commission indicates that it gave consideration to the statements of the two appellees here. Given the "open-ended" nature of the proceedings, and the Commission's announced willingness to consider proposals for modification after operating experience had been acquired, we think the hearing requirement of § 1 (14)(a) of the Act was met. . . .

[The opinion then turns to the basic distinction between rule making and adjudication, as illustrated in the Supreme Court cases of *Londoner* v. *Denver* and *Bi-Metallic Investment Co.* v. *State Board of Equalization*. This passage is quoted above, page 153]

The Commission's procedure satisfied both the provisions of § 1 (14)(a) of the Interstate Commerce Act and of the Administrative Procedure Act, and were not inconsistent with prior decisions of this Court. We, therefore, reverse the judgment of the District Court, and remand the case so that it may consider those contentions of the parties that are not disposed of by this opinion.

It is so ordered.

Reversed and Remanded.

Mr. Justice POWELL took no part in the consideration or decision of this case.

[The dissenting opinion of Mr. Justice Douglas, with whom Mr. Justice Stewart concurs, is omitted.]

The change effected by the *Florida East Coast* decision was quite significant. Justice Douglas, in his dissent, called it "a sharp break with traditional concepts of procedural due process."[28] One commentator said that the Court redefined "the procedural ingredients that traditionally defined the term 'hearing.'"[29] Henry J. Friendly, a long-time federal appeals court judge, said the decision "signals a large expansion of what can be done by notice and comment rule making and a corresponding retraction of the area where a trial type hearing is required in the regulatory field."[30]

The *Florida East Coast* decision was a stimulus to an already-developing trend toward greater use of rule making at the federal level. This development, in turn, began giving rise to attempts to place checks on agency rule making. We will discuss below the efforts of Congress and the president in this area.

Even before the *Florida East Coast* decision, some lower courts, led by the Court of Appeals for the D.C. Circuit, had sometimes imposed additional procedural requirements for informal rule making even when not mandated by statute. After *Florida East Coast* this practice continued, to the point where, as Antonin Scalia put it (prior to the commencement of his career as a judge), "the D.C. Circuit was in the process of replacing the rudimentary procedural mandates" of the APA.[31] This development set the stage for the landmark *Vermont Yankee* decision of 1978.

---

[28] 410 U.S. 224 at 246.

[29] Verkuil, above, note 12, at 284.

[30] Henry J. Friendly, "Some Kind of Hearing," 123 *University of Pennsylvania Law Review* 1267, 1308 (1975).

[31] Antonin Scalia, "Vermont Yankee: The A.P.A., the D.C. Circuit, and The Supreme Court," in Philip B. Kurland and Gerhard Casper (eds.), *The Supreme Court Review, 1978* 359 (1979).

Vermont Yankee Nuclear Power Corp. v. *Natural Resources Defense Council, Inc.*

SUPREME COURT OF THE UNITED STATES, 1978.
435 U.S. 519, 98 S.Ct. 1197, 55 L.Ed. 2d 460.

[This long and complex case concerned a number of issues growing out of the licensing of two nuclear power plants. The most important issue for our purposes was the procedure used by the Atomic Energy Commission in promulgating a "spent-fuel-cycle rule." The licensing proceedings employed full adjudicatory hearings, but the rule making, although it included oral comment, did not allow for discovery or cross-examination, and thus did not utilize full adjudicatory procedures. The Court of Appeals for the D.C. Circuit overturned the rule because of shortcomings in the procedures, and the Supreme Court reviewed on certiorari. Justice Rehnquist's opinion represented the unanimous view of the seven participating members of the Court.]

Mr. Justice REHNQUIST delivered the opinion of the Court. . . .

Interpreting [§ 553 of the APA] in *United States* v. *Allegheny-Ludlum Steel Corp.*, 406 U.S. 742 (1972), and *United States* v. *Florida East Coast Ry. Co.*, 410 U.S. 224 (1973), we held that generally speaking this section of the APA established the maximum procedural requirements which Congress was willing to have the courts impose upon agencies in conducting rulemaking procedures. Agencies are free to grant additional procedural rights in the exercise of their discretion, but reviewing courts are generally not free to impose them if the agencies have not chosen to grant them. This is not to say necessarily that there are no circumstances which would ever justify a court in overturning agency action because of a failure to employ procedures beyond those required by the statute. But such circumstances, if they exist, are extremely rare.

Even apart from the Administrative Procedure Act this Court has for more than four decades emphasized that the formulation of procedures was basically to be left within the discretion of the agencies to which Congress had confided the responsibility for substantive judgments. It is in the light of this background of statutory and decisional law that we granted certiorari to review two judgments of the Court of Appeals for the District of Columbia Circuit because of our concern that they had seriously misread or misapplied this statutory and decisional law cautioning reviewing courts against engrafting their own notions of proper procedures upon agencies entrusted with substantive functions by Congress. . . . We conclude that the Court of Appeals has done just that in these cases. . . .

[After disposing of other matters, the Court turned to the rule-making issue.]

We next turn to the invalidation of the fuel cycle rule. But before determining whether the Court of Appeals reached a permissible result, we must determine exactly what result it did reach, and in this case that is no mean feat. Vermont Yankee argues that the court invalidated the rule because of the inadequacy of the procedures employed in the proceedings. Respondents, on the other hand, labeling petitioner's view of the decision a "straw man," argue to this Court that the court merely held that the record was inadequate to enable the reviewing court to determine whether the agency had fulfilled its statutory obligation. But we unfortunately have not found the parties' characterization of the opinion to be entirely reliable; it appears here, as in *Orloff* v. *Willoughby*, 345 U.S. 83, 87 (1953), that "in this Court the parties changed positions as nimbly as if dancing a quadrille."

After a thorough examination of the opinion itself, we conclude that while the matter is not entirely free from doubt, the majority of the Court of Appeals struck down the rule because of the perceived inadequacies of the procedures employed in the rulemaking proceedings. The court first determined the intervenors' primary argument to be "that the decision to preclude 'discovery or cross-examination' denied them a meaningful opportunity to participate in the proceedings as guaranteed by due process." . . . The court then went on to frame the issue for decision thus: "Thus, we are called upon to decide whether the procedures provided by the agency were sufficient to ventilate the issues." . . . The court conceded that absent extraordinary circumstances it is improper for a reviewing court to prescribe the procedural format an agency must follow, but it likewise clearly thought it entirely appropriate to "scrutinize the record as a whole to insure that genuine opportunities to participate in a meaningful way were provided. . . ." The court also refrained from actually ordering the agency to follow any specific procedures, . . . but there is little doubt in our minds that the ineluctable mandate of the court's decision is that the procedures afforded during the hearings were inadequate. . . .

In prior opinions we have intimated that even in a rule-making proceeding when an agency is making a "quasi-judicial" determination by which a very small number of persons are "exceptionally affected, in each case upon individual grounds," in some circumstances additional procedures may be required in order to afford the aggrieved individuals due process. *United States* v. *Florida East Coast R. Co.*, 410 U.S., at 242, 245, quoting from *Bi-Metallic Investment Co.* v. *State Board of Equalization*, 239 U.S. 441, 446 (1915). It might also be true, although we do not think the issue is presented in this case and accordingly do not

decide it, that a totally unjustified departure from well-settled agency procedures of long standing might require judicial correction.

But this much is absolutely clear. Absent constitutional constraints or extremely compelling circumstances the "administrative agencies 'should be free to fashion their own rules of procedure and to pursue methods of inquiry capable of permitting them to discharge their multitudinous duties.'" *FCC* v. *Schreiber* 381 U.S. 279 at 290 (1965), quoting *FCC* v. *Pottsville Co.* 309 U.S. 134 at 143 (1940). . . .

Respondent NRDC argues that § 553 of the Administrative Procedure Act merely establishes lower procedural bounds and that a court may routinely require more than the minimum when an agency's proposed rule addresses complex or technical factual issues or "Issues of Great Public Import." We have, however, previously shown that our decisions reject this view. . . .

There are compelling reasons for construing § 553 in this manner. In the first place, if courts continually review agency proceedings to determine whether the agency employed procedures which were, in the court's opinion, perfectly tailored to reach what the court perceives to be the "best" or "correct" result, judicial review would be totally unpredictable. And the agencies, operating under this vague injunction to employ the "best" procedures and facing the threat of reversal if they did not, would undoubtedly adopt full adjudicatory procedures in every instance. Not only would this totally disrupt the statutory scheme, through which Congress enacted "a formula upon which opposing social and political forces have come to rest," *Wong Yang Sung* v. *McGrath*, 339 U.S., at 40, but all the inherent advantages of informal rulemaking would be totally lost.

Secondly, it is obvious that the court in these cases reviewed the agency's

choice of procedures on the basis of the record actually produced at the hearing, . . .
and not on the basis of the information
available to the agency when it made the
decision to structure the proceedings in a
certain way. This sort of Monday morning
quarterbacking not only encourages but
almost compels the agency to conduct all
rulemaking proceedings with the full pan-
oply of procedural devices normally associated only with adjudicatory hearings.

Finally, and perhaps most importantly, this sort of review fundamentally
misconceives the nature of the standard
for judicial review of an agency rule. The
court below uncritically assumed that additional procedures will automatically result in a more adequate record because it
will give interested parties more of an opportunity to participate in and contribute
to the proceedings. But informal rulemaking need not be based solely on the transcript of a hearing held before an agency.
Indeed, the agency need not even hold a
formal hearing. . . . Thus, the adequacy of
the "record" in this type of proceeding is
not correlated directly to the type of procedural devices employed, but rather
turns on whether the agency has followed

the statutory mandate of the Administrative Procedure Act or other relevant statutes. If the agency is compelled to support
the rule which it ultimately adopts with
the type of record produced only after a
full adjudicatory hearing, it simply will
have no choice but to conduct a full adjudicatory hearing prior to promulgating
every rule. In sum, this sort of unwarranted judicial examination of perceived
procedural shortcomings of a rulemaking
proceeding can do nothing but seriously
interfere with that process prescribed by
Congress. . . .

In short, nothing in the APA, NEPA,
the circumstances of this case, the nature
of the issues being considered, past
agency practice, or the statutory mandate
under which the Commission operates
permitted the court to review and overturn the rulemaking proceeding on the
basis of the procedural devices employed
(or not employed) by the Commission so
long as the Commission employed at least
the statutory *minima*, a matter about
which there is no doubt in this case. . . .

Reversed and remanded. Mr. Justice
BLACKMUN and Mr. Justice POWELL
took no part in the consideration or decision of these cases.

DEREGULATION AND RULE MAKING

During some periods of recent American history, the election of a new president (particularly a Republican president) has been associated with im-
pulses toward reducing the role of government in American life, toward, in
a word, deregulation. Thus, for instance, when George W. Bush succeeded
Bill Clinton in 2001, dozens of regulations announced in the last days of the
Clinton administration that had not yet taken effect were suspended by the
Bush administration so that they could be reviewed by newly appointed
agency heads.[32] A number of these regulations were cancelled or changed
significantly.

---

[32] See "Regulatory Review Plan," a memorandum by Andrew H. Card, Jr., Assistant to President
Bush and Chief of Staff, dated January 20, 2001, and published in the *Federal Register* on January
24, 2001, Volume 66, No. 16, pages 7701–7702. For a comment on the Card memorandum, see "Mr.
Card's Dangerous Memo," *New York Times on the Web*, February 12, 2001, http://www.nytimes.com/
2001/02/12/opinion/12MON2.html.

Another option available to a new administration is to rescind or change a rule that has already taken effect. On this matter the Supreme Court has spoken several times, particularly in the 1980s, in the years of the first Reagan administration. Two important Supreme Court cases, both still cited frequently by courts and discussed by commentators, will be examined in this section: the *State Farm* case (1983) and the *Chevron* case (1984). Although both cases manifest a number of interesting facets, the main focus of our attention here will be on the subject of rescinding or changing rules.

Motor Vehicle Manufacturers Association v. *State Farm Mutual Automobile Insurance Company*

SUPREME COURT OF THE UNITED STATES, 1983.
463 U.S. 29, 103 S.Ct. 2856, 77 L.Ed. 2d 443.

[Congress in 1966 enacted the National Traffic and Motor Vehicle Safety Act[33] for the purpose of reducing "traffic accidents and deaths and injuries to persons resulting from traffic accidents." The act directs the secretary of transportation or his delegate to issue motor vehicle safety standards that "shall be practicable, shall meet the need for motor vehicle safety, and shall be stated in objective terms."

The regulation at issue in this case, according to Justice Byron R. White in his majority opinion, "bears a complex and convoluted history." A standard requiring that passive restraints (air bags or automatic seat belts) be installed in automobiles was first proposed in 1969. But it was not until 1977 that Modified Standard 208 was adopted. It mandated the installation of passive restraints in large cars in model year 1982 and the phasing in of the requirement to cover all cars by model year 1984.

In February 1981, however, the new secretary of transportation reopened the rule-making process. Acting for the secretary, the National Highway Traffic Safety Administration (NHTSA) first ordered a one-year delay in the application of the standard and later rescinded the passive restraint requirement altogether.

The respondent brought suit for review of the rescission, and the U.S. Court of Appeals for the District of Columbia ruled in 1982 that the rescission was arbitrary and capricious. The Supreme Court granted certiorari to review the court of appeals' decision. As indicated above, the main issue covered below is the court's view of the appropriate process for rescinding a regulation.]

Justice WHITE delivered the opinion of the Court. . . .

Both the Act and the 1974 Amendments concerning occupant crash protection standards indicate that motor vehicle safety standards are to be promulgated under the informal rulemaking procedures of the Administrative Procedure Act. . . . The agency's action in promulgating such standards therefore may be set aside if found to be "arbitrary, capricious, an abuse of discretion, or otherwise not in accordance with law." . . . We believe that the rescission or modification of an occupant-protection standard is subject to the same test. Section 103(b) of the Act . . . states that the procedural and judicial re-

---

[33] 15 U.S.C. §§ 1381 et seq.

view provisions of the Administrative Procedure Act "shall apply to all orders establishing, amending, or revoking a Federal motor vehicle safety standard," and suggests no difference in the scope of judicial review depending upon the nature of the agency's action.

Petitioner Motor Vehicle Manufacturers Association (MVMA) disagrees, contending that the rescission of an agency rule should be judged by the same standard a court would use to judge an agency's refusal to promulgate a rule in the first place—a standard petitioner believes considerably narrower than the traditional arbitrary-and-capricious test. We reject this view. The Act expressly equates orders "revoking" and "establishing" safety standards; neither that Act nor the APA suggests that revocations are to be treated as refusals to promulgate standards. Petitioner's view would render meaningless Congress' authorization for judicial review of orders revoking safety rules. Moreover, the revocation of an extant regulation is substantially different than a failure to act. Revocation constitutes a reversal of the agency's former views as to the proper course. . . .

Accordingly, an agency changing its course by rescinding a rule is obligated to supply a reasoned analysis for the change beyond that which may be required when an agency does not act in the first instance. . . .

The ultimate question before us is whether NHTSA's rescission of the passive restraint requirement of Standard 208 was arbitrary and capricious. We conclude, as did the Court of Appeals, that it was. We also conclude . . . that further consideration of the issue by the agency is therefore required. . . .

[J]ust as an agency reasonably may decline to issue a safety standard if it is uncertain about its efficacy, an agency may also revoke a standard on the basis of serious uncertainties if supported by the record and reasonably explained. Rescis-

sion of the passive restraint requirement would not be arbitrary and capricious simply because there was no evidence in direct support of the agency's conclusion. It is not infrequent that the available data do not settle a regulatory issue, and the agency must then exercise its judgment in moving from the facts and probabilities on the record to a policy conclusion. Recognizing that policymaking in a complex society must account for uncertainty, however, does not imply that it is sufficient for an agency to merely recite the terms "substantial uncertainty" as a justification for its actions. As previously noted, the agency must explain the evidence which is available, and must offer a "rational connection between the facts found and the choice made." *Burlington Truck Lines, Inc*. v. *United States, supra*, at 168. Generally, one aspect of that explanation would be a justification for rescinding the regulation before engaging in a search for further evidence.

In these cases, the agency's explanation for rescission of the passive restraint requirement is *not* sufficient to enable us to conclude that the rescission was the product of reasoned decisionmaking. . . .

"An agency's view of what is in the public interest may change, either with or without a change in circumstances. But an agency changing its course must supply a reasoned analysis. . . ." *Greater Boston Television Corp*. v. *FCC*, 143 U.S. App. D.C. 383, 394, 444 F.2d 841, 852 (1970) (footnote omitted), cert. denied, 403 U.S. 923 (1971). We do not accept all of the reasoning of the Court of Appeals but we do conclude that the agency has failed to supply the requisite "reasoned analysis" in this case. Accordingly, we vacate the judgment of the Court of Appeals and remand the cases to that court with directions to remand the matter to the NHTSA for further consideration consistent with this opinion.

So ordered.

Justice REHNQUIST, with whom THE CHIEF JUSTICE, Justice POWELL, and Justice O'CONNOR join, concurring in part and dissenting in part. . . .

The agency's changed view of the standard seems to be related to the election of a new president of a different political party. It is readily apparent that the responsible members of one administration may consider public resistance and uncertainties to be more important than do their counterparts in a previous administration. A change in administration brought about by the people casting their votes is a perfectly reasonable basis for an executive agency's reappraisal of the costs and benefits of its programs and regulations. As long as the agency remains within the bounds established by Congress, it is entitled to assess administrative records and evaluate priorities in light of the philosophy of the administration.

Chevron U.S.A., Inc. v. *Natural Resources Defense Council, Inc.*, 467 U.S. 837, 104 S.Ct. 2778, 81 L.Ed. 2d 694 (1984), has been called "one of the most important decisions in the history of administrative law."[34] The two-step test articulated by the Supreme Court in this case for reviewing agency interpretations of statutes was discussed in chapter 4. *Chevron* also has relevance to the present discussion of political aspects of agency rule making. The 1977 amendments to the Clean Air Act required states that had not achieved national air-quality standards to create a permit program regulating "new or modified major stationary sources" of air pollution. Of considerable significance was the meaning of *stationary source*, which was not explicitly defined in the 1977 amendments. The so-called bubble concept involved adopting a plant-wide definition of a stationary source. Under this definition, a plant containing pollution devices could install or modify one piece of pollution equipment as long as this alteration would not increase total emissions from the plant. Thus, to quote from the Supreme Court opinion in the case, "all of the pollution-emitting devices within the same industrial grouping" would be treated "as though they were encased within a single bubble." In 1980 the EPA adopted a regulation that precluded using the bubble concept in the particular circumstances that became the issue in this case. But, as the Supreme Court noted in its opinion, the EPA view changed after the 1980 election: "[I]n 1981 a new administration took office and initiated a 'government-wide reexamination of regulatory burdens and complexities.'[35] In the context of that review, the EPA reevaluated the various arguments that had been advanced in connection with the proper definition of the term 'source.' . . ."[36] It concluded that the plant-wide definition of source

---

[34] Pierce 1, above, note 2, 140. In 1996 Judge Patricia M. Wald called *Chevron* "as much of a landmark decision as exists in administrative law." Patricia M. Wald, "Judicial Review in Midpassage: The Uneasy Partnership between Courts and Agencies Plays On," 32 *Tulsa Law Journal* 221, 241 (1996). On this point see also "The Notoriety of Chevron" in Peter L. Strauss, Todd Rakoff, Roy A. Schotland, and Cynthia R. Farina, *Administrative Law: Cases and Comments* 620 (9th ed., 1995).

[35] 46 Fed.Reg. 16281.

[36] 467 U.S. 837, 840.

was appropriate, and thus embraced the bubble concept as a general standard.[37]

The Natural Resources Defense Council brought suit in the court of appeals, which ruled the regulation invalid on the ground that the bubble concept as applied to the pollution-control areas in question was contrary to law. In reviewing this decision, the Supreme Court addressed two basic issues: (1) whether the regulation allowing the use of the bubble concept was a reasonable construction by the EPA of legislative intent, and (2) the degree of judicial deference that should be given to the agency's ruling. The Supreme Court reversed the decision of the court of appeals. In a unanimous decision for the six members of the Court who participated, Justice Stevens stated that the use of the bubble concept was "a reasonable policy choice for the agency to make." It was "a permissible construction of the statute which seeks to accommodate progress in reducing air pollution with economic growth." Regarding the fact that the agency had changed its definition of the term *source*, the Court said:

> [this] does not, as respondents argue, lead us to conclude that no deference should be accorded to the agency's interpretation of the statute. An initial agency interpretation is not instantly carved in stone. On the contrary, the agency, to engage in informed rulemaking, must consider varying interpretations and the wisdom of its policy on a continuing basis.

Stevens added that policy arguments of this sort should not be waged in court. They "are more appropriately addressed to legislators or administrators, not to judges." Among the "well-settled principles" that the court of appeals ignored in its decision was the following: "Sometimes the legislative delegation to an agency on a particular question is implicit rather than explicit. In such a case, a court may not substitute its own construction of a statutory provision for a reasonable interpretation made by the administrator of an agency."

The *State Farm* and *Chevron* cases, decided one year apart, make clear the difficulty of articulating a firm guideline regarding the appropriate judicial role in reviewing agency rule making. As a recent book on rule making has put it, *Chevron* "appears to grant latitude to agencies as broad as that which the earlier *State Farm* case appeared to grant to the judiciary."[38]

RULE MAKING AND ITS CONTROL

Kenneth Culp Davis, one of the leading specialists on American administrative law during the last half of the twentieth century, called rule-making

---

[37] This example of rule changing by a new presidential administration is not unusual. When George W. Bush came into office in 2001, a number of rules from the Clinton administration were amended or rescinded. An important example that pertains to the present discussion was the adoption of less stringent rules under the Clean Air Act that led the Environmental Protection Agency to drop investigations against a number of power plants. The rule changes grew out of recommendations made by Vice President Dick Cheney's energy task force. For details see Christopher Drew and Richard A. Oppel, Jr., "Lawyers at E.P.A. Say It Will Drop Pollution Cases," *New York Times*, November 11, 2003, A1.

[38] Kerwin, above, note 23, 249.

procedure "one of the greatest inventions of modern government."[39] And as countless examinations of the subject have made clear, the past fifty years have seen a dramatic rise in the use of rule making as a vehicle for developing governmental policy. The tremendous increase in rule making has not been without problems and critics, however. The economic impact of regulations on private parties, particularly business organizations, can be considerable, and representatives of this area of the public have long called for restraints on the regulators. At the same time, other segments of the public increasingly want to make sure that their views, on matters of pollution control and other environmental issues, for instance, are not ignored in administrative rule making. Whether in direct response to these appeals or not, a view that appears to be expressed increasingly in recent years states, in effect, "Let's try to keep a closer check on what the agencies are doing by means of rules and regulations." The developments and recommendations relevant to this point involve Congress, the president, and the courts.

The Role of Congress

Congress performs a number of general functions of oversight and control that may have an effect on rule making. These include the Senate's advice and consent on agency heads appointed by the president; congressional review and approval of agency budgets; congressional committee hearings on the activities of administrative agencies; and requirements that agencies report to Congress. In addition, individual members of Congress make "casework" contacts with agencies on behalf of constituents. But Congress has also made use of or considered a number of more specific measures that affect rule making directly. In this category are the following:

Increased Formality for Rule Making in Certain Agencies

Congress has, in some cases, required that agencies go beyond the requirements of § 553 in rule making. But the attractiveness of either formal or hybrid rule making, both discussed earlier in this chapter, seems to have waned in recent years.

Congressional Voiding of Regulations by Statute

The congressional-voiding device is rarely used, but it is a legitimate exercise of legislative power. An example of its use is a 1975 statute that suspended a food-stamp cost increase that had been promulgated under Department of Agriculture regulations.[40] Since the device involves the exercise of statutory power by Congress, the president is also involved by either assenting to or vetoing the legislation. This device seems to have been replaced recently by Congress's "joint resolution of disapproval." See below under "Congressional Review of Agency Rule Making."

---

[39] Kenneth Culp Davis, *Administrative Law: Cases—Text—Problems* 241 (6th ed., 1977).

[40] Public Law 94-4, 89 Stat. 6, February 22, 1975.

Legislative Veto

The term *legislative veto* refers to congressional authority to annul executive or administrative action—including administrative rules—by resolution of one or both houses or by a congressional committee. As discussed in chapter 3, however, in 1983 the Supreme Court declared the legislative veto to be unconstitutional in *Immigration and Naturalization Service* v. *Chadha*.[41] As Justice White pointed out in dissent in this case, legislative veto provisions in nearly 200 statutes were invalidated by this decision. Among several reasons cited by the majority for finding the legislative veto deficient was that it violated the presentment clauses of the Constitution, which require that all congressional measures having the force of law be presented to the president for signature or veto.

Sunset Legislation

Sunset provisions have been written into a number of statutes in recent years. They require periodic congressional review of agency programs. If, after a specified period of time, Congress does not act to renew or revise a program, spending authority is terminated. A recent example is the four-year sunset provision in the antiterrorism law adopted by Congress in the wake of the September 11, 2001, attacks.[42] While sunset measures are not specifically aimed at agency rule making, certain regulations would clearly make some agencies likely targets.[43]

Environmental Impact Statements

The National Environmental Policy Act of 1969[44] requires environmental impact statements (EISs) on every recommendation for legislation "or other major Federal actions significantly affecting the quality of the human environment." Thousands of such statements have been prepared since the act was adopted, some of them running to thousands of pages and costing millions of dollars to compile. The process of adopting an EIS is not significantly different from APA rule-making procedures.[45]

Cost-Benefit Analysis

In recent years Congress has adopted a number of statutes, in areas such as health, education, transportation, housing, and the environment, that require an assessment of the economic impact of regulations. These laws have been passed at least in part in response to charges from critics that

---

[41] 462 U.S. 919 (1983).

[42] Public Law 107-56, 115 Stat. 272, October 26, 2001.

[43] For details on this point see Chris Mooney, "A Short History of Sunsets," *Legal Affairs*, January/February 2004, www.legalaffairs.org/issues/January-February-2004/story_mooney_janfeb04.html.

[44] 83 Stat. 852, 42 U.S.C. §§ 4321, 4331–4347.

[45] Kerwin, above, note 23, 68.

overregulation hurts business and that it is reasonable to ask for some relative balancing by administrators between the benefits to be gained and the costs incurred as a result of the regulations they adopt. Cost-benefit analysis is part of a broader impulse toward regulatory reform known as regulatory analysis. Attempts to adopt broad legislation requiring cost-benefit analysis by all administrative agencies have so far failed in Congress.[46] But the subject continues to generate widespread interest as well as numerous critics.[47]

Congress has adopted two pieces of legislation that bear on this subject, however. The Regulatory Flexibility Act, adopted in 1980, requires agencies to consider the impact of proposed rules on small entities, including businesses and other organizations. The agencies, in the course of rule making, must look into alternatives that are less burdensome to small entities and, if not adopted, explain why such alternatives were rejected.[48] The Paperwork Reduction Act has among its objectives the reduction of the paperwork burden on the public. To this end, agencies are required to gain the approval of the Office of Management and Budget (OMB) before engaging in the collection of information from the public.[49] Because of the relationship between information collected by agencies and rule making, agencies must routinely indicate whether a rule to be adopted imposes new reporting or record-keeping requirements on those parties to whom it applies.

Congressional Review of Agency Rule Making

President Clinton signed "The Contract with America Advancement Act of 1996,"[50] which covered a number of diverse subjects, including raising the exempt-earnings limit for social security recipients and giving the president the line-item veto. The part of this package of laws of interest here is "The Small Business Regulatory Enforcement Fairness Act of 1996," and specifically its chapter 8, "Congressional Review of Agency Rulemaking."[51] Under the chapter's provisions, every rule that a federal agency seeks to adopt must be submitted to both houses of Congress and the comptroller general (the head of the General Accounting Office, an arm of Congress). The rule is accompanied by a concise general statement regarding the rule and by other information, including the cost-benefit analysis, if any. The statute distin-

---

[46] Robert W. Hahn, "State and Federal Regulatory Reform: A Comparative Analysis," 29 *Journal of Legal Studies* 973, 888 (2000). This was one of a number of articles presented at "Cost-Benefit Analysis: Legal, Economic, and Philosophical Perspectives: A Conference Sponsored by the John M. Olin Foundation and the University of Chicago Law School." Several other articles from the conference, which was held at the University of Chicago Law School in September 1999, were published in the same issue of *Journal of Legal Studies*.

[47] On the latter point, see, e.g., Thomas O. McGarity, "A Cost-Benefit State," 50 *Administrative Law Review* 7 (1998); Henry S. Richardson, "The Stupidity of the Cost-Benefit Standard," 29 *Journal of Legal Studies* 971 (2000).

[48] Public Law 96-354, 94 Stat. 1156 (1980), 5 U.S.C. §§ 601–612.

[49] Public Law 96-511, 94 Stat. 2812 (1980), 44 U.S.C. §§ 3501–3520.

[50] Public Law 104-121 (110 Stat. 847).

[51] Chapter 8 is codified as a new part of the APA, §§ 801–808.

guishes between major rules and all other rules. A major rule is a regulation that the OMB has deemed likely to have one or more specified economic characteristics, such as "an annual effect on the economy of $100,000,000 or more."[52] The effective date of major rules is delayed for at least sixty days during congressional review. This restriction does not apply to nonmajor rules. But for both types of rules, Congress may adopt a joint resolution of disapproval, the result of which is that "such rule shall have no force or effect."[53] The joint resolution of disapproval requires the president's signature (or passage over a presidential veto) and is treated as a statute.[54]

Some commentators have questioned whether this most recent effort at congressional control of rule making will be successful. They believe that it will result in increased costs for rule making and that agencies will seek ways around its provisions. Moreover, it is predicted that because of the cumbersome nature of its procedures, this method of congressional control is likely to be little used.[55] It is true that few joint resolutions of disapproval have been introduced since the law came into effect, and fewer still have been adopted. Still, a determined Congress can, on occasion, thwart a regulation it opposes, particularly with a sympathetic president heading the executive branch. A leading example is the fate of the so-called ergonomics rule, adopted by the Occupational Safety and Health Administration late in 2000 after an extended period of discussion and a large number of public hearings. This controversial regulation, which ran to about 1,000 pages of text, was aimed at lessening the number of work-related musculoskeletal injuries caused by repetitive-motion jobs. Soon after the effective date of the rule in January 2001, the two houses of Congress adopted a joint resolution of disapproval, which President George W. Bush quickly signed.[56]

But to expect Congress to play a constant oversight role through this mechanism is probably unrealistic; Congress simply has too many other important functions, including its own legislative agenda, to be able to spend significantly more time on review of administrative regulations. Even more unrealistic are other proposals emanating from Congress that would, in effect, take over from agencies the function of approving *all* regulations.[57]

---

[52] § 804 (2) (A).

[53] § 802 (a).

[54] The president's signature is required to avoid violating the presentment clauses of the Constitution, one of the bases for declaring the legislative veto unconstitutional. See the discussion of the legislative veto earlier in this chapter.

[55] See, e.g., Daniel Cohen and Peter L. Strauss, "Congressional Review of Agency Actions," 49 *Administrative Law Review* 95 (1997); Morton Rosenberg, "Whatever Happened to Congressional Review of Agency Rulemaking?: A Brief Overview, Assessment, and Proposal for Reform," 51 *Administrative Law Review* 1051 (1999).

[56] The final Ergonomics Rule appeared in 65 FR no. 220, p. 68262, on November 14, 2000. The joint resolution of disapproval, signed by the president, became Public Law 107-5, 115 Stat. 7 (March 20, 2001). The notice from OSHA removing the rule from the *Code of Federal Regulations* appeared in 66 FR no. 78, p. 20403 (April 23, 2001).

[57] Several legislative proposals that would have this effect have been introduced in Congress in recent years. See, e.g., H.R. 1036, introduced in the House of Representatives March 12, 1997, which "ensures that Federal regulations will not take effect unless passed by a majority of the members of the Senate and House of Representatives and signed by the President." This bill was discussed in

The Role of the President

All recent presidents from Richard Nixon on have shown an interest in asserting greater control over administrative rule making. Presidential oversight of rule making is said to serve at least two purposes: to help the president carry out what he sees as his electoral mandate and to resolve conflicts and achieve coordination among rules adopted by different agencies.[58] Several presidents have issued executive orders on rule making.[59] Although these documents have differed in their details from president to president, their general thrust has been similar. A major role in review of rule making is assigned to the OMB, particularly to its Office of Information and Regulatory Affairs (OIRA). Agencies are required to provide OIRA with information about their rules, including a cost-benefit analysis for major rules, before promulgation. The scope of activity performed by OIRA is considerable; it may have hundreds of rules under review at any given time.[60]

These executive orders seek to place rule making under closer scrutiny of the president and the president's advisors, although, given the great number of rules processed by OIRA, the degree to which that body can give a considered, expert review of the documents it receives is at least open to question. Nor is this the only potential problem with OIRA review. It is argued by some critics, for instance, that Congress has delegated rule-making power to particular agencies, and when presidential representatives outside of these agencies effect changes in the rules, the spirit of the legislation is violated. It is further suggested that off-the-record intervention from OIRA, perhaps after the notice-and-comment period has ended, violates the intent of the APA. Moreover, considerable delays in the adoption of some rules have been inevitable. Perhaps as a result of these concerns, the Clinton executive order established time limits for review of regulations, barred ex parte contacts between employees of OIRA and the agencies, and provided other changes to meet criticisms of previous practices.[61] These changes notwithstanding, it seems clear that the White House has gained the upper hand over Congress in supervising agency rule making. Certainly some of Congress's legislative efforts in this area in recent years indicate the desire to reassert itself in this continuing struggle.[62]

"The Role of Congress in Monitoring Administrative Rulemaking," Hearing before the Subcommittee on Commercial and Administrative Law of the Committee on the Judiciary, House of Representatives, 105th Congress, 1st Session, September 25, 1997 (Serial No. 54), 13–19. Another example of a legislative proposal of this kind may be found in "Role of Congress in Monitoring Administrative Rulemaking," Hearing before the Subcommittee on Commercial and Administrative Law of the Committee on the Judiciary, House of Representatives, 104th Congress, 2nd Session, September 12, 1996 (Serial No. 93), (H.R. 47), 2–3.

[58] Kerwin, above, note 23, 224.

[59] As of this writing (late 2002), the Bush administration is still operating under Executive Order 12866, which was adopted in 1993, during the first Clinton administration. For a review of recent presidential executive orders on rule making, see Hahn, above, note 45, 886–892 (2000).

[60] See "Regulations Currently under E.O. 12866 Review," http://www.whitehouse.gov/omb/inforeg/regpol.html.

[61] See the discussion of these changes in Pierce, Shapiro, and Verkuil, above, note 22, 488.

[62] Kerwin, above, note 23, 224.

The Role of the Courts

Several cases discussed earlier in the chapter set forth the notice and comment provisions of § 553 of the APA as the standard format for agency rule making. *Florida East Coast Railway* made this point explicitly. The *Vermont Yankee* case prohibited the lower courts from imposing additional rule making requirements beyond notice and comment, absent a statutory provision directing such procedures. And in the *Chevron* case, the Supreme Court reversed a court of appeals decision that had barred the Environmental Protection Agency from changing its mind (after a presidential election) about the suitability of a rule that embraced the bubble concept. With these decisions the role of the courts in overseeing the rule-making process has been restricted. But there are still countless issues regarding administrative rule making that come to the courts for resolution. And in a number of these cases, lower courts have found agency rule making inadequate because the agency failed to provide a "reasoned explanation" for the rule.[63] This "excessively demanding judicial review" (as it is termed by one source[64]) is one of the factors that has led in recent years to considerably greater difficulty in promulgating administrative rules, the subject of the final section of this chapter.

CONCLUSION

As just indicated, several leading Supreme Court decisions leaning toward simplicity in rule making have to some extent been diminished in their effect by lower-court decisions that have been more demanding of rule-making proceedings. But this is not the only factor that has complicated rule making in recent years. The formidable oversight mechanisms created by Congress and the president have contributed to what numerous commentators have come to call the "ossification" of the rule-making process. In addition to long delays in rule adoption, some rules just die because of the inability of agencies to sustain the momentum needed to reach promulgation. And while rule making was once seen as superior to adjudication for agency policy making, recent evidence suggests that some agencies are now increasingly using adjudication or seeking alternative, less participatory vehicles for rule making, such as invoking the "good cause" and other exemptions to regular notice and comment. The ways around traditional notice and comment are referred to by political scientist Cornelius Kerwin as "exceptions, exemptions, and evasions."[65] The literature is replete with suggested ways to fight ossification, but for the moment the federal government seems destined to face a rule-making procedure far more extended and complicated than the relatively simple provisions written into § 553 almost sixty years ago.

---

[63] See, e.g., Thomas O. McGarity, "Some Thoughts on 'Deossifying' the Rulemaking Process," 41 *Duke Law Journal* 1385, 1400 (1992); Pierce, Shapiro, and Verkuil, above, note 22, 328–330. This standard for overturning a rule seems close to the "reasoned analysis" language found in the *State Farm Mutual* case discussed earlier in this chapter.

[64] Pierce, Shapiro and Verkuil, above, note 22, 329–330.

[65] Kerwin, above, note 23, 71.

The Right to Be Heard and Adjudicatory Policy Making

THE RIGHT TO BE HEARD

As noted in the last chapter, rule making may at times resemble adjudication in the procedural requirements that are built into the process. But in general, discussions of "the right to a hearing" imply adjudication, a quasi-judicial, as opposed to quasi-legislative, process. A list of the types of such hearings would be nearly endless; a few examples include proceedings to receive a license of some kind or to be awarded a television channel by the Federal Communications Commission (FCC), or renewal or revocation of such licenses; proceedings involving the firing, supervision, or disciplining of a government employee; a conference or interview involving one's pension or tax problems; a discussion with school authorities about the suspension or expulsion of one's child from school; an appeal of a zoning ruling concerning one's property; and many more. Whatever the matter at issue, the right to be heard involves some form of oral participation by the party affected by the administrative action. The degree of required formality of the hearing may vary from situation to situation. If a hearing is required, there may be a question as to when it must be held. And there are some situations when no hearing of any kind is necessary. These are the matters that will be examined in this chapter.

The question of who has a right to a hearing has been a controversial one in administrative law for decades. While there has been considerable judicial attention to this matter in recent years, controversies still arise frequently, and it is impossible to state with precision the conditions that will or will not require a hearing. One should start by looking at the applicable legislation, both general statutes and those applying specifically to the administrative agency in question. Typically, the general statute will reference particular statutes. For instance, § 554 of the Administrative Procedure Act (APA), on adjudication, applies to "every case of adjudication required by statute to be determined on the record after opportunity for agency hearing."

The absence of a particular statute providing for a hearing may not be conclusive, however. Much litigation has involved allegations that the denial of a hearing, even when no hearing is mandated by the legislature, contravenes the constitutional rights of the plaintiff. The constitutional basis for most such litigation is the provisions of the Fifth and Fourteenth Amendments, stating that a person may not be deprived of "life, liberty, or property, without due process of law."

The Right-Privilege Distinction

In applying these provisions to concrete cases, how do courts determine if a deprivation of life, liberty, or property actually is involved? A test frequently applied in earlier years was the so-called right-privilege distinction, which essentially holds that if a privilege rather than a right is at stake, then due process does not require a hearing. The distinction has a long history and is usually traced to Judge Oliver Wendell Holmes, Jr.[1] It has been stated many times by the courts, but perhaps nowhere was it put more succinctly than in a 1950 Supreme Court opinion upholding the exclusion from the country without a hearing of the alien wife of a U.S. citizen, "solely upon a finding by the Attorney General that her admission would be prejudicial to the interests of the United States. . . . we are dealing here with a matter of *privilege*. Petitioner has no vested *right* of entry . . ." [*United States of America* ex rel. *Knauff* v. *Shaughnessy* 338 U.S. 537, 539, 544 (1950); emphasis in the original].

By the 1970s, however, the impact of the right-privilege distinction had been eroded to a considerable extent. Commentators wrote of a "due process explosion,"[2] which, among other things, discredited the right-privilege distinction and extended the requirement of a hearing into areas in which it would not have been deemed necessary some years earlier. Courts stopped using the language of rights and privileges to determine whether due process requirements were to be provided. But this "revolution," as it was sometimes termed, did not proceed as far as most analysts, either proponents or critics, had prophesied. By the end of the decade, a drawing back from the expectations of the early and mid-1970s regarding the development of due process was clear. The dominant theme of those assessing the Supreme Court's role in this development has been the inconsistency and lack of clarity in the Court's pronouncements. These assessments will be discussed further below. But first the outlines of the abbreviated "revolution" should be sketched.

---

[1] The kernel of the Holmes position is contained in his statement that a "petitioner may have a constitutional right to talk politics, but he has no constitutional right to be a policeman," made in *McAuliffe* v. *Mayor of New Bedford*, 155 Mass. 216, 220, 29 N.E. 517 (Supreme Judicial Court of Massachusetts, 1892). This quotation, as well as a general discussion of the case, provides the introduction to Professor William W. Van Alstyne's comprehensive article on the right-privilege distinction: "The Demise of the Right-Privilege Distinction in Constitutional Law," 81 *Harvard Law Review* 1439 (1968).

[2] The term was used by Judge Henry J. Friendly in "Some Kind of Hearing," 123 *University of Pennsylvania Law Review* 1267, 1268 (1975). In this article Judge Friendly stated (at 1273) that "we have witnessed a greater expansion of procedural due process in the last five years than in the entire period since ratification of the Constitution."

The first key case is *Goldberg* v. *Kelly*, a 1970 decision that spoke to the right-privilege distinction in the course of spelling out the due process status of a welfare recipient.[3]

Goldberg v. *Kelly*

SUPREME COURT OF THE UNITED STATES, 1970.
397 U.S. 254; 90 S.Ct. 1011; 25 L.Ed. 2d 287.

Mr. Justice BRENNAN delivered the opinion of the Court.

The question for decision is whether a State that terminates public assistance payments to a particular recipient without affording him the opportunity for an evidentiary hearing prior to termination denies the recipient procedural due process in violation of the Due Process Clause of the Fourteenth Amendment. . . .

Pursuant to [a relevant regulation], the New York City Department of Social Services promulgated Procedure No. 68-18. A caseworker who has doubts about the recipient's continued eligibility must first discuss them with the recipient. If the caseworker concludes that the recipient is no longer eligible, he recommends termination of aid to a unit supervisor. If the latter concurs, he sends the recipient a letter stating the reasons for proposing to terminate aid and notifying him that within seven days he may request that a higher official review the record, and may support the request with a written statement prepared personally or with the aid of an attorney or other person. If the reviewing official affirms the determination of ineligibility, aid is stopped immediately and the recipient is informed by letter of the reasons for the action. Appellees' challenge to this procedure emphasizes the absence of any provisions for the personal appearance of the recipient before the reviewing official, for oral presentation of evidence, and for confrontation and cross-examination of adverse witnesses. However, the letter does inform the recipient that he may request a post-termination "fair hearing." . . .

The constitutional issue to be decided, therefore, is the narrow one whether the Due Process Clause requires that the recipient be afforded an evidentiary hearing *before* the termination of benefits. The District Court held that only a pre-termination evidentiary hearing would satisfy the constitutional command, and rejected the argument of the state and city officials that the combination of the post-termination "fair hearing" with the informal pre-termination review disposed of all due process claims. The court said: "While post-termination review is relevant, there is one overpowering fact which controls here. By hypothesis, a welfare recipient is destitute, without funds or assets. . . . Suffice it to say that to cut off a welfare recipient in the face of . . . 'brutal need' without a prior hearing of some sort is unconscionable, unless overwhelming considerations justify it." *Kelly* v. *Wyman*, 294 F. Supp. 893, 899, 900 (1968). The court rejected the argument that the need to protect the public's tax revenues supplied the requisite "overwhelming consideration." "Against the justified desire to protect public funds must be weighed the individual's overpowering need in this unique situation not to be wrongfully deprived of assistance. . . . While the problem of additional expense must be kept in mind, it

---

[3] So important is this case that one scholar, writing in the 1970s, referred to the "*Goldberg* v. *Kelly* revolution" [Bernard Schwartz, "Administrative Law: The Third Century," 29 *Administrative Law Review* 291, 300 (1977)].

does not justify denying a hearing meeting the ordinary standards of due process. Under all the circumstances, we hold that due process requires an adequate hearing before termination of welfare benefits, and the fact that there is a later constitutionally fair proceeding does not alter the result." . . .

Appellant does not contend that procedural due process is not applicable to the termination of welfare benefits. Such benefits are a matter of statutory entitlement for persons qualified to receive them. Their termination involves state action that adjudicates important rights. The constitutional challenge cannot be answered by an argument that public assistance benefits are "a 'privilege' and not a 'right.'" *Shapiro* v. *Thompson*, 394 U.S. 618, 627 n. 6 (1969). . . .

It is true, of course, that some governmental benefits may be administratively terminated without affording the recipient a pre-termination evidentiary hearing. But we agree with the District Court that when welfare is discontinued, only a pre-termination evidentiary hearing provides the recipient with procedural due process. . . . Welfare recipients must . . . be given an opportunity to confront and cross-examine witnesses relied on by the department. . . . We do not say that counsel must be provided at the pre-termination hearing, but only that the recipient must be allowed to retain an attorney if he so desires. Counsel can help delineate the issues, present the factual contentions in an orderly manner, conduct cross-examination, and generally safeguard the interests of the recipient. . . . We agree with the District Court that prior involvement in some aspects of a case will not necessarily bar a welfare official from acting as a decision maker. He should not, however, have participated in making the determination under review.

Affirmed.

[The dissenting opinion of Justice Black is omitted.]

Two years after *Goldberg* came *Morrissey* v. *Brewer*, 408 U.S. 471 (1972), a case involving the liberty rather than the property aspects of due process. The Supreme Court in *Morrissey* ruled that the due process clause of the Fourteenth Amendment afforded an individual the right to be heard prior to the revocation of his parole. The Court stated: "it is hardly useful any longer to try to deal with this problem in terms of whether the parolee's liberty is a 'right' or a 'privilege.' By whatever name the liberty is valuable and must be seen as within the protection of the Fourteenth Amendment" (408 U.S. 482). The Court called for a two-stage parole revocation process, with a preliminary hearing at the time of arrest and a more formal revocation hearing later. While the Court said that it "cannot write a code of procedure," it did lay down "minimum requirements of due process" for the second hearing, including written notice, disclosure of evidence against the parolee, opportunity to be heard in person and to present witnesses and documentary evidence, the right to confront and cross-examine adverse witnesses ("unless the hearing officer specifically finds good cause for not allowing confrontation"), a neutral and detached hearing body, and a written statement as to the evidence relied on and the reasons for revoking parole. The Court did not decide the question of the parolee's entitlement to retain counsel, however, as it had in *Goldberg*.

In another opinion on the same day as *Morrissey*, the Supreme Court appeared to dispense completely with the right-privilege distinction when it stated that "the Court has fully and finally rejected the wooden distinction between 'rights' and 'privileges' that once seemed to govern the applicability of procedural due process rights" [*Board of Regents* v. *Roth*, 408 U.S. 564, 571 (1972)]. But in this case, the majority of the Supreme Court held that Roth, an assistant professor at a state university hired on a one-year contract, was not entitled under the Fourteenth Amendment to either a statement of reasons or a hearing on the decision not to rehire him. As Justice Potter Stewart stated for the majority, "the range of interests protected by procedural due process is not infinite."[4]

Roth, then, was a decision that cut both ways: it continued the condemnation of the right-privilege distinction, but it ruled that Roth's due process interest was sufficiently minor that a hearing was not required. Some commentators trace to the *Roth* case a change in direction in the Supreme Court's treatment of right-to-be-heard cases. Thereafter, in the words of Victor G. Rosenblum, "the lack of a coherent methodology in dealing with this area of law" was discernible.[5] Moreover, in spite of the Supreme Court's abandonment of the *language* of rights versus privileges, it has not been able to dispense altogether with the *substance* of that distinction.[6] The new orientation was particularly manifested in the 1976 case of *Mathews* v. *Eldridge*, which is close to *Goldberg* in that both involved the right to a pretermination hearing over the continued receipt of benefit payments.

Mathews v. *Eldridge*

Supreme Court of the United States, 1976.
424 U.S. 319; 96 S.Ct. 893; 47 L.Ed. 2d 18.

Mr. Justice POWELL delivered the opinion of the Court.

The issue in this case is whether the Due Process Clause of the Fifth Amendment requires that prior to the termination of Social Security disability benefit payments the recipient be afforded an opportunity for an evidentiary hearing.

I

Cash benefits are provided to workers during periods in which they are completely disabled under the disability insurance benefits program created by the 1956 amendments to Title II of the Social Security Act. . . . Respondent Eldridge

---

[4] In the companion case of *Perry* v. *Sinderman*, the Court ruled that a professor who had been employed for a number of years at the same institution was entitled to attempt to show that a de facto tenure system existed at his institution and that proof of such a system would entitle him to a hearing on the matter of his dismissal [408 U.S. 593 (1972)].

[5] Victor G. Rosenblum, "Schoolchildren: Yes, Policemen: No—Some Thoughts about the Supreme Court's Priorities Concerning the Right to a Hearing in Suspension and Removal Cases," 72 *Northwestern University Law Review* 146 (1977), at 155.

[6] In the words of Pierce and associates, writing in 1999: "Thus, while the Court says it has abandoned the distinction between 'rights' subject to protection and 'privileges' not subject to protection, it is actually in the process of changing the boundary that separates 'rights' from 'privileges.' It probably will no longer call interests on each side of that boundary 'rights' and 'privileges,' but it is continuing to draw a distinction with the same effect" [Richard J. Pierce, Jr., Sidney A. Shapiro, and Paul R. Verkuil, *Administrative Law and Process* 234 (3rd ed., 1999)].

was first awarded benefits in June 1968. In March 1972, he received a questionnaire from the state agency charged with monitoring his medical condition. Eldridge completed the questionnaire, indicating that his condition had not improved and identifying the medical sources, including physicians, from whom he had received treatment recently. The state agency then obtained reports from his physician and a psychiatric consultant. After considering these reports and other information in his file the agency informed Eldridge by letter that it had made a tentative determination that his disability had ceased in May 1972. The letter included a statement of reasons for the proposed termination of benefits, and advised Eldridge that he might request reasonable time in which to obtain and submit additional information pertaining to his condition.

In his written response, Eldridge disputed one characterization of his medical condition and indicated that the agency already had enough evidence to establish his disability. The state agency then made its final determination that he had ceased to be disabled in May 1972. This determination was accepted by the Social Security Administration (SSA), which notified Eldridge in July that his benefits would terminate after that month. The notification also advised him of his right to seek reconsideration by the state agency of this initial determination within six months.

Instead of requesting reconsideration Eldridge commenced this action challenging the constitutional validity of the administrative procedures established by the Secretary of Health, Education, and Welfare for assessing whether there exists a continuing disability. . . .

The District Court concluded that the administrative procedures pursuant to which the Secretary had terminated Eldridge's benefits abridged his right to procedural due process. The court viewed the

interest of the disability recipient in uninterrupted benefits as indistinguishable from that of the welfare recipient in *Goldberg*. . . . Relying entirely upon the District Court's opinion, the Court of Appeals for the Fourth Circuit affirmed the injunction barring termination of Eldridge's benefits prior to an evidentiary hearing. . . . We reverse. . . .

Procedural due process imposes constraints on governmental decisions which deprive individuals of "liberty" or "property" interests within the meaning of the Due Process Clause of the Fifth or Fourteenth Amendment. The Secretary does not contend that procedural due process is inapplicable to terminations of Social Security disability benefits. . . .

This Court consistently has held that some form of hearing is required before an individual is finally deprived of a property interest. . . .

Eldridge agrees that the review procedures available to a claimant before the initial determination of ineligibility becomes final would be adequate if disability benefits were not terminated until after the evidentiary hearing stage of the administrative process. The dispute centers upon what process is due prior to the initial termination of benefits, pending review.

In recent years this Court increasingly has had occasion to consider the extent to which due process requires an evidentiary hearing prior to the deprivation of some type of property interest even if such a hearing is provided thereafter. In only one case, *Goldberg* v. *Kelly*, 397 U.S., at 266–271, has the Court held that a hearing closely approximating a judicial trial is necessary. . . . [R]esolution of the issue whether the administrative procedures provided here are constitutionally sufficient requires analysis of the governmental and private interests that are affected. More precisely, our prior decisions indicated that identification of the specific dictates of due process generally requires consideration of three distinct factors: first the private interest that will be affected by the official action; second, the risk of an erroneous deprivation of such interest through the procedures used, and the probable value, if any, of additional or substitute procedural safeguards; and finally, the Government's interest, including the function involved and the fiscal and administrative burdens that the additional or substitute procedural safeguards would entail.

[The Court then described the legally mandated procedures for determining disability and monitoring continuing eligibility for disability payments. This monitoring is carried out by mail or telephone, supplemented by information from the recipient's source of medical treatment. If a recipient's benefits are to be terminated, he or she is notified, provided with a summary of the evidence on which the proposed termination is based, and given an opportunity "to respond in writing and submit additional evidence." No pretermination hearing is provided, although the procedures do allow for a posttermination evidentiary hearing.]

Despite the elaborate character of the administrative procedures provided by the Secretary, the courts below held them to be constitutionally inadequate, concluding that due process requires an evidentiary hearing prior to termination. In light of the private and governmental interests at stake here and the nature of the existing procedures, we think this was error.

Since a recipient whose benefits are terminated is awarded full retroactive relief if he ultimately prevails, his sole interest is in the uninterrupted receipt of this source of income pending final administrative decision on his claim. His potential injury is thus similar in nature to that of the welfare recipient in *Goldberg*, see 397 U.S., at 263–264, the nonprobationary federal employee in *Arnett*, see

416 U.S., at 146, and the wage earner in *Sniadach*. See 395 U.S., at 341–342.

Only in *Goldberg* has the Court held that due process requires an evidentiary hearing prior to a temporary deprivation. It was emphasized there that welfare assistance is given to persons on the very margin of subsistence:

> "The crucial factor in this context—a factor not present in the case of . . . virtually anyone else whose governmental entitlements are ended—is that termination of aid pending resolution of a controversy over eligibility may deprive an *eligible* recipient of the very means by which to live while he waits." 397 U.S. at 264 (emphasis in original) . . .

Eligibility for disability benefits, in contrast, is not based upon financial need. Indeed, it is wholly unrelated to the worker's income or support from many other sources, such as earnings of other family members, workmen's compensation awards, tort claims awards, savings, private insurance, public or private pensions, veterans' benefits, food stamps, public assistance, or the "many other important programs, both public and private, which contain provisions for disability payments affecting a substantial portion of the work force. . . ." *Richardson* v. *Belcher*, 404 U.S., at 85-87 (Douglas, J., dissenting).

As *Goldberg* illustrates, the degree of potential deprivation that may be created by a particular decision is a factor to be considered in assessing the validity of any administrative decision making process. . . . The potential deprivation here is generally likely to be less than in *Goldberg*, although the degree of difference can be overstated. As the District Court emphasized, to remain eligible for benefits a recipient must be "unable to engage in substantial gainful activity." . . . Thus, in contrast to the discharged federal employee in *Arnett*, there is little possibility that the terminated recipient will be able to find even temporary employment to ameliorate the interim loss. . . . The Secretary concedes that the delay between a request for a hearing before an administrative law judge and a decision on the claim is currently between 10 and 11 months. Since a terminated recipient must first obtain a reconsideration decision as a prerequisite to invoking his right to an evidentiary hearing, the delay between the actual cutoff of benefits and final decision after a hearing exceeds one year.

In view of the torpidity of this administrative review process, and the typically modest resources of the family unit of the physically disabled worker, the hardship imposed upon the erroneously terminated disability recipient may be significant. Still, the disabled worker's need is likely to be less than that of a welfare recipient. In addition to the possibility of access to private resources, other forms of government assistance will become available where the termination of disability benefits places a worker or his family below the subsistence level. In view of these potential sources of temporary income, there is less reason here than in *Goldberg* to depart from the ordinary principle, established by our decisions, that something less than an evidentiary hearing is sufficient prior to adverse administrative action. . . .

An additional factor to be considered here is the fairness and reliability of the existing pretermination procedures, and the probable value, if any, of additional procedural safeguards. Central to the evaluation of any administrative process is the nature of the relevant inquiry. In order to remain eligible for benefits the disabled worker must demonstrate by means of "medically acceptable clinical and laboratory diagnostic techniques," . . . that he is unable "to engage in any substantial gainful activity by reason of any *medically determinable* physical or mental impairment. . . ." In short, a medical assessment of the worker's physical or

mental condition is required. This is a more sharply focused and easily documented decision than the typical determination of welfare entitlement. . . .

The decision in *Goldberg* also was based on the Court's conclusion that written submissions were an inadequate substitute for oral presentation because they did not provide an effective means for the recipient to communicate his case to the decision maker. Written submissions were viewed as an unrealistic option, for most recipients lacked the "educational attainment necessary to write effectively" and could not afford professional assistance. In addition, such submissions would not provide the "flexibility of oral presentations" or "permit the recipient to mold his argument to the issues the decision maker appears to regard as important." . . . In the context of the disability-benefits-entitlement assessment the administrative procedures under review here fully answer these objections.

The detailed questionnaire which the state agency periodically sends the recipient identifies with particularity the information relevant to the entitlement decision, and the recipient is invited to obtain assistance from the local SSA office in completing the questionnaire. More important, the information critical to the entitlement decision usually is derived from medical sources, such as the treating physician. Such sources are likely to be able to communicate more effectively through written documents than are welfare recipients or the lay witnesses supporting their cause. The conclusions of physicians often are supported by X-rays and the results of clinical or laboratory tests, information typically more amenable to written than to oral presentation. . . .

In striking the appropriate due process balance the final factor to be assessed is the public interest. This includes the administrative burden and other societal costs that would be associated with requiring, as a matter of constitutional right, an evidentiary hearing upon demand in all cases prior to the termination of disability benefits. The most visible burden would be the incremental cost resulting from the increased number of hearings and the expense of providing benefits to ineligible recipients pending decision. No one can predict the extent of the increase, but the fact that full benefits would continue until after such hearings would assure the exhaustion in most cases of this attractive option. . . .

In assessing what process is due in this case, substantial weight must be given to the good-faith judgments of the individuals charged by Congress with the administration of social welfare programs that the procedures they have provided assure fair consideration of the entitlement claims of individuals. This is especially so where, as here, the prescribed procedures not only provide the claimant with an effective process for asserting his claim prior to any administrative action,

but also assure a right to an evidentiary hearing, as well as to subsequent judicial review, before the denial of his claim becomes final.

We conclude that an evidentiary hearing is not required prior to the termination of disability benefits and that the present administrative procedures fully comport with due process.

The judgment of the Court of Appeals is

Reversed.

Mr. Justice STEVENS took no part in the consideration or decision of this case.

Mr. Justice BRENNAN, with whom Mr. Justice MARSHALL concurs, dissenting.

For the reasons stated in my dissenting opinion in *Richardson* v. *Wright*, 405 U.S. 208, 212 (1972), I agree with the District Court and the Court of Appeals that, prior to termination of benefits, Eldridge must be afforded an evidentiary hearing of the type required for welfare beneficiaries. . . .

Application of the Mathews *Doctrine*

It is without question that *Mathews* v. *Eldridge* has been the key case with regard to property interests and due process for more than a quarter century. Its three-part test for due process balancing cited above (the private interest affected by government action; the risk of erroneous deprivation of that interest as a result of the procedures provided; and the government's interest) has become the primary decision tool for courts in handling such cases.

A good example is *Gilbert* v. *Homar*, 520 U.S. 924 (1997), in which the Supreme Court upheld the suspension without pay of an employee of a state university in Pennsylvania. A unanimous Court ruled that no presuspension hearing was required as long as a prompt postsuspension hearing was provided. The Court's reasoning focused on balancing the three factors cited above from *Mathews* v. *Eldridge*. It asserted that the state had "a significant interest in immediately suspending" the employee, who had been arrested on a felony drug charge, which was later dismissed (520 U.S. 926–927, 932).

The need for *immediate* governmental action mentioned in *Gilbert* v. *Homar* has been a factor in a number of other cases that have relied on *Mathews* v. *Eldridge*. One of these is *Mackey* v. *Montrym*, 443 U.S. 1 (1979), in which the Supreme Court upheld the suspension of the driver's license of a driver who refused to take a Breathalyzer test upon arrest for driving while intoxicated. One of the justifications for not requiring a prior hearing in this case was the assertion that it would forestall necessary administrative action. The point was even made that removing drunken drivers from the highways is within the ambit of "summary procedures" which the courts "have traditionally accorded the states great leeway in adopting" (441 U.S. 1). This is one of the illustrations of the recent expansion of the concept of summary powers. The use of such authority, according to one scholar, "had its roots in the common law of nuisance."[7] Its early application was typically premised on the existence of "extraordinary" or "emergency"[8] circumstances, upon a "pressing need for quick action."[9]

If the grounds for employing summary authority have been expanded in recent years, there are still occasions when summary administrative activity, in the more traditional sense, is necessary. In such cases, the need for swift administrative action will obviate any possible justification for a prior hearing. The following case is an example.

Hodel v. *Virginia Surface Mining and Reclamation Association, Inc.*

SUPREME COURT OF THE UNITED STATES, 1981.
452 U.S. 264, 101 S.Ct. 2352, 69 L.Ed. 2d 1.

[An association of coal producers brought suit challenging the constitutionality of parts of the Surface Mining Control and Reclamation Act of 1977, which was designed to combat the adverse effects of surface coal-mining operations.[10] The act was administered by the secretary of the interior in cooperation with the state governments. The Office of Surface Mining Reclamation and Enforcement (OSM), within the Department of the Interior, actually carried out the regulatory and enforcement programs, including inspecting surface-mining operations for violations of the act. The complaints alleged that several of the act's provisions were unconstitutional. The district court ruled in favor of some of the plaintiff's constitutional claims and against others. The issue of relevance here is the association's assertion that the act violated procedural due process requirements, a claim the district court supported. In its review the Supreme Court ruled against the association on all of its constitutional challenges. The excerpt below, from the long majority opinion of Justice Marshall, involves only the part of the decision pertaining to the procedural due process implications of summary action permitted under the act. As the numerous citations included in this excerpt indicate, the Supreme Court has been called upon on numerous occasions to rule on the constitutionality of the exercise of summary powers.]

Justice MARSHALL delivered the opinion of the Court. . . .

The District Court next ruled that the Act contravenes the Fifth Amendment because a number of its enforcement provi-

---

[7] James O. Freedman, *Crisis and Legitimacy: The Administrative Process and American Government* 208 (1978).

[8] Ibid., 209.

[9] Jerry L. Mashaw and Richard A. Merrill, *Introduction to the American Public Law System* 374 (1975).

[10] 30 U.S.C. § 1201 et seq.

sions offend the Amendment's Due Process Clause. One such provision is § 521 (a)(2), . . . which instructs the Secretary immediately to order total or partial cessation of a surface mining operation whenever he determines, on the basis of a federal inspection, that the operation is in violation of the Act or a permit condition required by the Act and that the operation

> creates an immediate danger to the health or safety of the public, or is causing, or can reasonably be expected to cause significant, imminent environmental harm to land, air, or water resources. . . .

The District Court held that § 521 (a)(2)'s authorization of immediate cessation orders violates the Fifth Amendment because the statute does not provide sufficiently objective criteria for summary administrative action. . . .

Our cases have indicated that due process ordinarily requires an opportunity for "some kind of hearing" prior to the deprivation of a significant property interest. . . . The Court has often acknowledged, however, that summary administrative action may be justified in emergency situations. . . . The question then, is whether the issuance of immediate cessation orders under § 521 (a) falls under this emergency situation exception to the normal rule that due process requires a hearing prior to deprivation of a property right. We believe that it does.

The immediate cessation order provisions reflect Congress' concern about the devastating damage that may result from mining disasters. They represent an attempt to reach an accommodation between the legitimate desire of mining companies to be heard before submitting to administrative regulation and the governmental interest in protecting the public health and safety and the environment from imminent danger. Protection of the health and safety of the public is a paramount governmental interest which justi-

fies summary administrative action. Indeed, deprivation of property to protect the public health and safety is "[one] of the oldest examples" of permissible summary action. *Ewing* v. *Mytinger & Casselberry, Inc.*, supra, at 599. See *Mackey* v. *Montrym*, 443 U.S. 1, 17-18 (1979); id., at 21, n. 1, 25 (STEWART, J., dissenting); *North American Cold Storage Co.* v. *Chicago*, supra, at 315-316. Moreover, the administrative action provided through immediate cessation orders responds to situations in which swift action is necessary to protect the public health and safety. This is precisely the type of emergency situation in which this Court has found summary administrative action justified. See *Ewing* v. *Mytinger & Casselberry, Inc.*, supra; *North American Cold Storage Co.* v. *Chicago*, supra.

Rather than taking issue with any of these principles, the District Court held that the Act does not establish sufficiently objective criteria governing the issuance of summary cessation orders. We disagree. In our judgment, the criteria established by the Act and the Secretary's implementing regulations are specific enough to control governmental action and reduce the risk of erroneous deprivation. Section 701 (8) of the Act . . . , defines the threat of "imminent danger to the health and safety of the public" as the existence of a condition or practice which could

> [reasonably] be expected to cause substantial physical harm to persons outside the permit area before such condition, practice, or violation can be abated. A reasonable expectation of death or serious injury before abatement exists if a rational person, subjected to the same conditions or practices giving rise to the peril, would not expose himself or herself to the danger during the time necessary for abatement.

If anything, these standards are more specific than the criteria in other statutes authorizing summary administrative action that have been upheld against due process challenges. See, e. g., *Ewing* v. *Mytinger & Casselberry, Inc.*, supra, at 595-596 ("'dangerous to health . . . or would be in a material respect misleading to the injury or damage of the purchaser or consumer'"); *Fahey* v. *Mallonee*, supra, at 250-251, n. 1 ("is unsafe or unfit to manage a Federal savings and loan association" or "[is] in imminent danger of becoming impaired"); *Air East, Inc.* v. *National Transportation Safety Board*, 512 F.2d 1227, 1232 (CA3) ("emergency requiring immediate action . . . in respect to air safety in commerce").

The fact that OSM inspectors have issued immediate cessation orders that were later overturned on administrative appeal does not undermine the adequacy of the Act's criteria but instead demonstrates the efficacy of the review procedures. The relevant inquiry is not whether a cessation order should have been issued in a particular case, but whether the statutory procedure itself is incapable of affording due process. . . . The possibility of administrative error inheres in any regulatory program; statutory programs authorizing emergency administrative action prior to a hearing are no exception. As we explained in *Ewing* v. *Mytinger & Casselberry, Inc.*, 339 U.S., at 599:

> Discretion of any official action may be abused. Yet it is not a requirement of due process that there be judicial inquiry before discretion can be exercised. It is sufficient, where only property rights are concerned, that there is at some stage an opportunity for a hearing and a judicial determination.

Here, mine operators are afforded prompt and adequate post-deprivation administrative hearings and an opportunity for judicial review. We are satisfied that the Act's immediate cessation order provisions comport with the requirements of due process. . . .

[The concurring opinions of the Chief Justice and Justice Powell and the opinion of Justice Rehnquist concurring in the judgment are omitted.]

The authority for the use of summary power in cases of seizure or dangerous or illegal products has been sanctioned by the Supreme Court at least as far back as the late nineteenth century. In some of the early cases, the Court upheld statutes providing not only for seizure but also for summary destruction of the offending objects. See, for instance *Lawton* v. *Steele*, 152 U.S. 133, 14 S.Ct. 499 (1894) (illegal fish nets), and *North American Cold Storage Co.* v. *Chicago*, 211 U.S. 306 (1908) (allegedly putrid poultry). Although the *North American Cold Storage* case is still cited approvingly by the Supreme Court, it seems unlikely that the Court would today approve summary administrative action that involved destruction of private property unless that destruction were absolutely necessary.

CIVIL FORFEITURE AND DUE PROCESS

Asset forfeiture is a legal concept whose roots can be traced to ancient times.[11] In American law two forms are recognized. Criminal forfeiture is

---

[11] Leonard W. Levy, *A License to Steal: The Forfeiture of Property* 7–20 (1996).

assessed against the person (in personam). Civil forfeiture is against the thing in question (in rem), inanimate property that is seen as having a relationship to alleged or actual criminal activity committed by a person. Thus, cases involving civil forfeiture that get to court sometimes have curious names, such as *One 1958 Plymouth Sedan* v. *Commonwealth of Pennsylvania* (380 U.S. 693), an important case decided by the Supreme Court in 1965.

Civil forfeiture has long existed in U.S. law, both on the federal level and in the states. But its importance has increased considerably in recent years, largely as a result of federal legislation adopted in the 1970s and 1980s to fight the war against illegal drugs.[12] Civil forfeiture is justified by two rationales:

1. That the asset in question facilitated the commission of an illegal act (it was an "instrument of the crime," as it was sometimes put) and is therefore subject to confiscation. A car or boat used to carry illegal goods would be examples, as would a house used to prepare narcotics or carry out narcotics transactions.
2. Or that the asset was acquired as a result of illegal actions. Examples would be the cash proceeds from drug deals or property purchased with such proceeds.

Since in rem proceedings are against things rather than people, they are not classified as criminal proceedings (or at least not quite criminal; the term *quasi-criminal* is sometimes used with regard to civil forfeiture[13]). And the level of protection, including constitutional protection, available to persons whose property has been subject to forfeiture has traditionally been decidedly lower than that available to defendants in purely criminal cases.

In recent years, however, public attention to problems associated with civil forfeiture has increased.[14] And the courts, including the Supreme Court, have heard large numbers of cases growing out of the hundreds of thousands of seizures of property.[15] The following case, decided by the Supreme Court in 1993, is one of the Court's most important decisions in this area. Note in the part of the decision excerpted below the reliance on *Mathews* v. *Eldridge* and discussion of summary powers.

---

[12] See 18 U.S.C. §§ 981 et seq. and 21 U.S.C. §§ 801 et seq. Another forfeiture measure was adopted as part of the comprehensive antiterrorism legislation that Congress passed after the September 11, 2001, terrorist attacks in the United States. It allows for seizure of funds in accounts in foreign banks that have interbank accounts in the United States [Public Law 107-56, 115 Stat. 272 (October 26, 2001)]. Section 319 of this law, "forfeiture of funds in United States interbank accounts," was codified as subsection k of 18 U.S.C. § 981.

[13] "Finally as Justice Bradley aptly pointed out in *Boyd*, a forfeiture proceeding is quasi-criminal in character" [Justice Goldberg for eight members of the Supreme Court in *One 1958 Plymouth Sedan* v. *Commonwealth of Pennsylvania*, 380 U.S. 693, at 700 (1965)].

[14] See, e.g., Levy's book, above, note 11, and the many sources cited therein; also the sources cited in "Civil Asset Forfeiture Reform Act," report number 106-92, Committee on the Judiciary, U.S. House of Representatives, June 18, 1999. A search in the Lexis data base for "civil forfeiture" for the last half of the 1990s produced 847 entries. And at least two documentary videos were produced during the 1990s, one a *Sixty Minutes* segment from 1992 entitled "You're under Arrest," and the other a Films for the Humanities and Sciences video titled *Guilty until Proven Innocent* (FFH 4286).

[15] On numbers of seizures, see Levy, above, note 11, 139, and Judd J. Balmer, "Note: Civil Forfeiture Under 21 U.S.C. § 881 and the Eighth Amendment's Excessive Fines Clause," 38 *Arizona Law Review* 999, 1000 (1996).

United States v. *James Daniel Good Real Property*

SUPREME COURT OF THE UNITED STATES, 1993.
510 U.S. 43, 114 S.Ct. 492, 126 L.Ed. 2d 490.

[After illegal drugs and drug paraphernalia were found in James Daniel Good's house in Hawaii as a result of a search with a warrant, Good pleaded guilty to violating state drug laws and was sentenced. Four and a half years after the drugs were found, the United States sought forfeiture of Good's house and four acres of land on which the house was situated under 21 U.S.C. 881 (a) (7), which authorizes civil forfeiture of property used to commit or facilitate the commission of a federal drug offense.

In a proceeding at which Good was not present (a so-called ex parte proceeding, from Latin, meaning "on one side only"), a U.S. magistrate judge, after hearing evidence, authorized seizure of the property by the U.S. government. Good was renting the house at the time of this proceeding. In addition to seizure of the house, future rent payments were directed to the government.

Good filed suit against the government's action, asserting that the seizure deprived him of his property without due process of law. He also claimed that the forfeiture was invalid because it had not been initiated in a timely fashion. Although this and other matters were also examined by the court of appeals and the Supreme Court, the focus of our analysis will be on the due process issue.

The district court ruled in the government's favor, agreeing to its motion for summary judgment and entering an order forfeiting the property. The court of appeals reversed on the main issue, holding that the seizure without prior notice and hearing violated due process.

The Supreme Court's examination of the case produced a complex set of responses from the justices. Four separate opinions were written, three of them concurring in part and dissenting in part. Although all nine justices were able to agree that the government's appeal had been filed in a timely fashion, they split five to four on the crucial issue of due process. The excerpt below is from the majority's analysis of this issue.]

Justice KENNEDY delivered the opinion of the Court.

The principal question presented is whether, in the absence of exigent circumstances, the Due Process Clause of the Fifth Amendment prohibits the Government in a civil forfeiture case from seizing real property without first affording the owner notice and an opportunity to be heard. We hold that it does. . . .

The Due Process Clause of the Fifth Amendment guarantees that "no person shall . . . be deprived of life, liberty, or property, without due process of law." Our precedents establish the general rule that individuals must receive notice and an opportunity to be heard before the Government deprives them of property.

The Government does not, and could not, dispute that the seizure of Good's home and 4-acre parcel deprived him of property interests protected by the Due Process Clause. By the Government's own submission, the seizure gave it the right to charge rent, to condition occupancy, and even to evict the occupants. Instead, the Government argues that it afforded Good all the process the Constitution requires. The Government makes two separate points in this regard. First, it contends that compliance with the Fourth Amendment suffices when the Government seizes property for purposes of forfeiture. In the alternative, it argues that the seizure of real property under the drug forfeiture laws justifies an exception to the usual due process requirement of preseizure notice and hearing. We turn to these issues.

A

The Government argues that because civil forfeiture serves a "law enforcement purpose," the Government need comply only with the Fourth Amendment when seizing forfeitable property. We disagree. The Fourth Amendment does place restrictions on seizures conducted for purposes of civil forfeiture, *One 1958 Plymouth Sedan* v. *Pennsylvania*, 380 U.S. 693, 696, 14 L.Ed. 2d 170, 85 S.Ct. 1246 (1965) (holding that the exclusionary rule applies to civil forfeiture), but it does not follow that the Fourth Amendment is the sole constitutional provision in question when the Government seizes property subject to forfeiture.

We have rejected the view that the applicability of one constitutional amendment pre-empts the guarantees of another. As explained in *Soldal* v. *Cook County*, 506 U.S. 56, 70, 121 L.Ed. 2d 450, 113 S.Ct. 538 (1992):

> Certain wrongs affect more than a single right and, accordingly, can implicate more than one of the Constitution's commands. Where such multiple violations are alleged, we are not in the habit of identifying as a preliminary matter the claim's 'dominant' character. Rather, we examine each constitutional provision in turn.

Though the Fourth Amendment places limits on the Government's power to seize property for purposes of forfeiture, it does not provide the sole measure of constitutional protection that must be afforded property owners in forfeiture proceedings. So even assuming that the Fourth Amendment were satisfied in this case, it remains for us to determine whether the seizure complied with our well-settled jurisprudence under the Due Process Clause.

B

Whether ex parte seizures of forfeitable property satisfy the Due Process Clause is a question we last confronted in *Calero-Toledo* v. *Pearson Yacht Leasing Co.*, [416 U.S. 663, 40 L.Ed. 2d 452, 94 S.Ct. 2080 (1974)], which held that the Government could seize a yacht subject to civil forfeiture without affording prior notice or hearing. Central to our analysis in *Calero-Toledo* was the fact that a yacht was the "sort [of property] that could be removed to another jurisdiction, destroyed, or concealed, if advance warning of confiscation were given." . . . The ease with which an owner could frustrate the Government's interests in the forfeitable property created a "'special need for very prompt action'" that justified the postponement of notice and hearing until after the seizure. . . .

We had no occasion in *Calero-Toledo* to decide whether the same considerations apply to the forfeiture of real property, which, by its very nature, can be neither moved nor concealed. In fact, when *Calero-Toledo* was decided, both the Puerto Rican statute, . . . and the federal forfeiture statute upon which it was modeled, . . . authorized the forfeiture of personal property only. It was not until 1984, 10 years later, that Congress amended § 881 to authorize the forfeiture of real property. . . .

We tolerate some exceptions to the general rule requiring predeprivation notice and hearing, but only in "'extraordinary situations where some valid governmental interest is at stake that justifies postponing the hearing until after the event.'" . . . Whether the seizure of real property for purposes of civil forfeiture justifies such an exception requires an examination of the competing interests at stake, along with the promptness and adequacy of later proceedings. The three-part inquiry set forth in *Mathews* v. *Eldridge*, 424 U.S. 319, 47 L.Ed. 2d 18, 96

S.Ct. 893 (1976), provides guidance in this regard. The *Mathews* analysis requires us to consider the private interest affected by the official action; the risk of an erroneous deprivation of that interest through the procedures used, as well as the probable value of additional safeguards; and the Government's interest, including the administrative burden that additional procedural requirements would impose. . . .

Good's right to maintain control over his home, and to be free from governmental interference, is a private interest of historic and continuing importance. The seizure deprived Good of valuable rights of ownership, including the right of sale, the right of occupancy, the right to unrestricted use and enjoyment, and the right to receive rents. All that the seizure left him, by the Government's own submission, was the right to bring a claim for the return of title at some unscheduled future hearing. . . .

The Government makes much of the fact that Good was renting his home to tenants, and contends that the tangible effect of the seizure was limited to taking the $900 a month he was due in rent. But even if this were the only deprivation at issue, it would not render the loss insignificant or unworthy of due process protection. The rent represents a significant portion of the exploitable economic value of Good's home. It cannot be classified as *de minimis* for purposes of procedural due process. In sum, the private interests at stake in the seizure of real property weigh heavily in the *Mathews* balance.

The practice of *ex parte* seizure, moreover, creates an unacceptable risk of error. Although Congress designed the drug forfeiture statute to be a powerful instrument in enforcement of the drug laws, it did not intend to deprive innocent owners of their property. The affirmative defense of innocent ownership is allowed by statute. . . .

The *ex parte* preseizure proceeding affords little or no protection to the innocent owner. . . . The purpose of an adversary hearing is to ensure the requisite neutrality that must inform all governmental decision-making. That protection is of particular importance here, where the Government has a direct pecuniary interest in the outcome of the proceeding.

This brings us to the third consideration under *Mathews*, "the Government's interest, including the function involved and the fiscal and administrative burdens that the additional or substitute procedural requirement would entail." 424 U.S. at 335. The governmental interest we consider here is not some general interest in forfeiting property but the specific interest in seizing real property before the forfeiture hearing. The question in the civil forfeiture context is whether *ex parte* seizure is justified by a pressing need for prompt action. We find no pressing need here.

This is apparent by comparison to *Calero-Toledo*, where the Government's interest in immediate seizure of a yacht subject to civil forfeiture justified dispensing with the usual requirement of prior notice and hearing. Two essential considerations informed our ruling in that case: First, immediate seizure was necessary to establish the court's jurisdiction over the property, . . . and second, the yacht might have disappeared had the Government given advance warning of the forfeiture action. . . . Neither of these factors is present when the target of forfeiture is real property.

Because real property cannot abscond, the court's jurisdiction can be preserved without prior seizure. It is true that seizure of the res has long been considered a prerequisite to the initiation of *in rem* forfeiture proceedings. This rule had its origins in the Court's early admiralty cases, which involved the forfeiture of vessels and other movable personal property. Justice Story, writing for the Court in *The Brig Ann*, explained the justification for the rule as one of fixing and preserving jurisdiction: "Before judicial cognizance can attach upon a forfeiture *in rem*, . . . there must be a seizure; for until seizure it is impossible to ascertain what is the competent forum." [13 U.S. 289, at 291, 9 Cranch 289, 3 L.Ed. 734 (1815)]. But when the res is real property, rather than personal goods, the appropriate judicial forum may be determined without actual seizure.

As *The Brig Ann* held, all that is necessary "in order to institute and perfect proceedings *in rem*, [is] that the thing should be actually or constructively within the reach of the Court." . . .

Requiring the Government to postpone seizure until after an adversary hearing creates no significant administrative burden. A claimant is already entitled to an adversary hearing before a final judgment of forfeiture. No extra hearing would be required in the typical case, since the Government can wait until after the forfeiture judgment to seize the property. From an administrative standpoint it makes little difference whether that hearing is held before or after the seizure. And any harm that results from delay is minimal in comparison to the injury occasioned by erroneous seizure.

C

It is true that, in cases decided over a century ago, we permitted the *ex parte* seizure of real property when the Government was collecting debts or revenue. Without revisiting these cases, it suffices to say that their apparent rationale—like that for allowing summary seizures during wartime, and seizures of contaminated food—was one of executive urgency. "The prompt payment of taxes," we noted, "may be vital to the existence of a government."

A like rationale justified the *ex parte* seizure of tax-delinquent distilleries in the late 19th century, since before passage of the Sixteenth Amendment, the Federal Government relied heavily on liquor, customs, and tobacco taxes to generate operating revenues. . . .

The federal income tax code adopted in the first quarter of [the twentieth] century, however, afforded the taxpayer notice and an opportunity to be heard by the Board of Tax Appeals before the Government could seize property for nonpayment of taxes. In *Phillips* v. *Commissioner*, 283 U.S. 589, 75 L. Ed. 1289, 51 S.Ct. 608 (1931), the Court relied upon the availability, and adequacy, of these preseizure administrative procedures in holding that no judicial hearing was required prior to the seizure of property. These constraints on the Commissioner could be overridden, but only when the Commissioner made a determination that a jeopardy assessment was necessary. . . . Writing for a unanimous Court, Justice Brandeis explained that under the tax laws "formal notice of the tax liability is thus given; the Commissioner is required to answer; and there is a complete hearing *de novo*. . . . These provisions amply protect the [taxpayer] against improper administrative action." . . .

Similar provisions remain in force today. The current Internal Revenue Code prohibits the Government from levying upon a deficient taxpayer's property without first affording the taxpayer notice and an opportunity for a hearing, unless exigent circumstances indicate that delay will jeopardize the collection of taxes due. . . .

Just as the urgencies that justified summary seizure of property in the 19th century had dissipated by the time of *Phillips*, neither is there a plausible claim of urgency today to justify the summary seizure of real property under § 881(a)(7). Although the Government relies to some extent on forfeitures as a means of defraying law enforcement expenses, it does not, and we think could not, justify the prehearing seizure of forfeitable real property as necessary for the protection of its revenues.

D

The constitutional limitations we enforce in this case apply to real property in general, not simply to residences. That said, the case before us well illustrates an essential principle: Individual freedom finds tangible expression in property rights. At stake in this and many other forfeiture cases are the security and privacy of the home and those who take shelter within it.

Finally, the suggestion that this one claimant must lose because his conviction was known at the time of seizure, and because he raises an as applied challenge to the statute, founders on a bedrock proposition: Fair procedures are not confined to the innocent. The question before us is the legality of the seizure, not the strength of the Government's case.

In sum, based upon the importance of the private interests at risk and the absence of countervailing Government needs, we hold that the seizure of real property under § 881(a)(7) is not one of those extraordinary instances that justify the postponement of notice and hearing. Unless exigent circumstances are present, the Due Process Clause requires the Government to afford notice and a meaningful opportunity to be heard before seizing real property subject to civil forfeiture.

To establish exigent circumstances, the Government must show that less restrictive measures—*i.e.*, a *lis pendens* [a pending suit], restraining order, or bond—would not suffice to protect the Government's interests in preventing the sale, destruction, or continued unlawful use of the real property. We agree with the Court of Appeals that no showing of exigent circumstances has been made in this case, and we affirm its ruling that the *ex parte* seizure of Good's real property violated due process. . . .

[The opinions of Chief Justice Rehnquist (joined by Justice Scalia and in part by Justice O'Connor), Justice O'Connor, and Justice Thomas, concurring in part and dissenting in part, are omitted].

The due process requirements of the *Good* decision were written into a comprehensive Civil Asset Forfeiture Reform Act of 2000, Public Law 106-185, 114 Stat. 202.[16] This legislation did not accomplish everything that reformers wanted,[17] but it is generally agreed that the new law addressed some of the issues of basic fairness in forfeiture proceedings.

DEGREE OF FORMALITY

Justice Black complained in a dissenting opinion in *Goldberg* v. *Kelly* (not included in the excerpt printed earlier in this chapter) that the procedural

---

[16] Public Law 106-185, 114 Stat. 202. These provisions were codified as 18 U.S.C. § 985. For a discussion of the *Good* case and its relationship to the 2000 legislation, see Clinton P. Sanko, "The Appropriate Remedy for Failing to Comply with Constitutional Mandates in a Civil In Rem Forfeiture of Real Property," 105 *Dickinson Law Review* 129 (2000).

[17] On this point see David Rovella, "Defenders argue asset seizure bill is too mild," *The National Law Journal*, April 24, 2000, A1.

complexity ordered in that case would work against welfare recipients by inducing welfare agencies to carry out more exhaustive investigations before putting claimants on the welfare rolls in the first place. Beyond the area of welfare benefits, a more general concern about overjudicialization of administrative processes has been expressed by numerous analysts. Something is to be said, therefore, for protecting due process rights through less formal procedures. The following case represents an example of the Supreme Court's efforts to mandate an approach of that kind.

Goss v. Lopez

SUPREME COURT OF THE UNITED STATES, 1975.
419 U.S. 565, 95 S.Ct. 729, 42 L.Ed. 2d 725.

[Several Columbus, Ohio, school students were temporarily suspended without a hearing, either prior to the suspensions or within a reasonable time thereafter. The students sued for a declaration that the Ohio statute under which they were suspended was unconstitutional. The U.S. district court ruled that the students had been denied due process and ordered school administrators to remove all references to the suspensions from the students' records. The school administrators appealed.]

Mr. Justice WHITE delivered the opinion of the Court. . . .

At the outset, appellants contend that because there is no constitutional right to an education at public expense, the Due Process Clause does not protect against expulsions from the public school system. This position misconceives the nature of the issue and is refuted by prior decisions. The Fourteenth Amendment forbids the State to deprive any person of life, liberty, or property without due process of law. Protected interests in property are normally "not created by the Constitution. Rather, they are created and their dimensions are defined" by an independent source such as state statutes or rules entitling the citizen to certain benefits. *Board of Regents* v. *Roth*, 408 U.S. 564, 577 (1972).

Accordingly, a state employee who

under state law, or rules promulgated by state officials, has a legitimate claim of entitlement to continued employment absent sufficient cause for discharge may demand the procedural protections of due process. So may welfare recipients who have statutory rights to welfare as long as they maintain the specified qualifications. . . .

Here, on the basis of state law, appellees plainly had legitimate claims of entitlement to a public education. . . . Having chosen to extend the right to an education to people of appellees' class generally, Ohio may not withdraw that right on grounds of misconduct, absent fundamentally fair procedures to determine whether the misconduct has occurred. . . .

Appellants proceed to argue that even if there is a right to a public education protected by the Due Process Clause generally, the Clause comes into play only when the State subjects a student to a "severe detriment or grievous loss." The loss of 10 days, it is said, is neither severe nor grievous and the Due Process Clause is therefore of no relevance. . . . The Court's view has been that as long as a property deprivation is not *de minimis*, its gravity is irrelevant to the question whether account must be taken of the Due Process Clause. A 10-day suspension from school is not *de minimis* in our view and may not be imposed in complete disregard of the

Due Process Clause. . . . Disciplinarians, although proceeding in utmost good faith, frequently act on the reports and advice of others; and the controlling facts and the nature of the conduct under challenge are often disputed. The risk of error is not at all trivial, and it should be guarded against if that may be done without prohibitive cost or interference with the educational process.

The difficulty is that our schools are vast and complex. Some modicum of discipline and order is essential if the educational function is to be performed. Events calling for discipline are frequent occurrences and sometimes require immediate, effective action. Suspension is considered not only to be a necessary tool to maintain order but a valuable educational device. The prospect of imposing elaborate hearing requirements in every suspension case is viewed with great concern, and many school authorities may well prefer the untrammeled power to act unilaterally, unhampered by rules about notice and hearing. But it would be a strange disciplinary system in an educational institution if no communication was sought by the disciplinarian with the student in an effort to inform him of his dereliction and to let him tell his side of the story in order to make sure that an injustice is not done. . . .

We do not believe that school authorities must be totally free from notice and hearing requirements if their schools are to operate with acceptable efficiency. Students facing temporary suspension have interests qualifying for protection of the Due Process Clause, and due process requires, in connection with a suspension of 10 days or less, that the student be given oral or written notice of the charges against him and, if he denies them, an explanation of the evidence the authorities have and an opportunity to present his side of the story. The Clause requires at least these rudimentary precautions against unfair or mistaken findings of misconduct and arbitrary exclusion from school.

There need be no delay between the time "notice" is given and the time of the hearing. In the great majority of cases the disciplinarian may informally discuss the alleged misconduct with the student minutes after it has occurred. We hold only that, in being given an opportunity to explain his version of the facts at this discussion, the student first be told what he is accused of doing and what the basis of the accusation is. Lower courts which have addressed the question of the *nature* of the procedures required in short suspension cases have reached the same conclusion. Since the hearing may occur almost immediately following the misconduct, it follows that as a general rule notice and hearing should precede removal of the student from school. We agree with the District Court, however, that there are recurring situations in which prior notice and hearing cannot be insisted upon. Students whose presence poses a continuing danger to persons or property or an ongoing threat of disrupting the academic process may be immediately removed from school. In such cases, the necessary notice and rudimentary hearing should follow as soon as practicable, as the District Court indicated.

In holding as we do, we do not believe that we have imposed procedures on school disciplinarians which are inappropriate in a classroom setting. Instead we have imposed requirements which are, if anything, less than a fair-minded school principal would impose upon himself in order to avoid unfair suspensions. Indeed, according to the testimony of the principal of Marion-Franklin High School, that school had an informal procedure, remarkably similar to that which we now require, applicable to suspensions generally but which was not followed in this case. . . .

We stop short of construing the Due Process Clause to require, countrywide, that hearings in connection with short suspensions must afford the student the opportunity to secure counsel, to confront and cross-examine witnesses supporting the charge, or to call his own witnesses to verify his version of the incident. Brief disciplinary suspensions are almost countless. To impose in each such case even truncated trial-type procedures might well overwhelm administrative facilities in many places and, by diverting resources, cost more than it would save in educational effectiveness. Moreover, further formalizing the suspension process and escalating its formality and adversary nature may not only make it too costly as a regular disciplinary tool but also destroy its effectiveness as part of the teaching process.

On the other hand, requiring effective notice and informal hearing permitting the student to give his version of the events will provide a meaningful hedge against erroneous action. At least the disciplinarian will be alerted to the existence of disputes about facts and arguments about cause and effect. He may then determine himself to summon the accuser, permit cross-examination, and allow the student to present his own witnesses. In more difficult cases, he may permit counsel. In any event, his discretion will be more informed and we think the risk of error substantially reduced.

Requiring that there be at least an informal give-and-take between student and disciplinarian, preferably prior to the suspension, will add little to the factfinding function where the disciplinarian himself has witnessed the conduct forming the basis for the charge. But things are not always as they seem to be, and the student will at least have the opportunity to characterize his conduct and put it in what he deems the proper context.

We should also make it clear that we have addressed ourselves solely to the short suspension, not exceeding 10 days. Longer suspensions or expulsions for the remainder of the school term, or permanently, may require more formal procedures. Nor do we put aside the possibility that in unusual situations, although involving only a short suspension, something more than the rudimentary procedures will be required.

IV

The District Court found each of the suspensions involved here to have occurred without a hearing, either before or after the suspension, and that each suspension was therefore invalid and the statute unconstitutional insofar as it permits such suspensions without notice or hearing. Accordingly, the judgment is

Affirmed.

[The dissenting opinion of Justice Powell, joined by the Chief Justice, Justice Blackmun, and Justice Rehnquist, is omitted].

A leading analyst asserts that the "principles and reasoning" of the *Goss* decision should be applied "on a near universal basis." He argues as follows: "Agencies rarely take actions whose adverse effects on an individual are so trivial that the action should be taken without notice and the opportunity for an informal hearing. The few minutes required to provide the kind of hearing described in *Goss* imposes little burden on an agency relative to its benefits in the form of enhanced fairness and accuracy."[18]

A case decided just two years after *Goss* indicates, however, that the

---

[18] Richard J. Pierce, Jr., 2 *Administrative Law Treatise* 574 (4th ed., 2002).

Supreme Court is not ready to take this step. In *Ingraham* v. *Wright*, 430 U.S. 651, 97 S.Ct. 1401, 51 L.Ed. 2d 711 (1977), two students in a Dade County, Florida, school were subjected to disciplinary paddling without prior notice and hearing. The plaintiffs alleged that the severity of the paddling constituted cruel and unusual punishment under the Eighth Amendment, and that the procedure leading up to their punishment violated the Due Process Clause of the Fourteenth Amendment. Two lower courts ruled against the plaintiffs, and the Supreme Court, by a five-to-four majority, affirmed.

Justice Powell, writing for the majority, asserted that the original purpose of the Eighth Amendment's prohibition was to limit punishment in the true criminal law context. He concluded that the school setting provided "an inadequate basis for wrenching the Eighth Amendment from its historical context and extending it to traditional disciplinary practices in the public schools" (430 U.S. 651 at 669). He also pointed out that to the extent that a school official employed excessive or unreasonable force in disciplining a student, traditional common-law remedies, including a damage suit against the official, were available.

Turning to the due process issue, Powell called on the formulation put forth in *Mathews* v. *Eldridge* to balance the private and public interests involved. He concluded as follows:

> In view of the low incidence of abuse, the openness of our schools, and the common-law safeguards that already exist, the risk of error that may result in violation of a schoolchild's substantive rights can only be regarded as minimal. Imposing additional administrative safeguards as a constitutional requirement might reduce that risk marginally, but would also entail a significant intrusion into an area of primary educational responsibility. We conclude that the Due Process Clause does not require notice and a hearing prior to the imposition of corporal punishment in the public schools, as that practice is authorized and limited by the common law (*Ingraham*, at 682).

Justice White, who wrote the majority opinion in *Goss*, spoke for the four dissenters in *Ingraham* v. *Wright*. He pointed out that the Eighth Amendment prohibits "cruel and unusual punishments," not just criminal punishments. He would have extended Eighth Amendment protection to the school children in this case. On the due process issue, his numerous references to his majority opinion in *Goss* make it clear that, in his view, *Goss* should be controlling in this case. The voting lineup in these two similar cases is interesting to note: White for the five-member majority in *Goss*, Powell for the four dissenters; Powell for the five-member majority in *Ingraham*, White for the four dissenters. The swing vote from the first case to the second was Justice Stewart.[19] Richard Pierce and his associates no doubt spoke for many who have analyzed these cases when they concluded, "we are unable to reconcile *Goss* and *Ingraham*."[20]

---

[19] Between the two cases, Justice Douglas was replaced by Justice Stevens. Douglas voted with the majority in *Goss* and Stevens with the minority in *Ingraham*.

[20] Pierce, Shapiro, and Verkuil, above, note 6, 272.

ADJUDICATION AND POLICY MAKING

Agencies can develop policies through adjudication as well as through rule making. Commentators and judges often express a preference for rule making, and as discussed in the last chapter, the use of rule making has increased significantly in recent decades. Among the advantages of rule making are the following:

- the notice and opportunity-for-comment provisions in rule making offer the chance for wider public participation than is the case in adjudicatory hearings;
- the use of rule making allows an agency to plan a broad administrative program to carry out its legislative mandate rather than proceeding on a piecemeal basis;
- since rules are basically prospective, they avoid the problem of retroactivity of application that sometimes characterizes administrative decisions;
- rules guarantee a uniformity of application that a case-by-case approach might not achieve;
- rules, which are normally direct statements of agency policy, are published or otherwise available to the public; and
- they thereby have the qualities of accessibility and clarity of formulation that adjudicatory decisions may not possess.[21]

Some agencies do not have clear rule-making power, however, and some manifest a definite preference for adjudication, even when rule-making authority exists. (A prime example is the National Labor Relations Board, whose aversion to rule making is discussed later in this chapter.) Among the reasons that agencies might resort to adjudication rather than rule making are the following:

- a greater ability of adjudicatory decisions to survive judicial challenge, especially if rule-making authority is unclear;
- a greater freedom to depart from prior adjudicatory decisions than from regulations;[22]
- the fact that some problem areas under an agency's charge are unforeseeable and therefore not susceptible to the application of general rules; and
- a need to retain flexibility in administering complex matters of administrative management.[23]

Three key Supreme Court cases dealing with the general issue of rule making versus adjudication will be discussed. The most recent was decided over a quarter century ago. The first case, *Securities and Exchange Commission* v. *Chenery*, came to the Supreme Court twice during the 1940s. The

---

[21] See David L. Shapiro, "The Choice of Rulemaking or Adjudication in the Development of Administrative Policy," 78 *Harvard Law Review* 921 (1965).

[22] Ibid.

[23] Pierce, Shapiro, and Verkuil, above, note 6, 289–290.

majority opinion contains a good discussion of the choice between rule making and adjudication in agency policy making.

Securities and Exchange Commission v. Chenery Corporation

SUPREME COURT OF THE UNITED STATES, 1947.
332 U.S. 194, 67 S.Ct. 1575, 91 L.Ed. 1995.

[In the first *Chenery, Securities and Exchange Commission* v. *Chenery Corporation*, 318 U.S. 80, 63 S.Ct. 454, 87 L.Ed. 626 (1943), the Court ruled that the Securities and Exchange Commission's (SEC's) order could not be upheld because it was based on judicial precedents that did not support the order. The case was remanded, the SEC reconsidered the issue, and on the basis of a new rationale, the commission reached the same result.

Several matters of importance are treated in Justice Murphy's opinion for the majority: whether the SEC's recast reasoning supported the decision and order; the choice between rule making and adjudication for developing agency policy; and the issue of retroactive application of decisions reached in adjudicatory proceedings.]

Mr. Justice MURPHY delivered the opinion of the Court. . . .

The Commission had been dealing with the reorganization of the Federal Water Service Corporation (Federal), a holding company registered under the Public Utility Holding Company Act of 1935. . . . During the period when successive reorganization plans proposed by the management were before the Commission, the officers, directors and controlling stockholders of Federal purchased a substantial amount of Federal's preferred stock on the over-the-counter market. Under the fourth reorganization plan, this preferred stock was to be converted into common stock of a new corporation; on the basis of the purchases of preferred stock, the management would have received more than 10% of this new common stock. It was frankly admitted that the management's purpose in buying the preferred stock was to protect its interest in the new company. It was also plain that there was no fraud or lack of disclosure in making these purchases.

But the Commission would not approve the fourth plan so long as the preferred stock purchased by the management was to be treated on a parity with the other preferred stock. It felt that the officers and directors of a holding company in process of reorganization under the Act were fiduciaries and were under a duty not to trade in the securities of that company during the reorganization period. . . . And so the plan was amended to provide that the preferred stock acquired by the management, unlike that held by others, was not to be converted into the new common stock; instead, it was to be surrendered at cost plus dividends accumulated since the purchase dates. As amended, the plan was approved by the Commission over the management's objections. . . .

After the case was remanded to the Commission, Federal Water and Gas Corp. (Federal Water), the surviving corporation under the reorganization plan, made an application for approval of an amendment to the plan to provide for the issuance of new common stock of the reorganized company. This stock was to be distributed to the members of Federal's management on the basis of the shares of the old preferred stock which they had acquired during the period of reorganization, thereby placing them in the same position as the public holders of the old preferred stock. The intervening members of Federal's management joined in this request. The Commission denied the application in an order issued on February 8, 1945. . . . That order was reversed by the Court of Appeals . . . , which felt that our prior decision precluded such action by the Commission.

The latest order of the Commission definitely avoids the fatal error of relying on judicial precedents which do not sustain it. This time, after a thorough reexamination of the problem in light of the purposes and standards of the Holding Company Act, the Commission has concluded that the proposed transaction is inconsistent with the standards of §§ 7 and 11 of the Act. It has drawn heavily upon its accumulated experience in dealing with utility reorganizations. And it has expressed its reasons with a clarity and thoroughness that admit of no doubt as to the underlying basis of its order.

The argument is pressed upon us, however, that the Commission was foreclosed from taking such a step following our prior decision. It is said that, in the absence of findings of conscious wrongdoing on the part of Federal's management, the Commission could not determine by an order in this particular case that it was inconsistent with the statutory standards to permit Federal's management to realize a profit through the reorganization purchases. All that it could do was to enter an order allowing an amendment to the plan so that the proposed transaction could be consummated. Under this view, the Commission would be free only to promulgate a general rule outlawing such profits in future utility reorganizations; but such a rule would have to be prospective in nature and have no retroactive effect upon the instant situation.

We reject this contention, for it grows out of a misapprehension of our prior decision and of the Commission's statutory duties. We held no more and no less than that the Commission's first order was un-

supportable for the reasons supplied by that agency. But when the case left this Court, the problem whether Federal's management should be treated equally with other preferred stockholders still lacked a final and complete answer. It was clear that the Commission could not give a negative answer by resort to prior judicial declarations. And it was also clear that the Commission was not bound by settled judicial precedents in a situation of this nature. . . . Still unsettled, however, was the answer the Commission might give were it to bring to bear on the facts the proper administrative and statutory considerations, a function which belongs exclusively to the Commission in the first instance. The administrative process had taken an erroneous rather than a final turn. Hence we carefully refrained from expressing any views as to the propriety of an order rooted in the proper and relevant considerations.

When the case was directed to be remanded to the Commission for such further proceedings as might be appropriate, it was with the thought that the Commission would give full effect to its duties in harmony with the views we had expressed. This obviously meant something more than the entry of a perfunctory order giving parity treatment to the management holdings of preferred stock. The fact that the Commission had committed a legal error in its first disposition of the case certainly gave Federal's management no vested right to receive the benefits of such an order. After the remand was made, therefore, the Commission was bound to deal with the problem afresh, performing the function delegated to it by Congress. It was again charged with the duty of measuring the proposed treatment of the management's preferred stock holdings by relevant and proper standards. Only in that way could the legislative policies embodied in the Act be effectuated. . . .

It is true that our prior decision explicitly recognized the possibility that the Commission might have promulgated a general rule dealing with this problem under its statutory rule-making powers, in which case the issue for our consideration would have been entirely different from that which did confront us. . . . But we did not mean to imply thereby that the failure of the Commission to anticipate this problem and to promulgate a general rule withdrew all power from that agency to perform its statutory duty in this case. To hold that the Commission had no alternative in this proceeding but to approve the proposed transaction, while formulating any general rules it might desire for use in future cases of this nature, would be to stultify the administrative process. That we refuse to do.

Since the Commission, unlike a court, does have the ability to make new law prospectively through the exercise of its rule-making powers, it has less reason to rely upon ad hoc adjudication to formulate new standards of conduct within the framework of the Holding Company Act. The function of filling in the interstices of the Act should be performed, as much as possible, through this quasi-legislative promulgation of rules to be applied in the future. But any rigid requirement to that effect would make the administrative process inflexible and incapable of dealing with many of the specialized problems which arise. Not every principle essential to the effective administration of a statute can or should be cast immediately into the mold of a general rule. Some principles must await their own development, while others must be adjusted to meet particular, unforeseeable situations. In performing its important functions in these respects, therefore, an administrative agency must be equipped to act either by general rule or by individual order. To insist upon one form of action to the exclusion of the other is to exalt form over necessity.

In other words, problems may arise in a case which the administrative agency could not reasonably foresee, problems which must be solved despite the absence of a relevant general rule. Or the agency may not have had sufficient experience with a particular problem to warrant rigidifying its tentative judgment into a hard and fast rule. Or the problem may be so specialized and varying in nature as to be impossible of capture within the boundaries of a general rule. In those situations, the agency must retain power to deal with the problems on a case-to-case basis if the administrative process is to be effective. There is thus a very definite place for the case-by-case evolution of statutory standards. And the choice made between proceeding by general rule or by individual, ad hoc litigation is one that lies primarily in the informed discretion of the administrative agency.

Hence we refuse to say that the Commission, which had not previously been confronted with the problem of management trading during reorganization, was forbidden from utilizing this particular proceeding for announcing and applying a new standard of conduct. That such action might have a retroactive effect was not necessarily fatal to its validity. Every case of first impression has a retroactive effect, whether the new principle is announced by a court or by an administrative agency. But such retroactivity must be balanced against the mischief of producing a result which is contrary to a statutory design or to legal and equitable principles. If that mischief is greater than the ill effect of the retroactive application of a new standard, it is not the type of retroactivity which is condemned by law.

And so in this case, the fact that the Commission's order might retroactively prevent Federal's management from securing the profits and control which were the objects of the preferred stock purchases may well be outweighed by the dangers inherent in such purchases from the statutory standpoint. If that is true, the argument of retroactivity becomes nothing more than a claim that the Commission lacks power to enforce the standards of the Act in this proceeding. Such a claim deserves rejection.

The problem in this case thus resolves itself into a determination of whether the Commission's action in denying effectiveness to the proposed amendment to the Federal reorganization plan can be justified on the basis upon which it clearly rests. As we have noted, the Commission avoided placing its sole reliance on inapplicable judicial precedents. Rather it has derived its conclusions from the particular facts in the case, its general experience in reorganization matters and its informed view of statutory requirements. It is those matters which are the guide for our review.

The Commission concluded that it could not find that the reorganization plan, if amended as proposed, would be "fair and equitable to the persons affected thereby" within the meaning of § 11 (e) of the Act, under which the reorganization was taking place. Its view was that the amended plan would involve the issuance of securities on terms "detrimental to the public interest or the interest of investors" contrary to §§ 7 (d) (6) and 7 (e), and would result in an "unfair or inequitable distribution of voting power" among the Federal security holders within the meaning of § 7 (e). It was led to this result "not by proof that the interveners [Federal's management] committed acts of conscious wrongdoing but by the character of the conflicting interests created by the interveners' program of stock purchases carried out while plans for reorganization were under consideration." . . .

Drawing upon its experience, the Commission indicated that all these normal and special powers of the holding company management during the course of a § 11 (e) reorganization placed in the management's command "a formidable battery of devices that would enable it, if

it should choose to use them selfishly, to affect in material degree the ultimate allocation of new securities among the various existing classes, to influence the market for its own gain, and to manipulate or obstruct the reorganization required by the mandate of the statute." In that setting, the Commission felt that a management program of stock purchase would give rise to the temptation and the opportunity to shape the reorganization proceeding so as to encourage public selling on the market at low prices. No management could engage in such a program without raising serious questions as to whether its personal interests had not opposed its duties "to exercise disinterested judgment in matters pertaining to subsidiaries' accounting, budgetary and dividend policies, to present publicly an unprejudiced financial picture of the enterprise, and to effectuate a fair and feasible plan expeditiously." . . .

The scope of our review of an administrative order wherein a new principle is announced and applied is no different from that which pertains to ordinary administrative action. The wisdom of the principle adopted is none of our concern. Our duty is at an end when it becomes evident that the Commission's action is based upon substantial evidence and is consistent with the authority granted by Congress.

We are unable to say in this case that the Commission erred in reaching the result it did. The facts being undisputed, we are free to disturb the Commission's conclusion only if it lacks any rational and statutory foundation. . . . There is thus a reasonable basis for a judgment that the benefits and profits accruing to the management from the stock purchases should be prohibited, regardless of the good faith involved. And it is a judgment that can justifiably be reached in terms of fairness and equitableness, to the end that the interests of the public, the investors and the consumers might be protected. But it is a judgment based upon public policy, a judgment which Congress has indicated is of the type for the Commission to make.

The Commission's conclusion here rests squarely in that area where administrative judgments are entitled to the greatest amount of weight by appellate courts. It is the product of administrative experience, appreciation of the complexities of the problem, realization of the statutory policies, and responsible treatment of the uncontested facts. It is the type of judgment which administrative agencies are best equipped to make and which justifies the use of the administrative process. Whether we agree or disagree with the result reached, it is an allowable judgment which we cannot disturb.

Reversed.

Mr. Justice BURTON concurs in the result.

The CHIEF JUSTICE and Mr. Justice DOUGLAS took no part in the consideration or decision of these cases.

[The dissenting opinion of Mr. Justice Jackson, joined by Mr. Justice Frankfurter, is omitted.]

As suggested above, some administrative bodies manifest a definite preference for adjudication over rule making. One such agency is the National Labor Relations Board (NLRB), which, in spite of criticism by commentators and prodding by courts and many in Congress, long resisted the use of rule making.[24] It is not surprising, therefore, that the two other key cases in this section involve the NLRB. *National Labor Relations Board* v. *Wyman-Gordon Co.*, 394 U.S. 759, was decided in 1969. So divided were the justices on the main issues in the case that none of the four opinions was able to command a majority.

On petition by a labor union, the NLRB (it is often referred to simply as "the Board") ordered an election among Wyman-Gordon's production and maintenance employees. Two unions contested for the right to become the employees' exclusive bargaining unit. The NLRB instructed Wyman-Gordon to supply a list of names and addresses of employees for the unions' election activities. Wyman-Gordon refused, the election was held without the list of employees, and both unions lost.

Upon objection by the unions, the NLRB issued a subpoena ordering Wyman-Gordon to provide either the employee list or personnel and payroll records containing employee names. The NLRB petitioned a U. S. district court for enforcement of the subpoena. The district court supported the NLRB's position, but the court of appeals reversed.

The appeals court held the NLRB order invalid because it was based on a decision reached in an earlier adjudication, involving Excelsior Underwear, Inc., which the NLRB had designated as a rule. But the *Excelsior* rule had not been promulgated in accordance with the rule-making provisions of the APA, § 553. In the *Excelsior* proceeding, the NLRB had "invited certain interested parties" to file briefs and participate in oral arguments regarding the issue of requiring employers to furnish employee lists in connection with union elections. Several employee groups and trade unions did so. What happened next is summarized in Justice Abe Fortas's plurality opinion:

---

[24] On this matter see, for instance, Mark H. Grunewald, "The NLRB's First Rulemaking: An Exercise in Pragmatism," 1991 *Duke Law Journal* 274 (1991). The NLRB completed its first notice-and-comment rule making in 1989.

After these proceedings, the Board issued its decision in *Excelsior*. It purported to establish a general rule that such a list must be provided, but it declined to apply the new rule to the companies involved in the *Excelsior* case. Instead, it held that the rule would apply "only in those elections that are directed, or consented to, subsequent to 30 days from the date of [the *Excelsior*] Decision." *NLRB* v. *Wyman-Gordon*, 393 U.S. 759 at 763.

Basically, two distinct but related issues were presented to the Supreme Court in this case: the appropriateness of the NLRB's rule-making procedure and the question of whether the NLRB's order in the *Wyman-Gordon* case should be upheld. The case generated four opinions by the justices, representing three distinct points of view. Justices Douglas and Harlan, in separate opinions, concluded that the NLRB had violated the APA's rule-making procedure, thereby making its actions invalid and requiring the Court to affirm the decision of the court of appeals. But Douglas's and Harlan's were *dissenting* opinions.

Justice Fortas's plurality opinion represented the views of four members of the Court. It indicated unequivocal disapproval of the NLRB "rule-making" procedure:

> The board asks us to hold that it has discretion to promulgate new rules in adjudicatory proceedings, without complying with the requirements of the Administrative Procedure Act.
>
> The rule-making provisions of that Act, which the Board would avoid, were designed to assure fairness and mature consideration of rules of general application. They may not be avoided by the process of making rules in the course of adjudicatory proceedings. There is no warrant in law for the Board to replace the statutory scheme with a rule-making procedure of its own invention. Apart from the fact that the device fashioned by the Board does not comply with statutory command, it obviously falls short of the substance of the requirements of the Administrative Procedure Act. The "rule" created in *Excelsior* was not published in the Federal Register, which is the statutory and accepted means of giving notice of a rule as adopted; only selected organizations were given notice of the "hearing," whereas notice in the Federal Register would have been general in character; under the Administrative Procedure Act, the terms or substance of the rule would have to be stated in the notice of hearing, and all interested parties would have an opportunity to participate in the rule making. *Ibid.*, at 764.

Having condemned the NLRB's effort at rule making in *Excelsior*, Fortas proceeded (somewhat incongruously, to some analysts) to consider the Board's action in the Wyman-Gordon proceeding as a stand-alone adjudication:

> In the present case, however, the respondent itself was specifically directed by the Board to submit a list of names and addresses of its employees for use by the unions in connection with the election. This direction, which was part of the order directing that an election be held, is unquestionably valid. Even though the direction to furnish the list was followed by citation to "Excelsior Underwear Inc., 156 NLRB No. 111," it is an order in the present case that the respondent was required to obey. Absent this direction by the Board, the respondent was under no compulsion to furnish the list because no statute and no validly adopted rule required it to do so.
>
> Because the Board in an adjudicatory proceeding directed the respondent

itself to furnish the list, the decision of the Court of Appeals for the First Circuit must be reversed. . . . *Ibid.*, 766.

The other opinion in this case was written by Justice Black, with whom Justices Brennan and Marshall concurred. In effect, it supported the Board on both issues. Black agreed with Fortas on the requirement that the employees' names be disclosed. He called the Board's order "valid on its merits." But he took issue with Fortas's criticism of the *Excelsior* proceeding. Black expressed his conviction "that the Excelsior practice was adopted by the Board as a legitimate incident to the adjudication of a specific case before it, and for that reason I would hold that the board properly followed the procedures applicable to 'adjudication' rather than 'rule making.'" As to the Board's not applying its adjudicatory decision in the *Excelsior* case itself, Black said that the NLRB was merely avoiding the problem of retroactive application of a new directive: "[W]hile fully agreeing that disclosure should be required, the Board did not feel that it should upset the Excelsior Company's justified reliance on previous refusals to command disclosure by setting aside this particular election" (Ibid., 769, 770, 774). For Black, then, *Excelsior* was pure adjudication, even though the Board had purported to adopt a rule.

The lineup of the nine justices on the two issues was thus as follows: six justices (Fortas for four, plus dissenters Douglas and Harlan) stated that the NLRB did not comply with rule-making procedures in adopting the *Excelsior* rule. But seven justices (Fortas for four and Black for three) concluded that the order issued by the Board in *Wyman-Gordon* was valid. This split caused some confusion several years later (at the court of appeals level) in *National Labor Relations Board* v. *Bell Aerospace Co.*, 416 U.S. 267 (1974).

The NLRB had long taken the position that managerial personnel were not "employees" under the National Labor Relations Act and were thus outside the collective bargaining process. A union petitioned the NLRB for a representation election among a group of buyers for Bell Aerospace. The Board, in an adjudicatory proceeding, ruled that even if buyers were to be considered managerial employees, they would be covered by the act unless it was shown that a union of buyers would be a conflict of interest in labor relations.

The court of appeals, in *Bell Aerospace Co.* v. *National Labor Relations Board*, 475 F.2d 485, rejected, as contrary to congressional intent, the Board's change in policy that introduced the conflict of interest standard. It allowed as how the Board might conclude that buyers are not managerial employees and could thus fall within the act. But it held that such a change could be effected only by rule making, not by adjudication. In reaching this conclusion, the court of appeals quoted from the opinions representing the six Supreme Court justices in *Wyman-Gordon* who disapproved of how the NLRB's "Excelsior rule" was adopted.

Five members of the Supreme Court agreed with the court of appeals that managerial employees are outside the scope of the act. But on the issue of rule making versus adjudication, the Court unanimously reversed the court of appeals and supported the NLRB. In taking this position, the Supreme Court repeatedly cited the second *Chenery* case and *Wyman-Gordon* as authority. A key passage is the following:

> The views expressed in *Chenery II* and *Wyman-Gordon* make plain that the Board is not precluded from announcing the new principles in an adjudicative proceeding and that the choice between rulemaking and adjudication lies in the first instance within the Board's discretion. Although there may be situations where the Board's reliance on adjudication would amount to an abuse of discretion or a violation of the Act, nothing in the present case would justify such a conclusion. Indeed, there is ample indication that adjudication is especially appropriate in the instant context. As the Court of Appeals noted, "[t]here must be tens of thousands of manufacturing, wholesale and retail units which employ buyers, and hundreds of thousands of the latter." . . . Moreover, duties of buyers vary widely depending on the company or industry. It is doubtful whether any generalized standard could be framed which would have more than marginal utility. The Board thus has reason to proceed with caution, developing its standards in a case-by-case manner with attention to the specific character of the buyers' authority and duties in each company. The Board's judgment that adjudication best serves this purpose is entitled to great weight (416 U.S. 267 at 294).

Bell Aerospace is the last time that the Supreme Court considered restricting an agency's use of adjudication for policy making. The Court's position on this issue may not be embraced by all commentators.[25] But it is surely a realistic view, given the complexities of regulation in the twenty-first century. As Davis and Pierce have put it: "Congress shares the same concerns the Court expressed in *Chenery* and repeated in *Bell Aerospace*. There are simply too many circumstances in which an agency cannot anticipate all of the problems that a rule must address and accommodate."[26]

---

[25] See, e.g., Alfred C. Aman, Jr., and William T. Mayton, *Administrative Law* 115 (2nd ed., 2001).

[26] Kenneth Culp Davis and Richard J. Pierce, Jr., 1 *Administrative Law Treatise* 273 (3rd ed., 1994).

Chapter 8

Informal Activity and the Exercise of Discretion

This chapter involves an area that has received relatively less attention from commentators. This is not to suggest that students of administrative law do not appreciate the importance of the informal aspects of the subject. One can go all the way back to the founders of the discipline in the United States and find concern expressed about the dangers of uncontrolled administrative discretion.[1] During the course of the adoption of the Administrative Procedure Act (APA) more than five decades ago, it was asserted that over 90 percent of administrative activity was informal.[2] In more recent times, Warner W. Gardner, chairman of the Committee on Informal Action of the Administrative Conference of the United States, offered the view that the 90 percent figure was "much too low."[3] In an article published in the early 1970s, Gardner expressed the hope that an "Informal Procedure Act" could be adopted, and he sketched the general contours that he hoped such an act would take.[4] But by later in that decade he expressed skepticism that such

---

[1] Ernst Freund wrote in 1894 that "the greatest drawback of our system . . . lies in the fact that it makes no provision for the review of discretionary action" [as quoted in Oscar Kraines, *The World and Ideas of Ernst Freund: The Search for General Principles of Legislation and Administrative Law* 104 (1974)]. Frank Goodnow, in 1905, stated that "it is the purpose of all administrative legislation to lessen as far as possible the realm of administrative discretion and to fix limits within which the administration must move" [*The Principles of the Administrative Law of the United States* 368 (1905)].

[2] See *Hearings before the Subcommittee of the Committee on the Judiciary on S. 674, S. 675 and S. 918*, 79th Congress 804 (1941) (testimony of Dean Acheson); Todd D. Rakoff, "The Choice between Formal and Informal Modes of Administrative Regulation," 51 *Administrative Law Review* 159, at 162 (2000).

[3] Warner G. Gardner, "The Informal Actions of the Federal Government," 26 *American University Law Review* 799 (1977).

[4] "The Procedures by Which Informal Action Is Taken," 24 *Administrative Law Review* 155 (1972).

legislation could or should be undertaken, concluding that informal activity can be well understood and evaluated only in the context of the substantive governmental program to which it applies.[5]

Yet discussion continues about the wide variety of informal actions that administrators perform and the potential problems for private parties that are thereby created. One recent article was devoted to "administrative arm-twisting," which the author identified as "a threat by an agency to impose a sanction or withhold a benefit in hopes of encouraging 'voluntary' compliance with a request that [the] agency could not impose directly on a regulated entity."[6] Although the author understood the advantage of the flexibility the agency gained through arm-twisting, he saw the tactic as often allowing administrators "to stretch the outer boundaries of their delegated powers."[7]

A number of other forms of informal persuasion, such as jawboning, raising an eyebrow, recommending, and threatening, have also been identified by commentators.[8]

But informal actions are not limited to administrative efforts to induce particular private parties to behave in certain ways. They may be more generalized with regard to the audience to whom they are directed. And their aim may not be to persuade or induce, but simply to provide aid to parties. With regard to informal action of a generalized nature, many agencies adopt policy statements, advisory opinions, and the like, including what one commentator terms *guidance*.[9] These devices are meant to inform the public of an agency's view of one or another aspect of its mission, but they generally do not have the force of law. Interpretive rules, as discussed in chapter 6, may supplement statutes or legislative-type rules and need not be adopted according to the rule-making provisions of the APA. But if interpretive rules are not published in the *Federal Register*, they may be declared to have no legal effect [*Morton* v. *Ruiz*, 415 U.S. 199 (1974)].

Aid by agencies to individual parties also takes a variety of forms. The Internal Revenue Service (IRS) issues "letter rulings" to individuals on tax matters. But the tax authorities do not consider themselves bound by these rulings in dealings with other taxpayers.[10] And many agencies provide advice with regard to a multitude of matters that touch the lives of ordinary individuals and organizations.

---

[5] Gardner, above, note 3, 804.

[6] Lars Noah, "Administrative Arm-Twisting in the Shadow of Congressional Delegation of Authority," 1997 *Wisconsin Law Review* 873, at 874 (1997).

[7] Ibid., 941.

[8] See, e.g., Takehisa Nakagawa, "Administrative Informality in Japan: Governmental Activities outside Statutory Authorization," 52 *Administrative Law Review* 175, 205 (2000) (the author is speaking here about the United States); Florence Heffron with Neil McFeeley, *The Administrative Regulatory Process* 213–214 (1983).

[9] Todd D. Rakoff, "The Choice between Formal and Informal Modes of Administrative Regulation," 52 *Administrative Law Review* 159 (2000).

[10] See the discussion in Peter L. Strauss, Todd Rakoff, Roy A. Schotland, and Cynthia R. Farina, *Administrative Law: Cases and Comments* 658–659 (9th ed., 1995).

ADVICE FROM GOVERNMENTAL OFFICIALS: AN EXAMPLE OF INFORMAL ACTIVITY

As Professor Michael Asimow put it in *Advice to the Public from Federal Administrative Agencies*: "Providing advice to the public on proposed private transactions is a significant government function. It consumes an appreciable quantity of the resources of many agencies; it provides an invaluable benefit to a vast number of citizens each year."[11] It is also an activity, however, from which unfortunate consequences—and legal problems—may ensue for the unwary citizen.

Almost all citizens need to consult a government agency at one time or another for advice or information: Is a certain expenditure tax deductible? Is a building permit needed to build an addition to the house or a zoning variance needed to build in a certain part of the city? Am I entitled to this specific kind of benefit from the government, and if so, what must I do to get it? On such questions as these, and many others that one could imagine, an individual might turn to a government agency before proceeding to take action. But what if the advice that one relied on in such situations turned out to be erroneous, and one stood to suffer a loss as a result? The doctrine of equitable estoppel is relevant to this problem. Under this doctrine, a person "may be precluded by his act or conduct from asserting a right or defense which he otherwise would have had."[12]

An actual example is the following: A worker was assured by his employer that he could initiate a compensation claim for an industrial accident within a seven-year period. However, under the Federal Employees' Liability Act,[13] the actual period of limitation was three years. The worker, who brought his claim after the three-year period had elapsed, sued to estop his employer from raising the three-year limitation as a defense. The Supreme Court unanimously ruled in his favor, quoting the maxim that "no man may take advantage of his own wrong."[14]

Estopping the Government

One problem with equitable estoppel in administrative law is that it traditionally has been held not to apply to governmental units. As "an offshoot of sovereign immunity,"[15] a doctrine that will be discussed in more detail in chapter 9, it has often been held by courts that the government cannot be estopped. An often-cited decision is the 1947 case of *Federal Crop Insurance Corporation* v. *Merrill*, 332 U.S. 380. Merrill, an Idaho farmer, received ad-

---

[11] *Advice to the Public from Federal Administrative Agencies* 2 (1973).

[12] "Annotation: Equitable Estoppel as Precluding Reliance on Statute of Limitations—Federal Cases," 3 L.Ed. 2d 1886 (1959). A useful summary and analysis of equitable estoppel is provided by David K. Thompson, "Equitable Estoppel of the Government," 79 *Columbia Law Review* 551 (1979).

[13] 35 Stat. 65, as amended, 45 U.S.C. §§ 51–60.

[14] *Glus* v. *Brooklyn Eastern Dist. Terminal*, 359 U.S. 231 (1959).

[15] "Modern Status of Applicability of Doctrine of Estoppel against Federal Government and Its Agencies," 27 A.L.R. Fed. 702, 708 (1976).

vice from the local agent of the Federal Crop Insurance Corporation (FCIC), a wholly government-owned enterprise, that a certain crop was insurable, and the FCIC accepted the application. The advice was inaccurate, however (the Wheat Crop Insurance Regulations, published in the *Federal Register*, prohibited insuring the type of crop in question), and when the crop was destroyed by drought, the corporation refused to pay the loss. In a five-to-four decision, the Supreme Court reversed the Idaho Supreme Court, which found for the farmer, and ruled that the government could not be estopped in this case. Although assuming "that recovery could be had against a private insurance company," Justice Frankfurter for the Court stated that it "is too late in the day to urge that the Government is just another private litigant" and that "anyone entering into an arrangement with the Government takes the risk of having accurately ascertained that he who purports to act for the government stays within the bounds of his authority." For good measure the majority added, quoting from an earlier Supreme Court case: "Men must turn square corners when they deal with the Government."[16]

Since *Merrill*, the Supreme Court has decided a number of cases involving estoppel against the government. The most recent of these was *Office of Personnel Management* v. *Richmond* (1990), which will be examined next. Although the *Richmond* case reaches a result with regard to estoppel similar to that rendered in *Merrill*, *Richmond* is by no means the last word by the Supreme Court (or other courts) on estoppel-type remedies.

Office of Personnel Management v. Richmond

UNITED STATES SUPREME COURT, 1990.
496 U.S. 414, 110 S.Ct. 2465, 110 L.Ed. 2d 387.

[Charles Richmond, a civilian working for the U.S. Navy, was granted disability benefits due to impaired eyesight, which prevented him from performing his job as a welder. Under the statutory rules applicable at the time he left his position, Richmond would become ineligible for continued disability payments if his income after retirement equaled at least 80 percent of his pay with the Navy for two years in a row.

In 1982, the year after Richmond's retirement, Congress changed the measuring period for determining continued eligibility from two years to one. Richmond took a part-time job as a school bus driver, and from 1982 to 1985 his earnings were under the 80 percent limit, thus leaving

him eligible for continued disability payments. In 1986 he had an opportunity to earn more money, and he consulted an employee relations specialist at the personnel department of the Navy Public Works Center, his former employer.

Relying on the provisions of the repealed pre-1982 statute, the personnel officer gave Richmond incorrect advice, advice which he repeated in a second consultation with Richmond in 1987. He also gave Richmond a copy of an outdated Federal Personnel Manual Letter, which stated the erroneous two-year eligibility rule.

When Richmond exceeded the statutory earnings limit, his disability payments were terminated by the U.S. Office

---

[16] 332 U.S. 380 at 383, 384, 385 (1947). Quoting *Rock Island Arkansas & Louisiana Railroad Co.* v. *United States*, 254 U.S. 141, 143 (1920).

of Personnel Management (OPM). Later, when his outside earnings dropped below the level allowed by the statute, his disability annuity was restored. Richmond appealed to the administrative appeal body, the Merit Systems Protection Board (MSPB), asserting that the erroneous advice given him should estop the government from discontinuing the disability payments. The MSPB rejected his claim, but the court of appeals reversed, holding the government estopped because of the misinformation Richmond received from Navy personnel].

Justice KENNEDY delivered the opinion of the Court. . . .

The Court of Appeals acknowledged the longstanding rule that "ordinarily the government may not be estopped because of erroneous or unauthorized statements of government employees when the asserted estoppel would nullify a requirement prescribed by Congress." . . . Nonetheless, the Court of Appeals focused on this Court's statement in an earlier case that "we are hesitant . . . to say that there are *no cases*" where the Government might be estopped. *Heckler* v. *Community Health Services of Crawford County, Inc.*, 467 U.S. 51, 60 (1984). The Court of Appeals then discussed other Circuit and District Court opinions that had applied estoppel against the Government.

The Court of Appeals majority decided that "based on the Supreme Court's acknowledgment that the estoppel against the government is not foreclosed and based on court of appeals rulings applying estoppel against the government, our view is that estoppel is properly applied against the government in the present case." . . . The Court reasoned that the provision of the out-of-date OPM form was "affirmative misconduct" that should estop the Government from denying respondent benefits in accordance with the statute. The facts of this case, it held, are "sufficiently unusual and extreme that no concern is warranted about

exposing the public treasury to estoppel in broad or numerous categories of cases." . . .

From our earliest cases, we have recognized that equitable estoppel will not lie against the Government as against private litigants. . . .

The principles of these and many other cases were reiterated in *Federal Crop Insurance Corporation* v. *Merrill . . .* (1947), the leading case in our modern line of estoppel decisions. . . .

Despite the clarity of these earlier decisions, dicta in our more recent cases have suggested the possibility that there might be some situation in which estoppel against the Government could be appropriate. . . .

Our own opinions have continued to mention the possibility, in the course of rejecting estoppel arguments, that some type of "affirmative misconduct" might give rise to estoppel against the Government. See *INS* v. *Hibi*, 414 U.S. 5, 8 (1973) (per curiam) ("While the issue of whether 'affirmative misconduct' on the part of the Government might estop it from denying citizenship was left open in *Montana* v. *Kennedy*, 366 U.S. 308, 314, 315, no conduct of the sort there adverted to was involved here."); *Schweiker* v. *Hansen*, 450 U.S. 785, 788 (1981) (per curiam) (denying an estoppel claim for Social Security benefits on the authority of *Merrill* . . . but observing that the Court "has never decided what type of conduct by a Government employee will estop the Government from insisting upon compliance with valid regulations governing the distribution of welfare benefits"); *INS* v. *Miranda*, 459 U.S. 14, 19 (1982) (per curiam) ("This case does not require us to reach the question we reserved in *Hibi*, whether affirmative misconduct in a particular case would estop the Government from enforcing the immigration laws."); *Heckler* v. *Community Health Services*, 467 U.S., at 60 ("We have left the issue open in the past, and do so again today.").

The language in our decisions has spawned numerous claims for equitable estoppel in the lower courts. As Justice MARSHALL stated in dissent in *Hansen* . . . "the question of when the Government may be equitably estopped has divided the distinguished panel of the Court of Appeals in this case, has received inconsistent treatment from other Courts of Appeals, and has been the subject of considerable ferment." 450 U.S., at 791 (citing cases). Since that observation was made, federal courts have continued to accept estoppel claims under a variety of rationales and analyses. In sum, courts of appeals have taken our statements as an invitation to search for an appropriate case in which to apply estoppel against the Government, yet we have reversed every finding of estoppel that we have reviewed. Indeed, no less than three of our most recent decisions in this area have been summary reversals of decisions upholding estoppel claims. . . .

The Solicitor General proposes to remedy the present confusion in this area of the law with a sweeping rule. As it has in the past, the Government asks us to adopt "a flat rule that estoppel may not in any circumstances run against the Government." *Community Health Services*, supra, at 60. The Government bases its broad rule first upon the doctrine of sovereign immunity. Noting that the "United States, as sovereign, is immune from suit save as it consents to be sued," *United States* v. *Mitchell*, 445 U.S. 535, 538 (1980), the Government asserts that the courts are without jurisdiction to entertain a suit to compel the Government to act contrary to a statute, no matter what the context or circumstances. The Government advances as a second basis for this rule the doctrine of separation of powers. The Government contends that to recognize estoppel based on the misrepresentations of Executive Branch officials would give those misrepresentations the force of law, and thereby invade the legislative province reserved to Congress. This rationale, too, supports the Government's contentions that estoppel may never justify an order requiring executive action contrary to a relevant statute, no matter what statute or what facts are involved.

We have recognized before that the "arguments the Government advances for the rule are substantial." *Community Health Services*, supra, at 60. And we agree that this case should be decided under a clearer form of analysis than "we will know an estoppel when we see one." *Hansen*, supra, at 792 (MARSHALL, J., dissenting). But it remains true that we need not embrace a rule that no estoppel will lie against the Government in any case in order to decide this case. We leave for another day whether an estoppel claim could ever succeed against the Government. A narrower ground of decision is sufficient to address the type of suit presented here, a claim for payment of money from the Public Treasury contrary to a statutory appropriation.

The Appropriations Clause of the Constitution, Art. I, § 9, cl. 7, provides that: "No Money shall be drawn from the Treasury, but in Consequence of Appropriations made by Law." For the particular type of claim at issue here, a claim for money from the Federal Treasury, the Clause provides an explicit rule of decision. Money may be paid out only through an appropriation made by law; in other words, the payment of money from the Treasury must be authorized by a statute. . . .

Our cases underscore the straightforward and explicit command of the Appropriations Clause. "It means simply that no money can be paid out of the Treasury unless it has been appropriated by an act of Congress." *Cincinnati Soap Co.* v. *United States*, 301 U.S. 308, 321 (1937) (citing *Reeside* v. *Walker*, 52 U.S. 272, 11 How. 272, 291 (1851)). . . .

We have held, for example, that while the President's pardon power may remove all disabilities from one convicted of treason, that power does not extend to an order to repay from the Treasury the proceeds derived from the sale of the convict's forfeited property. . . .

Just as the pardon power cannot override the command of the Appropriations Clause, so too judicial use of the equitable doctrine of estoppel cannot grant respondent a money remedy that Congress has not authorized. . . .

The whole history and practice with respect to claims against the United States reveals the impossibility of an estoppel claim for money in violation of a statute. Congress' early practice was to adjudicate each individual money claim against the United States, on the ground that the Appropriations Clause forbade even a delegation of individual adjudicatory functions where payment of funds from the treasury was involved. . . .

Respondent points to no authority in precedent or history for the type of claim he advances today. Whether there are any extreme circumstances that might support estoppel in a case not involving payment from the Treasury is a matter we need not address. As for monetary claims, it is enough to say that this Court has never upheld an assertion of estoppel against the Government by a claimant seeking public funds. In this context there can be no estoppel, for courts cannot estop the Constitution. The judgment of the Court of Appeals is Reversed.

[The concurring opinion of Justice White, joined by Justice Blackmun, is omitted].

Justice STEVENS, concurring in the judgment.

Although I join the Court's judgment, I cannot accept its reasoning. The Appropriations Clause of the Constitution has nothing to do with this case. Payments of pension benefits to retired and disabled federal servants are made "in Consequence of Appropriations made by Law" even if in particular cases they are the product of a mistaken interpretation of a statute or regulation. The Constitution contemplates appropriations that cover programs—not individual appropriations for individual payments. The Court's creative reliance on constitutional text is nothing but a red herring. . . .

Respondent's loss of benefits was serious but temporary, and, even if we assume that respondent was not adequately compensated for the stress of his increased workload, his additional earnings certainly mitigated the shortfall in benefits. I agree with JUSTICE MARSHALL that there are strong equities favoring respondent's position, but I am persuaded that unless the 5-to-4 decision in *Federal Crop Ins. Corp.* v. *Merrill* . . . is repudiated by Congress or this Court, this kind of maladministration must be tolerated. . . .

Justice MARSHALL, with whom Justice BRENNAN joins, dissenting. . . .

The majority hints that it is unsympathetic to Richmond's claim that he was treated unfairly, but it does not rule on that basis. Rather, the majority resolves the issue by holding as a general rule that a litigant may not succeed on a claim for payment of money from the Treasury in the absence of a statutory appropriation. Although the Constitution generally forbids payments from the Treasury without a congressional appropriation, that proposition does not resolve this case. Most fundamentally, Richmond's collection of disability benefits would be fully consistent with the relevant appropriation. And even if the majority is correct that the statute cannot be construed to appropriate funds for claimants in Richmond's position, the Government may nonetheless be estopped, on the basis of its prelitigation conduct, from arguing that the Appropriations Clause bars his recovery. Both the statutory construction and the estoppel arguments turn on the equities, and the equities favor Richmond. . . .

Significant policy concerns would of course be implicated by an indiscriminate use of estoppel against the Government. But estoppel is an equitable doctrine. As such, it can be tailored to the circumstances of particular cases, ensuring that fundamental injustices are avoided without seriously endangering the smooth operation of statutory schemes. In this case, the Federal Circuit undertook a thorough examination of the circumstances and concluded that denying Richmond his pension simply because he followed the Government's advice would be fundamentally unjust.

The majority does not reject the court's findings on the facts but rejects Richmond's claim on the theory that, except where the Constitution requires otherwise, equitable estoppel may not be applied against the Government where the claimant seeks unappropriated funds from the Treasury. This Court has never so much as mentioned the Appropriations Clause in the context of a discussion of equitable estoppel . . . , nor has the majority's theory ever before been discussed, much less adopted, by any court. This lack of precedent for the majority's position is not surprising because the Appropriations Clause does not speak either to the proper interpretation of any statute or to the question whether the Government should be estopped from invoking the Clause in a particular case. I dissent.

In *Richmond*, then, the Supreme Court continued its refusal to estop the government. Several statements in Justice Kennedy's majority opinion indicated, however, that not all issues in this area of law are thereby resolved. The Court refused again the government's proposal to adopt a complete bar to estopping the government. In quoting from earlier Supreme Court opinions, Kennedy left the door open for the possibility, in some future set of circumstances ("affirmative misconduct" on the part of the government was referred to in several earlier cases), that estoppel might be an appropriate remedy. And he noted that some federal courts have found reason to estop the government in previous cases. Although the Supreme Court has overturned such estoppels in cases that have reached it, not all lower court cases estopping the government have come to the high court, and thus on some occasions before *Richmond*, federal court rulings declared the government estopped. This has continued to be the case since *Richmond* as well.[17]

An instructive post-*Richmond* case is the following. Note Judge Ruggero J. Aldersert's reference to "affirmative misconduct" and the assertion that his court "is among the majority of circuits recognizing estoppel as an equitable defense against government claim." His opinion, only the highlights of which are reproduced here, provides a thorough examination of the subject of estopping the government.

---

[17] See, e.g., the cases cited in Kenneth Culp Davis and Richard J. Pierce, Jr., *1998 Supplement, Administrative Law Treatise* 346–348 (1998); also see Alfred C. Aman, Jr., and William T. Mayton, *Administrative Law* 333–336 (2nd ed., 2001).

Barry I. Fredericks v. *Commissioner of Internal Revenue*

UNITED STATES COURT OF APPEALS FOR THE THIRD CIRCUIT, 1997.
125 F.3d 433.

[Barry Fredericks's 1977 tax return was being examined by the IRS with regard to a tax shelter. The agency requested that Fredericks fill out and return a Form 872-A, which provided an indefinite extension for examining the return. Although the extension was indefinite, the form was revocable by Fredericks any time after ninety days from its receipt by the IRS. Fredericks completed and sent in the form but was told by the IRS that it had not been received and was probably "lost in the mail." During each of the next three years, the agency requested that Fredericks complete another extension form (Form 872), each form extending the statute of limitations for one year. The last of these extensions would have expired in 1984. Unbeknownst to Fredericks, some time before the end of the last extension, the IRS claimed to have "discovered" the lost form 872-A. It did not inform Fredericks, who could have revoked the effect of the form at any time. On the basis of the "found" form, the IRS in 1992 (fourteen years after Fredericks had filed a timely tax return) assessed Fredericks $28,360 and approximately $158,000 in interest on the basis of the disallowed tax shelter.

Fredericks took the case to the U.S. Tax Court, contending that the IRS was estopped, based on its misrepresentation and misconduct with regard to its use of the extension forms. The tax court ruled for the IRS, asserting that Fredericks had failed to prove the elements of estoppel. He then appealed to the court of appeals].

Judge ALDERSERT delivered the opinion of the Court. . . .

The Tax Court has set forth the essential elements of estoppel:

1) a false representation or wrongful misleading silence; 2) an error in a statement of fact and not in an opinion or statement of law; 3) person claiming the benefits of estoppel must be ignorant of the true facts; and 4) person claiming estoppel must be adversely affected by the acts or statements of the person against whom estoppel is claimed. *Estate of Emerson* v. *Commissioner,* 67 T.C. 612, 617-618 (1977). This court is among the majority of circuits recognizing estoppel as an equitable defense against government claims, but in such a context we impose an additional burden on claimants to establish some affirmative misconduct on the part of the government officials. The additional element reflects the need to balance both the public interest in ensuring government can enforce the law without fearing estoppel and citizens' interests "in some minimum standard of decency, honor, and reliability in their relations with their Government." [*U.S.* v. *Asmar,* 827 F.2d 907, 911, n. 4, 912 (3d Cir., 1987)] . . . Here, the IRS did not refute evidence that it told Fredericks the Form 872-A "was probably lost in the mail." On three occasions over a period of two years the IRS induced Fredericks to sign Forms 872, establishing an agreement to three consecutive specific dates on which the statute of limitations would expire. The government's misrepresentation went beyond mere erroneous oral advice from an IRS agent; it consisted of affirmative, authorized acts inducing Fredericks to sign and rely on the terms of the Form 872 on three different occasions in three different years. Moreover, the IRS' misleading silence after finding and deciding to rely on the Form 872-A, coupled with its failure to notify Fredericks of its decision and its effective revocation of the third Form 872, constitute affirmative misconduct.

Case law in this and other jurisdictions supports our conclusion. We have recognized that the authority to act, as well as the failure to do so when such authority exists, can give rise to an estoppel claim. In *Ritter* v. *United States,* 28 F.2d 265 (3d Cir. 1928), we stated: "The acts *or omissions* of the officers of the government, if they be authorized to bind the United States in a particular transaction, will work estoppel against the government. . . ." *Id.* at 267 (emphasis added).

In *Dana Corp.* v. *United States,* 200 Ct. Cl. 200, 470 F.2d 1032 (Ct. Cl. 1972), the court held that the Post Office Department was estopped from denying the effects of its agent's decision to continue to pay, *and not inform,* the plaintiff-supplier that it was performing in excess of contract requirements. . . .

In the case at bar, the agent who misrepresented that the IRS did not have a Form 872-A, and the agents who solicited and executed the subsequent Form 872 one-year extensions had authority to act as they did. As in *Dana Corp.,* because of the government's silence after its discovery of, and decision to rely on, the Form 872-A, the IRS agents induced Fredericks to continue to rely on the Forms 872. Had the taxpayer been informed of the IRS' discovery and its decision to adopt an alternative plan of action, he could have—and testified that he would have—exercised his right to terminate the Form 872-A.

When the IRS discovered its mistake in denying the existence of a previously executed Form 872-A, any number of agents presumably had authority to alert Fredericks to the prior misrepresentation that the form did not exist. We assume that these agents were also authorized to inform Fredericks that the IRS decided to disregard the third Form 872—which extended the statute until June 30, 1984—and decided to rely on this alternative form, which created an indefinite extension period. Instead, the IRS waited eight years before notifying Fredericks that it possessed the form, then filed an assess-

ment and precluded him from exercising his right to terminate the Form 872-A. The IRS should be bound by the authorized acts and omissions of its agents and estopped from relying on the Form 872-A, and from denying the validity of the last Form 872 it executed with the taxpayer . . .

The IRS' conduct in this case is more unconscionable than that in *Dana Corp.* and similar case law. See, e.g., *Stockstrom* v. *Commissioner*, 88 U.S. App. D.C. 286, 190 F.2d 283 (D.C. Cir. 1951) (holding IRS estopped from assessing taxpayer for failure to file return where the omission was induced by a ruling of the Commissioner). . . . Here, the IRS claims authority to assess a tax in 1992 based on Fredericks' failure to terminate a Form 872-A when it was the IRS' acts and omissions that lulled Fredericks into inaction. The IRS prevented Fredericks from terminating the Form 872-A by misrepresenting that it did not possess such a form, by affirmatively maintaining that misrepresentation and by failing for eight years to notify the taxpayer after discovering its error and adopting an alternative course of action.

In response to the question raised at oral argument whether the IRS had any obligation to notify the taxpayer when it discovered its possession of the Form 872-A, counsel for the IRS responded:

> I think that as a matter of fairness, and not as a matter of what is statutorily required in this case, that if there was someone at the IRS who realized that Mr. Fredericks had been misled, I do believe that they had an obligation to notify him. That is a different question than the question that we should be asking, which is: is it the proper case to apply equitable estoppel.

We disagree. We reject the notion that IRS agents examining Fredericks' file sometime in 1984 could have discovered a Form 872-A that was signed in 1980 and not known that the taxpayer had been misled as to its existence given that the three subsequently executed Forms 872 were also in Fredericks' file. It is exactly this combination of written agreements entered into by the IRS and Fredericks that prompted the IRS to forgo soliciting additional one-year extensions.

The IRS was the only party with knowledge of all the facts in this case. The IRS' secreting of the reappearance of the Form 872-A, its failure to inform Fredericks of the form's reappearance, its decision to revoke without notice the third Form 872 agreement which limited the extension to June 30, 1984, and its filing of an assessment eight years later constitutes affirmative misconduct and gives rise to the most impressive case for estoppel against the IRS that our research has disclosed. . . .

The Commissioner may not challenge the only permissible inference that can be drawn: that the IRS discovered the presence of the executed Form 872-A prior to the expiration of the third Form 872 extension on June 30, 1984. The precise date is information within the sole possession of the IRS. As previously stated, the Commissioner's counsel confessed at oral argument that she could not supply this information to the court, and that her file did not disclose this information. Nor did the Commissioner see fit to introduce any direct evidence on this issue at the Tax Court trial. We are thus left with circumstantial evidence, but the evidence here has a quality of probability that gives rise to what the logicians describe as a compellable inference. Consider the following uncontroverted evidence: (1) the IRS' misrepresentation that it did not have the Form 872-A; (2) the IRS' three requests for, and execution of, annual extensions of the statute of limitations; (3) *the absence of any requests for annual extensions after June 30, 1984;* (4) the IRS' eight-year delay and production of the Form 872-A in 1992; and (5) the IRS' admission that the investigation of the tax shelter was

actively ongoing until 1992. The only reasonable conclusion that can be drawn from the evidence is that the IRS had actual knowledge of the Form 872-A's existence at least prior to June 30, 1984. Otherwise, the government would have sought additional annual extensions because, as stated at oral argument, the investigation was ongoing.

The IRS confirmed its earlier misrepresentations by failing to notify the taxpayer that it possessed the Form 872-A and that the Commissioner intended to rely upon that form. The government's misleading silence was a perpetuation of its misrepresentation that the Form 872-A was never signed or received by the IRS. It was an affirmative decision to usurp the Form 872 agreement entered by the IRS setting June 30, 1984 as the expiration of the statute of limitations. The IRS' decision to lie doggo, and induce the taxpayer into thinking all was well, coupled with its additional eight-year delay in producing a document it previously represented as non-existent, compels us to conclude that the IRS was guilty of affirmative misconduct at least as of June 30, 1984. Fredericks has met his burden of establishing the misrepresentation and affirmative-misconduct elements of an estoppel claim against the government. We, therefore, proceed to an examination of the reliance and detriment elements of this doctrine. . . .

Fredericks argues that if he had known the IRS was in possession of the Form 872-A, he would have filed the necessary document (Form 872-T to terminate the indefinite consent). Relying on the IRS' misrepresentation that the Form 872-A was not in his file, followed by the IRS' repeated requests for Form 872 agreements, Fredericks concluded that it was unnecessary to terminate a consent agreement which the IRS maintained that it never received. He concluded that the subsequent Forms 872 were the only agreements relevant to his 1977 return.

On June 30, 1984, when the last one-year Form 872 extension expired, Fredericks believed that the statute of limitations prevented the IRS from assessing any deficiencies.

We conclude that Fredericks acted reasonably in relying on the IRS' misrepresentation that the Form 872-A was not in his file, and in relying on the subsequent Forms 872 executed by him and the IRS. Fredericks' reliance would have been unreasonable had it been based solely on the initial oral misrepresentation that the Form 872-A was "probably lost in the mail." But in this case, the IRS repeatedly confirmed its stated position for three years by requesting on three separate occasions the one-year Form 872 extensions. The language of the Form 872 agreements is clear and unequivocal. The third Form 872 executed by the taxpayer stated: [Fredericks] and the District director of Internal Revenue consent and agree to the following:

> (1) that the amount of any Federal [Income] tax due on any return(s) made or for the above taxpayer(s) for the period(s) ended [December 31, 1977 . . .] may be assessed at any time on or before [June 30, 1984].

We believe that Fredericks' reliance on the text of this written IRS form was reasonable. Reading this form in conjunction with the IRS' earlier statements, Fredericks reasonably concluded that June 30, 1984 was the last date for the IRS to assess a deficiency on his 1977 tax return. . . .

Fredericks argues that he suffered a substantial economic detriment by relying on the IRS' misrepresentations. He reasonably relied on the third Form 872 and reasonably believed that the statute of limitations expired on June 30, 1984. He relied on the IRS' misrepresentations that there was no Form 872-A indefinite extension of the statute of limitations and, to his detriment, did not terminate that form. Fredericks permanently lost

his right to terminate the Form 872-A and he lost the benefit of the statute of limitations in the third Form 872. Moreover, he was penalized by the IRS' application of an enhanced rate of interest that continues to be compounded daily. This interest accrued while the IRS waited eight years after the June 30, 1984 statute of limitations expired to assess a deficiency.

To understand the nature of the detriment Fredericks suffered, we must consider the interest rate charged on his underpayment. . . .

The detriment Fredericks suffered becomes readily apparent by comparing the penalty-enhanced rates to those he could have earned in savings accounts, certificates of deposit, treasury securities or top-rated corporate bonds. Concededly, Fredericks retained and could have earned interest on $28,361 that he owed to the IRS, but even in a best-case scenario he could not have earned the amount of interest the government now seeks to collect. . . .

The Supreme Court has not directly met the issue whether estoppel against the IRS may be appropriate in certain circumstances. However, contrary to counsel for the Commissioner's emphatic statement at oral argument that in no case has estoppel been asserted successfully against the IRS, this court and others have applied the doctrine of estoppel to the IRS under various circumstances [citations omitted]. . . .

The IRS is not the only federal agency against which courts have applied the doctrine of estoppel. Case law demonstrates that courts have invoked estoppel against the Post Office Department, the Department of Housing and Urban Development, the Land Management Office, the Postal Service, the Parole Commission, the Farmer's Home Administration, the War Department, the Department of Interior, the Department of Commerce and Labor and the General Land Office [citations omitted]. This plethora of precedent suggests that "it is well settled that the doctrine of equitable estoppel, in proper circumstances, and with appropriate caution, may be invoked against the United States in cases involving internal revenue taxation," and in a variety of other contexts. *Simmons* v. *United States,* 308 F.2d 938, 945 (5th Cir. 1962). . . .

Courts are more likely to estop the government when the public fisc—in particular, Congress' power to control public expenditures—is only minimally impacted, if at all. . . .

The public-fisc consideration cuts in favor of estopping the government in the case at bar. By enacting a three-year statute of limitations on the time within which the IRS must assess tax deficiencies, Congress clearly contemplated that in some instances taxpayers would retain funds—because the statute of limitations had run—to which they were not initially entitled. Therefore, invoking the statute of limitations to bar an IRS assessment cannot be deemed an intrusion into Congress' power to expend and allocate public funds. Neither Congress' power to control

public expenditures nor its authority to enact statutes of limitations is impacted when a taxpayer invokes such a statute, either at the end of its original life or 11 years later pursuant to written agreements between the taxpayer and IRS. . . .

Having concluded that the IRS is estopped from relying on the Form 872-A to extend the statute of limitations, we hold that the Commissioner was time-barred from making any assessment, in full or in part, in 1992. The original three-year statute of limitations had run, as had the three one-year extensions agreed to by the parties. Any assessment by the IRS on Fredericks' 1977 tax return was time-barred by 1984. The taxpayer asserted the statute of limitations as a defense to a 1992 assessment, and the Commissioner is thus estopped from refusing to recognize that defense and from denying the effectiveness of the 1984 statute of limitations. . . .

Because we rule the Commissioner is estopped from asserting a deficiency in the 1977 tax return of Barry I. Fredericks, the decision of the Tax Court will be reversed.

Estoppel Remedies without Estoppel

The previous section demonstrated that while the Supreme Court has been reluctant to estop the government, lower federal courts have found a number of occasions to do so. It is also clear, however, that the Supreme Court has found ways to avoid its bar on estoppel and rule in favor of private parties by estopping the government without labeling it as such. One commentator refers to this practice as "remedial due process."[18] In cases of this kind, the Supreme Court avoids the estoppel language and label but pronounces a remedy that amounts to estopping the government. The most important (but by no means the only[19]) case in this category is *Moser* v. *United States*, 341 U.S. 41 (1951). This decision is made more noteworthy because

---

[18] Joshua I. Schwartz, "The Irresistible Force Meets the Immovable Object: Estoppel Remedies for an Agency's Violation of Its Own Regulations or Other Misconduct," 44 *Administrative Law Review* 653, 660, 736 (1992).

[19] See Ibid., esp. 668–742.

it came just four years after *Merrill*, the leading case among the Court's modern pronouncements barring estoppel of the government.

In *Moser*, the Supreme Court reversed a court of appeals decision and ruled that a Swiss national residing in the United States did not waive his right to gain American citizenship even though a form he signed in connection with being relieved from serving in the U.S. Army expressly stated that under the applicable statute, a person who in such circumstances did seek to be excused from the military service "shall thereafter be debarred from becoming a citizen of the United States."

The Supreme Court said that there was "no need" to consider the matter of estoppel in this case. Moser, the Court stated, "never had an opportunity to make an intelligent election between diametrically opposed courses required as a matter of strict law." Therefore, the Court concluded, "elementary fairness" required that Moser not be barred from citizenship (341 U.S. 47).

The inconsistency between the *Merrill* and *Moser* decisions has bothered commentators for decades.[20] The Supreme Court's resort, on occasion, to estoppel-avoiding devices in order to render remedial due process may be laudable. But when viewed alongside its continued aversion to governmental estoppel, the inconsistency of the mid–twentieth century continues to resound to the present time. As Richard Pierce has put it: "*Richmond* seems patently inconsistent with *Moser*. *Moser* may well have been wrongly decided, but the plurality should either have overruled *Moser* or distinguished it. Clarity in the law is not well-served by the Court's too frequent practice of simply ignoring precedents inconsistent with its holding in a case."[21]

DISCRETION AND ITS CONTROL

As suggested at the beginning of this chapter, commentators have long been aware of the significance of discretion in administrative law and of the desirability of keeping it within reasonable bounds. The problem has been to find ways to limit discretion without unduly restricting the flexibility of the administrator. Kenneth Culp Davis, in his pioneering study *Discretionary Justice* (1969), recommended the increased use of administrative rule making to curb unreasonable discretion. The great rise in the use of rule making in the last decades of the twentieth century no doubt had some effect in this area. More recently, however, some commentators have argued that the legal system is being choked by too many rules. What is needed, to such

---

[20] See, e.g., Kenneth Culp Davis, *Administrative Law: Cases—Text—Problems* 540 (6th ed., 1977); Schwartz, "The Irresistible Force," 661f. Davis, in the work just cited, argued that it would make more sense if the result in each case were reversed, with estoppel being granted in *Merrill* and denied in *Moser*. As Davis put it, "Merrill must read the Federal Register, but Moser need not read what he signs."

[21] Richard J. Pierce, Jr., 2 *Administrative Law Treatise* 875 (4th ed., 2002). To avoid the inconsistency discussed here, Schwartz urged the Court to reconsider *Richmond*. See Schwartz, "The Irresistible Force," 744.

critics, is to allow greater room for administrative officials to exercise judgment (i.e., discretion).[22]

The tension between rules and discretion, and the appropriate balance of the two, is one of the enduring problems of law.[23] Commentators, including Supreme Court justices, have recognized that discretion may have multiple meanings. Justice Brennan, in *Board of Pardons* v. *Allen*, 482 U.S. 369 (1987), put it this way:

> In one sense of the word, an official has discretion when he or she "is simply not bound by standards set by the authority in question." R. Dworkin, *Taking Rights Seriously* 32 (1977). . . . But the term discretion may instead signify that "an official must use judgment in applying the standards set him [or her] by authority"; in other words, an official has discretion when the standards set by a statutory or regulatory scheme "cannot be applied mechanically." Dworkin, supra, at 31, 32. . . . [T]he presence of official discretion in this sense is not incompatible with the existence of a liberty interest in parole release when release is *required* after the Board determines (in its broad discretion) that the necessary prerequisites exist.[24]

In some cases discretion is specifically accorded to administrators by law. For instance, a section of the immigration laws, 8 USC § 1229b, provides that "where the Attorney General exercises discretion to grant a waiver," the deportation of certain otherwise deportable aliens may be canceled. And the government receives an extraordinary degree of protection in connection with the exercise of discretion by officials. The most important exemption to the Federal Tort Claims Act, 28 USC § 2680(a), a statute that will be discussed in the next chapter, denies governmental liability for any act "based upon the exercise or performance or the failure to exercise or perform a discretionary function or duty . . . , whether or not the discretion involved be abused." Section 701 of the APA precludes judicial review where "agency action is committed to agency discretion by law." As discussed in chapter 4, this provision is considered to be a rather narrow exception to a broad right of judicial review of administrative activity. Section 706 of the same act provides that the reviewing court shall "hold unlawful and set aside agency action, findings, and conclusions found to be—a. arbitrary, capricious, and abuse of discretion, or otherwise not in accordance with law. . . ." But discretion may be provided by law whether or not the word itself is used in the statute. As Ernst Freund wrote in 1928,

---

[22] See, for instance, Philip Howard, *The Death of Common Sense: How Law Is Suffocating America* (1994). And see the discussion of the issue in Mark Seidenfeld, "Bending the Rules: Flexible Regulation and Constraints on Agency Discretion," 51 *Administrative Law Review* 429 (1999). Seidenfeld believes that in general agencies now have sufficient flexibility and do not need additional discretion for their operation. His article presents a thorough analysis of the arguments on both sides of the issue.

[23] Keith Hawkins, "Issues in the Use of Discretion," in Keith Hawkins, ed., *The Uses of Discretion*, 1992, 3.

[24] 482 U.S. at 375–376. For further comments on the meanings of discretion, see in general Hawkins, ed., *The Uses of Discretion*. Because of the term's ambiguity, one writer has recently gone so far as to recommend "abandoning the idea of discretion" in favor of "a different set of concepts." But even he concluded that the term "is too familiar to replace." Edward L. Rubin, "Discretion and Its Discontents," 72 *Chicago-Kent Law Review* 1299, at 1300, 1336 (1997).

a statute confers discretion when it refers an official for the use of his power to beliefs, expectations, or tendencies, instead of facts, or to such terms as "adequate," "advisable," "appropriate," "beneficial," "convenient," "detrimental," "expedient," "equitable," "fair," "fit," "necessary," "practicable," "proper," "reasonable," "reputable," "safe," "sufficient," "wholesome," or their opposites.[25]

Such legislative language confers considerable room for judgment on administrators. It is largely the job of the courts, therefore, to try to rein in the too broad use of discretion. As already noted, the APA limits judicial review where the law commits a matter to agency discretion. In a more general sense, courts are reluctant to substitute their judgment for that of administrative experts, although they are sometimes willing to consider whether agencies have overstepped reasonable limits on the use of discretionary authority. Some commentators assert that the power of the courts in this area has been restricted in recent years.[26] If this turns out to be the case, then the last line of defense against the overzealous administrator has been weakened to some extent. The following two cases illustrate two approaches by the courts on this matter. In the first case, all members of the Supreme Court concluded that the Securities and Exchange Commission (SEC) had exercised discretion beyond its statutory grant of power. In the second, a case freighted with international political significance, a court of appeals provided wide latitude to the government in its exercise of discretion.

Securities and Exchange Commission v. Sloan

SUPREME COURT OF THE UNITED STATES, 1978.
436 U.S. 103, 98 S.Ct. 1702, 56 L.Ed. 2d 148.

Mr. Justice REHNQUIST delivered the opinion of the Court.

Under the Securities Exchange Act of 1934 . . . the Securities and Exchange Commission has the authority "summarily to suspend trading in any security . . . for a period not exceeding ten days" if "in its opinion the public interest and the protection of investors so require." Acting pursuant to this authority the Commission issued a series of consecutive orders suspending trading in the common stock of Canadian Javelin, Ltd. (CJL), for over a

year. The Court of Appeals for the Second Circuit held that such a series of suspensions was beyond the scope of the Commission's statutory authority. . . . We granted certiorari to consider this important question . . . and, finding ourselves in basic agreement with the Court of Appeals, we affirm. We hold that even though there be a periodic redetermination of whether such action is required by "the public interest" and for "the protection of investors," the Commission is not empowered to issue, based upon a single

---

[25] *Administrative Powers over Persons and Property* 71, as quoted in Kraines, above, note 1, at 112.

[26] Pierce sees the Supreme Court's landmark *Chevron* case of 1984 (467 U.S. 837), which is discussed at length in chapter 6, as marking a "doctrinal shift": "By holding that reviewing courts must affirm any reasonable interpretation of ambiguous language in an agency-administered statute, the Court [in *Chevron*] reduced significantly the discretion of individual judges to attribute to Congress intentions that are based more on the judge's policy preferences than on the language Congress chose to express its intent" (4 *Administrative Law Treatise* 1237, above, note 19). See also Aman and Mayton, above, note 17 , 478–479.

set of circumstances, a series of summary orders which would suspend trading beyond the initial 10-day period. . . .

Turning to the merits, we note that this is not a case where the Commission, discovering the existence of a manipulative scheme affecting CJL stock, suspended trading for 10 days and then, upon the discovery of a second manipulative scheme or other improper activity unrelated to the first scheme, ordered a second 10-day suspension. Instead it is a case in which the Commission issued a series of summary suspension orders lasting over a year on the basis of evidence revealing a single, though likely sizable, manipulative scheme. Thus, the only question confronting us is whether, even upon a periodic redetermination of "necessity," the Commission is statutorily authorized to issue a series of summary suspension orders based upon a single set of events or circumstances which threaten an orderly market. This question must, in our opinion, be answered in the negative.

The first and most salient point leading us to this conclusion is the language of the statute. Section 12 (k) authorizes the Commission "summarily to suspend trading in any security . . . *for a period not exceeding ten days. . . .*" The Commission would have us read the [italicized phrase] as a limitation only upon the duration of a single suspension order. So read, the Commission could indefinitely suspend trading in a security without any hearing or other procedural safeguards as long as it redetermined every 10 days that suspension was required by the public interest and for the protection of investors. While perhaps not an impossible reading of the statute, we are persuaded it is not the most natural or logical one. The duration limitation rather appears on its face to be just that—a maximum time period for which trading can be suspended for any single set of circumstances.

Apart from the language of the stat-ute, which we find persuasive in and of itself, there are other reasons to adopt this construction of the statute. In the first place, the power to summarily suspend trading in a security even for 10 days, without any notice, opportunity to be heard, or findings based upon a record, is an awesome power with a potentially devastating impact on the issuer, its shareholders, and other investors. A clear mandate from Congress, such as that found in § 12 (k), is necessary to confer this power. No less clear a mandate can be expected from Congress to authorize the Commission to extend, virtually without limit, these periods of suspension. But we find no such unmistakable mandate in § 12 (k). Indeed, if anything, that section points in the opposite direction.

Other sections of the statute reinforce the conclusion that in this area Congress considered summary restrictions to be somewhat drastic and properly used only for very brief periods of time. When explicitly longer term, though perhaps temporary, measures are to be taken against some person, company, or security, Congress invariably requires the Commission to give some sort of notice and opportunity to be heard. For example, § 12 (j) of the Act authorizes the Commission, as it deems necessary for the protection of investors, to suspend the registration of a security for a period not exceeding 12 months if it makes certain findings "*on the record after notice and opportunity for hearing. . . .*" Another section of the Act empowers the Commission to suspend broker-dealer registration for a period not exceeding 12 months upon certain findings made only "*on the record after notice and opportunity for hearing.*" Still another section allows the Commission, pending final determination whether a broker-dealer's registration should be revoked, to temporarily suspend that registration, but only "*after notice and opportunity for hearing.*" . . . In light of the explicit congressional recognition in other sections of the Act . . . that any long-term sanctions or any continuation of summary restrictions must be accompanied by notice and an opportunity for a hearing, it is difficult to read the silence in § 12 (k) as an authorization for an extension of summary restrictions without such a hearing, as the Commission contends. The more plausible interpretation is that Congress did not intend the Commission to have the power to extend the length of suspensions under § 12 (k) at all, much less to repeatedly extend such suspensions without any hearing. . . .

[T]he Commission argues that for a variety of reasons Congress should be considered to have approved the Commission's construction of the statute as correct. Not only has Congress re-enacted the summary suspension power without disapproving the Commission's construction, but the Commission participated in the drafting of much of this legislation and on at least one occasion made its views known to Congress in Committee hearings. Furthermore, at least one Committee indicated on one occasion that it understood and approved of the Commission's practice. . . .

We are extremely hesitant to presume general congressional awareness of the Commission's construction based only upon a few isolated statements in the thousands of pages of legislative documents. That language in a committee report, without additional indication of more widespread congressional awareness, is simply not sufficient to invoke the presumption in a case such as this. For here its invocation would result in a construction of the statute which is not only at odds with the language of the section in question and the pattern of the statute taken as a whole, but is extremely far reaching in terms of the virtually untrammeled and unreviewable power it would vest in a regulatory agency. . . .

In sum, had Congress intended the Commission to have the power to summarily suspend trading virtually indefinitely we expect that it could and would have authorized it more clearly than it did in § 12 (k). The sweeping nature of that power supports this expectation. The absence of any truly persuasive legislative history to support the Commission's view, and the entire statutory scheme suggesting that in fact the Commission is not so empowered, reinforce our conclusion that the Court of Appeals was correct in concluding no such power exists. Accordingly, its judgment is Affirmed.

Mr. Justice BRENNAN, with whom Mr. Justice MARSHALL joins, concurring in the judgment.

Although I concur in much of the Court's reasoning and in its holding that "the Commission is not empowered to issue, based upon a single set of circumstances, a series of summary orders which would suspend trading beyond the initial 10-day period," ante, at 106, I cannot join the Court's opinion because of its omissions and unfortunate dicta. . . .

The Court's opinion does not reveal how flagrantly abusive the Security and Exchange Commission's use of its § 12 (k) authority has been. That section authorizes the Commission "summarily to suspend trading in any security . . . for a period not exceeding ten days. . . ." As the Court says, this language "is persuasive in and of itself" that 10 days is the "maximum time period for which trading can be suspended for any single set of circumstances." . . . But the Commission has used § 12 (k), or its predecessor statutes . . . to suspend trading in a security for up to 13 *years*. And, although the 13-year suspension is an extreme example, the record is replete with suspensions lasting the better part of a year. I agree that § 12 (k) is clear on its face and that it prohibits this administrative practice. But even if § 12 (k) were unclear, a 13-year suspension, or even a 1-year suspension as here, without notice or hearing so obviously violates fundamentals of due process and fair play that no reasonable individual could suppose that Congress intended to authorize such a thing.

Moreover, the SEC's procedural implementation of its § 12 (k) power mocks any conclusion other than that the SEC simply could not care whether its § 12 (k) orders are justified. So far as this record shows, the SEC never reveals the reasons for its suspension orders. To be sure, here respondent was able long after the fact to obtain some explanation through a Freedom of Information Act request, but even the information tendered was heavily excised and none of it even purports to state the reasoning of the Commissioners under whose authority § 12 (k) orders issue. Nonetheless, when the SEC finally agreed to give respondent a hearing on the suspension of Canadian Javelin stock, it required respondent to state, in a verified petition (that is, under oath) why he thought the unrevealed conclusions of the SEC to be wrong. This is obscurantism run riot.

Accordingly, while we today leave open the question whether the SEC could tack successive 10-day suspensions if this were necessary to meet first one and then a different emergent situation, I for one would look with great disfavor on any effort to tack suspension periods unless the SEC concurrently adopted a policy of stating its reasons for each suspension. Without such a statement of reasons, I fear our holding today will have no force since the SEC's administration of its suspension power will be reviewable, if at all, only by the circuitous and time-consuming path followed by respondent here. . . .

Mr. Justice BLACKMUN, concurring in the judgment. . . .

Here, the Commission indulged in 37 suspension orders, all but the last issued "quite bare of any emergency findings," to borrow Professor Loss' phrase. Beyond the opaque suggestion in an April 1975 Release . . . that the Commission was awaiting the "dissemination of information concerning regulatory action by Canadian authorities," shareholders of CJL were given no hint why their securities were to be made nonnegotiable for over a year. Until April 22, 1976 . . . the SEC provided no opportunity to shareholders to dispute the factual premises of a suspension, and, in the absence of any explanation by the Commission of the basis for its suspension orders, such a right to comment would be useless. As such, I conclude that the use of suspension orders in this case exceeded the limits of the Commission's discretion. . . .

Elian Gonzalez v. *Reno*

UNITED STATES COURT OF APPEALS FOR THE ELEVENTH CIRCUIT, 2000.
212 F.3d 1338.

[Elian Gonzalez's parents, both citizens of Cuba, separated when Elian was about three years old. In 1999, when he was six, Elian was taken by his mother to live in the United States. But the small ship in which they were traveling met rough seas and capsized. Most of those aboard died, including Elian's mother. Elian was rescued and taken to Miami for medical treatment. On his release from the hospital, the Immigration and Naturalization Service (INS), an agency of the U.S. Department of Justice, decided not to send Elian back to Cuba immediately but instead paroled him into the care and custody of Miami resident Lazaro Gonzalez, a great-uncle of Elian.

Shortly thereafter, a series of applications for asylum were filed on Elian's behalf, including one signed by Elian (which is why he is sometimes referred to as "the Plaintiff" in the excerpt from the decision set forth below). A state court awarded Lazaro temporary custody of Elian.

Soon after Elian was rescued at sea, however, Elian's father, Juan Miguel Gonzalez, requested through Cuban officials that Elian be returned to Cuba. The Cuban government sent this request to the INS.

After lengthy interviews by the INS with Elian's father in Cuba and with his Miami relatives, the INS commissioner rejected all claims of asylum. The commissioner, in the words of the appeals court decision, asserted that "parents generally speak for their children and finding that no circumstances in this case warranted a departure from that custom—concluded that the asylum applications submitted by Plaintiff and Lazaro were legally void and required no further consideration" (212 F.3d 1346).

The attorney general declined to overturn the INS commissioner's ruling, after which a federal district court dismissed a complaint against the INS decision. It was on this basis that the case came to the court of appeals.

During the course of these proceedings, the Justice Department had been negotiating with Elian's Miami relatives to turn the boy over to his father, who had come to the United States. A court order was issued instructing Juan Miguel Gonzalez not to return to Cuba with his son until all judicial issues concerning the matter of asylum had been resolved. When the protracted negotiations with the Miami relatives failed to persuade them to turn over Elian, armed U.S. marshals and Border Patrol agents made an early-morning raid on the house where Elian was staying and took him away, to be reunited with his father. This act by the government spawned further lawsuits, charging excessive use of force by federal agents against relatives of Elian and protesters outside the residence where Elian was staying.

Six weeks after the raid, on June 1, 2000, the Court of Appeals issued its decision. The excerpts provided below focus on the government's use of and possible abuse of discretion. Note the court's reliance in the opinion that follows on some of the leading cases discussed in this book, *Chevron* and *Chenery* among them.]

Judge EDMONDSON delivered the opinion of the Court.

This case, at first sight, seems to be about little more than a child and his father. But, for this Court, the case is mainly about the separation of powers under our constitutional system of government: a statute enacted by Congress, the permissible scope of executive discretion under that statute, and the limits on judicial review of the exercise of that executive discretion.

On appeal, Plaintiff argues that the district court erred (1) by dismissing Plaintiff's claim under 8 U.S.C. § 1158, [and] (2) by dismissing Plaintiff's due process claim. . . . We have reviewed carefully the record and the briefs filed by all parties. We conclude that Plaintiff's due process claim lacks merit and does not warrant extended discussion. . . . We now turn, however, to a more difficult question: the district court's dismissal of Plaintiff's statutory claim.

Plaintiff contends that the district court erred in rejecting his statutory claim based on 8 U.S.C. § 1158. Section 1158 provides that "[a]ny alien . . . may apply for asylum." . . . Plaintiff says that, because he is "any alien," he may apply for asylum. Plaintiff insists that, by the applications signed and submitted by himself and Lazaro, he, in fact, did apply for asylum within the meaning of section 1158. In addition, Plaintiff argues that the summary rejection by the INS of his applications as invalid violated the intent of Congress as set out in the statute.

The INS responds that section 1158 is silent about the validity of asylum applications filed on behalf of a six-year-old child, by the child himself and a non-parental relative, against the wishes of the child's parent. The INS argues that, because the statute does not spell out how a young child files for asylum, the INS was free to adopt a policy requiring, in these circumstances, that any asylum claim on Plaintiff's behalf be filed by Plaintiff's father. As such, the INS urges that the rejection of Plaintiff's purported asylum applications as legally void was lawful. According to the INS, because the applications had no legal effect, Plaintiff never applied at all within the meaning of the statute.

Guided by well-established principles of statutory construction, judicial restraint, and deference to executive agencies, we accept that the rejection by the INS of Plaintiff's applications as invalid did not violate section 1158.

Our consideration of Plaintiff's statutory claim must begin with an examination of the scope of the statute itself. . . . In *Chevron* [, *U.S.A., Inc.* v. *Natural Resources Defense Council, Inc.* (1984)], the Supreme Court explained: "First, always, is the question whether Congress has directly spoken to the precise question at issue. If the intent of Congress is clear, that is the end of the matter; for the court, as well as the agency, must give effect to the unambiguously expressed intent of Congress." 104 S.Ct. at 2781. We turn, therefore, to the plain language of the statute.

Section 1158 provides, in pertinent part:

> *Any alien* who is physically present in the United States or who arrives in the United States (whether or not at a designated port of arrival and including an alien who is brought to the United States after having been interdicted in international or United States waters), irrespective of such alien's status, *may apply for asylum* in accordance with this section or, where applicable, section 1225(b) of this title. . . .

Section 1158 is neither vague nor ambiguous. The statute means exactly what it says: "any alien . . . may apply for asylum." . . . That "any alien" includes Plaintiff seems apparent. . . . Section 1158, therefore, plainly would permit Plaintiff to apply for asylum.

When an alien does apply for asylum within the meaning of the statute, the INS—according to the statute itself and INS regulations—must consider the merits of the alien's asylum claim. . . . The important legal question in this case, therefore, is not whether Plaintiff *may* apply for asylum; that a six-year-old is eligible to apply for asylum is clear. The ultimate inquiry, instead, is whether a six-year-old child *has* applied for asylum within the meaning of the statute when he, or a non-parental relative on his behalf, signs and submits a purported application against the express wishes of the child's parent.

About this question, more important than what Congress said in section 1158 is what Congress left unsaid. In reading statutes, we consider not only the words Congress used, but the spaces between those words. Section 1158 is silent on the precise question at issue in this case. Although section 1158 gives "any alien" the right to "apply for asylum," the statute does not command how an alien applies for asylum. The statute includes no definition of the term "apply." The statute does not set out procedures for the proper filing of an asylum application. Furthermore, the statute does not identify the necessary contents of a valid asylum application. In short, although the statute requires the existence of some application procedure so that aliens may apply for asylum, section 1158 says nothing about the particulars of that procedure. . . .

Because the statute is silent on the issue, Congress has left a gap in the statutory scheme. From that gap springs executive discretion. As a matter of law, it is not for the courts, but for the executive agency charged with enforcing the statute (here, the INS), to choose how to fill such gaps. . . . Moreover, the authority of the executive branch to fill gaps is especially great in the context of immigration policy. . . .

That the courts owe some deference to executive policy does not mean that the executive branch has unbridled discretion in creating and in implementing policy. Executive agencies must comply with the procedural requirements imposed by statute . . . . Agencies must respect their own procedural rules and regulations. . . . And the policy selected by the agency must be a reasonable one in the light of the statutory scheme. . . . To this end, the courts retain the authority to check agency policymaking for procedural compliance and for arbitrariness. But the courts cannot properly reexamine the wisdom of an agency-promulgated policy. . . .

In this case, because the law—particularly section 1158—is silent about the validity of Plaintiff's purported asylum applications, it fell to the INS to make a discretionary policy choice. The INS, exercising its gap-filling discretion, determined these things: (1) six-year-old children lack the capacity to sign and to submit personally an application for asylum; (2) instead, six-year-old children must be represented by an adult in immigration matters; (3) absent special circumstances, the only proper adult to represent a six-year-old child is the child's parent, even when the parent is not in this country; and, (4) that the parent lives in a communist-totalitarian state (such as Cuba), in and of itself, does not constitute a special circumstance requiring the selection of a non-parental representative. Our duty is to decide whether this policy might be a reasonable one in the light of the statutory scheme. . . .

We accept that the INS policy at issue here comes within the range of reasonable choices. First, we cannot say that the foundation of the policy—the INS determination that six-year-old children necessarily lack sufficient capacity to assert, on their own, an asylum claim—is unreasonable. . . . Because six-year-old children must have some means of applying for asylum . . . and because the INS has decided that the children cannot apply personally, the next element of the INS policy—that a six-year-old child must be represented by some adult in applying for asylum—necessarily is reasonable. . . .

Critically important, the INS policy does not neglect completely the independent and separate interest that a child may have, apart from his parents, in applying for asylum. . . . Instead, according to the INS policy, special circumstances may exist that render a parent an inappropriate representative for the child. Where such circumstances do exist, the INS policy appears to permit other persons, besides a parent, to speak for the child in immigration matters. So, to some extent, the policy does protect a child's own right to apply for asylum under section 1158 despite the contrary wishes of his parents. . . .

And we cannot invalidate the policy—one with international relations implications—selected by the INS merely because we personally might have chosen another. . . . Because we cannot say that this element of the INS policy—that, ordinarily, a parent, and only a parent, can act for a six-year-old child in immigration matters—is unreasonable, we defer to the INS policy. . . .

[The court then discussed at some length the fact that Cuba is widely viewed as a communist-totalitarian state and the tradition of giving greater deference to executive branch decisions in the foreign affairs arena. It concluded as follows:] Something even close to a per se rule—that, for immigration purposes, no parent living in a totalitarian state has sufficient liberty to represent and to serve the true, best interests of his own child in the United States—likely would have significant consequences for the President's conduct of our Nation's international affairs: such a rule would focus not on the qualities of the particular parent, but on the qualities of the government of the parent's country. As we understand the legal precedents, they, in effect, direct that a court of law defer especially to this international-relations aspect of the INS policy.

We are obliged to accept that the INS policy, on its face, does not contradict and does not violate section 1158, although section 1158 does not require the approach that the INS has chosen to take. . . .

We now examine the INS's application of its facially reasonable policy to Plaintiff in this case. Although based on a policy permissible under *Chevron*, if the ultimate decision of the INS—to treat Plaintiff's asylum applications as invalid—was "arbitrary, capricious, [or] an abuse of discretion," the decision is unlawful. But whatever we personally might think about the decisions made by the Government, we cannot properly conclude that the INS acted arbitrarily or abused its discretion here.

The application signed and submitted by Plaintiff himself, insofar as the INS has decided that six-year-old children cannot file for asylum themselves, necessarily was a nullity under the INS policy. As we have explained, the INS's per se rule—prohibiting six-year-old children from personally filing asylum applications against their parents' wishes—is entitled to deference under the law. The INS, therefore, did not act arbitrarily or abuse its discretion in rejecting Plaintiff's

own purported asylum application as void. . . .

We have not the slightest illusion about the INS's choices: the choices—about policy and about application of the policy—that the INS made in this case are choices about which reasonable people can disagree. Still, the choices were not unreasonable, not capricious and not arbitrary, but were reasoned and reasonable. The INS's considerable discretion was not abused.

CONCLUSION

As policymakers, it is the duty of the Congress and of the executive branch to exercise political will. Although courts should not be unquestioning, we should respect the other branches' policymaking powers. The judicial power is a limited power. It is the duty of the judicial branch not to exercise political will, but only to render judicial judgment under the law.

When the INS was confronted with Plaintiff's purported asylum applications, the immigration law of the United States provided the INS with no clear answer. The INS accordingly developed a policy to deal with the extraordinary circumstances of asylum applications filed on behalf of a six-year-old child, by the child himself and a non-parental relative, against the express wishes of the child's parents (or sole parent). The INS then applied this new policy to Plaintiff's purported asylum applications and rejected them as nullities.

Because the preexisting law compelled no particular policy, the INS was entitled to make a policy decision. The policy decision that the INS made was within the outside border of reasonable choices. And the INS did not abuse its discretion or act arbitrarily in applying the policy and rejecting Plaintiff's purported asylum applications. The Court neither approves nor disapproves the INS's decision to reject the asylum applications filed on Plaintiff's behalf, but the INS decision did not contradict 8 U.S.C. § 1158.

The judgment of the district court is AFFIRMED.

On June 28, 2000, the Supreme Court refused to stay the court of appeals' decision and denied certiorari in the case (*Gonzalez* v. *Reno*, 530 U.S. 1270). Hours later Elian and his father flew back to Havana.

INFORMAL REMEDIES: OMBUDSMEN AND OTHERS

The heightened awareness of the significance of informal administrative action has given rise to a number of efforts to find new mechanisms to cope with its problems. Clearly the most important of these is the ombudsman, an institution of Swedish origin, emulated around the world, for handling complaints against administration. Since the ombudsman idea began to spread in the 1960s, an enormous amount of attention and study has been devoted to the institution. The American Bar Association's Administrative Law and Regulatory Practice Section has an Ombudsman Committee that has adopted recommendations, standards, and model legislation on ombudsmen. A United States Ombudsman Association serves public sector ombudsman offices in the United States and abroad.[27] The International Ombudsman Institute, with headquarters at the University of Alberta, in Canada, links citizen defender offices in six large regions around the world. It reported that in 2001 national-level ombudsman offices existed in about 110 countries.[28] Regional, provincial, state, and municipal offices are also found in a number of countries.

In the United States, in addition to hundreds of public sector ombudsman offices, bodies of similar purpose exist in a large number of nongovernmental organizations in such areas as higher education, long-term care, mental health care, and the prevention of domestic violence.

Given the proliferation of ombudsman offices in recent years, any overall assessment of the effectiveness of the institution is clearly impossible. Its presence no doubt provides some aid to individuals facing formidable bureaucracies that may have treated them unfairly. A fairly typical comment in the literature, however, is that performing the ombudsman function is often impeded by such factors as limited funding, staffing problems, and restrictions on the office's authority and autonomy.[29]

A kind of citizen complaint not usually handled by ombudsmen involves the activities of local police. The traditional manner of dealing with allega-

---

[27] See www.usombudsman.org.

[28] "The International Ombudsman Institute Information Booklet," http://www.law.ualberta.ca/centres/ioi/history.htm.

[29] See, e.g., Elizabeth B. Herrington, "Strengthening the Older Americans Act's Long-Term Protection Provisions: A Call for Further Improvement of Important State Ombudsman Programs," 5 *Elder Law Journal* 321 (1997).

tions of "police brutality" and like complaints has been through internal police department disciplinary proceedings. But because, as one commentator has put it, "when five policemen hear a complaint against another policeman, the policeman is always right,"[30] pressures for some form of independent review grew in the 1950s and 1960s.

Resistance from powerful police departments and police lobbies discredited these early efforts. But in what a leading commentator has called "the rise, fall, and revival of citizen oversight,"[31] agencies that exercise oversight of police activities have made a considerable comeback in recent years.[32] Not all such agencies have uniform success in their efforts. A number of civilian police review bodies lack truly independent authority, and many face hostility and noncooperation from the police departments whose activities they are charged with reviewing.[33] In spite of these problems, outside monitoring of police behavior has again become a factor in governmental operations at the municipal level.

CONCLUSION

This chapter has ranged across a number of subjects, all of them controversial. What these issues make clear is that government agencies feel constrained at times to act informally in ways that can affect important interests of private parties. One of the continuing challenges to administrative law is to fashion a suitable balance between public needs and private interests in this area.

---

[30] Arnold Trebach, *The Rationing of Justice* 215 (1964).

[31] This is the title of chapter 2 of Samuel Walker's 2001 book *Police Accountability: The Role of Citizen Oversight*, 19–50.

[32] Ibid., 6, 44.

[33] Ibid., 182.

PART FOUR

Remedies

CHAPTER 9

Remedies against Improper Administrative Acts

CHAPTER 10

Open Government

Chapter 9

Remedies against Improper Administrative Acts

As chapter 4 made clear, there are a number of avenues available for obtaining judicial review, including both statutory review and the various forms of nonstatutory review. In this chapter we examine the forms of relief that a private party might seek with regard to administrative actions taken against him or her. To put the matter in its simplest form, a private party who considers an administrative act illegal or improper would want, depending on the timing of the act, (1) to halt or prevent the action or (2) to have it declared illegal and rescinded. If accomplishing these objectives still left the party injured by the governmental act, compensation might be sought from an official or from the government itself. These are the matters that will be discussed in this chapter, with special attention given to compensation to citizens injured by governmental acts. Another remedy of sorts, which has grown considerably in importance in recent years, has to do with the individual's right to gain information about government operations. This will be the subject of the next chapter.

DECLARATORY AND INJUNCTIVE RELIEF

Many of the cases we have discussed in early chapters have involved either (1) or (2) above. For example, in *Marshall* v. *Barlow's* (1978),[1] presented in chapter 5, Bill Barlow sued to prevent a warrantless search that OSHA sought to conduct at his electrical and plumbing installation business. In other words, he asked for injunctive relief, or an injunction. In *Kent* v. *Dulles* (1958),[2] in chapter 3, a suit was brought against the secretary of state for failure to issue a passport to Kent after Kent had refused to file an affidavit

---

[1] 436 U.S. 307 (1978).

[2] 357 U.S. 116 (1958).

concerning his membership in the Communist Party. Kent sought declaratory relief, or a declaratory judgment, an assertion by the court that the secretary of state's action was beyond the bounds of the law. Sometimes plaintiffs will ask for both an injunction and a declaratory judgment. Thus, in *Ingraham* v. *Wright* (1977),[3] described in chapter 7, both injunctive and declaratory relief were sought by the students in connection with the school paddling incidents. The students also sued for damages, a subject that will be discussed below.

Even with the doctrine of estoppel, discussed in chapter 8, the objective is to prevent the government from acting in a way contrary to a private party's interest. Thus, for instance, in *Federal Crop Insurance Corporation* v. *Merrill* (1947),[4] Merrill, the Idaho farmer, sued to estop the government from denying the validity of an insurance contract. As discussed in chapter 8, the law has changed somewhat from the traditional rule that governmental units cannot be estopped. That rule apparently had its roots in the doctrine of sovereign immunity: "the king cannot be estopped, for it cannot be presumed that the king would wrong any person."[5]

Sovereign immunity also has relevance to other kinds of suits against the government. In the past, for instance, sovereign immunity was often used successfully to bar suits against the federal government seeking a declaratory judgment, an injunction, or other specific relief.[6] In 1976, however, Congress abolished this aspect of sovereign immunity by amending section 702 of the Administrative Procedure Act (APA) to provide that an action against the United States for relief other than money damages "shall not be dismissed nor relief denied on the ground that it is against the United States or that the United States is an indispensable party."

TORT SUITS AGAINST THE GOVERNMENT

Sovereign immunity, one of the common-law inheritances of the United States from England, still applies, however, in the area of damage suits against the government. The basis for the sovereign immunity doctrine is the ancient notion that "the king can do no wrong." How a doctrine such as this, originally connected purely with the personality of the English king, ever came to be applied to the United States is "one of the mysteries of legal evolution."[7] Whatever the explanation, the main principle of the doctrine, that the government cannot be sued without its consent, became a bedrock maxim of American jurisprudence. Justice Holmes expressed the principle as: "The United States has not consented to be sued for torts, and therefore

---

[3] 430 U.S. 651 (1977).

[4] 332 U.S. 380 (1947).

[5] 15 *Halsbury's Laws of England* 248 (1956), quoting from *Bacon's Abridgements,* as quoted in Kenneth Culp Davis, *Administrative Law Text* 343 (3rd ed., 1972).

[6] See ibid., 494–507.

[7] Edwin M. Borchard, "Governmental Liability in Tort," 34 *Yale Law Journal* 4 (1924).

it cannot be said that in the legal sense the United States has been guilty of a tort. For a tort is a tort in a legal sense only because the law has made it so" [*United States* v. *Thompson*, 257 U.S. 419, 433 (1922)].

Until the 1940s, the government had consented to be sued only in a very narrow range of circumstances. In most cases, sovereign immunity prevailed, and many victims who otherwise would have been entitled to compensation were left empty handed because the harm visited on them was inflicted by the government. The only recourse in such cases was either a suit against the wrongdoing official (such suits will be discussed below) or the congressional enactment of a private bill giving relief to the individual as a matter of legislative grace. The latter course was a time-consuming and unsure method that depended greatly on one's having a powerful "angel" in Congress who could carry the fight for a private bill through both houses of the legislature.

A long effort by opponents of sovereign immunity culminated in 1946 in the adoption by Congress of the Federal Tort Claims Act (FTCA), 60 Stat. 842. The key provision of the act reads as follows:

> The United States shall be liable, respecting the provisions of this title relating to tort claims, in the same manner and to the same extent as a private individual under like circumstances. . . .

The direct implication of this passage is that the regular rules of tort law, including the basic requirement of negligence or fault on the part of the wrongdoer, apply to the government. Since tort rules are part of state law, not federal law, the act meant that governmental liability would depend to some extent on the law of the state in which the tortious act took place.

What has caused controversy is the strictness with which the courts have interpreted this passage. What the courts initially said, in effect, was that there could be governmental liability only in those instances in which private persons traditionally have been found liable. Thus, in *Feres* v. *United States*, a case that involved injuries inflicted on soldiers on active duty by other members of the armed services, the Supreme Court could find no analogy in the tort relationships between private individuals, and so it rejected the claims of the soldiers: "We find no parallel liability before and we think no new one has been created by this act. Its effect is to waive immunity from recognized causes of action and was not to visit the government with novel and unprecedented liabilities" [340 U.S. 135 (1950)]. In spite of considerable criticism of the decision over the years, the *Feres* doctrine still stands.

Besides the main provision of the FTCA discussed above, the act contains thirteen specific exceptions—circumstances in which there can be no governmental liability. Of these, two are of greatest importance. The first bars tort actions based on certain intentional torts, such as libel, slander, misrepresentation, deceit, and others, by public officers.[8] The second excep-

---

[8] A 1974 amendment to the Federal Tort Claims Act reduced considerably the scope of this intentional torts exception. The legislation provided that the government would be liable for claims based on acts of U.S. investigative or law enforcement officers involved in "assault, battery, false imprisonment, false arrest, abuse of process or malicious prosecution" (Public Law 93–253, 88 Stat. 50). The adoption of this amendment followed a particularly shocking act of forced entry and unau-

tion, which has further-reaching implications, is the so-called discretionary-function exception. It states in part that the act does not extend to claims "based upon the exercise or performance or the failure to exercise or perform a discretionary function or duty on the part of a federal agency or an employee of the Government, whether or not the discretion involved be abused."

This exception has been called "the most litigated provision of a much-litigated statute."[9] It has also proved to be the most challenging part of the FTCA for the courts, which have struggled mightily to explain when governmental action should be classified as a discretionary function and when it should not. A key early case was *Dalehite* v. *United States* (1953). It is significant not only because of the huge losses involved (560 deaths, 3,000 persons injured, personal and property claims totaling $200 million), but also because of the significant pronouncements concerning the interpretation of the statute made by the Supreme Court.

Dalehite v. *United States*

SUPREME COURT OF THE UNITED STATES, 1953.
346 U.S. 15, 73 S.Ct. 956, 97 L.Ed. 1427.

[As part of the foreign aid program after World War II, the United States government decided to produce fertilizer for shipment to Europe and elsewhere. Production took place at deactivated ordnance plants used during the war. The fertilizer was manufactured under plans developed by responsible governmental officials, but the plants were actually operated by private companies that had entered into contracts with the government. The basic ingredient of the fertilizer was FGAN—fertilizer grade ammonium nitrate, long used as a component in explosives. In undertaking to manufacture the fertilizer, government officials drew up detailed specifications regarding its production.

In April 1947, almost three thousand tons of FGAN were loaded onto two ships in the harbor at Texas City, Texas. A fire started, and as the Supreme Court put it

in summing up the accident, "[b]oth ships exploded and much of the city was leveled and many people were killed."

The suit brought by the relatives of Henry G. Dalehite, who was killed in the explosion, represented some 300 personal and property claims against the U.S. government. The U.S. district court found that the government had been negligent in several ways, from the drafting and adoption of the fertilizer export program, to the manufacturing of the fertilizer, to failures in shipboard loading and fire-fighting. It awarded damages of $75,000 to each of the individual plaintiffs. The court of appeals unanimously reversed.

The Supreme Court's decision in the case took up a number of issues. The brief excerpt reproduced below is limited, in both the principal opinion and the dissent, to the two most important of these: the range of acts covered by the discre-

---

thorized search—at the wrong address—by federal narcotics agents. For a vivid description of the incident, see J. Boger, M. Gitenstein, and P. Verkuil, "The Federal Tort Claims Act Intentional Tort Amendment: An Interpretive Analysis," 54 *North Carolina Law Review* 497, 500–501 (1976).

[9] D. Scott Barash, "The Discretionary Function Exception and Mandatory Regulations," 54 *University of Chicago Law Review* 1300, 1301 (1987).

tionary function exception and the so-called private person analogy, that is, the question of whether some of the allegedly negligent acts were, as in *Feres*, uniquely governmental in nature.]

Mr. Justice REED delivered the opinion of the Court. . . .

It is unnecessary to define, apart from this case, precisely where discretion ends. It is enough to hold, as we do, that the "discretionary function or duty" that cannot form a basis for suit under the Tort Claims Act includes more than the initiation of programs and activities. It also includes determinations made by executives or administrators in establishing plans, specifications or schedules of operations. Where there is room for policy judgment and decision there is discretion. It necessarily follows that acts of subordinates in carrying out the operations of government in accordance with official directions cannot be actionable. . . .

In short, the alleged "negligence" does not subject the Government to liability. *The decisions held culpable were all responsibly made at a planning rather than operational level*[10] and involved considerations more or less important to the practicability of the Government's fertilizer program. . . .

The findings of negligence on the part of the Coast Guard in failing to supervise the storage of the FGAN, and in fighting the fire after it started, were rejected by a majority of the Court of Appeals. We do not enter into an examination of these factual findings. We prefer, again, to rest our decision on the Act.

The District Court's holding that the Coast Guard and other agencies were negligent in failing to prevent the fire by regulating storage or loading of the fertilizer in some different fashion is like his [the district court judge's] specific citations of negligence discussed above. They are classically within the exception. . . .

As to the alleged failure in fighting the fire, we think this too without the Act. The Act did not create new causes of action where none existed before. . . .

It did not change the normal rule that an alleged failure or carelessness of public firemen does not create private actionable rights. Our analysis of the question is determined by what was said in the *Feres* case. The Act, as was there stated, limited United States liability to "the same manner and to the same extent as a private individual under like circumstances." Here, as there, there is no analogous liability; in fact, if anything is doctrinally sanctified in the law of torts it is the immunity of communities and other public bodies for injuries due to fighting fire. . . .

Affirmed

Mr. Justice DOUGLAS and Mr. Justice CLARK took no part in the consideration or decision of this case.

Mr. Justice JACKSON, joined by Mr. Justice BLACK and Mr. Justice FRANKFURTER, dissenting. . . .

We think that the statutory language, the reliable legislative history, and the common-sense basis of the rule regarding municipalities, all point to a useful and proper distinction preserved by the statute other than that urged by the Government. When an official exerts governmental authority in a manner which legally binds one or many, he is acting in a way in which no private person could. Such activities do and are designed to affect, often deleteriously, the affairs of individuals, but courts have long recognized the public policy that such official shall be controlled solely by the statutory or administrative mandate and not by the added threat of private damage suits. For example, the Attorney General will not be

---

[10] Italics supplied by the authors. The planning-operational distinction articulated here long served as the key element used by federal courts for applying the discretionary function exception. This matter is discussed in the section titled "Effects of the *Dalehite* Case."

liable for false arrest in circumstances where a private person performing the same act would be liable, and such cases could be multiplied. The official's act might inflict just as great an injury and might be just as wrong as that of the private person, but the official is not answerable. The exception clause of the Tort Claims Act protects the public treasury where the common law would protect the purse of the acting public official.

But many acts of government officials deal only with the housekeeping side of federal activities. The Government, as landowner, as manufacturer, as shipper, as warehouseman, as shipowner and operator, is carrying on activities indistinguishable from those performed by private persons. In this area, there is no good reason to stretch the legislative text to immunize the Government or its officers from responsibility for their acts, if done without appropriate care for the safety of others. Many official decisions even in this area may involve a nice balancing of various considerations, but this is the same kind of balancing which citizens do at their peril and we think it is not within the exception of the statute.

The Government's negligence here was not in policy decisions of a regulatory or governmental nature, but involved actions akin to those of a private manufacturer, contractor, or shipper. Reading the discretionary exception as we do, in a way both workable and faithful to legislative intent, we would hold that the Government was liable under these circumstances. Surely a statute so long debated was meant to embrace more than traffic accidents. If not, the ancient and discredited doctrine that "The King can do no wrong" has not been uprooted; it has merely been amended to read, "The King can do only little wrongs."

[The *Dalehite* decision was eventually "appealed" to Congress, where relief was granted by means of private legislation.[11] When the last claim had been processed in 1957, 1,394 awards, totaling nearly $17,000,000, had been made.[12]]

Effects of the Dalehite *Case*

Some of the rules laid down in the *Dalehite* case were modified during the next several years. In *Indian Towing Co.* v. *United States*, 360 U.S. 61 (1955), the company sued the government for damages to one of its tugboats, which ran aground because of the alleged negligence of the Coast Guard in allowing the light in a lighthouse to become extinguished. The government argued in defense that a close analogy to the extinguishing of a lighthouse would be the faulty operation of a traffic light and that since, under the municipal law of Louisiana (in whose waters the accident happened), the operation of traffic lights was a "governmental" function, for which there could be no liability, the same should apply to the present case. But the Supreme Court refused to be pushed into the "'governmental-non-governmental' quagmire," referring to this distinction as "inherently unsound."

---

[11] Public Law 378, 69 Stat. 707 (1955).

[12] Milton Mackay, "Death on the Waterfront," *Saturday Evening Post* 100 (October 27, 1957). The irony of this result is that the FTCA was adopted, in part, to obviate the need for private legislation. The act was adopted as Title IV of the broader Congressional Reorganization Act of 1946, "an Act to provide increased efficiency in the legislative branch of government" [Public Law 601, 60 Stat. 812 (1946)].

The Court also rejected the contentions of the *Feres* and *Dalehite* cases that there can be no liability for negligence in the performance of activities that private persons do not perform. The majority opinion stated:

> [I]f the United States were to permit the operation of a private lighthouse—not at all inconceivable—the Government's basis of differentiation would be gone and the negligence charged in this case would be actionable. . . . [A]ll Government activity is inescapably "uniquely governmental" in that it is performed by the Government. . . . On the other hand, it is hard to think of any governmental activity on the "operational level," . . . which is "uniquely governmental," in the sense that its kind has not at one time or another been, or could not conceivably be, privately performed.[13]

The decision in *Indian Towing Co.* did not clear up the meaning of the exception for discretionary functions, but it came to some different conclusions concerning discretion. It was held that once the Coast Guard "exercised its discretion" to maintain the lighthouse light "and engendered reliance on the guidance afforded by the light, it was obligated to use due care to make certain that the light was kept in working order."[14]

A similar conclusion was reached in the lower court case of *United States* v. *Union Trust Co.*, 221 F.2d 62 (D.C. Cir. 1954), cert. denied 350 U.S. 907 (1955). This case was brought against the government as a result of a collision of two airplanes caused when a government control tower operator directed the two planes to land on the same airstrip at the same time. The government contended that the tower operators' duties involved discretion and that, therefore, the government should be exempted from liability. The court held, however, that "discretion was exercised when it was decided to operate the tower, but the tower personnel had no discretion to operate it negligently." And in 1963 the Supreme Court partially denied another aspect of *Dalehite* and *Feres* by holding that prisoners in federal prisons can recover from the government for injuries sustained while in prison, even though private parties at that time did not run prisons and no analogous liability had existed before the adoption of the FTCA [*United States* v. *Muniz*, 374 U.S. 150 (1963)].

Note the use of the term "operational level" in the *Indian Towing* excerpt above. This is a direct reference to one of *Dalehite*'s most important contributions to interpreting the discretionary function exception. To the objection by the appellees that the chain of events leading to the disaster may have been "born in discretion," but that the allegedly tortious acts themselves (the packaging, handling, and loading of the fertilizer; the fighting of the fire; and so on) were not discretionary, the Court stated that the decisions upon which these actions were based "were all responsibly made at a planning rather than operational level." This distinction, whether or not it was applied correctly in *Dalehite* (and some commentators argue that

---

[13] 360 U.S. at 66, 67, 68.

[14] It is important to note that the Supreme Court did not hold the government liable to pay damages to the Indian Towing Company. It merely stated that the immunity defenses the government sought to assert would not be allowed. When the case was finally tried on the merits, the plaintiffs did not succeed in persuading the lower court that the government was negligent. See *Indian Towing Company* v. *United States*, 276 F.2d 300 (5th Cir. 1960).

it was not), served as a key to interpreting the discretionary function exception in large numbers of cases over the next thirty years. In effect, if a court found that a government activity was on the planning level, it was protected by the discretionary function exception; if the activity was deemed operational, it was not. But in the 1980s this understanding began to break down.

Two cases were largely responsible for this breakdown. The first was *United States* v. *Varig Airlines*, 467 U.S. 797 (1984). This case consolidated two separate actions involving aircraft crashes that led to suits against the United States under the FTCA. Federal aviation authorities are responsible for certifying aircraft design and manufacture as well as for policing compliance with minimum safety standards by air carriers. Plaintiffs alleged in one case that the government had conducted a negligent inspection of the aircraft and in the other that the government had approved the faulty installation of a gas heater in a plane. The government offered several defenses in these cases, including the discretionary function exception. Although the district courts had come to opposite conclusions (one ruling for the government's position, the other rejecting it), the Court of Appeals for the Ninth Circuit, in deciding both cases on the same day, ruled against the government. Although the court of appeals did not mention the planning-operational distinction, it made clear that this formulation was at the heart of its reasoning. As it stated in one of the cases: "The duties undertaken by the [Federal Aviation Administration, or FAA] inspectors are more like those of the lighthouse keepers in *Indian Towing* than those of the cabinet level secretaries in *Dalehite*. The United States is not protected from liability under the discretionary function exception to the Federal Tort Claims Act in this case."[15]

With the two cases combined, the Supreme Court unanimously reversed. Several considerations were important to the Court in reaching this conclusion. First, it said, "it is the nature of the conduct, rather than the status of the actor, that governs whether the discretionary function exception applies in a given case. . . . Thus, the basic inquiry concerning the application of the discretionary function exception is whether the challenged acts of a Government employee—whatever his or her rank—are of the nature and quality that Congress intended to shield from tort liability" (467 U.S. 813). Second, the Court agreed with the government that main responsibility for satisfying air safety standards rested with the manufacturer and operator of the aircraft rather than with the government. The job of the government was limited to spot-checking aircraft. The Court even italicized a quotation from the Civil Aviation Authority manual of procedure to emphasize this point:

> It is obvious that complete detailed checking of data is not possible. Instead, an overriding check method should be used . . . with sufficient spot-checking to ascertain that the design complies with the minimum air-worthiness requirements [467 U.S. 818].

Finally and most importantly, the Court ruled that spot-checking activity qualified as a discretionary function under the FTCA:

---

[15] *Varig Airlines* v. *United States*, 692 F.2d 1205 (1982). The other case, decided the same day, was *United Scottish Insurance* v. *United States*, 692 F.2d 1209 (1982).

In administering the "spot-check" program, these FAA engineers and inspectors necessarily took certain calculated risks, but those risks were encountered for the advancement of a governmental purpose and pursuant to the specific grant of authority in the regulations and operating manuals. Under such circumstances, the FAA's alleged negligence in failing to check certain specific items in the course of certificating a particular aircraft falls squarely within the discretionary function exception . . . [467 U.S. 820].

Thus, without talking about the planning-operational distinction or using the term *operational*, the Supreme Court included operational-level discretion within the exception. Given the Supreme Court's somewhat indirect language, it is not surprising that some lower courts did not understand the Supreme Court's new direction immediately. This is demonstrated by the second key case in the Court's reinterpretation of the discretionary function doctrine, *United States* v. *Gaubert,* 499 U.S. 315 (1991).

Thomas Gaubert was chairman of the board and the largest stockholder in the Independent American Savings Association (IASA), a savings and loan company. The Federal Home Loan Bank Board (FHLBB), a federal agency, was authorized by statute to regulate such organizations. Upon examining the operation of IASA, FHLBB exerted pressure on Gaubert to remove himself from IASA's management. Thereafter, the Dallas branch of FHLBB took over much of the day-to-day operation of the company. When IASA was later declared insolvent, Gaubert sued the government for negligence, seeking compensation for the lost value of his shares in the company and for the value of a security that he had posted at the request of FHLBB.

The district court ruled that the discretionary function exception of the FTCA protected the government from suit and dismissed the case. The court of appeals reversed in part, holding that only a portion of the government's action was so protected: "Only policy oriented decisions enjoy . . . immunity. Thus, the FHLBB and FHLB-Dallas officials were only protected by the discretionary function exception until their actions became operational in nature. . . ." The appeals court concluded that the district court "should not have dismissed" the parts of the complaint alleging "negligent operational activities, liability for which is not barred by the discretionary function exception to the FTCA" [885 F.2d 1284, 1289–1290 (5th Cir.1989)]. The Supreme Court unanimously reversed. The essence of the Court's rationale for its decision is found in the following statement:

> In light of our cases and their interpretation of § 2680(a) [the discretionary function exception], it is clear that the Court of Appeals erred in holding that the exception does not reach decisions at the operational or management level of the bank involved in this case. A discretionary act is one that involves choice or judgment; there is nothing in that description that refers exclusively to policy-making or planning functions. Day-to-day management of banking affairs, like the management of other businesses, regularly requires judgment as to which of a range of permissible courses is the wisest. Discretionary conduct is not confined to the policy or planning level (499 U.S. 325).

The Supreme Court went on to note that the planning-operational distinction was first mentioned in the *Dalehite* case. It stated that in *Dalehite* this distinction "was merely description of the level at which the challenged conduct occurred. There was no suggestion that decisions made at an operational level could not also be based on policy" (499 U.S. 326). But to assert this is to deny three decades of interpretation of the discretionary exception based on *Dalehite* and its progeny, including *Indian Towing.* This is no doubt what Richard Pierce meant when he said that the Supreme Court in *Gaubert* "interpreted (or, more accurately, reinterpreted) *Dalehite* and *Indian Towing* as not establishing such a distinction and held that there is no distinction between planning and operational level decisions for purposes of applying the discretionary function exception."[16]

Although the judgment of the Supreme Court in *Gaubert* was unanimous as to the disposition of the case, Justice Scalia wrote a concurring opinion in which he appeared to question the complete abandonment of the old interpretation.

> [T]here is something to the planning vs. operational dichotomy. . . . [T]he level at which the decision is made is often *relevant* to the discretionary function inquiry, since the answer to that inquiry turns on *both* the subject matter *and* the office of the decisionmaker. In my view a choice is shielded from liability by the discretionary function exception if the choice is, under the particular circumstances, one that ought to be informed by considerations of social, economic, or political policy and is made by an officer whose official responsibilities include assessment of those considerations [499 U.S. 335; emphasis in the original].

In fact, a body of opinion holds that the recent interpretations of the Supreme Court have brought about at least a partial return to sovereign immunity.[17] Some critics believe that the level of protection now afforded by the discretionary function exception has "swallowed" the FTCA as a whole and rendered it of little practical meaning.[18] But it is unlikely that the Supreme Court, having chosen the course that led it to the *Gaubert* decision,

---

[16] Richard J. Pierce, Jr., 3 *Administrative Law Treatise* 1444 (4th ed., 2002).

[17] See, e.g., Bruce A. Peterson and Mark E. Van Der Weide, "Susceptibility to Faulty Analysis: United States v. *Gaubert* and the Resurrection of Federal Sovereign Immunity," 72 *Notre Dame Law Review* 447 (1997).

[18] A sampling of scholarly commentary after *Gaubert* includes the following: "This broad language [in *Gaubert*] may allow the exception to swallow the rule that allows tort actions against the United States Government" [Barry R. Goldman, "Can the King Do No Wrong? A New Look at the Discretionary Function Exception to the Federal Tort Claims Act," 26 *Georgia Law Review* 837, 860 (1992)]; "[*Gaubert*] has greatly restricted the federal government's tort liability for all but the most mundane transgressions. Since *Gaubert*, the government has been winning far more discretionary function exception cases, and it has been winning them more often without going to trial" (Peterson and Van Der Weide, "Susceptibility to Faulty Analysis" 448); *Gaubert* "extended the exception beyond its underlying purpose" ["Government Tort Liability," 111 *Harvard Law Review* 2009, 2023 (1998)]; "In sum, the core language of the FTCA—that the federal government shall be liable in tort like a private actor—has been severely undermined in its application. The FTCA has merely carved out a thin slice of liability, allowing citizens to collect only on claims that meet a limited standard set of criteria. There is wide scholarly agreement on the failings of the FTCA caused by the discretionary function exception" [James R. Levine, "The Federal Tort Claims Act: A Proposal for Institutional Reform," 100 *Columbia Law Review* 1538, 1547 (2000)].

Among comments by lower court judges on the new interpretation of the discretionary function exception: Judge McKay, concurring in *Allen* v. *United States*, 816 F.2d 1417, 1424–1425 (10th Cir. 1987): The FTCA has become a "false promise." "[T]he rule that 'the king can do no wrong' still prevails at the federal level in all but the most trivial of matters." Judge Merritt, dissenting in *Rosebush* v. *United States*, 119 F.3d 438, 444 (6th Cir. 1997): The discretionary function exception has "swallowed, digested, and excreted the liability-creating sections of the Federal Tort Claims Act."

will modify its interpretation anytime soon. This leaves Congress to fix the problem. However, given that Congress has not paid much attention to the FTCA since its adoption in 1946 (an important 1974 amendment was discussed earlier, and 1988 amendments will be examined below), one should not be optimistic about early congressional action either. Congress does, however, from time to time pass private bills to aid victims of governmental activity in noteworthy cases where the courts have denied relief. As indicated earlier, it was the press of such special legislation that led Congress to adopt the FTCA in the first place.

STATE TORT LIABILITY

States have a dual protection against tort suits: the common-law doctrine of sovereign immunity and the Eleventh Amendment to the U.S. Constitution. That amendment will be discussed in further detail below. As on the federal level, the extent to which a state can be liable for the torts of its agents depends on the extent of its waiver of immunity. States have waived their immunity to varying degrees, a number of them having created amenability to suit approximately equivalent to that on the federal level.[19] But a number of states continue to maintain a high level of immunity.[20]

State sovereign immunity cases are handled largely by the state courts, but recently the United States Supreme Court has become significantly involved in the issue. The Eleventh Amendment to the U.S. Constitution, which was adopted in 1798, has been interpreted to mean that a state cannot be sued by an individual in the *federal* courts without its consent.[21] What is different about recent cases, including a handful of five-to-four decisions, is that the Court is now saying that legislation adopted by the United States Congress protecting citizens against actions by states must yield to a state's claim of sovereign immunity.[22] To be sure, these cases have not involved damage suits against the states and are in this sense outside the scope of

---

[19] A standard textbook on torts from the 1980s asserts that "about 30 states, the largest single group, have abrogated the immunity in a substantial or general way," and that in these states "liability . . . is approximately as broad as, or broader than, the liability of the Federal Tort Claims Act." The rest of the states are said to maintain a higher level of immunity [*Prosser and Keeton on the Law of Torts* (W. Page Keeton, general ed.) 1045 (1984)].

[20] See the opinion of Justice Stevens, dissenting in *Florida Prepaid* v. *College Savings Bank*, 527 U.S. 627 (1999). At 527 U.S. 659, Stevens describes, for illustrative purposes, the high level of immunity still existing in five U.S. states, including West Virginia, whose constitution, article VI, section 35, provides: "The State of West Virginia shall never be made a defendant in any court of law or equity. . . ."

[21] The Eleventh Amendment provides: "The Judicial power of the United States shall not be construed to extend to any suit in law or equity, commenced or prosecuted against one of the United States by Citizens of another State, or by Citizens or Subjects of any Foreign State." The amendment has been interpreted to bar suits by in-state plaintiffs as well. See the discussion in Henry Paul Monaghan, "The Sovereign Immunity 'Exception,'" 110 *Harvard Law Review* 102, 104–107 (1996).

[22] Among these cases, selected from several years of recent court decisions, are the following: *Seminole Tribe of Florida* v. *Florida* 527 U.S. 44 (1996); *Alden* v. *Maine* 527 U.S. 706 (1999); *Kimel* v. *Florida Board of Regents*, 528 U.S. 62 (2000); *Board of Trustees of the University of Alabama* v. *Garrett*, 531 U.S. 350 (2001).

the present discussion. But they indicate an inclination on the part of the Supreme Court to raise the level of immunity protection of government. And in this sense they are consistent with tort law decisions discussed in the previous section.

THE LIABILITY OF INDIVIDUAL OFFICERS

Although the government has traditionally been protected by sovereign immunity, this doctrine did not extend the cloak of protection to individual governmental servants. As the great English jurist A. V. Dicey said, in an oft-quoted statement, "every official, from the Prime Minister down to a constable or a collector of taxes, is under the same responsibility for every act done without justification as any other citizen."[23] And indeed, some early American cases ruled that public officials could be held liable for improper acts, even if undertaken reasonably and in good faith.[24] But the modern law on the subject is much different. Generally speaking, it is fair to say that if a public official is performing a function requiring judgment or discretion, if that function is within the sphere of his or her duties, and if it is performed in good faith and in a reasonable manner, the official will not be held liable by a court for injuries or property damage that might ensue.[25]

There are varying levels of official protection, depending on the functions being performed. Judges performing judicial functions are usually said to have "absolute immunity," meaning that they are protected from liability even if acting maliciously or in bad faith. The same level of immunity was long considered applicable to legislators, but this has been modified to some extent since the 1970s. Other public officials were not put in the same category as those performing judicial or legislative functions, and their level of immunity has varied with the circumstances. What is termed *qualified immunity* has traditionally protected public servants from liability unless it can be shown that the official in question acted maliciously or in bad faith.[26] Some examination of concrete cases may be helpful, but first the legal basis for suits against governmental officials should be discussed.

Basically, a person may sue a governmental official on the basis of common-law principles, civil rights legislation, and the Constitution. Common-law tort liability will be discussed in some of the cases presented below and needs no further examination here. The Civil Rights Act of 1871, 42 U.S.C. § 1983, provides in part: "Every person who, under color of any statute, ordinance, regulation, custom, or usage, of any State or Territory, sub-

---

[23] A. V. Dicey, *Introduction to the Study of the Law of the Constitution* 189 (8th ed., 1915).

[24] A frequently cited case is *Miller* v. *Horton*, 152 Mass. 540, 26 N.E. 100 (1891). This much-criticized case was overruled in 1973 in *Gildea* v. *Ellershaw*, 363 Mass. 800, 298 N.E. 847.

[25] See generally Bernard Schwartz, *Administrative Law* 598–602 (3rd ed., 1991).

[26] The standard of "bad faith" is discussed by Jerry L. Mashaw in "Civil Liability of Government Officers: Property Rights and Official Accountability," 42 *Law and Contemporary Problems* 8, esp. at 20 (1976). But see below, p. 252. In *Harlow* v. *Fitzgerald*, 457 U.S. 800 (1982), the Supreme Court attempted to refine the meaning of qualified immunity.

jects or causes to be subjected, any citizen of the United States or other person within the jurisdiction thereof to the deprivation of any rights, privileges or immunities secured by the Constitution and laws, shall be liable to the party injured in an action at law, suit in equity, or other proper proceeding for redress." So-called Section 1983 suits are brought in federal courts against officials who operate under state law. The constitutional basis for suing officials in tort was articulated in *Bivins* v. *Six Unknown Named Agents of the Fed. Bureau of Narcotics*, 403 U.S. 388 (1971). In this case the Supreme Court ruled that the Fourth Amendment could provide the basis for a damage suit when federal agents made a warrantless, early morning raid at the plaintiff's apartment and ransacked the premises in a fruitless and illegal attempt to find evidence.[27]

Liability of Judges

Under common law, it has long been clear that judges are absolutely immune from tort suits.[28] Suits against judges based on § 1983 of the Civil Rights Act date from more recent times, but the Supreme Court ruled in favor of absolute immunity in this kind of suit in 1967 (*Pierson* v. *Ray*, 386 U.S. 547). The following case is an affirmation of that principle, but the contrasting views of the majority and the dissenters are interesting to consider.

Stump v. Sparkman

SUPREME COURT OF THE UNITED STATES, 1978.
435 U.S. 349, 98 S.Ct. 1099, 55 L.Ed.2d 331.

[Ora Spitler McFarlin, the mother of the respondent, Linda Kay Spitler Sparkman, petitioned the Circuit Court of De-Kalb County, Indiana, to have her "somewhat retarded" fifteen-year-old daughter sterilized. The petition was approved by Judge Stump on the same day. The operation was performed, the daughter having been told that she was to have her appendix removed. Two years later the daughter married Leo Sparkman and, when she discovered that she had been sterilized, the Sparkmans sued the judge and others under § 1983 seeking damages for the alleged violation of her constitutional rights. The district court ruled that Judge

Stump was absolutely immune from liability, but the court of appeals reversed, holding that the judge had not "acted within his jurisdiction" and had forfeited his immunity for "failure to comply with elementary principles of procedural due process."]

Mr. Justice WHITE delivered the opinion of the Court. . . .

The governing principle of law is well established and is not questioned by the parties. As early as 1872, the Court recognized that it was "a general principle of the highest importance to the proper administration of justice that a judicial officer, in exercising the authority vested in

---

[27] The Supreme Court remanded the case to the court of appeals for consideration of the question of official immunity. That court ruled that the officers were entitled to qualified rather than absolute immunity [456 F.2d 1339 (2nd Cir., 1972)].

[28] See the discussion and cases cited by Mashaw, above, note 26, 15.

him, [should] be free to act upon his own convictions, without apprehension of personal consequences to himself." *Bradley* v. *Fisher* [13 Wall. 335], at 347. For that reason the Court held that "judges of courts of superior or general jurisdiction are not liable to civil actions for their judicial acts, even when such acts are in excess of their jurisdiction, and are alleged to have been done maliciously or corruptly." 13 Wall., at 351.

Later we held that this doctrine of judicial immunity was applicable in suits under § 1 of the Civil Rights Act of 1871, 42 U.S.C. § 1983, for the legislative record gave no indication that Congress intended to abolish this long-established principle. . . . The Court of Appeals correctly recognized that the necessary inquiry in determining whether a defendant judge is immune from suit is whether at the time he took the challenged action he had jurisdiction over the subject matter before him. . . .

We cannot agree that there was a "clear absence of all jurisdiction" in the DeKalb County Circuit Court to consider the petition presented by Mrs. McFarlin [Sparkman's mother]. As an Indiana Circuit Court Judge, Judge Stump had "original exclusive jurisdiction in all cases at law and in equity whatsoever . . . ;" jurisdiction over the settlement of estates and over guardianships, appellate jurisdiction as conferred by law, and jurisdiction over "all other causes, matters and proceedings where exclusive jurisdiction thereof is not conferred by law upon some other court, board or officer." Ind. Code § 33-4-4-3 (1975). This is indeed a broad jurisdictional grant; yet the Court of Appeals concluded that Judge Stump did not have jurisdiction over the petition authorizing Linda Sparkman's sterilization.

In so doing, the Court of Appeals noted that the Indiana statutes provided for the sterilization of institutionalized persons under certain circumstances . . . but otherwise contained no express authority for judicial approval of tubal ligations. It is true that the statutory grant of general jurisdiction to the Indiana circuit courts does not itemize types of cases those courts may hear and hence does not expressly mention sterilization petitions presented by the parents of a minor. But in our view, it is more significant that there was no Indiana statute and no case law in 1971 prohibiting a circuit court, a court of general jurisdiction, from considering a petition of the type presented to Judge Stump. The statutory authority for the sterilization of institutionalized persons in the custody of the State does not warrant the inference that a court of general jurisdiction has no power to act on a petition for sterilization of a minor in the custody of her parents, particularly where the parents have authority under the Indiana statutes to "consent to and contract for medical or hospital care or treatment of [the minor] including surgery." Ind. Code § 16-8-4-2 (1973). The District Court concluded that Judge Stump had jurisdiction under § 33-4-4-3 to entertain and act upon Mrs. McFarlin's petition. We agree with the District Court, it appearing that neither by statute nor by case law has the broad jurisdiction granted to the circuit courts of Indiana been circumscribed to foreclose consideration of a petition for authorization of a minor's sterilization. . . .

Perhaps realizing the broad scope of Judge Stump's jurisdiction, the Court of Appeals stated that, even if the action taken by him was not foreclosed under the Indiana statutory scheme, it would still be "an illegitimate exercise of his common law power because of his failure to comply with elementary principles of procedural due process." 552 F. 2d, at 176. This misconceives the doctrine of judicial immunity. A judge is absolutely immune from liability for his judicial acts even if his exercise of authority is flawed by the commission of grave procedural errors. . . .

We conclude that the Court of Appeals, employing an unduly restrictive view of the scope of Judge Stump's jurisdiction, erred in holding that he was not entitled to judicial immunity. Because the court over which Judge Stump presides is one of general jurisdiction, neither the procedural errors he may have committed nor the lack of a specific statute authorizing his approval of the petition in question rendered him liable in damages for the consequences of his actions.

The respondents argue that even if Judge Stump had jurisdiction to consider the petition presented to him by Mrs. McFarlin, he is still not entitled to judicial immunity because his approval of the petition did not constitute a "judicial" act. It is only for acts performed in his "judicial" capacity that a judge is absolutely immune, they say. We do not disagree with this statement of the law, but we cannot characterize the approval of the petition as a nonjudicial act. . . .

The relevant cases demonstrate that the factors determining whether an act by a judge is a "judicial" one relate to the nature of the act itself, i.e., whether it is a function normally performed by a judge, and to the expectations of the parties, i.e., whether they dealt with the judge in his judicial capacity. Here, both factors indicate that Judge Stump's approval of the sterilization petition was a judicial act. State judges with general jurisdiction not infrequently are called upon in their official capacity to approve petitions relating to the affairs of minors, as for example, a petition to settle a minor's claim. Furthermore, as even respondents have admitted, at the time he approved the petition presented to him by Mrs. McFarlin, Judge Stump was "acting as a county circuit court judge." We may infer from the record that it was only because Judge Stump served in that position that Mrs. McFarlin, on the advice of counsel, submitted the petition to him for his approval. Because Judge Stump performed the type of act normally performed only by judges and because he did so in his capacity as a Circuit Court Judge, we find no merit to respondents' argument that the informality with which he proceeded rendered his action nonjudicial and deprived him of his absolute immunity.

Both the Court of Appeals and the respondents seem to suggest that, because of the tragic consequences of Judge Stump's actions, he should not be immune. . . . Disagreement with the action taken by the judge, however, does not justify depriving that judge of his immunity. Despite the unfairness to litigants that sometimes results, the doctrine of judicial immunity is thought to be in the best interests of "the proper administration of justice . . . [, for it allows] a judicial officer, in exercising the authority vested in him [, to] be free to act upon his own convictions, without apprehension of personal consequences to himself." *Bradley* v. *Fisher*, 13 Wall., at 347. The fact that the issue before the judge is a controversial one is all the more reason that he should be able to act without fear of suit. . . .

The Indiana law vested in Judge Stump the power to entertain and act upon the petition for sterilization. He is, therefore, under the controlling cases, immune from damages liability even if his approval of the petition was in error. Accordingly, the judgment of the Court of Appeals is reversed, and the case is remanded for further proceedings consistent with this opinion.

It is so ordered.

Mr. Justice BRENNAN took no part in the consideration or decision of this case.

Mr. Justice STEWART, with whom Mr. Justice MARSHALL and Mr. Justice POWELL join, dissenting.

It is established federal law that judges of general jurisdiction are absolutely immune from monetary liability "for their judicial acts, even when such acts are in excess of their jurisdiction, and are alleged to have been done maliciously or corruptly." *Bradley* v. *Fisher*, 13 Wall.

335, 351. It is also established that this immunity is in no way diminished in a proceeding under 42 U.S.C. § 1983. . . . But the scope of judicial immunity is limited to liability for "judicial acts" and I think that what Judge Stump did on July 9, 1971, was beyond the pale of anything that could sensibly be called a judicial act.

Neither in *Bradley* v. *Fisher* [1872] nor in *Pierson* v. *Ray* [1967] was there any claim that the conduct in question was not a judicial act, and the Court thus had no occasion in either case to discuss the meaning of that term. Yet the proposition that judicial immunity extends only to liability for "judicial acts" was emphasized no less than seven times in Mr. Justice Field's opinion for the Court in the Bradley case. And if the limitations inherent in that concept have any realistic meaning at all, then I cannot believe that the action of Judge Stump in approving Mrs. McFarlin's petition is protected by judicial immunity.

The Court finds two reasons for holding that Judge Stump's approval of the sterilization petition was a judicial act. First, the Court says, it was "a function normally performed by a judge." Second, the Court says, the act was performed in Judge Stump's "judicial capacity." With all respect, I think that the first of these grounds is factually untrue and that the second is legally unsound. When the Court says that what Judge Stump did was an act "normally performed by a judge," it is not clear to me whether the Court means that a judge "normally" is asked to approve a mother's decision to have her child given surgical treatment generally, or that a judge "normally" is asked to approve a mother's wish to have her daughter sterilized. But whichever way the Court's statement is to be taken, it is factually inaccurate. In Indiana, as elsewhere in our country, a parent is authorized to arrange for and consent to medical and surgical treatment of his minor child. . . . And when a parent decides to call a physician to care for his sick child or arranges to have a surgeon remove his child's tonsils, he does not, "normally" or otherwise, need to seek the approval of a judge. On the other hand, Indiana did in 1971 have statutory procedures for the sterilization of certain people who were institutionalized. But these statutes provided for administrative proceedings before a board established by the superintendent of each public hospital. Only if, after notice and an evidentiary hearing, an order of sterilization was entered in these proceedings could there be review in a circuit court. . . .

In sum, what Judge Stump did on July 9, 1971, was in no way an act "normally performed by a judge." Indeed, there is no reason to believe that such an act has ever been performed by any other Indiana judge, either before or since.

When the Court says that Judge Stump was acting in "his judicial capacity" in approving Mrs. McFarlin's petition, it is not clear to me whether the Court means that Mrs. McFarlin submitted the petition to him only because he was a judge, or that, in approving it, he said that he was acting as a judge. But however the Court's test is to be understood, it is, I think, demonstrably unsound.

It can safely be assumed that the Court is correct in concluding that Mrs. McFarlin came to Judge Stump with her petition because he was a County Circuit Court Judge. But false illusions as to a judge's power can hardly convert a judge's response to those illusions into a judicial act. In short, a judge's approval of a mother's petition to lock her daughter in the attic would hardly be a judicial act simply because the mother had submitted her petition to the judge in his official capacity.

If, on the other hand, the Court's test depends upon the fact that Judge Stump *said* he was acting in his judicial capacity, it is equally invalid. It is true that Judge Stump affixed his signature to the approval of the petition as "Judge, DeKalb Circuit Court." But the conduct of a judge surely does not become a judicial act merely on his own say-so. A judge is not free, like a loose cannon, to inflict indiscriminate damage whenever he announces that he is acting in his judicial capacity.

If the standard adopted by the Court is invalid, then what is the proper measure of a judicial act? Contrary to implications in the Court's opinion, my conclusion that what Judge Stump did was not a judicial act is not based upon the fact that he acted with informality, or that he may not have been "in his judge's robes," or "in the courtroom itself." And I do not reach this conclusion simply "because the petition was not given a docket number, was not placed on file with the clerk's office, and was approved in an ex parte proceeding without notice to the minor, without a hearing, and without the appointment of a guardian ad litem." . . .

The petitioners' brief speaks of "an aura of deism which surrounds the bench . . . essential to the maintenance of respect for the judicial institution." Though the rhetoric may be overblown, I do not quarrel with it. But if aura there be, it is hardly protected by exonerating from liability such lawless conduct as took place here. And if intimidation would serve to deter its recurrence, that would surely be in the public interest.

MR. Justice POWELL, dissenting.

While I join the opinion of MR. Justice STEWART, I wish to emphasize what I take to be the central feature of this case—Judge Stump's preclusion of any possibility for the vindication of respondents' rights elsewhere in the judicial system.

Bradley v. *Fisher*, 13 Wall. 335 (1872), which established the absolute judicial immunity at issue in this case, recognized that the immunity was designed to further the public interest in an independent judiciary, sometimes at the expense of legitimate individual grievances. . . . Underlying the *Bradley* immunity . . . is the notion that private rights can be sacrificed in some degree to the achievement of the greater public good deriving from a completely independent judiciary, because there exist alternative forums and methods for vindicating those rights.

But where a judicial officer acts in a manner that precludes all resort to appellate or other judicial remedies that otherwise would be available, the underlying assumption of the Bradley doctrine is inoperative. . . . The complete absence of normal judicial process foreclosed resort to any of the "numerous remedies" that "the law has provided for private parties." *Bradley*, supra, at 354.

In sum, I agree with MR. JUSTICE STEWART that petitioner judge's actions were not "judicial," and that he is entitled to no judicial immunity from suit under 42 U.S.C. § 1983.

Some limited restrictions on the absolute immunity of judges have begun to emerge more recently, as *Pulliam* v. *Allen* and *Forrester* v. *White* illustrate. Gladys Pulliam, a state magistrate in Virginia, imposed bail on Richmond R. Allen and Jesse W. Nicholson for nonjailable offenses and then jailed them when they couldn't post bail. They brought a § 1983 action against her, and the district court both enjoined the practice of committing persons to jail in such circumstances and awarded the respondents more than $7,000 in costs and attorney's fees (the money award was made under § 1988, a related part of the statute). Over the vigorous dissent of four justices, the Supreme Court majority ruled that absolute judicial immunity prohibited neither the injunction nor the awarding of attorney's fees [*Pulliam* v. *Allen*, 466 U.S. 522 (1984)].

Howard Lee White, a circuit judge in Illinois, had the authority to hire and dismiss probation officers. He employed Cynthia A. Forrester in this capacity in 1977 and later promoted her to a supervisory position. In 1980 he demoted and then dismissed her. Forrester, alleging that she was discriminated against on the basis of her sex, brought suit against White under Title VII of the Civil Rights Act of 1964 and § 1983. A jury found that White had discriminated against Forrester and awarded her more than $81,000 in compensatory damages. But the U.S. district court accepted White's motion for summary judgment on the basis of his "judicial immunity" from a civil damage suit, and the court of appeals affirmed. A unanimous Supreme Court reversed on the matter of Judge White's absolute immunity. The key to the Court's decision was its characterization of the function White was performing in connection with hiring and dismissing Forrester:

> Here, as in other contexts, immunity is justified and defined by the *functions* it protects and serves, not by the person to whom it attaches. This Court has never undertaken to articulate a precise and general definition of the class of acts entitled to immunity. The decided cases, however, suggest an intelligible distinction between judicial acts and administrative, legislative, or executive functions that judges may on occasion be assigned to perform. . . . In the case before us, we think it clear that Judge White was acting in an administrative capacity when he demoted and discharged Forrester. Those acts—like many others involved in supervising court employees and overseeing the efficient operation of a court—may have been quite important in providing the necessary conditions of a sound adjudicative system. The decisions at issue, however, were not judicial or adjudicative. . . . Such decisions, like personnel decisions made by judges, are often crucial to the efficient operation of public institutions . . . yet no one suggests that they give rise to absolute immunity from liability in damages under 1983. . . . We conclude that Judge White was not entitled to absolute immunity for his decision to demote and discharge Forrester [emphasis in the original; *Forrester* v. *White*, 484 U.S. 219 (1988)].

Prosecutors, like judges, have been accorded absolute immunity under common law, and in *Imbler* v. *Pachtman*, 424 U.S. 409 (1976), the Supreme Court unanimously ruled that absolute immunity for prosecutors applies to § 1983 suits as well. However, three of the eight justices participating felt that the immunity extended by the majority was broader than necessary and that, in general, prosecutors are not entitled to absolute immunity in suits based on claims of unconstitutional suppression of evidence, because such an act "is beyond the scope of duties constituting an integral part of the judicial process" (424 U.S. 443). In a 1997 case, the Supreme Court ruled that a prosecutor was entitled to only qualified immunity when testifying as a "complaining witness" in a probable cause proceeding. The Supreme Court cited *Forrester* in support of its conclusion that in this case the prosecutor was not performing "the traditional functions of an advocate" [*Kalina* v. *Fletcher*, 522 U.S. 118 (1997)].

Liability of Legislators

The speech and debate clause of the Constitution, as interpreted by the Supreme Court, provides members of Congress with broad protection from tort suits.[29] This principle has been expressed on numerous occasions by the Supreme Court, although it has also been indicated that such blanket protection does not extend to subordinate employees of legislators.[30] But when legislators "act outside of this 'sphere of legitimate legislative activity,' they enjoy no special immunity from local laws protecting the good name or the reputation of the ordinary citizens" [*Doe* v. *McMillan*, 412 U.S. 306 (1973)].

Thus, members of Congress are wholly immune for speeches made in Congress, which are published in the *Congressional Record*, and for committee reports and associated work. But newsletters and press releases by individual members are outside of this protection. This distinction was the basis for the Supreme Court's 1979 ruling that Senator William Proxmire was not immune from a defamation suit by a behavioral scientist based on a "Golden Fleece Award" aimed at allegedly egregious examples of wasteful government spending. The so-called award was announced by the senator in a news release in 1975 [*Hutchinson* v. *Proxmire*, 443 U.S. 111 (1979)].

In 1998 the Supreme Court examined the issue of legislators' immunity again, this time on the municipal level. The Court ruled in *Bogan* v. *Scott-Harris* that local legislators are absolutely immune under § 1983 for legislative functions. Here the city council adopted an ordinance that eliminated a one-person department. The ordinance had been proposed by the vice president of the city council and the city's mayor, and the latter signed it into law. A jury had ruled in the case that the two officials just mentioned were liable for violating Scott-Harris's First Amendment rights, concluding, as the Supreme Court put it, that her "constitutionally protected speech was a substantial or motivating factor in the elimination of her position." The Supreme Court unanimously brushed aside these considerations, ruling that "petitioners' activities were undoubtedly legislative" and thus entitled to absolute immunity [*Bogan* v. *Scott-Harris*, 523 U.S. 44 (1998)].

Liability of Other Officials

By a five-to-four vote, the Supreme Court ruled in 1982 that a former president "is entitled to absolute immunity from damage liability predicated on his official acts." The justification for absolute liability was "the special nature of the President's constitutional office and functions" (*Nixon* v. *Fitzgerald*, 457 U.S. 731, 749, 756). *Clinton* v. *Jones* was decided by the Supreme Court fifteen years later. It involved a civil suit against the president based on alleged conduct before he took office. The Supreme Court ruled unanimously that *Nixon* v. *Fitzgerald* "provides no support for an immunity for *unofficial* conduct" (emphasis in the original). The president's plea for a postponement of judicial proceedings until the end of his term of office was unanimously rejected [*Clinton* v. *Jones*, 520 U.S. 681, 694 (1997)].

---

[29] Article I, Section 6, Clause 1 provides: "They shall in all Cases, except Treason, Felony and Breach of the Peace, be privileged from Arrest during their Attendance at the Session of their respective Houses, and in going to and returning from the same; and for any Speech or Debate in either House, they shall not be questioned in any other Place."

[30] *Tenney* v. *Brandhove*, 342 U.S. 367 (1951); *Dombrowski* v. *Eastland*, 387 U.S. 82 (1967); *Doe* v. *McMillan*, 412 U.S. 306 (1973).

Bryce Harlow and Alexander Butterfield, former presidential aides, were codefendants in the 1982 civil damage suit against President Nixon referred to above. They also sought the protection of absolute immunity. But in a separate decision, the Supreme Court ruled by a vote of eight to one that they were entitled to only qualified immunity. Noting that for "executive officials in general . . . our cases make plain that qualified immunity represents the norm," the Court concluded that public policy did not require that presidential aides be afforded absolute immunity [*Harlow* v. *Fitzgerald*, 457 U.S. 800, 807 (1982)].

A notable further point made in *Harlow* involved the standard for determining whether qualified immunity applies. It was suggested above[31] that qualified immunity protects an official unless maliciousness or bad faith can be shown. In *Harlow* the Court asserted that "substantial costs attend the litigation of the subjective good faith of governmental officials," allowing some cases to go to trial that should be dismissed as falling within the protection of qualified immunity. The Court therefore ruled that henceforth "governmental officials performing discretionary functions generally are shielded from liability for civil damages insofar as their conduct does not violate clearly established constitutional rights of which a reasonable person would have known" (457 U.S. 818). But applying this "clearly established" standard in practice has proved difficult.[32]

What happens to qualified immunity when an activity traditionally performed by a governmental agency is turned over to a private organization? A sharply divided Supreme Court addressed this question in the 1997 case set forth below.

Richardson v. *McKnight*

SUPREME COURT OF THE UNITED STATES, 1997.
521 U.S. 399, 117 S.Ct. 2100, 138 L.Ed. 2d 540.

[The defendants in this case, Daryll Richardson and John Walker, were guards at a Tennessee correctional center whose management had been privatized. Ronnie Lee McKnight, a prisoner in the facility, sued the guards under § 1983, asserting that he had been injured by their actions. A motion by the guards to dismiss the suit on qualified immunity grounds was denied in federal district court. A court of appeals affirmed.]

Justice BREYER delivered the opinion of the Court.

The issue before us is whether prison guards who are employees of a private prison management firm are entitled to a qualified immunity from suit by prisoners charging a violation of 42 U.S.C. § 1983. We hold that they are not. . . .

History does not reveal a "firmly rooted" tradition of immunity applicable to privately employed prison guards. Correctional services in the United States have undergone various transformations. . . . *Government*-employed prison guards may have enjoyed a kind of immunity de-

---

[31] See note 48.

[32] See Pierce, 3 *Administrative Law Treatise*, above, note 16, 1416–1417; also Alfred C. Aman, Jr., and William T. Mayton, *Administrative Law* 561–564 (2nd ed., 2001).

fense arising out of their status as public employees at common law. . . . But correctional functions have never been exclusively public. . . . Private individuals operated local jails in the 18th century, . . . and private contractors were heavily involved in prison management during the 19th century. . . .

Our research, including the sources that the parties have cited, reveals that in the 19th century (and earlier) sometimes private contractors and sometimes government itself carried on prison management activities. And we have no found no conclusive evidence of an historical tradition of immunity for private parties carrying out these functions. History therefore does not provide significant support for the immunity claim. . . .

Earlier precedent described immunity as protecting the public from unwarranted timidity on the part of public officials by, for example, "encouraging the vigorous exercise of official authority," *Butz* v. *Economou*, 438 U.S. 478, 506, 57 L.Ed. 2d 895, 98 S.Ct. 2894 (1978), by contributing to "'principled and fearless decision-making,'" *Wood* v. *Strickland*, 420 U.S. 308, 319, 43 L.Ed. 2d 214, 95 S.Ct. 992 (1975), and by responding to the concern that threatened liability would, in Judge Hand's words, "'dampen the ardour of all but the most resolute, or the most irresponsible'" public officials. *Harlow* [v. *Fitzgerald*] 457 U.S. at 814 (quoting *Gregoire v. Biddle*, 177 F.2d 579, 581 (CA2 1949) (L. Hand, J.), cert. denied, 339 U.S. 949, 94 L. Ed. 1363, 70 S.Ct. 803 (1950). . . .

[But] marketplace pressures provide the private firm with strong incentives to avoid overly timid, insufficiently vigorous, unduly fearful, or "non-arduous" employee job performance. And the contract's provisions[33]—including those that might permit employee indemnification and avoid many civil-service restrictions—grant this private firm freedom to respond to those market pressures through rewards and penalties that operate directly upon its employees. To this extent, the employees before us resemble those of other private firms and differ from government employees.

This is not to say that government employees, in their efforts to act within constitutional limits, will always, or often, sacrifice the otherwise effective performance of their duties. Rather, it is to say that government employees typically act within a different system. They work within a system that is responsible through elected officials to voters who, when they vote, rarely consider the performance of individual subdepartments or civil servants specifically and in detail. And that system is often characterized by multidepartment civil service rules that, while providing employee security, may limit the incentives or the ability of individual departments or supervisors flexibly to reward, or to punish, individual employees. Hence a judicial determination that "effectiveness" concerns warrant *special* immunity-type protection in respect to this latter (governmental) system does not prove its need in respect to the former. Consequently, we can find no special immunity-related need to encourage vigorous performance. . . .

Our examination of history and purpose thus reveals nothing special enough about the job or about its organizational structure that would warrant providing these private prison guards with a governmental immunity. The job is one that private industry might, or might not, perform; and which history shows private firms did sometimes perform without relevant immunities. The organizational

---

[33] This is the contract between the state and the private firm managing the prison (Authors).

structure is one subject to the ordinary competitive pressures that normally help private firms adjust their behavior in response to the incentives that tort suits provide—pressures not necessarily present in government departments. Since there are no special reasons significantly favoring an extension of governmental immunity, and since [*Wyatt* v. *Cole*, 504 U.S. 158 (1992)] makes clear that private actors are not automatically immune (i. e., § 1983 immunity does not automatically follow § 1983 liability), we must conclude that private prison guards, unlike those who work directly for the government, do not enjoy immunity from suit in a § 1983 case. . . .

For these reasons the judgment of the Court of Appeals is *affirmed*.

Justice SCALIA, with whom The Chief Justice, Justice KENNEDY and Justice THOMAS join, dissenting.

In *Procunier* v. *Navarette*, 434 U.S. 555, 55 L.Ed. 2d 24, 98 S.Ct. 855 (1978), we held that state prison officials, including both supervisory and subordinate officers, are entitled to qualified immunity in a suit brought under 42 U.S.C. § 1983. Today the Court declares that this immunity is unavailable to employees of private prison management firms, who perform the same duties as state-employed correctional officials, who exercise the most palpable form of state police power, and who may be sued for acting "under color of state law." This holding is supported neither by common-law tradition nor public policy, and contradicts our settled practice of determining § 1983 immunity on the basis of the public function being performed. . . .

I respectfully dissent.

Bivins *Actions*

As mentioned above, the 1971 case of *Bivins* v. *Six Unknown Named Agents of the Federal Bureau of Narcotics*, 403 U.S. 388, serves as the basis for suing officials for so-called constitutional torts. Much litigation has been initiated under *Bivins*, but plaintiffs have seldom prevailed.[34] Subsequent Supreme Court decisions have narrowed the field of application of *Bivins*, but so far calls for the Court to overrule the decision[35] have gone unheeded.

The Supreme Court, in *Federal Deposit Insurance Corp.* v. *Myer*, 510 U.S. 127 (1994), refused to extend the reach of the *Bivins* decision to include federal agencies. And in 2001 it declined to apply *Bivins* to a private corporation operating a halfway house under contract with the Bureau of Prisons (*Correctional Service Corporation* v. *Malesko*, 534 U.S. 61). After more than three decades, what one critic has termed "the failure of *Bivins*"[36] has led to recommendations to transfer liability for constitutional torts from federal officials to the government.

---

[34] William P. Kratzke, "Some Recommendations Concerning Tort Liability of Government and Its Employees for Torts and Constitutional Torts," 9 *Administrative Law Journal of American University* 1105 (1996).

[35] See, e.g., Pierce, 3 *Administrative Law Treatise*, above, note 16, 260.

[36] The term is Kratzke's, above, note 34, 1149. Pierce, 3 *Administrative Law Treatise*, above, note 16, 1471, calls the *Bivins* opinion "a mistake."

THE INTEGRATION OF GOVERNMENT AND OFFICERS' LIABILITY

A notable development of recent decades has been the partial substitution of the government for the public official as the responsible party in tort actions. This trend has been effected in several ways.

Legislation Protecting Government Employees from Liability

Legislation making the government the sole defendant in tort suits that might be filed against individuals has been adopted on several occasions. A 1961 amendment to the FTCA provided that for personal injuries resulting from a government employee's operation of a motor vehicle, only the government and not the employee could be sued, upon certification by the attorney general that the employee was acting within the scope of his office.[37]

Other such legislation protects certain government contractors from liability. For example, a 1976 statute provided that the exclusive remedy for claimants seeking damages for liability arising from the swine flu immunization program being administered at that time would be a suit against the United States.[38] And a 1984 statute substituted the United States as a defendant in all suits against private contractors with the government arising out of injuries connected with the atomic weapons testing program.[39]

In 1988 legislation by Congress extended this principle more generally with the Federal Employees Liability Reform and Tort Compensation Act, Public Law 100–694, 102 Stat. 4563. This law, which amended the FTCA, made a suit against the United States the exclusive remedy "for injury or loss of property, or personal injury or death arising from the negligent or wrongful act or omission of any employee of the Government while acting within the scope of his employment."

This legislation is known as the Westfall Act, after *Westfall* v. *Erwin*, 484 U.S. 292 (1988), in which the Supreme Court refused to grant absolute immunity in a negligence suit to several federal employees performing nondiscretionary functions. At the end of its unanimous decision, the Supreme Court invited Congress to provide "standards governing the immunity of federal employees" in such circumstances (484 U.S. 300). Congress passed the above-mentioned legislation within the year, leaving only the liability of officials for constitutional torts outside the law's protection. As discussed above, several commentators have advocated legislation protecting governmental officials in this area as well.[40]

Liability under Section 1983

Monroe v. *Pape*, 365 U.S. 167 (1961), was an important case that, according to the *Harvard Law Review*, "resurrected Section 1983 from ninety years of

---

[37] Public Law 87–258, 75 Stat. 539 (1961) as amended by Public Law 89–506, 80 Stat. 306 (1966).

[38] Public Law 94–380, 90 Stat. 1115 (1976).

[39] Public Law 98–525, 98 Stat. 2646.

[40] See, e.g., Pierce, 3 *Administrative Law Treatise*, above, note 16, 1392, 1471–1472; Kratzke, above, note 34, 1152.

obscurity."[41] It allowed Chicago police officers to be held liable for illegal acts against individuals even if the acts were done without state authority. But the Supreme Court ruled that the City of Chicago was immune from liability under § 1983, reasoning that a municipality could not be considered a "person" whose acts, which deprived others of their civil rights, the statute was designed to remedy. In 1978 the Supreme Court overruled the latter aspect of *Monroe* v. *Pape*, holding that that case had been based on an erroneous interpretation of legislative history and that local governments, municipal corporations, and school boards were "persons" subject to liability under § 1983 [*Monell* v. *Department of Social Services of the City of New York*, 436 U.S. 658 (1978)]. Since then, many § 1983 suits that might otherwise have been brought against individual officials are now initiated against municipalities.

Paying Judgments against Officials from Public Funds

On some occasions governmental units (federal, state, and local) protect their officials from tort liability by assuming the obligations themselves, either through the payment of insurance premiums or by settling claims against officials from public funds. Examples of governmental units' assuming financial responsibility for potentially large damage awards occasionally come to light. An important example on the state level was the state of Ohio's $675,000 out-of-court settlement in 1978 of a suit against Governor Rhodes and a number of National Guardsmen, brought by the victims and families of victims of the Kent State University shootings.[42] On the federal level, the government or individual agencies sometimes pay to settle constitutional tort ("*Bivins*") suits against federal officials. In 1994, for example, the Internal Revenue Service paid a Miami lawyer, Daniel Heller, $500,000 to settle a taxpayer abuse suit that Heller had brought against three IRS agents.[43]

WHERE DOES LIABILITY GO FROM HERE?

The government is a unique kind of entity. And as the foregoing discussion has shown, the present law provides it with a significant level of protection for the injury-causing acts of its agents. Some take the view, however, that the government ought not to be less liable than a private party for acts of this kind, but more liable. The bases for this kind of thinking are the rise of the welfare state and the greater ability of the government than of most

---

[41] "Developments in the Law: Section 1983 and Federalism," 90 *Harvard Law Review* 1133, 1169 (1977).

[42] *New York Times*, January 5, 1978, 12.

[43] *New York Times*, February 9, 1994, D1; John D. McKinnon, "IRS Pays Lawyer $500,000: His Lawsuit Had Alleged a Vendetta by Three Agents," 80 *American Bar Association Journal* 28 (May 1994).

private parties to pay for damages caused by it. Professor Davis has summarized the relevant reasoning as follows:

> . . . After all, a governmental unit differs significantly from a private party: it is supported by taxation, and it is not dependent on private investment or private profit. A large enough governmental unit is the best of all possible loss spreaders, especially, perhaps, if its taxes are geared to ability to pay. The basic fact, which so far has been given too little heed, will in time lead us to see that the basis for governmental liability should not be fault but should be equitable loss spreading. The ultimate principle may be that the taxpaying public should usually bear the fortuitous and heavy losses that result from governmental activity. . . . The key idea will be simply that a beneficent governmental unit ought not to allow exceptional losses to be borne by those upon whom the governmental activity has happened to inflict harm.[44]

This line of thinking is quite different from more traditional views. It is not argued today (as it was put in an old English case) that "it is better that an individual should sustain in injury than that the public should suffer an inconvenience."[45] But there are still many who do not favor so-called collectivization of risk, who hold that "individual well-being is not in itself absolutely assured by any government. . . . The individual must pay for the privilege of living in an organized society."[46]

Even if one favors the further extension of governmental liability, there remains the question of how far the government should be held liable for its acts. Nearly all governmental activity, legislative, executive, judicial, and administrative, hurts someone, but should there be liability for all such acts? This would be neither reasonable or possible. The government must be given some latitude in performing its functions. As Justice Jackson has stated, "it is not a tort for the government to govern" [*Dalehite* v. *United States*, 346 U.S. 15, 57 (1953)].

Up to the present, the basis of governmental tort liability, as of tort liability in general in the United States, has been the concept of negligence or fault. In most cases it must be shown that injury was based on negligence before a judgment can be made against a defendant. In private tort law, an important development of modern times has been the replacement of the fault principle in certain circumstances (the use of dangerous substances or the conducting of ultrahazardous activity, for instance) by the principle of "strict liability" or liability regardless of fault. But *Dalehite* v. *United States* ruled that liability under the FTCA could be based only on negligence [346 U.S. 15, 45 (1953)]. The principle was reaffirmed in *Laird* v. *Nelms*, 406 U.S. 797 (1972), in which the Supreme Court ruled that a plaintiff could not recover damages caused by sonic booms by military aircraft because no negligence was shown to have taken place in the flight. Yet many would argue that this cost of living in a highly technological society should not be borne by an individual.

---

[44] 3 *Administrative Law Treatise* 503–504 (1958).

[45] *Russell* v. *Men of Devon*, 100 Eng. Rep. 359, as cited in *Muskopf* v. *Corning Hospital Dist.*, 55 Cal.3d 211, 11 Cal. Rptr. 89, 359 P.2d 457 (1961).

[46] Harry Street, "Governmental Liability for Tort in Britain and the United States," 18 *Public Administration* 48 (1950).

Most people would probably agree that a person who has been arrested, convicted, and has served time in prison for a crime of which he is innocent should have recourse against the government for compensation. And indeed such recourse does exist, at least in some jurisdictions. On the federal level, the Unjust Conviction Statute provides this kind of possibility of compensation. But an award of damages may not exceed $5,000.[47]

Private Legislation and Administrative Settlement of Claims

As indicated earlier, the avenue of private legislation is still resorted to when a suit against the government fails or the government is declared immune. Here are some examples. The victims of the Texas City disaster benefited from private legislation, although the test case, *Dalehite* v. *United States* (1953), was lost in the courts. Several sets of plaintiffs sued for damages based on injuries alleged to have been caused by government negligence in connection with nuclear testing: civilians downwind of nuclear test sites, military personnel subject to radiation during testing, and civilian and military test site workers. All three groups were ultimately denied the right to have their cases decided on the merits because of the FTCA's discretionary function exception.[48] Some of the civilian downwinders actually won their case at the district court level and were awarded substantial compensation. But the decision was overturned on appeal on the basis of the revised interpretation of the discretionary function exception discussed earlier.

At about the same time that the courts were ruling on these matters (the late 1980s), other U.S. courts were immunizing the government from liability, partly on the basis of the discretionary function exception, in suits brought by servicemen and their families for injuries related to exposure to the defoliant Agent Orange.[49] Later, in 1996, the Supreme Court ruled that the United States could not be made to share litigation expenses and the costs of a settlement made by chemical manufacturers who produced Agent Orange.[50]

An earlier example of mass government action that resulted in litigation was the internment of Japanese Americans during World War II. When the government argued the cases for internment before the Supreme Court in the 1940s, it concealed reports that contradicted the so-called military necessity of internment.[51] In spite of this deception, federal courts in the 1980s

---

[47] 52 Stat. 438 (1938), 28 U.S.C. §§ 1495m 2513.

[48] The three cases are, respectively: *Allen* v. *United States*, 816 F.2d 1417 (10th Cir., 1987), cert. denied 484 U.S. 1004 (1988); *In re Consolidated United States Atmospheric Testing Litigation*, 820 F.2d 982 (9th Cir., 1987), cert. denied 485 U.S. 905 (1988); and *Prescott* v. *United States*, 858 F. Supp. 1461 (D. Nev., 1994).

[49] *In re "Agent Orange" Product Liability Litigation; Thomas Adams et al.* v. *United States*, 818 F.2d 201 (2nd Cir., 1987), cert. denied 484 U.S. 1004 (1988).

[50] *Hercules, Inc.* v. *United States*, 516 U.S. 417 (1996). For background on the Agent Orange litigation, see Peter H. Schuck, *Agent Orange on Trial: Mass Toxic Disasters in the Courts*, enlarged edition, 1987.

[51] The 1940s cases were *Hirabayshi* v. *United States*, 320 U.S. 81 (1943), and *Korematsu* v. *United States*, 323 U.S. 214 (1944). Forty years later a U.S. District Court vacated Korematsu's con-

denied damages to plaintiff-internees, in part on the basis of sovereign immunity.[52]

In every one of the cases just discussed, the Congress took up the matter after the courts had rejected plaintiffs' suits on the basis of sovereign immunity and, through special legislation, provided millions of dollars in compensation for the victims of government action.[53]

Another avenue of compensation is by administrative settlement of claims. Section 2672 of the FTCA provides for administrative settlement by the heads of appropriate federal agencies. The amount of such settlement is unlimited, but any award in excess of $25,000 must be approved by the attorney general. And § 2677 of the same title provides that the attorney general or his designee may arbitrate, compromise, or settle any claim against the United States that has already been commenced.

There have been some notable awards under these sections. A $9 million settlement was made in 1975 in a suit against the United States Public Health Service for a forty-year study of the effects of untreated syphilis in which 600 black males were subjects.[54] A more recent settlement against the United States involved the so-called human radiation experiments (HRE). These secret Cold War–era experiments, which were sponsored by the federal government between 1944 and 1974, involved exposure of soldiers and civilians to radiation, in some cases through direct injection of radioactive materials. They were conducted without the victims' consent or knowledge. In a number of cases the subjects were persons from vulnerable populations, such as prisoners, indigent hospital patients, and retarded children.[55] The experiments came to light only in 1992. In 1996 the government agreed to pay $4.8 million to twelve victims of the human radiation experiments. At that time numerous other claims were still being examined.[56]

---

viction for violating the internment order on the grounds of government misconduct. Judge Marilyn Patel, in ruling for Korematsu, stated the following:

> [T]here is substantial support in the record that the government deliberately omitted relevant information and provided misleading information in papers before the court. The information was critical to the court's determination. . . . Because the information was of the kind peculiarly within the government's knowledge, the court was dependent on the government to provide a full and accurate account. . . . The judicial process is seriously impaired when the government's law enforcement officers violate their ethical obligations to the court [*Korematsu* v. *United States*, 584 F. Supp. 1406, 1420 (1984)].

[52] *Hohri* v. *United States*, 847 F.2d 779 (Federal Cir., 1988) (affirming district court decision, 586 F. Supp. 769).

[53] These laws are as follows: Public Law 101-426, 104 Stat. 920 (1990) ("Radiation Exposure Compensation Act"); Public Law 102-4, 105 Stat. 11 (1991) ("Agent Orange Act of 1991"); and Public Law 100-383, 102 Stat. 903 (1988) ("Civil Liberties Act of 1988"). This last act, in addition to providing compensation to the interned Japanese Americans and their families, apologized "on behalf of the people of the United States for the evacuation, relocation, and internment of such citizens and permanent resident aliens." Under the legislation, an estimated 60,000 surviving Japanese Americans were to be awarded $20,000 each, a sum described by one constitutional law specialist as "completely inadequate." See Craig R. Ducat, 1 *Constitutional Interpretation* 193 (7th ed., 2000).

[54] See James H. Jones, *Bad Blood: The Tuskegee Syphilis Experiment* 217 (1981).

[55] Nestor M. Davidson, "Constitutional Mass Torts: Sovereign Immunity and the Human Radiation Experiments," 96 *Columbia Law Review* 1203, 1229 (1996).

[56] *New York Times*, November 20, 1996, A1. On the human radiation experiments and other government-sponsored human experiments more generally, see Jonathan D. Moreno, *Undue Risk: Secret State Experiments on Humans*, 2000.

The case of Dr. Frank Olson, a civilian biochemist working for the federal government, was not part of the HRE. But his fate at the hands of government officials was perhaps more tragic. In 1953 he plunged to his death from a Manhattan hotel room after CIA agents, engaged in testing the effects of LSD on humans, placed the drug in his after-dinner drink during a conference of government scientists. The real cause of Dr. Olson's death was kept secret for decades. In 1976 Congress provided $750,000 to his family.[57]

Is private legislation a reasonable answer to the kinds of government-caused wrongs discussed in this section? Hardly. After all, one of the justifications for the adoption of the FTCA in the first place was to remove Congress from the business of dealing with such matters. Special legislation is an uncertain and unreliable device that leaves the principle of broad governmental immunity in place. Administrative settlement of claims also has its shortcomings. While an agency head or the attorney general may be prepared to settle claims for rather modest amounts, it would likely require really egregious government misbehavior to persuade such officials to recommend large payments. Moreover, the administrative settlement of claims by agency heads carries at least the suggestion of conflict of interest. It amounts to admitting that the agency did something wrong. It may be unreasonable to expect consistent objectivity from high-level bureaucrats under this arrangement.

Governments engage in a great deal of activity, and some of it causes harm. This is a normal state of affairs. But when the activity is as shocking and secretive as in some of the examples just presented, when, as one commentator put it, the government "does fundamental violence to the liberties of the citizens of the United States,"[58] the principles of justice and the rule of law call for better remedies than are now available.

---

[57] The private legislation on behalf of the Olson family is Private Law 94-126, 90 Stat. 3006 (1976). The facts surrounding Dr. Olson's death were widely reported in the press in the mid-1970s, including the *New York Times*, December 19, 1975, 24. A 2001 article in the *New York Times Magazine* tells a much darker story about Dr. Olson's demise and the government's role in it: Michael Ignatieff, "What Did the C.I.A. Do to His Father?" *New York Times Magazine*, April 1, 2001, 56.

[58] Davidson, above, note 55, 1251.

Chapter 10

Open Government

The late 1960s and the 1970s saw a significant shift in the direction of increased public access to government operations. This shift was accomplished largely through legislation, but the contours of the movement were shaped by judicial and administrative action as well. The most important aspects of this development, which will be discussed in this chapter, are the following: the federal Freedom of Information Act, the Privacy Act, government-in-the-sunshine laws, and the concept of executive privilege.[1] The movement toward open government has met resistance along the way from a variety of sources. And in recent years both Congress and the courts have leaned toward greater protection of government information. Nevertheless, the developments mentioned above evidence an impressive change, since the middle of the twentieth century, in the direction of opening up government operations to public view.

THE FREEDOM OF INFORMATION ACT

A key development was the adoption of the federal Freedom of Information Act (FOIA) in 1966 (Public Law 89-487, 80 Stat. 250). Before the adoption of the act, government records were required to be revealed only to "persons properly and directly concerned" with such records. Any records could be kept secret if such a policy was "in the public interest" or if the records related "solely to the internal management of an agency."[2] The FOIA, described by the House Committee on Government Operations as "milestone legislation that reversed long-standing government practices,"[3] provides, by

---

[1] See the detailed analysis of most of the matters examined in this chapter in James T. O'Reilly, *Federal Information Disclosure*, 2 vols. (3rd ed., 2000).

[2] 60 Stat. 237 (1946) (section 3 of the original Administrative Procedure Act).

[3] *A Citizen's Guide on How to Use the Freedom of Information Act and the Privacy Act in Requesting Government Documents*, Thirteenth Report by the Committee on Government Operations, 95th Congress, 1st session, House Report No. 95-793, Washington, 1977, 5.

contrast, that "each agency" shall make available records or other information requested by "any person." The burden of proof for withholding information is placed on the agency, which is required to respond to all requests for information within twenty working days after receipt of a request, except when "unusual circumstances" permit an extension of ten more working days. A denial of information may be appealed to a higher level in the agency, and if the information request is still denied, the party may go to federal district court to seek an order that the records be produced.

Not all information in the hands of the government need be released, of course. The act lists nine specific matters to which the disclosure section does not apply, including such information as "trade secrets and commercial or financial information obtained from a person," which are deemed "privileged or confidential," and "personnel and medical files and similar files the disclosure of which would constitute a clearly unwarranted invasion of personal privacy." Perhaps the most important exemption is for information "specifically authorized under criteria established by Executive order to be kept secret in the interest of national defense or foreign policy."

Whether the disclosure of certain files *would* constitute an unwarranted invasion of privacy and whether information in a government's possession *is* privileged or confidential are matters about which opinions may differ. These questions (as well as issues related to the other exemptions under the act) are matters that the courts are called upon to decide. The exemption involving information pertaining to national defense and foreign policy has been the subject of some significant litigation. A number of Americans are fearful that the provision could be used unreasonably to keep information from the public. In the first few years of the FOIA's operation, courts seemed quite willing to go along with the government's use of the exemption. A key case was *Environmental Protection Agency* v. *Mink* (1973).

Environmental Protection Agency v. Mink

SUPREME COURT OF THE UNITED STATES (1973).
410 U.S. 73, 93 S.Ct. 827, 35 L.Ed. 2d 119.

[Congresswoman Patsy Mink and others took the government to court to gain access to documents relating to underground nuclear testing. The district court ruled in favor of the government, partly on the basis of the "national defense and foreign policy" exemption. The court of appeals reversed, concluding that this exemption permitted withholding only the secret portions of documents. It ordered the district judge to examine the documents in camera (behind closed doors) for purposes of separating the secret from the nonsecret components and allowing the latter to be disclosed.]

Mr. Justice White delivered the opinion of the Court. . . .

Respondents' lawsuit began with an article that appeared in a Washington, D. C., newspaper in late July 1971. The article indicated that the President had received conflicting recommendations on the advisability of the underground nuclear test scheduled for that coming fall and, in particular, noted that the "latest recommendations" were the product of "a departmental under-secretary committee named to investigate the controversy." Two days later, Congresswoman Patsy Mink, a respondent, sent a telegram to the President urgently requesting the "immediate release of recommendations and report by inter-departmental committee. . . ." When the request was denied, an action under the Freedom of Information Act was commenced by Congresswoman Mink and 32 of her colleagues in the House. . . .

Subsection (b)(1) of the Act [hereafter sometimes "Exemption 1"] exempts from forced disclosure matters "specifically required by Executive order to be kept secret in the interest of the national defense or foreign policy." According to the Irwin affidavit,[4] the six documents for which Exemption 1 is now claimed were all duly classified Top Secret or Secret, pursuant to Executive Order 10501. . . . That order was promulgated under the authority of the President in 1953 . . . and, since that time, has served as the basis for the classification by the Executive Branch of information "which requires protection in the interests of national defense." We do not believe that Exemption 1 permits compelled disclosure of documents, such as the six here that were classified pursuant to this Executive Order. Nor does the Exemption permit *in camera* inspection of such documents to sift out so-called "nonsecret components." Obviously, this test was not the only alternative available. But Congress chose to follow the Executive's determination in these matters and that choice must be honored. . . .

What has been said thus far makes wholly untenable any claim that the Act intended to subject the soundness of executive security classifications to judicial review at the insistence of any objecting citizen. It also negates the proposition that Exemption 1 authorizes or permits *in camera* inspection of a contested document bearing a single classification so that the court may separate the secret

from the supposedly nonsecret and order disclosure of the latter. The Court of Appeals was thus in error. The Irwin affidavit stated that each of the six documents for which Exemption 1 is now claimed "are and have been classified" Top Secret and Secret "pursuant to Executive Order No. 10501" and as involving "highly sensitive matter that is vital to our national defense and foreign policy."

The fact of those classifications and the documents' characterizations have never been disputed by respondents. Accordingly, upon such a showing and in such circumstances, petitioners had met their burden of demonstrating that the documents were entitled to protection under Exemption 1, and the duty of the District Court under § 552 (a)(3) was therefore at an end. . . .

The judgment is reversed and the case is remanded for further proceedings consistent with this opinion. . . .

Mr. Justice Rehnquist took no part in the consideration or decision of this case.

Mr. Justice Stewart, concurring. . . .

[The] Court's opinion demonstrates that Congress has conspicuously failed to attack the problem that my Brother Douglas [in the dissenting opinion below] discusses. Instead, it has built into the Freedom of Information Act an exemption that provides no means to question an Executive decision to stamp a document "secret," however cynical, myopic, or even corrupt that decision might have been. . . . [In] enacting § 552 (b)(1) Congress chose . . . to decree blind acceptance of Executive fiat.

Mr. Justice Brennan, with whom Mr. Justice Marshall joins, concurring in part and dissenting in part. . . . The Court's interpretation of Exemption 1 as a complete bar to judicial inspection of matters claimed by the Executive to fall within it

---

[4] Authors' note: John N. Irwin II, undersecretary of state, headed a committee that annually reviewed the underground nuclear test program and reported to the president. He submitted an affidavit supporting the EPA's view that the materials sought were exempt under the FOIA.

wholly frustrates the objective of the Freedom of Information Act. That interpretation makes a nullity of the Act's requirement of de novo judicial review. The judicial role becomes "meaningless judicial sanctioning of agency action," . . . the very result Congress sought to prevent by incorporating the de novo requirement. . . .

Mr. Justice DOUGLAS, dissenting. . . .

The Government is aghast at a federal judge's even looking at the secret files and views with disdain the prospect of responsible judicial action in the area. It suggests that judges have no business declassifying "secrets," that judges are not familiar with the stuff with which these "Top Secret" or "Secret" documents deal. That is to misconceive and distort the judicial function under § 552 (a)(3) of the Act. The Court of Appeals never dreamed that the trial judge would declassify documents. His first task would be to determine whether nonsecret material was a mere appendage to a "Secret" or "Top Se-

cret" file. His second task would be to determine whether under normal discovery procedures contained in Fed. Rule Civ. Proc. 26, factual material in these "Secret" or "Top Secret" materials is detached from the "Secret" and would, therefore, be available to litigants confronting the agency in ordinary lawsuits.

Unless the District Court can do those things, the much-advertised Freedom of Information Act is on its way to becoming a shambles. Unless federal courts can be trusted, the Executive will hold complete sway and by *ipse dixit* make even the time of day "Top Secret." Certainly, the decision today will upset the "workable formula," at the heart of the legislative scheme, "which encompasses, balances, and protects all interests, yet places emphasis on the fullest responsible disclosure." . . . The Executive Branch now has *carte blanche* to insulate information from public scrutiny whether or not that information bears any discernible relation to the interests sought to be protected by subsection (b)(1) of the Act. . . .

Amendments to the Freedom of Information Act

The FOIA has been amended a number of times, most significantly in 1974 and 1996. As was evident from the separate opinions in *Mink*, there was considerable dissatisfaction with exemption 1 as interpreted by the Court, since it left the executive completely unfettered with regard to assertions of national defense and foreign policy. Nor was such concern limited to the four justices whose views were quoted above. It is not too much to say that some of the changes written into the 1974 amendments amounted to Congress's overruling *Mink*.[5]

The relevant amendments provided that information classified under the exemptions must be "in fact properly classified"; that the court may make in camera examination of documents that the Supreme Court had denied in *Mink* "to determine whether such records or any part thereof shall be withheld" under any of the exemptions; and that "[a]ny reasonably segregable portion of a record shall be provided to any person requesting such

---

[5] See "National Security and the Amended Freedom of Information Act," 85 *Yale Law Journal* 401, 402 (1976); "National Security and the Public's Right to Know: A New Role for the Courts under the Freedom of Information Act," 123 *University of Pennsylvania Law Review* 1438, 1448 (1975); Bernard Schwartz, *Administrative Law* 148 (3rd ed., 1991).

record after deletion of the portions which are exempt under this subsection."

Other important 1974 amendments set a ten-day time limit for responding to information requests (this was raised to twenty days by the 1996 amendments), provided for discipline of persons responsible for arbitrary and capricious withholding of information, and allowed court costs and attorney fees to be awarded if the plaintiff "substantially prevailed" in a case taken to court under the FOIA.[6]

But the scope of disclosure of governmental information still depends to a considerable extent on the attitude of the executive branch. For instance, the FOIA's "national security and foreign policy" exemption covers matters "specifically required by Executive order to be kept secret." President Reagan enacted a rather broad secrecy order in comparison with that of his predecessors. President Clinton's executive order on the subject effected the declassification of a large number of documents, especially older information. President George W. Bush moved back in the direction of restricting information available to the public, especially after the attacks on New York and Washington of September 11, 2001.[7]

Some congressional action in more recent years has further limited the scope of the FOIA. The Central Intelligence Information Act of 1984 allows the Central Intelligence Agency (CIA) director to exempt most operational files from the reach of the FOIA.[8] As part of a comprehensive Anti-Drug Enforcement Act of 1986, Congress broadened exemption 7 of the FOIA (law enforcement information) to provide further protection for law enforcement records.[9]

The Electronic Freedom of Information Act Amendments of 1996, Public Law 104-231, 110 Stat. 3048, made a number of significant changes to the FOIA. In the introductory passages of the act, Congress encouraged agencies to "use new technology to enhance public access to agency records and information." Accordingly, the new law made it clear that "agency records" included material stored in electronic form, a matter about which there had been some dispute. It required agencies to make policy statements and other general information available by electronic means. And it charged agencies with providing information in the form requested (including electronically) if the records were readily reproducible in that format. To facilitate access

---

[6] Public Law 93-502, 88 Stat. 1561.

[7] On the executive branch's role in information access, see, e.g., Mark S. Zaid, "Too Many Secrets," *The National Law Journal*, March 25, 2002, A17; Richard Reeves, "Writing History to Executive Order," *New York Times on the Web*, November 16, 2001; Peter L. Strauss, Todd Rakoff, Roy A. Schotland, and Cynthia R. Farina, *Administrative Law: Cases and Comments* 915 (9th ed., 1995); Richard J. Pierce, Jr., Sidney A. Shapiro, and Paul R. Verkuil, *Administrative Law and Process* 428 (3rd ed., 1999).

[8] Public Law 98-477, 98 Stat. 2209. Herbert N. Foerstel asserts that this legislation has encouraged the CIA to interpret the statute's restrictions on information disclosure more broadly than Congress intended and has led the federal judiciary to defer unreasonably to CIA information policy. See his *Freedom of Information and the Right to Know* 106–114 (1999).

[9] Public Law 99-570, 100 Stat. 3207. The "Freedom of Information Reform Act of 1986" is Subtitle N of the Anti-Drug Abuse Act. In addition to broadening exemption 7, the act includes amended fee and waiver provisions.

to information, agencies were instructed to prepare descriptions of available information, including indexes of records.

Some of the other important provisions of the amendments dealt with matters not necessarily associated with electronic information. The ten-day time limit for responding to FOIA requests was lengthened to twenty days. As before, however, the FOIA allows this period to be extended "in unusual circumstances." In reality, few agencies had been responding within ten days.[10] It was hoped that, by greater use of computer technology, backlogs that had delayed responses to FOIA requests could be brought under control. Moreover, agencies were directed to adopt multitrack processing of requests, under which, according to the amendments, a person could "limit the scope of the request in order to qualify for faster processing." Another provision stated that a person who demonstrated "compelling need" for records was entitled to "expedited processing of a request."

In the several years since their enactment, the 1996 amendments appear to have been less effective in reaching their objectives than had been hoped. Congress has given insufficient attention to funding the increased costs of providing public access to electronic information in agency hands. Perhaps in part for this reason, for many agencies the development of electronic information systems is seen as essentially an internal matter. Providing public access or complying with FOIA directives is at best secondary.[11]

If the mindset of Congress and the agencies has leaned toward protecting government information in recent years, the same can be said of the courts, which have shown little inclination to interpret FOIA provisions expansively.[12] Perhaps as a result, the number of FOIA cases brought to court in recent years has dropped considerably.[13]

THE PRIVACY ACT

Like the FOIA, the Privacy Act of 1974 (Public Law 93-579, 88 Stat. 1897) is codified as part of the Administrative Procedure Act (APA). In the words of a popular citizen's guide published by the U.S. government, the Privacy Act:

---

[10] Senator Patrick Leahy, "The Electronic FOIA Amendments of 1996: Reformatting the FOIA for On-Line Access," 50 *Administrative Law Review* 339, 342 (1998).

[11] On these matters see Martin E. Halstuk, "Speed Bumps on the Information Highway: A Study of Federal Agency Compliance with the Electronic Freedom of Information Act of 1996," 5 *Communication and Law Policy* 423 (2000); Foerstel, above, note 8, 60–61; David MacDonald, "The Electronic Freedom of Information Act Amendments: A Minor Upgrade to Public Access Law," 23 *Rutgers Computer and Technology Law Journal* 357 (1997).

[12] Pierce, et al., above, note 7, 423.

[13] The annual reports of the Director of the Administrative Office of the United States Courts show that the number of such cases dropped by over 43 percent between 1993 and 2001. See "2001 Annual Report of the Director," Table C-2A, 133, www.uscourts.gov/judbususc/judbus.html. Based on earlier annual reports, Aman and Mayton speculated that part of this drop in cases may have been based on the executive order of President Clinton that led to the declassification of a large number of historical documents [Alfred C. Aman, Jr., and William T. Mayton, *Administrative Law* 643 (2nd ed., 2001)].

provides safeguards against an invasion of privacy through the misuse of records by Federal agencies. In general, the act allows a citizen to learn how records are collected, maintained, used, and disseminated by the Federal Government. The act also permits an individual to gain access to most personal information maintained by Federal agencies and to seek amendment of any inaccurate, incomplete, untimely, or irrelevant information.[14]

General exemptions to the Privacy Act apply to files maintained by the CIA and to certain records of criminal law enforcement agencies. In addition, seven specific exemptions apply to all agencies and cover such matters as classified documents concerning national defense and foreign policy, Secret Service intelligence files, and certain materials pertaining to government employment.

The act establishes agency appeal procedures for individuals dissatisfied with agency responses to requests to amend records. After administrative appeal, a case may be taken to federal court. Some potential for conflict exists between the FOIA and the Privacy Act. While the Privacy Act contains a statement [§ 552a(b)(2)] mandating disclosure if it is "required under Section 552 of [the Freedom of Information Act]," the issue was raised in several cases as to whether the Privacy Act itself might be considered a "withholding statute" under exemption 3 of the FOIA. The lower courts had given inconsistent views on this question, and in 1984 Congress amended the Privacy Act to make clear that "[n]o agency shall rely on any exemption contained in section 552 of this title to withhold from an individual any record which is otherwise accessible to such individual under the provisions of this section" (Public Law 98-477, 98 Stat. 2209, 2211).

But provisions of the FOIA and the Privacy Act can intersect in other ways as well, as the following case shows. Note the Supreme Court's repeated reliance here on the important 1989 case *Department of Justice* v. *Reporters Committee for Freedom of the Press*, 489 U.S. 749.

United States Department of Defense v. *Federal Labor Relations Authority*

SUPREME COURT OF THE UNITED STATES, 1994.
510 U.S. 487, 114 S.Ct. 1006, 127 L.Ed. 2d 325.

Justice THOMAS delivered the opinion of the Court.

This case requires us to consider whether disclosure of the home addresses of federal civil service employees by their employing agency pursuant to a request made by the employees' collective-bargaining representative under the Federal Service Labor-Management Relations Statute . . . would constitute a "clearly unwarranted invasion" of the employees' personal privacy within the meaning of the Freedom of Information Act. . . . Concluding that it would, we reverse the judgment of the Court of Appeals.

The controversy underlying this case arose when two local unions requested the petitioner federal agencies to provide them with the names and home addresses

---

[14] *A Citizen's Guide on Using the Freedom of Information Act and the Privacy Act of 1974 to Request Government Records* 22, House Report 106-50, Committee on Government Reform, 1999.

of the agency employees in the bargaining units represented by the unions. The agencies supplied the unions with the employees' names and work stations, but refused to release home addresses.

In response, the unions filed unfair labor practice charges with respondent Federal Labor Relations Authority (Authority), in which they contended that the Federal Service Labor-Management Relations Statute (Labor Statute) . . . required the agencies to divulge the addresses. The Labor Statute generally provides that agencies must, "to the extent not prohibited by law," furnish unions with data that are necessary for collective-bargaining purposes. . . . The agencies argued that disclosure of the home addresses was prohibited by the Privacy Act of 1974 (Privacy Act). . . . [T]he Authority rejected that argument and ordered the agencies to divulge the addresses.

A divided panel of the United States Court of Appeals for the Fifth Circuit granted enforcement of the Authority's orders. . . . The panel majority agreed with the Authority that the unions' requests for home addresses fell within a statutory exception to the Privacy Act. That Act does not bar disclosure of personal information if disclosure would be "required under section 552 of this title [the FOIA]." The court below observed that FOIA, with certain enumerated exceptions, generally mandates full disclosure of information held by agencies. In the view of the Court of Appeals, only one of the enumerated exceptions—the provision exempting from FOIA's coverage personnel files "the disclosure of which would constitute a clearly unwarranted invasion of personal privacy," 5 U.S.C. § 552(b)(6) (Exemption 6)—potentially applied to this case.

In determining whether Exemption 6 applied, the Fifth Circuit balanced the public interest in effective collective bargaining embodied in the Labor Statute against the interest of employees in keeping their home addresses private. The court recognized that, in light of our decision in *Department of Justice* v. *Reporters Comm. for Freedom of Press*, 489 U.S. 749, 103 L.Ed. 2d 774, 109 S.Ct. 1468 (1989), other Courts of Appeals had concluded that the only public interest to be weighed in the Exemption 6 balancing analysis is the extent to which FOIA's central purpose of opening agency action to public scrutiny would be served by disclosure. Rejecting that view, however, the panel majority reasoned that *Reporters Committee* "has absolutely nothing to say about . . . the situation that arises when disclosure is initially required by some statute other than the FOIA, and the FOIA is employed only secondarily." In such cases, the court ruled that "it is proper for the federal court to consider the public interests embodied in the statute which generates the disclosure request."

Applying this approach, the court concluded that, because the weighty interest in public sector collective bargaining identified by Congress in the Labor Statute would be advanced by the release of the home addresses, disclosure "would not constitute a clearly unwarranted invasion of privacy." In the panel majority's view, because Exemption 6 would not apply, FOIA would require disclosure of the addresses; in turn, therefore, the Privacy Act did not forbid the agencies to divulge the addresses, and the Authority's orders were binding. . . .

We granted certiorari . . . to resolve a conflict among the Courts of Appeals concerning whether the Privacy Act forbids the disclosure of employee addresses to collective-bargaining representatives pursuant to information requests made under the Labor Statute.

To fulfill its good-faith bargaining obligation [under the Federal Service Labor-Management Relations Statute], an agency must, *inter alia*, "furnish to the exclusive representative involved, or its authorized representative, upon request and, *to the extent not prohibited by law,* data . . . (B) which is reasonably available and necessary for full and proper discussion, understanding, and negotiation of subjects within the scope of collective bargaining." . . . The Authority has determined that the home addresses of bargaining unit employees constitute information that is "necessary" to the collective-bargaining process because through them, unions may communicate with employees more effectively than would otherwise be possible. . . .

Petitioners contend that the Privacy Act prohibits disclosure. This statute provides in part:

> No agency shall disclose any record which is contained in a system of records by any means of communication to any person, or to another agency, except pursuant to a written request by, or with the prior written consent of, the individual to whom the record pertains, unless disclosure of the record would be . . . (2) required under section 552 of this title [the FOIA].

The employee addresses sought by the unions are "records" covered by the broad terms of the Privacy Act. Therefore, unless FOIA would require release of the addresses, their disclosure is "prohibited by law," and the agencies may not reveal them to the unions.

We turn, then, to FOIA. As we have recognized previously, FOIA reflects "a general philosophy of full agency disclosure unless information is exempted under clearly delineated statutory language." *Department of Air Force* v. *Rose,* 425 U.S. 352, 360–361, 48 L.Ed. 2d 11, 96 S.Ct. 1592 (1976). . . . Thus, while "disclosure, not secrecy, is the dominant objective of [FOIA]," there are a number of exemptions from the statute's broad reach. *Rose,* supra, at 361. The exemption potentially applicable to employee addresses is Exemption 6, which provides that FOIA's disclosure requirements do not apply to "personnel and medical files and similar files the disclosure of which would constitute a clearly unwarranted invasion of personal privacy." . . .

Thus, although this case requires us to follow a somewhat convoluted path of statutory cross-references, its proper resolution depends upon a discrete inquiry: whether disclosure of the home addresses "would constitute a clearly unwarranted invasion of [the] personal privacy" of bargaining unit employees within the meaning of FOIA. For guidance in answering this question, we need look no further than to our decision in *Department of Justice* v. *Reporters Comm. for Freedom of Press,* 489 U.S. 749, 103 L. Ed. 2d 774, 109 S.Ct. 1468 (1989).

Reporters Committee involved FOIA requests addressed to the Federal Bureau of Investigation that sought the "rap sheets" of several individuals. In the process of deciding that the FBI was prohibited from disclosing the contents of the rap sheets, we reaffirmed several basic principles that have informed our interpretation of FOIA. First, in evaluating whether a request for information lies within the scope of a FOIA exemption, such as Exemption 6, that bars disclosure when it would amount to an invasion of privacy that is to some degree "unwarranted," "a court must balance the public interest in disclosure against the interest Congress intended the exemption to protect." Id., at 776.

Second, the only relevant "public interest in disclosure" to be weighed in this balance is the extent to which disclosure would serve the "core purpose of the FOIA," which is "contributing significantly to public understanding of the operations or activities of the government." *Reporters Comm.,* supra, at 775. . . .

Third, "whether an invasion of privacy is warranted cannot turn on the purposes for which the request for information is made." *Reporters Comm.,* 489 U.S. at 771. . . .

The principles that we followed in *Re-*

porters Committee can be applied easily to this case. We must weigh the privacy interest of bargaining unit employees in nondisclosure of their addresses against the only relevant public interest in the FOIA balancing analysis—the extent to which disclosure of the information sought would "shed light on an agency's performance of its statutory duties" or otherwise let citizens know "what their government is up to." *Reporters Comm.*, supra, at 773.

The relevant public interest supporting disclosure in this case is negligible, at best. Disclosure of the addresses might allow the unions to communicate more effectively with employees, but it would not appreciably further "the citizens' right to be informed about what their government is up to." 489 U.S. at 773. Indeed, such disclosure would reveal little or nothing about the employing agencies or their activities. . . .

Apparently realizing that this conclusion follows ineluctably from an application of the FOIA tenets we embraced in *Reporters Committee*, respondents argue that *Reporters Committee* is largely inapposite here because it dealt with an information request made directly under FOIA, whereas the unions' requests for home addresses initially were made under the Labor Statute, and implicated FOIA only incidentally through a chain of statutory cross-references. In such a circumstance, contend respondents, to give full effect to the three statutes involved and to allow unions to perform their statutory representational duties, we should import the policy considerations that are made explicit in the Labor Statute into the FOIA Exemption 6 balancing analysis. If we were to do so, respondents are confident we would conclude that the Labor Statute's policy favoring collective bargaining easily outweighs any privacy interest that employees might have in nondisclosure.

We decline to accept respondents' ambitious invitation to rewrite the statutes before us and to disregard the FOIA principles reaffirmed in *Reporters Committee*. The Labor Statute does not, as the Fifth Circuit suggested, merely "borrow the FOIA's disclosure calculus for another purpose." Rather, it allows the disclosure of information necessary for effective collective bargaining only "to the extent not prohibited by law." . . . Disclosure of the home addresses is prohibited by the Privacy Act unless an exception to that Act applies. The terms of the Labor Statute in no way suggest that the Privacy Act should be read in light of the purposes of the Labor Statute. If there is an exception, therefore, it must be found within the Privacy Act itself. Congress could have enacted an exception to the Privacy Act's coverage for information "necessary" for collective-bargaining purposes, but it did not do so. In the absence of such a provision, respondents rely on the exception for information the disclosure of which would be "required under [FOIA]." . . . Nowhere, however, does the Labor Statute amend FOIA's disclosure requirements or grant information requesters under the Labor Statute special status under FOIA. Therefore, because all FOIA requesters have an equal, and equally qualified, right to information, the fact that respondents are seeking to vindicate the policies behind the Labor Statute is irrelevant to the FOIA analysis. . . .

Because the privacy interest of bargaining unit employees in nondisclosure of their home addresses substantially outweighs the negligible FOIA-related public interest in disclosure, we conclude that disclosure would constitute a "clearly unwarranted invasion of personal privacy." . . . FOIA, thus, does not require the agencies to divulge the addresses, and the Privacy Act, therefore, prohibits their release to the unions. . . .

For the foregoing reasons, the judgment of the Court of Appeals is reversed.

So ordered.

[The opinions of Justice SOUTER, concurring, and Justice GINSBURG, concurring in the judgment, are omitted].

SUNSHINE ACTS

Since 1950, government-in-the-sunshine, or open-meeting, statutes have been adopted in all fifty states and at the federal level. The last jurisdiction to do so was the federal government, in 1976 (Public Law 94-409, 90 Stat. 1241). Like the FOIA and the Privacy Act, the federal Sunshine Act was codified as part of the APA, 5 U.S.C. § 552b. The federal Sunshine Act applies only to multiheaded agencies. Executive-branch organizations headed by a single individual are not covered. The Federal Advisory Committee Act, Public Law 92-463, 86 Stat. 770 (1972), provides for public access to meetings of advisory committees, study panels, and ad hoc committees within the executive branch.

Obviously, the purpose of the sunshine laws is to enhance citizen access to government operations. The degree of openness provided varies considerably from statute to statute, however. On the federal level and in some states, a body can go into executive session and close a meeting to the public simply by a majority vote. In other states even informal meetings are required to be open. Most statutes allow for some exceptions to the principal of openness, as in the case of labor negotiations or other personnel matters. In the federal sunshine law there are ten such exceptions, a number of which parallel the exemptions in the FOIA.

As mentioned, the federal statute applies only to multiheaded agencies, even though some of the single-headed agencies perform similar functions. The implications of this point are well put in an analysis of the federal statute written shortly after its adoption: "The Securities and Exchange Commission, for instance, has enforcement powers comparable to the Attorney General and regulatory powers comparable to the Comptroller of the Currency; yet, of the three, only the Securities and Exchange Commission is covered by the Act."[15]

Relatively speaking, the FOIA has been the focus of considerable litigation, particularly in the early years after its adoption. Far fewer court cases have been based on the Privacy Act, and fewer still on the federal Sunshine Act. The Supreme Court has ruled on the latter only once, in *Federal Communications Commission* v. *ITT World Communications*, 466 U.S. 463 (1984). Members of the Federal Communications Commission (FCC) met with Canadian and European counterparts in conferences to discuss joint planning of telecommunications facilities. ITT brought suit, complaining, among other things, that these "Consultative Process" sessions were meetings within the meaning of the Sunshine Act and should be held in public. A unanimous Supreme Court ruled against ITT on two grounds: that the

---

[15] Howard I. Fox, "Government in the Sunshine," *1978 Annual Survey of American Law* 306 (1979).

sessions were not "meetings" since they could not, as the Sunshine Act provided, "determine or result in the joint conduct or disposition of official agency business"; and that the sessions were not meetings "of an agency" within the meaning of the act, since they were not subject to the FCC's unilateral control.

Public meetings under the federal Sunshine Act often lack the openness and spontaneity that the statute was designed to achieve. According to a report of an Administrative Conference of the United States committee, among the factors inhibiting the character of such agency meetings are the following:

> concern that providing initial deliberative views publicly, without sufficient thought and information, may harm the public interest by irresponsibly introducing uncertainty or confusion to industry or the general public; a desire on the part of members to speak with a uniform voice on matters of particular importance or to develop negotiating strategies which might be thwarted if debated publicly; reluctance of an agency member to embarrass another agency member, or to embarrass himself, through inadvertent, argumentative, or exaggerated statements; concern that an agency member's statements may be used against the agency in subsequent litigation, or misinterpreted or misunderstood by the public or the press, as for example, when the agency member is testing a position by "playing devil's advocate" or merely "thinking out loud"; and concerns that a member's statements may affect financial markets.[16]

After the federal Sunshine Act went into effect, a number of agencies found ways to dilute its impact. Some simply reduced the number of formal meetings. The role of staff assistants (who are not covered by the act) in working out crucial details of decisions was enhanced. The use of "notation voting" by agency members (written voting, without discussion) was increased. Thus, the greatest virtue of the Sunshine Act is not that it has encouraged open collective decision making. What the law does, to quote the Administrative Conference report again, is to "allow an agency to explain publicly the results of its prior decisionmaking."[17] Perhaps that is as much as can reasonably be expected under the law as presently written.

EXECUTIVE PRIVILEGE

The word *privilege* has several meanings in law. In the area of libel and slander, it refers to an exemption from liability for allegedly defamatory publication or speech. In the leading case of *Barr* v. *Matteo* (1959), for instance, a federal official was declared by the Supreme Court to have *absolute privilege* with regard to utterances made "within the outer perimeter" of his

---

[16] Special Committee, Administrative Conference of the United States, "Report & Recommendation by the Special Committee to Review the Government in the Sunshine Act," 49 *Administrative Law Review* 422 (1997). The Administrative Conference of the United States was abolished in 1995 when Congress ended its funding. This committee report was one of its final publications.

[17] Ibid., 423.

official duty [360 U.S. 564 at 575 (1959)]. Absolute privilege is the libel law equivalent of absolute immunity, discussed in the previous chapter.

Another use of the term *privilege* has to do with the protection of information or communications from access by the legal process. Examples of privileged communications that are recognized in some jurisdictions are those between physician and patient and those between husband and wife.

Executive privilege is a doctrine that has some relevance to administrative law. It is not mentioned in the FOIA, although the exemption for national defense and foreign policy information has to do with analogous matters. But there is a doctrine of executive privilege outside of the FOIA. A key case is *United States* v. *Reynolds*, 345 U.S. 1 (1953). The Supreme Court overruled a district court decision ordering that the government produce, for examination by the court, the air force's official accident investigation report sought by the widows of three deceased civilian observers who were killed in the crash of a military aircraft carrying secret electronic equipment. The plaintiffs were suing the government under the Federal Tort Claims Act, and the Supreme Court ruled that "the Court should not jeopardize the security which the privilege is meant to protect by insisting upon an examination of the evidence, even by the judge alone, in chambers."

In *United States* v. *Nixon*, 418 U.S. 683 (1974), the Watergate tapes case, the Supreme Court reaffirmed the principle of executive privilege, citing the *Reynolds* case, among others, as authority on the doctrine. But it ruled that executive privilege did not apply in the case at hand: "The generalized assertion of privilege must yield to the demonstrated, specific need for evidence in a pending criminal trial." Both before and since the *Nixon* case, presidents have regularly sought to use executive privilege to keep information from disclosure. Recently, however, the doctrine has seldom been asserted in an administrative law context (i.e., where the government is seeking to prevent disclosure to private parties) but more so in situations in which the executive wants to keep information from other agencies of government. Executive privilege was invoked numerous times during the Clinton presidency, perhaps most notably when his lawyers sought to avoid testifying before a grand jury about the investigation of Monica Lewinsky, with whom the president had had a sexual affair. A district court judge ruled that the White House had not met the burden of showing that communication with one of its lawyers "occurred in conjunction with advising the president" and that in any case the need for testimony by presidential aides outweighed Clinton's right to executive privilege.[18]

CONCLUSION

The federal Administrative Procedure Act (APA), adopted in 1946, has been in operation for about six decades. For its first twenty years, the section

---

[18] *In Re Grand Jury Proceedings*, 5 F. Supp. 2d 21 at 27 (1998). The court also rejected the attempt to use the attorney-client privilege to avoid giving testimony. On appeal, the president's aides dropped the executive privilege defense. The court of appeals affirmed the district court's order regarding the attorney-client privilege [*In Re Bruce R. Lindsey* 148 F.3d 1100 (1998)]. Certiorari was denied by the Supreme Court in *Office of the President* v. *Office of Independent Counsel*, 525 U.S. 996 (1998), as amended October 21, 1999.

dealing with the public's right to information was just several sentences long and quite restrictive. The Freedom of Information Act, adopted in 1966, was the first of several legislative enactments whose objective was to adjust the balance between the interests of government and the rights of private parties. The sections of the APA dealing with these matters now run to dozens of pages. As the cases discussed in this chapter demonstrate, however, this extensive statutory law still leaves plenty of room for controversy as to whether governmental or private interests should prevail in particular circumstances.

APPENDIXES

APPENDIX A

Source Materials in Administrative Law

APPENDIX B

Administrative Procedure Act

APPENDIX C

The Constitution of the United States of America

Source Materials in Administrative Law

Roseann Bowerman

The primary source materials for administrative law research are of four types. First are those legislative statutory sources that either create the administrative agencies or enable the agency to perform its functions. Second are the administrative rules and regulations themselves. Third is case law, the decisions of courts that have reviewed the actions of administrative agencies. Finally there are those sources that publish the administrative decisions of the agency hearing officers that result from the process of adjudication. This appendix will identify the official printed versions and in some cases commercial printings of these primary sources, indicate the format used when citing them, and list selected Internet access points. It should be noted that the Internet has made much of this material widely available, and this guide will not attempt to list every Internet access point. As with any legal resource, care should be taken to assess that the online material being consulted is the most recent or up-to-date version.

FEDERAL STATUTES

Statutes are the primary source materials that result from the federal legislative process. They are initially published in printed or electronic slip law form. At the end of the year in which the laws are passed, they appear as part of the *United States Statutes at Large*, a chronological publication of the laws enacted during a session of Congress. Every six years these new laws are codified and incorporated with other laws currently in force into the *United States Code*. The *United States Code* is an arrangement by subject (in fifty titles) of permanent general and public law. Supplements to the *U.S. Code* appear annually.

It should be noted that while statutes are the end result of the legislative process, a significant number of documentary publications are produced at the various steps along the path as a bill becomes law. These documents are significant to the understanding of the intent of the resulting statute, and the compilation and study of these documents is known as legislative history. Courts will examine these materials to determine legislative intent if there are questions or ambiguities concerning the language or meaning of a statute. The types of materials examined in conducting a legislative history include bills, House and Senate reports, hearings, floor debates, conference reports, and presidential statements. Tracking this history can be complex, and several sources of compiled legislative histories exist. These include:

> *United States Code Congressional and Administrative News* (*USCCAN*): This product includes the text of the Public Law and a selection of the congressional committee reports of significance to its passage.
>
> *Congressional Information Service CIS Index*: This printed index covers legislation back to 1970. Its legislative history section provides detailed indexing of all the varieties of documents pertinent to the history of these statutes.
>
> LexisNexis Congressional web service: This electronic service contains an electronic counterpart to the *CIS Index*. Its coverage goes back to 1970.

Citation Format

A uniform system of citation is used for many legal citations throughout the United States. It consists of three parts: volume number, name of publication, and page number or section number. For more information on citation style and legal research, see Morris. L. Cohen, *Legal Research in a Nutshell* (7th ed., 2000).

> *United States Statutes at Large* (abbreviated as Stat.)
> **For instance:** 60 Stat. 237
> *United States Code* (abbreviated as U.S.C.)
> **For instance:** 5 U.S.C. 551 *et seq.*

Internet Sources of Federal Statutes

> GPO Access: Public and Private Laws Database
> http://www.gpoaccess.gov/plaws/index.html
> GPO Access: United States Code Database[1]
> http://www.gpoaccess.gov/uscode/index.html
> U.S. House of Representatives: United States Code Database
> http://uscode.house.gov/

---

[1] Since the texts of laws published as public laws are identical to those that appear in the *U.S. Statutes at Large*, a search by Statutes at Large citation may be done in both the public laws and U.S. Code databases on GPO Access.

Cornell Law School, Legal Information Institute: United States Code
http://www4.law.cornell.edu/uscode/

Commercial Internet databases also provide access to public laws (statutes) and the United States Code. The latest edition of the United States Code Service, a privately published version of the United States Code, is available through LexisNexis Academic. The LexisNexis Congressional database also provides full text searching of the United States Code Service and is searchable by U.S.C. citation or Statutes at Large citation for public laws back to 1988. These sources are also made available to subscribers of the Westlaw research service
(http://web2.westlaw.com/signon/default.wl).

FEDERAL RULES AND REGULATIONS

The rules and regulations created by federal administrative agencies make their first appearance in a daily (weekdays, excepting federal holidays) publication, the *Federal Register*. This periodical has been published since 1936 and contains agency notices, proposed rules, final rules, and regulations. *Through the* Federal Register *the federal government provides notice that certain rules or changes to rules are being considered and informs the public of the dates that final rules and regulations become effective.* These rules and regulations are subsequently compiled on an annual basis into the *Code of Federal Regulations* (C.F.R.), a subject arrangement of only the regulations in full force or effect (in fifty titles.) While each title of the C.F.R. has its own index, a cumulative index volume for the entire set is also published annually. A monthly publication, the *List of Sections Affected* (LSA), indicates those rules that may have been changed or added since the publication of the C.F.R. It should be consulted when using the printed versions of these sources. All of these sources are currently published by the Office of the Federal Register, National Archives and Records Service, General Services Administration, through the U.S. Government Printing Office.

Citation Format

Federal Register (abbreviated as F.R.)
  Cited as volume, F.R., page number
  For instance: 65 F.R. 40776
Code of Federal Regulations (abbreviated as C.F.R.)
  Cited as Title, C.F.R., part and section
  For instance: 40 C.F.R § 405.53 (In this example 405 indicates the part and 53 indicates the section.)

Internet Sources for Federal Rules and Regulations

Federal Register Online via GPO Access
  http://www.gpoaccess.gov/fr/index.html
  contents: 1995 (vol. 60) to the present, updated by 6 a.m. daily

Code of Federal Regulations Online via GPO Access
  http://www.gpoaccess.gov/cfr/index.html
    contents: most recent edition, with past revision editions back to
      1996 available
List of Sections Affected via GPO Access
  http://www.gpoaccess.gov/lsa/about.html

Commercial Internet databases also make the *Federal Register* and the *Code of Federal Regulations* available to their subscribers. The LexisNexis Congressional service provides searches of the C.F.R. back to 1981 and the *Federal Register* back to 1980. LexisNexis Academic provides access to the latest edition of the C.F.R. Source statements in LexisNexis Academic indicate that "all adopted rules and regulations will be integrated and available in the CFR usually within 2 weeks after being published in the Federal Register." The coverage of the *Federal Register* on Academic Universe extends back to 1980. These sources are also made available to subscribers of the Westlaw research service
  (http://web2.westlaw.com/signon/default.wl).

CASE LAW

U.S. Supreme Court Cases

The texts of United States Supreme Court opinions appear in a variety of publications. All Supreme Court opinions are published, unlike the practice for lower courts. The official versions of these opinions are published by the U.S. Superintendent of Documents in a set entitled *United States Reports*. This official version often takes several years to appear in a bound form. However, the printed *U.S. Reports* decisions do show up in a few months in what is know as a slip opinion, without the official volume and page number. Softcover "advance pamphlets" known as Preliminary Prints replace the slip opinions. These are followed by the final casebound set of books known as the *United States Reports*. A citation to the official *United States Reports* version of an opinion is the preferred citation. Other commercial publishers also reproduce the exact texts of these decisions and supplement the texts with annotations and other editorial features. Two of these commercial publications are *West's Supreme Court Reporter* and *Lawyers' Cooperative's United States Supreme Court Reports, Lawyers' Edition*. These sets appear earlier than the final *U.S. Reports* volumes.

In this era of the Internet, the texts of Supreme Court opinions make their earliest accessible appearance as electronic publications through websites produced by the federal government or in legal database services. The Internet services listed below are just a small selection of those available. A complete list of Supreme Court opinion publishers is compiled and updated annually by the staff of the Supreme Court of the United States and can be found on the World Wide Web at the Supreme Court website.
  Where to Obtain Supreme Court Opinions
  http://www.supremecourtus.gov/opinions/obtainopinions.pdf

Citation format

> *United States Reports* (abbreviated as U.S.)
> **For instance:** 401 U.S. 402
> West's *Supreme Court Reporter* (abbreviated as S. Ct.)
> **For instance:** 91 S.Ct. 814
> *United States Supreme Court Reports, Lawyers' Edition* (abbreviated as L.Ed. followed by edition number)
> **For instance:** 28 L.Ed. 2d 136

Internet Sources for Supreme Court Opinions

> Supreme Court of the United States website
> Offers electronic versions of the bound *U.S. Reports* volumes issued since 1991 as well as recent slip opinions.
> http://www.supremecourtus.gov
> Findlaw's Supreme Court Opinions searchable database
> Includes decisions from 1893 to the present (U.S.Reports 150-, 1893-). Cases can be searched by citation, case title, and full text or browsed by year.
> http://www.findlaw.com/casecode/supreme.html

U.S. Courts of Appeals and U.S. District Courts

The opinions of the U.S. courts of appeals are printed in a serial publication, the *Federal Reporter*, produced by West Publishing Company. It is important to note that only a portion of cases considered by the U.S. courts of appeals or U.S. district courts are ever published. However, since its inception in 1880, the *Federal Reporter* has published selected court of appeals opinions in three consecutive series: *Federal Reporter*, covering 1880 to 1925; *Federal Reporter, Second Series*, 1925–1993; and *Federal Reporter, Third Series*, 1993–present. These series of publications contain over 1,400 volumes and often increase by as many as thirty volumes per year. Before 1932 the *Federal Reporter* contained both U.S. court of appeals and the U.S. district court cases. In 1932, West Publishing Company began a new publication, the *Federal Supplement*, to serve as a publication vehicle for U.S. district court opinions. A second series of the *Federal Supplement* was begun in 1998.

Citation format

> *Federal Reporter* (abbreviation reflects series number: F., F.2d, F.3d)
> **For instance:** 502 F.2d 79
> *Federal Supplement* (abbreviated as F. Supp., F. Supp.2d)
> **For instance:** 408 F. Supp. 331

Internet Sources of Court of Appeals and District Court Opinions

> Findlaw Databases of U.S. Court of Appeals by Circuit.
>> Can be browsed and searched by date, party name, or full text words. Coverage may vary but generally goes back to 1996.
>> http://www.findlaw.com/10fedgov/judicial/appeals_courts.html
> Findlaw Databases of U.S. District Courts
>> Provides links to District Courts websites, arranged by state. The availability of opinions varies by district and is frequently limited.
>> http://www.findlaw.com/10fedgov/judicial/district_courts.html

As with statutory and regulatory law, federal case law is also available electronically in the standard legal research subscription services, Lexis-Nexis Academic or Westlaw. Opinions published in the *U.S. Reports* volumes, the *Federal Reporter* series, or the *Federal Supplement* series are made available in their entirety through these services and appear with great rapidity, initially in unofficial versions, followed later by the official ones.

ADMINISTRATIVE DECISIONS

As indicated in chapters 7 and 8, federal administrative agencies are also involved in quasi-judicial activities. Some of these activities may be simply routine, such as issuing permits or licenses like those granted for broadcast stations by the Federal Communications Commission. They may also involve types of actions such as the granting of oil and gas exploration rights by the Bureau of Land Management or the Internal Revenue Service determination of tax consequences of particular activities for individual taxpayers. In other cases agency decision making may involve formal hearings of considerable complexity and length. In these situations the agency hearings may be presided over by an administrative law judge or panel and *may* result in a formal opinion that can in fact be appealed to higher authority either within the agency or in federal court.

There is a disconcerting lack of uniformity in the manner and methods agencies follow to distribute and make available the texts of their formal opinions or actions. And again, with the dynamic nature of the Internet, the publication patterns of federal agency opinions change frequently. Therefore, while some newer agency decisions are finding their way to agency websites, the texts of older materials will often be accessible only in the printed versions.

Some agencies (at this time numbering slightly more than a dozen) issue the texts of administrative decisions in bound published official reports not unlike those of the official federal court reporters. This is the practice followed by the Federal Trade Commission, which issues a publication entitled *Federal Trade Commission Decisions*. Others issue their decisions individually or in pamphlet form, an example being the *Agricultural Decisions* of the U.S. Department of Agriculture. Some, like the Federal Election Commission (FEC), distribute notices of their decisions in their Record or on their website but make the full text available only at their offices or on fee-based electronic distribution services. This practice has changed for the FEC, which now makes its *Advisory Opinions* back to 1977 available in full text on its website.

The practice of the Food and Drug Administration is to publish its orders in the *Federal Register*. Finally, there are agencies that do not officially publish decisions but rely on commercial publishers of looseleaf legal services to make the texts of these decisions available to interested parties. An example is the former Federal Home Loan Bank Board, whose General Counsel Opinions were not officially published but appeared in *Federal Banking Law Reports*, published by CCH (Commerce Clearing House).

A list of the agencies and the official or commercial sources of their adjudications, interpretations, and opinions can be found in Terry L. Swanlund, "Sources of Federal Regulatory Agency Rules, Regulations and Adjudications, Appendix D," in Morris L. Cohen, et al., *How to Find the Law* (9th ed., St. Paul: West Publishing Co.,1989), 665–674.

Internet Sources of Agency Decisions

As with the other forms of legal primary source material, the Internet now provides an important, although not complete, venue for accessing agency decisions. Most federal agencies maintain a presence on the web, and agencies that at one time released only texts of opinions and actions through Freedom of Information Act requests or in long-delayed official publications are beginning to migrate this information onto their websites. However, what is made available in the way of official decisions through the Internet varies among the agencies. One of the most comprehensive guides to the websites of federal agencies and their decisions is produced and maintained by the University of Virginia School of Law. Entitled Administrative Decisions & Other Actions, this project can be located at http://www.lib.virginia.edu/govdocs/fed_decisions_agency.html. It is an extensive compilation of annotated links to the websites of federal agencies, commissions, and boards, focusing on their decisions, opinions, actions, orders, and directives. The site can be browsed by agency name or by broad subject areas.

The major fee-based legal research subscription services, LexisNexis and WestLaw, are also excellent sources of agency decisions. The LexisNexis Academic service is geared toward general academic use, and while it is an excellent source for statutory law and federal court opinions, it does not at this time provide very much in the way of access to federal agency decisions.

A NOTE ON THE UNITED STATES CONSTITUTION

Students of administrative law often have a need to consult the United States Constitution and seek information on its history and interpretation by the courts. The text of the Constitution is provided in appendix C of this volume. Deeper analysis of the Constitution may be made by consulting the many textbooks and treatises on constitutional law that have been published. One of the most thorough of such works is produced by the Congressional Research Service of the Library of Congress. Entitled *The Constitution of the United States of America: Analysis and Interpretation*, this work not only contains the text and amendments but also offers historical background, commentary, and analysis. *It focuses on examining each provision of the Constitution and summarizing any applicable interpretation by the U.S. Supreme Court.* A new authoritative edition is published approximately every ten years and kept up to date with periodic pocket parts. The most recent complete edition was edited by Johnny H. Killian and George A. Costello. It was published in 1996 and covers relevant Supreme Court cases up to 1992. The latest pocket supplement was produced in 2000. The Congressional Research Service, American Law Division, will be finishing work on the next complete edition in June 2002, and it is expected to go to press after that.

This work is also made available, with supplements, on the Internet. This electronic version can be found at

> GPO Access—Constitution of the United States of America Analysis and Interpretation: Annotations of Cases Decided by the Supreme Court of the United States, http://www.gpoaccess.gov/constitution/index.html.

Two commercial publications also provide extended, annotated treatment of the U.S. Constitution. The *United States Code Service* (USCS) and the *United States Code Annotated* (USCA) not only publish the provisions of the United States Code but also print the text of each section of the Constitution with added historical annotations and references to relevant federal and state court decisions. An electronic version of the USCS, including the Constitution, is available to subscribers of LexisNexis Academic. WestLaw provides an analogous electronic version of the USCA.

Administrative Procedure Act

5 U.S.C. §§ 551 et seq. (Excerpts)

CHAPTER 5
Administrative Procedure

Sec.
551. Definitions.
552. Public Information; Agency Rules, Opinions, Orders, Records, and Proceedings.
552a. Records Maintained on Individuals.
552b. Open Meetings.
553. Rule Making.
554. Adjudications.
555. Ancillary Matters.
556. Hearings; Presiding Employees; Powers and Duties; Burden of Proof; Evidence; Record as Basis of Decision.
557. Initial Decisions; Conclusiveness; Review by Agency; Submissions by Parties; Contents of Decisions; Record.
558. Imposition of Sanctions; Determination of Applications for Licenses; Suspension, Revocation, and Expiration of Licenses.
559. Effect on Other Laws; Effect of Subsequent Statute.

§ 551. Definitions

For the purpose of this subchapter—

(1) "agency" means each authority of the Government of the United States, whether or not it is within or subject to review by another agency, but does not include—

    (A) the Congress;

    (B) the courts of the United States;

    (C) the governments of the territories or possessions of the United States;

    (D) the government of the District of Columbia; or except as to the requirements of section 552 of this title—

    (E) agencies composed of representatives of the parties or of representatives of organizations of the parties to the disputes determined by them;

    (F) courts martial and military commissions;

    (G) military authority exercised in the field in time of war or in occupied territory; or

    (H) functions conferred by sections 1738, 1739, 1743, and 1744 of title 12; chapter 2 of title 41; or sections 1622, 1884, 1891-1902, and former section 1641(b) (2), of title 50, appendix;

(2) "person" includes an individual, partnership, corporation, association, or public or private organization other than an agency;

(3) "party" includes a person or agency named or admitted as a party, or properly seeking and entitled as of right to be admitted as a party, in an agency proceeding, and a person or agency admitted by an agency as a party for limited purposes;

(4) "rule" means the whole or a part of an agency statement of general or particular applicability and future effect designed to implement, interpret, or prescribe law or policy or describing the organization, procedure, or practice requirements of an agency and includes the approval or prescription for the future of rates, wages, corporate or financial structures or reorganizations thereof, prices, facilities, appliances, services or allowances therefor or of valuations, costs, or accounting, or practices bearing on any of the foregoing;

(5) "rule making" means agency process for formulating, amending, or repealing a rule;

(6) "order" means the whole or a part of a final disposition, whether affirmative, negative, injunctive, or declaratory in form, of an agency in a matter other than rule making but including licensing;

(7) "adjudication" means agency process for the formulation of an order;

(8) "license" includes the whole or a part of an agency permit, certificate, approval, registration, charter, membership, statutory exemption or other form of permission;

(9) "licensing" includes agency process respecting the grant, renewal, denial, revocation, suspension, annulment, withdrawal, limitation, amendment, modification, or conditioning of a license;

(10) "sanction" includes the whole or a part of an agency—

(A) prohibition, requirement, limitation, or other condition affecting the freedom of a person;

(B) withholding of relief;

(C) imposition of penalty or fine;

(D) destruction, taking, seizure, or withholding of property;

(E) assessment of damages, reimbursement, restitution, compensation, costs, charges, or fees;

(F) requirement, revocation, or suspension of a license; or

(G) taking other compulsory or restrictive action;

(11) "relief" includes the whole or a part of an agency—

(A) grant of money, assistance, license, authority, exemption, exception, privilege, or remedy;

(B) recognition of a claim, right, immunity, privilege, exemption, or exception; or

(C) taking of other action on the application or petition of, and beneficial to, a person;

(12) "agency proceeding" means an agency process as defined by paragraphs (5), (7), and (9) of this section;

(13) "agency action" includes the whole or a part of an agency rule, order, license, sanction, relief, or the equivalent or denial thereof, or failure to act; and

(14) "ex parte communication" means an oral or written communication not on the public record with respect to which reasonable prior notice to all parties is not given, but it shall not include requests for status reports on any matter or proceeding covered by this subchapter.

§ 552. Public Information; Agency Rules, Opinions, Orders, Records, and Proceedings

(a) Each agency shall make available to the public information as follows:

(1) Each agency shall separately state and currently publish in the Federal Register for the guidance of the public—

(A) descriptions of its central and field organization and the established places at which, the employees (and in the case of a uniformed service, the members) from whom, and the methods whereby, the public may obtain information, make submittals or requests, or obtain decisions;

(B) statements of the general course and method by which its functions are channeled and determined, including the nature and requirements of all formal and informal procedures available;

(C) rules of procedure, descriptions of forms available or the places at which forms may be obtained, and instructions as to the scope and contents of all papers, reports, or examinations;

(D) substantive rules of general applicability adopted as authorized by law, and statements of general policy or interpretations of general applicability formulated and adopted by the agency; and

(E) each amendment, revision, or repeal of the foregoing. Except to the extent that a person has actual and timely notice of the terms thereof, a person may not in any manner be required to resort to, or be adversely affected by, a matter required to be published in the Federal Register and not so published. For the purpose of this paragraph, matter reasonably available to the class of persons affected thereby is deemed published in the Federal Register when incorporated by reference therein with the approval of the Director of the Federal Register.

(2) Each agency, in accordance with published rules, shall make available for public inspection and copying—

(A) final opinions, including concurring and dissenting opinions, as well as orders, made in the adjudication of cases;

(B) those statements of policy and interpretations which have been adopted by the agency and are not published in the Federal Register;

(C) administrative staff manuals and instructions to staff that affect a member of the public;

(D) copies of all records, regardless of form or format, which have been released to any person under paragraph (3) and which, because of the nature of their subject matter, the agency determines have become or are likely to become the subject of subsequent requests for substantially the same records; and

(E) a general index of the records referred to under subparagraph (D); unless the materials are promptly published and copies offered for sale. For records created on or after November 1, 1996, within one year after such date, each agency shall make such records available, including by computer telecommunications or, if computer telecommunications means have not been established by the agency, by other electronic means. To the extent required to prevent a clearly unwarranted invasion of personal privacy, an agency may delete identifying details when it makes available or publishes an opinion, statement of policy, interpretation, staff manual, instruction, or copies of records referred to in subparagraph (D). However, in each case the justification for the deletion shall be explained fully in writing, and the extent of such deletion shall be indicated on the portion of the record which is made available or published, unless including that indication would harm an interest protected by the exemption in subsection (b) under which the deletion is made. If technically feasible, the extent of the deletion shall be indicated at the place in the record where the deletion was made. Each agency shall also maintain and make available for public inspection and copying current indexes providing identifying information for the public as to any matter issued, adopted, or promulgated after July 4, 1967, and required by this paragraph to be made available or published. Each agency shall promptly publish, quarterly or more frequently, and distribute (by sale or otherwise) copies of each index or supplements thereto unless it determines by order published in the Federal Register that the publication would be unnecessary and impracticable, in which case the agency shall nonetheless provide copies of such index on request at a cost not to exceed the direct cost of duplication. Each agency shall make the index referred to in subparagraph (E) available by computer telecommunications by December 31, 1999. A final order, opinion, statement of policy, interpretation, or staff manual or instruction that affects a member of the public may be relied on, used, or cited as precedent by an agency against a party other than an agency only if—

(i) it has been indexed and either made available or published as provided by this paragraph; or

(ii) the party has actual and timely notice of the terms thereof.

(3)(A) Except with respect to the records made available under paragraphs (1) and (2) of this subsection, each agency, upon any request for records which (i) reasonably describes such records and (ii) is made in accordance with published rules stating the time, place, fees (if any), and procedures to be followed, shall make the records promptly available to any person.

(B) In making any record available to a person under this paragraph, an agency shall provide the record in any form or format requested by the person if the record is readily reproducible by the agency in that form or format. Each agency shall make reasonable efforts to maintain its records in forms or formats that are reproducible for purposes of this section.

(C) In responding under this paragraph to a request for records, an agency shall make reasonable efforts to search for the records in electronic form or format, except when such efforts would significantly interfere with the operation of the agency's automated information system.

(D) For purposes of this paragraph, the term "search" means to review, manually or by automated means, agency records for the purpose of locating those records which are responsive to a request.

(4)(A)(i) In order to carry out the provisions of this section, each agency shall promulgate regulations, pursuant to notice and receipt of public comment, specifying the schedule of fees applicable to the processing of requests under this section and establishing procedures and guidelines for determining when such fees should be waived or reduced. Such schedule shall conform to the guidelines which shall be promulgated, pursuant to notice and receipt of public comment, by the Director of the Office of Management and Budget and which shall provide for a uniform schedule of fees for all agencies.

(ii) Such agency regulations shall provide that—

(I) fees shall be limited to reasonable standard charges for document search, duplication, and review, when records are requested for commercial use;

(II) fees shall be limited to reasonable standard charges for document duplication when records are not sought for commercial use and the request is made by an educational or noncommercial scientific institution, whose purpose is scholarly or scientific research; or a representative of the news media; and

(III) for any request not described in (I) or (II), fees shall be limited to reasonable standard charges for document search and duplication.

(iii) Documents shall be furnished without any charge or at a charge reduced below the fees established under clause (ii) if disclosure of the information is in the public interest because it is likely to contribute significantly to public understanding of the operations or activities of the government and is not primarily in the commercial interest of the requester.

(iv) Fee schedules shall provide for the recovery of only the direct costs of search, duplication, or review. Review costs shall include only the direct costs incurred during the initial examination of a document for the purposes of determining whether the documents must be disclosed under this section and for the purposes of withholding any portions exempt from disclosure under this section. Review costs may not include any costs incurred in resolving issues of law or policy that may be raised in the course of processing a request under this section. No fee may be charged by any agency under this section—

(I) if the costs of routine collection and processing of the fee are likely to equal or exceed the amount of the fee; or

(II) for any request described in clause (ii) (II) or (III) of this subparagraph for the first two hours of search time or for the first one hundred pages of duplication.

(v) No agency may require advance payment of any fee unless the requester has previously failed to pay fees in a timely fashion, or the agency has determined that the fee will exceed $250.

(vi) Nothing in this subparagraph shall supersede fees chargeable under a statute specifically providing for setting the level of fees for particular types of records.

(vii) In any action by a requester regarding the waiver of fees under this section, the court shall determine the matter de novo: Provided, That the court's review of the matter shall be limited to the record before the agency.

(B) On complaint, the district court of the United States in the district in which the complainant resides, or has his principal place of business, or in which the agency records are situated, or in the District of Columbia, has jurisdiction to enjoin the agency from withholding agency records and to order the production of any agency records improperly withheld from the complainant. In such a case the court shall determine the matter de novo, and may examine the contents of such agency records in camera to determine whether such records or any part thereof shall be withheld under any of the exemptions set forth in subsection (b) of this section, and the burden is on the agency to sustain its action. In addition to any other matters to which a court accords substantial weight, a court shall accord substantial weight to an affidavit of an agency concerning the agency's determination as to technical feasibility under paragraph (2)(C) and subsection (b) and reproducibility under paragraph (3)(B).

(C) Notwithstanding any other provision of law, the defendant shall serve an answer or otherwise plead to any complaint made under this subsection within thirty days after service upon the defendant of the pleading in which such complaint is made, unless the court otherwise directs for good cause shown.

[(D) Repealed. Pub. L. 98-620, title IV, Sec. 402(2), Nov. 8,1984, 98 Stat. 3357]

(E) The court may assess against the United States reasonable attorney fees and other litigation costs reasonably incurred in any case under this section in which the complainant has substantially prevailed.

(F) Whenever the court orders the production of any agency records improperly withheld from the complainant and assesses against the United States reasonable attorney fees and other litigation costs, and the court additionally issues a written finding that the circumstances surrounding the withholding raise questions whether agency personnel acted arbitrarily or capriciously with respect to the withholding, the Special Counsel shall promptly initiate a proceeding to determine whether disciplinary action is warranted against the officer or employee who was primarily responsible for the withholding. The Special Counsel, after investigation and consideration of the evidence submitted, shall submit his findings and recommendations to the administrative authority of the agency concerned and shall send copies of the findings and recommendations to the officer or employee or his representative. The administrative authority shall take the corrective action that the Special Counsel recommends.

(G) In the event of noncompliance with the order of the court, the district court may punish for contempt the responsible employee, and in the case of a uniformed service, the responsible member.

(5) Each agency having more than one member shall maintain and make available for public inspection a record of the final votes of each member in every agency proceeding.

(6)(A) Each agency, upon any request for records made under paragraph (1), (2), or (3) of this subsection, shall—

    (i) determine within 20 days (excepting Saturdays, Sundays, and legal public holidays) after the receipt of any such request whether to comply with such request and shall immediately notify the person making such request of such determination and the reasons therefor, and of the right of such person to appeal to the head of the agency any adverse determination; and

(ii) make a determination with respect to any appeal within twenty days (excepting Saturdays, Sundays, and legal public holidays) after the receipt of such appeal. If on appeal the denial of the request for records is in whole or in part upheld, the agency shall notify the person making such request of the provisions for judicial review of that determination under paragraph (4) of this subsection.

(B)(i) In unusual circumstances as specified in this subparagraph, the time limits prescribed in either clause (i) or clause (ii) of subparagraph (A) may be extended by written notice to the person making such request setting forth the unusual circumstances for such extension and the date on which a determination is expected to be dispatched. No such notice shall specify a date that would result in an extension for more than ten working days, except as provided in clause (ii) of this subparagraph.

(ii) With respect to a request for which a written notice under clause (i) extends the time limits prescribed under clause (i) of subparagraph (A), the agency shall notify the person making the request if the request cannot be processed within the time limit specified in that clause and shall provide the person an opportunity to limit the scope of the request so that it may be processed within that time limit or an opportunity to arrange with the agency an alternative time frame for processing the request or a modified request. Refusal by the person to reasonably modify the request or arrange such an alternative time frame shall be considered as a factor in determining whether exceptional circumstances exist for purposes of subparagraph (C).

(iii) As used in this subparagraph, "unusual circumstances" means, but only to the extent reasonably necessary to the proper processing of the particular requests—

(I) the need to search for and collect the requested records from field facilities or other establishments that are separate from the office processing the request;

(II) the need to search for, collect, and appropriately examine a voluminous amount of separate and distinct records which are demanded in a single request; or

(III) the need for consultation, which shall be conducted with all practicable speed, with another agency having a substantial interest in the determination of the request or among two or more components of the agency having substantial subject-matter interest therein.

(iv) Each agency may promulgate regulations, pursuant to notice and receipt of public comment, providing for the aggregation of certain requests by the same requestor, or by a group of requestors acting in concert, if the agency reasonably believes that such requests actually constitute a single request, which would otherwise satisfy the unusual circumstances specified in this subparagraph, and the requests involve clearly related matters. Multiple requests involving unrelated matters shall not be aggregated.

(C)(i) Any person making a request to any agency for records under paragraph (1), (2), or (3) of this subsection shall be deemed to have exhausted his administrative remedies with respect to such request if the agency fails to comply with the applicable time limit provisions of this paragraph. If the Government can show exceptional circumstances exist and that the agency is exercising due diligence in responding to the request, the court may retain jurisdiction and allow the agency additional time to complete its review of the records. Upon any determination by an agency to comply with a request for records, the records shall be made promptly available to such person making such request. Any notification of denial of any request for records under this subsection shall set forth the names and titles or positions of each person responsible for the denial of such request.

(ii) For purposes of this subparagraph, the term "exceptional circumstances" does not include a delay that results from a predictable agency workload of requests under this section, unless the agency demonstrates reasonable progress in reducing its backlog of pending requests.

(iii) Refusal by a person to reasonably modify the scope of a request or arrange an alternative time frame for processing a request (or a modified request) under clause (ii) after being given an opportunity to do so by the agency to whom the person made the request shall be considered as a factor in determining whether exceptional circumstances exist for purposes of this subparagraph.

(D)(i) Each agency may promulgate regulations, pursuant to notice and receipt of public comment, providing for multitrack processing of requests for records based on the amount of work or time (or both) involved in processing requests.

(ii) Regulations under this subparagraph may provide a person making a request that does not qualify for the fastest multitrack processing an opportunity to limit the scope of the request in order to qualify for faster processing.

(iii) This subparagraph shall not be considered to affect the requirement under subparagraph (C) to exercise due diligence.

(E)(i) Each agency shall promulgate regulations, pursuant to notice and receipt of public comment, providing for expedited processing of requests for records—

(I) in cases in which the person requesting the records demonstrates a compelling need; and

(II) in other cases determined by the agency.

(ii) Notwithstanding clause (i), regulations under this subparagraph must ensure—

(I) that a determination of whether to provide expedited processing shall be made, and notice of the determination shall be provided to the person making the request, within 10 days after the date of the request; and

(II) expeditious consideration of administrative appeals of such determinations of whether to provide expedited processing.

(iii) An agency shall process as soon as practicable any request for records to which the agency has granted expedited processing under this subparagraph. Agency action to deny or affirm denial of a request for expedited processing pursuant to this subparagraph, and failure by an agency to respond in a timely manner to such a request shall be subject to judicial review under paragraph (4), except that the judicial review shall be based on the record before the agency at the time of the determination.

(iv) A district court of the United States shall not have jurisdiction to review an agency denial of expedited processing of a request for records after the agency has provided a complete response to the request.

(v) For purposes of this subparagraph, the term "compelling need" means—

(I) that a failure to obtain requested records on an expedited basis under this paragraph could reasonably be expected to pose an imminent threat to the life or physical safety of an individual; or

(II) with respect to a request made by a person primarily engaged in disseminating information, urgency to inform the public concerning actual or alleged Federal Government activity.

(vi) A demonstration of a compelling need by a person making a request for expedited processing shall be made by a statement certified by such person to be true and correct to the best of such person's knowledge and belief.

(F) In denying a request for records, in whole or in part, an agency shall make a reasonable effort to estimate the volume of any requested matter the provision of which is denied, and shall provide any such estimate to the person making the request, unless providing such estimate would harm an interest protected by the exemption in subsection (b) pursuant to which the denial is made.

(b) This section does not apply to matters that are—

(1)(A) specifically authorized under criteria established by an Executive order to be kept secret in the interest of national defense or foreign policy and (B) are in fact properly classified pursuant to such Executive order;

(2) related solely to the internal personnel rules and practices of an agency;

(3) specifically exempted from disclosure by statute (other than section 552b of this title), provided that such statute (A) requires that the matters be withheld from the public in such a manner as to leave no discretion on the issue, or (B) establishes particular criteria for withholding or refers to particular types of matters to be withheld;

(4) trade secrets and commercial or financial information obtained from a person and privileged or confidential;

(5) inter-agency or intra-agency memorandums or letters which would not be available by law to a party other than an agency in litigation with the agency;

(6) personnel and medical files and similar files the disclosure of which would constitute a clearly unwarranted invasion of personal privacy;

(7) records or information compiled for law enforcement purposes, but only to the extent that the production of such law enforcement records or information (A) could reasonably be expected to interfere with enforcement proceedings, (B) would deprive a person of a right to a fair trial or an impartial adjudication, (C) could reasonably be expected to constitute an unwarranted invasion of personal privacy, (D) could reasonably be expected to disclose the identity of a confidential source, including a State, local, or foreign agency or authority or any private institution which furnished information on a confidential basis, and, in the case of a record or information compiled by criminal law enforcement authority in the course of a criminal investigation or by an agency conducting a lawful national security intelligence investigation, information furnished by a confidential source, (E) would disclose techniques and procedures for law enforcement investigations or prosecutions, or would disclose guidelines for law enforcement investigations or prosecutions if such disclosure could reasonably be expected to risk circumvention of the law, or (F) could reasonably be expected to endanger the life or physical safety of any individual;

(8) contained in or related to examination, operating, or condition reports prepared by, on behalf of, or for the use of an agency responsible for the regulation or supervision of financial institutions; or

(9) geological and geophysical information and data, including maps, concerning wells.

Any reasonably segregable portion of a record shall be provided to any person requesting such record after deletion of the portions which are exempt under this subsection. The amount of information deleted shall be indicated on the released portion of the record, unless including that indication would harm an interest protected by the exemption in this subsection under which the deletion is made. If technically feasible, the amount of the information deleted shall be indicated at the place in the record where such deletion is made.

(c) (1) Whenever a request is made which involves access to records described in subsection (b)(7)(A) and—

(A) the investigation or proceeding involves a possible violation of criminal law; and

(B) there is reason to believe that (i) the subject of the investigation or proceeding is not aware of its pendency, and (ii) disclosure of the existence of the records could reasonably be expected to interfere with enforcement proceedings, the agency may, during only such time as that circumstance continues, treat the records as not subject to the requirements of this section.

(2) Whenever informant records maintained by a criminal law enforcement agency under an informant's name or personal identifier are requested by a third party according to the informant's name or personal identifier, the agency may treat the records as not subject to the requirements of this section unless the informant's status as an informant has been officially confirmed.

(3) Whenever a request is made which involves access to records maintained by the Federal Bureau of Investigation pertaining to foreign intelligence or counterintelligence, or international terrorism, and the existence of the records is classified information as provided in subsection (b)(1), the Bureau may, as long as the existence of the records remains classified information, treat the records as not subject to the requirements of this section.

(d) This section does not authorize withholding of information or limit the availability of records to the public, except as specifically stated in this section. This section is not authority to withhold information from Congress.

(e) (1) On or before February 1 of each year, each agency shall submit to the Attorney General of the United States a report which shall cover the preceding fiscal year and which shall include—

(A) the number of determinations made by the agency not to comply with requests for records made to such agency under subsection (a) and the reasons for each such determination;

(B)(i) the number of appeals made by persons under subsection (a)(6), the result of such appeals, and the reason for the action upon each appeal that results in a denial of information; and

(ii) a complete list of all statutes that the agency relies upon to authorize the agency to withhold information under subsection (b)(3), a description of whether a court has upheld the decision of the agency to withhold information under each such statute, and a concise description of the scope of any information withheld;

(C) the number of requests for records pending before the agency as of September 30 of the preceding year, and the median number of days that such requests had been pending before the agency as of that date;

(D) the number of requests for records received by the agency and the number of requests which the agency processed;

(E) the median number of days taken by the agency to process different types of requests;

(F) the total amount of fees collected by the agency for processing requests; and

(G) the number of full-time staff of the agency devoted to processing requests for records under this section, and the total amount expended by the agency for processing such requests.

(2) Each agency shall make each such report available to the public including by computer telecommunications, or if computer telecommunications means have not been established by the agency, by other electronic means.

(3) The Attorney General of the United States shall make each report which has been made available by electronic means available at a single electronic access point. The Attorney General of the United States shall notify the Chairman and ranking minority member of the Committee on Government Reform and Oversight of the House of Representatives and the Chairman and ranking minority member of the Committees on Governmental Affairs and the Judiciary of the Senate, no later than April 1 of the year in which each such report is issued, that such reports are available by electronic means.

(4) The Attorney General of the United States, in consultation with the Director of the Office of Management and Budget, shall develop reporting and performance guidelines in connection with reports required by this subsection by October 1, 1997, and may establish additional requirements for such reports as the Attorney General determines may be useful.

(5) The Attorney General of the United States shall submit an annual report on or before April 1 of each calendar year which shall include for the prior calendar year a listing of the number of cases arising under this section, the exemption involved in each case, the disposition of such case, and the cost, fees, and penalties assessed under subparagraphs (E), (F), and (G) of subsection (a)(4). Such report shall also include a descrip-

tion of the efforts undertaken by the Department of Justice to encourage agency compliance with this section.

(f)   For purposes of this section, the term—

(1) "agency" as defined in section 551(1) of this title includes any executive department, military department, Government corporation, Government controlled corporation, or other establishment in the executive branch of the Government (including the Executive Office of the President), or any independent regulatory agency; and

(2) "record" and any other term used in this section in reference to information includes any information that would be an agency record subject to the requirements of this section when maintained by an agency in any format, including an electronic format.

(g) The head of each agency shall prepare and make publicly available upon request, reference material or a guide for requesting records or information from the agency, subject to the exemptions in subsection (b), including—

(1) an index of all major information systems of the agency;

(2) a description of major information and record locator systems maintained by the agency; and

(3) a handbook for obtaining various types and categories of public information from the agency pursuant to chapter 35 of title 44, and under this section.

§ 552a.   Records Maintained on Individuals

(a) **Definitions**. For purposes of this section—

(1) the term "agency" means agency as defined in section 552[f](e);

(2) the term "individual" means a citizen of the United States or an alien lawfully admitted for permanent residence;

(3) the term "maintain" includes maintain, collect, use, or disseminate;

(4) the term "record" means any item, collection, or grouping of information about an individual that is maintained by an agency, including, but not limited to, his education, financial transactions, medical history, and criminal or employment history and that contains his name, or the identifying number, symbol, or other identifying particular assigned to the individual, such as a finger or voice print or a photograph;

(5) the term "system of records" means a group of any records under the control of any agency from which information is retrieved by the name of the individual or by some identifying number, symbol, or other identifying particular assigned to the individual;

(6) the term "statistical record" means a record in a system of records maintained for statistical research or reporting purposes only and not

used in whole or in part in making any determination about an identifiable individual, except as provided by section 8 of title 13;

(7) the term "routine use" means, with respect to the disclosure of a record, the use of such record for a purpose which is compatible with the purpose for which it was collected; and

(8) the term "matching program"—

(A) means any computerized comparison of—

(i) two or more automated systems of records or a system of records with non–Federal records for the purpose of—

(I) establishing or verifying the eligibility of, or continuing compliance with statutory and regulatory requirements by, applicants for, recipients or beneficiaries of, participants in, or providers of services with respect to, cash or in-kind assistance or payments under Federal benefit programs, or

(II) recouping payments or delinquent debts under such Federal benefit programs, or

(ii) two or more automated Federal personnel or payroll systems of records or a system of Federal personnel or payroll records with non-Federal records,

(B) but does not include—

(i) matches performed to produce aggregate statistical data without any personal identifiers;

(ii) matches performed to support any research or statistical project, the specific data of which may not be used to make decisions concerning the rights, benefits, or privileges of specific individuals;

(iii) matches performed, by an agency (or component thereof) which performs as its principal function any activity pertaining to the enforcement of criminal laws, subsequent to the initiation of a specific criminal or civil law enforcement investigation of a named person or persons for the purpose of gathering evidence against such person or persons;

(iv) matches of tax information (I) pursuant to section 6103(d) of the Internal Revenue Code of 1986, (II) for purposes of tax administration as defined in section 6103(b)(4) of such Code, (III) for the purpose of intercepting a tax refund due an individual under authority granted by section 464 or 1137 of the Social Security Act; or (IV) for the purpose of intercepting a tax refund due an individual under any other tax refund intercept program authorized by statute which has been determined by the Director of the Office of Management and Budget to contain verification, notice, and hearing requirements that are substantially similar to the procedures in section 1137 of the Social Security Act;

(v) matches—

(I) using records predominantly relating to Federal personnel, that are performed for routine administrative purposes (subject to guidance provided by the Director of the Office of Management and Budget pursuant to subsection (v)); or

(II) conducted by an agency using only records from systems of records maintained by that agency; if the purpose of the match is not to take any adverse financial, personnel, disciplinary, or other adverse action against Federal personnel; or

(vi) matches performed for foreign counterintelligence purposes or to produce background checks for security clearances of Federal personnel or Federal contractor personnel;

(vii) matches performed incident to a levy described in section 6103 (k) (8) of the Internal Revenue Code of 1986; or

(viii) matches performed pursuant to section 202 (x)(3) or 1611 (e)(1) of the Social Security Act 942 U.S.C. 402 (x)(3), 1382 (e)(1);

(9) the term "recipient agency" means any agency, or contractor thereof, receiving records contained in a system of records from a source agency for use in a matching program;

(10) the term "non-Federal agency" means any State or local government, or agency thereof, which receives records contained in a system of records from a source agency for use in a matching program;

(11) the term "source agency" means any agency which discloses records contained in a system of records to be used in a matching program, or any State or local government, or agency thereof, which discloses records to be used in a matching program;

(12) the term "Federal benefit program" means any program administered or funded by the Federal Government, or by any agent or State on behalf of the Federal Government, providing cash or in–kind assistance in the form of payments, grants, loans, or loan guarantees to individuals; and

(13) the term "Federal personnel" means officers and employees of the Government of the United States, members of the uniformed services (including members of the Reserve Components), individuals entitled to receive immediate or deferred retirement benefits under any retirement program of the Government of the United States (including survivor benefits).

(b) **Conditions of Disclosure**. No agency shall disclose any record which is contained in a system of records by any means of communication to any person, or to another agency, except pursuant to a written request by, or with the prior written consent of, the individual to whom the record pertains, unless disclosure of the record would be—

(1) to those officers and employees of the agency which maintains the record who have a need for the record in the performance of their duties;

(2) required under section 552 of this title;

(3) for a routine use as defined in subsection (a)(7) of this section and described under subsection (e)(4)(D) of this section;

(4) to the Bureau of the Census for purposes of planning or carrying out a census or survey or related activity pursuant to the provisions of title 13;

(5) to a recipient who has provided the agency with advance adequate written assurance that the record will be used solely as a statistical research or reporting record, and the record is to be transferred in a form that is not individually identifiable;

(6) to the National Archives and Records Administration as a record which has sufficient historical or other value to warrant its continued preservation by the United States Government, or for evaluation by the Archivist of the United States or the designee of the Archivist to determine whether the record has such value;

(7) to another agency or to an instrumentality of any governmental jurisdiction within or under the control of the United States for a civil or criminal law enforcement activity if the activity is authorized by law, and if the head of the agency or instrumentality has made a written request to the agency which maintains the record specifying the particular portion desired and the law enforcement activity for which the record is sought;

(8) to a person pursuant to a showing of compelling circumstances affecting the health or safety of an individual if upon such disclosure notification is transmitted to the last known address of such individual;

(9) to either House of Congress, or, to the extent of matter within its jurisdiction, any committee or subcommittee thereof, any joint committee of Congress or subcommittee of any such joint committee;

(10) to the Comptroller General, or any of his authorized representatives, in the course of the performance of the duties of the General Accounting Office;

(11) pursuant to the order of a court of competent jurisdiction; or

(12) to a consumer reporting agency in accordance with section 3711(f) of title 31.

(c) **Accounting of Certain Disclosures**. Each agency, with respect to each system of records under its control, shall—

(1) except for disclosures made under subsections (b)(1) or (b)(2) of this section, keep an accurate accounting of—

(A) the date, nature, and purpose of each disclosure of a record to any person or to another agency made under subsection (b) of this section; and

(B) the name and address of the person or agency to whom the disclosure is made;

(2) retain the accounting made under paragraph (1) of this subsection for at least five years or the life of the record, whichever is longer, after the disclosure for which the accounting is made;

(3) except for disclosures made under subsection (b)(7) of this section, make the accounting made under paragraph (1) of this subsection available to the individual named in the record at his request; and

(4) inform any person or other agency about any correction or notation of dispute made by the agency in accordance with subsection (d) of this section of any record that has been disclosed to the person or agency if an accounting of the disclosure was made.

(d) **Access to Records**. Each agency that maintains a system of records shall—

(1) upon request by any individual to gain access to his record or to any information pertaining to him which is contained in the system, permit him and upon his request, a person of his own choosing to accompany him, to review the record and have a copy made of all or any portion thereof in a form comprehensible to him, except that the agency may require the individual to furnish a written statement authorizing discussion of that individual's record in the accompanying person's presence;

(2) permit the individual to request amendment of a record pertaining to him and—

(A) not later than 10 days (excluding Saturdays, Sundays, and legal public holidays) after the date of receipt of such request, acknowledge in writing such receipt; and

(B) promptly, either—

(i) make any correction of any portion thereof which the individual believes is not accurate, relevant, timely, or complete; or

(ii) inform the individual of its refusal to amend the record in accordance with his request, the reason for the refusal, the procedures established by the agency for the individual to request a review of that refusal by the head of the agency or an officer designated by the head of the agency, and the name and business address of that official;

(3) permit the individual who disagrees with the refusal of the agency to amend his record to request a review of such refusal, and not later than 30 days (excluding Saturdays, Sundays, and legal public holidays) from the date on which the individual requests such review, complete such review and make a final determination unless, for good cause

shown, the head of the agency extends such 30-day period; and if, after his review, the reviewing official also refuses to amend the record in accordance with the request, permit the individual to file with the agency a concise statement setting forth the reasons for his disagreement with the refusal of the agency, and notify the individual of the provisions for judicial review of the reviewing official's determination under subsection (g)(1)(A) of this section;

(4) in any disclosure, containing information about which the individual has filed a statement of disagreement, occurring after the filing of the statement under paragraph (3) of this subsection, clearly note any portion of the record which is disputed and provide copies of the statement and, if the agency deems it appropriate, copies of a concise statement of the reasons of the agency for not making the amendments requested, to persons or other agencies to whom the disputed record has been disclosed; and

(5) nothing in this section shall allow an individual access to any information compiled in reasonable anticipation of a civil action or proceeding.

(e) **Agency Requirements**. Each agency that maintains a system of records shall—

(1) maintain in its records only such information about an individual as is relevant and necessary to accomplish a purpose of the agency required to be accomplished by statute or by executive order of the President;

(2) collect information to the greatest extent practicable directly from the subject individual when the information may result in adverse determinations about an individual's rights, benefits, and privileges under Federal programs;

(3) inform each individual whom it asks to supply information, on the form which it uses to collect the information or on a separate form that can be retained by the individual—

(A) the authority (whether granted by statute, or by executive order of the President) which authorizes the solicitation of the information and whether disclosure of such information is mandatory or voluntary;

(B) the principal purpose or purposes for which the information is intended to be used;

(C) the routine uses which may be made of the information, as published pursuant to paragraph (4)(D) of this subsection; and

(D) the effects on him, if any, of not providing all or any part of the requested information;

(4) subject to the provisions of paragraph (11) of this subsection, publish in the Federal Register upon establishment or revision a notice of

the existence and character of the system of records, which notice shall include—

 (A) the name and location of the system;

 (B) the categories of individuals on whom records are maintained in the system;

 (C) the categories of records maintained in the system;

 (D) each routine use of the records contained in the system, including the categories of users and the purpose of such use;

 (E) the policies and practices of the agency regarding storage, retrievability, access controls, retention, and disposal of the records;

 (F) the title and business address of the agency official who is responsible for the system of records;

 (G) the agency procedures whereby an individual can be notified at his request if the system of records contains a record pertaining to him;

 (H) the agency procedures whereby an individual can be notified at his request how he can gain access to any record pertaining to him contained in the system of records, and how he can contest its content; and

 (I) the categories of sources of records in the system;

(5) maintain all records which are used by the agency in making any determination about any individual with such accuracy, relevance, timeliness, and completeness as is reasonably necessary to assure fairness to the individual in the determination;

(6) prior to disseminating any record about an individual to any person other than an agency, unless the dissemination is made pursuant to subsection (b)(2) of this section, make reasonable efforts to assure that such records are accurate, complete, timely, and relevant for agency purposes;

(7) maintain no record describing how any individual exercises rights guaranteed by the First Amendment unless expressly authorized by statute or by the individual about whom the record is maintained or unless pertinent to and within the scope of an authorized law enforcement activity;

(8) make reasonable efforts to serve notice on an individual when any record on such individual is made available to any person under compulsory legal process when such process becomes a matter of public record;

(9) establish rules of conduct for persons involved in the design, development, operation, or maintenance of any system of records, or in maintaining any record, and instruct each such person with respect to such rules and the requirements of this section, including any other rules

and procedures adopted pursuant to this section and the penalties for noncompliance;

(10) establish appropriate administrative, technical, and physical safeguards to insure the security and confidentiality of records and to protect against any anticipated threats or hazards to their security or integrity which could result in substantial harm, embarrassment, inconvenience, or unfairness to any individual on whom information is maintained;

(11) at least 30 days prior to publication of information under paragraph (4)(D) of this subsection, publish in the Federal Register notice of any new use or intended use of the information in the system, and provide an opportunity for interested persons to submit written data, views, or arguments to the agency; and

(12) if such agency is a recipient agency or a source agency in a matching program with a non–Federal agency, with respect to any establishment or revision of a matching program, at least 30 days prior to conducting such program, publish in the Federal Register notice of such establishment or revision.

(f) **Agency Rules**. In order to carry out the provisions of this section, each agency that maintains a system of records shall promulgate rules, in accordance with the requirements (including general notice) of section 553 of this title, which shall—

(1) establish procedures whereby an individual can be notified in response to his request if any system of records named by the individual contains a record pertaining to him;

(2) define reasonable times, places, and requirements for identifying an individual who requests his record or information pertaining to him before the agency shall make the record or information available to the individual;

(3) establish procedures for the disclosure to an individual upon his request of his record or information pertaining to him, including special procedure, if deemed necessary, for the disclosure to an individual of medical records, including psychological records, pertaining to him;

(4) establish procedures for reviewing a request from an individual concerning the amendment of any record or information pertaining to the individual, for making a determination on the request, for an appeal within the agency of an initial adverse agency determination, and for whatever additional means may be necessary for each individual to be able to exercise fully his rights under this section; and

(5) establish fees to be charged, if any, to any individual for making copies of his record, excluding the cost of any search for and review of the record. The Office of the Federal Register shall biennially compile and publish the rules promulgated under this subsection and agency no-

tices published under subsection (e)(4) of this section in a form available to the public at low cost.

(g) **Civil Remedies**.

(1) Whenever any agency—

(A) makes a determination under subsection (d)(3) of this section not to amend an individual's record in accordance with his request, or fails to make such review in conformity with that subsection;

(B) refuses to comply with an individual request under subsection (d)(1) of this section;

(C) fails to maintain any record concerning any individual with such accuracy, relevance, timeliness, and completeness as is necessary to assure fairness in any determination relating to the qualifications, character, rights, or opportunities of, or benefits to the individual that may be made on the basis of such record, and consequently a determination is made which is adverse to the individual; or

(D) fails to comply with any other provision of this section, or any rule promulgated thereunder, in such a way as to have an adverse effect on an individual, the individual may bring a civil action against the agency, and the district courts of the United States shall have jurisdiction in the matters under the provisions of this subsection.

(2)(A) In any suit brought under the provisions of subsection (g)(1)(A) of this section, the court may order the agency to amend the individual's record in accordance with his request or in such other way as the court may direct. In such a case the court shall determine the matter de novo.

(B) The court may assess against the United States reasonable attorney fees and other litigation costs reasonably incurred in any case under this paragraph in which the complainant has substantially prevailed.

(3)(A) In any suit brought under the provisions of subsection (g)(1)(B) of this section, the court may enjoin the agency from withholding the records and order the production to the complainant of any agency records improperly withheld from him. In such a case the court shall determine the matter de novo, and may examine the contents of any agency records in camera to determine whether the records or any portion thereof may be withheld under any of the exemptions set forth in subsection (k) of this section, and the burden is on the agency to sustain its action.

(B) The court may assess against the United States reasonable attorney fees and other litigation costs reasonably incurred in any case under this paragraph in which the complainant has substantially prevailed.

(4) In any suit brought under the provisions of subsection (g)(1)(C) or (D) of this section in which the court determines that the agency acted

in a manner which was intentional or willful, the United States shall be liable to the individual in an amount equal to the sum of—

(A) actual damages sustained by the individual as a result of the refusal or failure, but in no case shall a person entitled to recovery receive less than the sum of $1,000; and

(B) the costs of the action together with reasonable attorney fees as determined by the court.

(5) An action to enforce any liability created under this section may be brought in the district court of the United States in the district in which the complainant resides, or has his principal place of business, or in which the agency records are situated, or in the District of Columbia, without regard to the amount in controversy, within two years from the date on which the cause of action arises, except that where an agency has materially and willfully misrepresented any information required under this section to be disclosed to an individual and the information so misrepresented is material to establishment of the liability of the agency to the individual under this section, the action may be brought at any time within two years after discovery by the individual of the misrepresentation. Nothing in this section shall be construed to authorize any civil action by reason of any injury sustained as the result of a disclosure of a record prior to September 27, 1975.

(h) **Rights of Legal Guardians**. For the purposes of this section, the parent of any minor, or the legal guardian of any individual who has been declared to be incompetent due to physical or mental incapacity or age by a court of competent jurisdiction, may act on behalf of the individual.

(i) **Criminal Penalties**.

(1) Any officer or employee of an agency, who by virtue of his employment or official position, has possession of, or access to, agency records which contain individually identifiable information the disclosure of which is prohibited by this section or by rules or regulations established thereunder, and who knowing that disclosure of the specific material is so prohibited, willfully discloses the material in any manner to any person or agency not entitled to receive it, shall be guilty of a misdemeanor and fined not more than $5,000.

(2) Any officer or employee of any agency who willfully maintains a system of records without meeting the notice requirements of subsection (e)(4) of this section shall be guilty of a misdemeanor and fined not more than $5,000.

(3) Any person who knowingly and willfully requests or obtains any record concerning an individual from an agency under false pretenses shall be guilty of a misdemeanor and fined not more than $5,000.

(j) **General Exemptions**. The head of any agency may promulgate rules, in accordance with the requirements (including general notice) of sections 553(b)(1), (2), and (3), (c), and (e) of this title, to exempt any system of records within the agency from any part of this section except subsections (b), (c)(1) and (2), (e)(4)(A) through (F), (e)(6), (7), (9), (10), and (11), and (i) if the system of records is—

(1) maintained by the Central Intelligence Agency; or

(2) maintained by an agency or component thereof which performs as its principal function any activity pertaining to the enforcement of criminal laws, including police efforts to prevent, control, or reduce crime or to apprehend criminals, and the activities of prosecutors, courts, correctional, probation, pardon, or parole authorities, and which consists of (A) information compiled for the purpose of identifying individual criminal offenders and alleged offenders and consisting only of identifying data and notations of arrests, the nature and disposition of criminal charges, sentencing, confinement, release, and parole and probation status; (B) information compiled for the purpose of a criminal investigation, including reports of informants and investigators, and associated with an identifiable individual; or (C) reports identifiable to an individual compiled at any stage of the process of enforcement of the criminal laws from arrest or indictment through release from supervision. At the time rules are adopted under this subsection, the agency shall include in the statement required under section 553(c) of this title, the reasons why the system of records is to be exempted from a provision of this section.

(k) **Specific Exemptions**. The head of any agency may promulgate rules, in accordance with the requirements (including general notice) of sections 553(b)(1), (2), and (3), (c), and (e) of this title, to exempt any system of records within the agency from subsections (c)(3), (d), (e)(1), (e)(4)(G), (H), and (I) and (f) of this section if the system of records is—

(1) subject to the provisions of section 552(b)(1) of this title;

(2) investigatory material compiled for law enforcement purposes, other than material within the scope of subsection (j)(2) of this section: Provided, however, That if any individual is denied any right, privilege, or benefit that he would otherwise be entitled by Federal law, or for which he would otherwise be eligible, as a result of the maintenance of such material, such material shall be provided to such individual, except to the extent that the disclosure of such material would reveal the identity of a source who furnished information to the Government under an express promise that the identity of the source would be held in confidence, or, prior to the effective date of this section, under an implied promise that the identity of the source would be held in confidence;

(3) maintained in connection with providing protective services to the President of the United States or other individuals pursuant to section 3056 of title 18;

(4) required by statute to be maintained and used solely as statistical records;

(5) investigatory material compiled solely for the purpose of determining suitability, eligibility, or qualifications for Federal civilian em-

ployment, military service, Federal contracts, or access to classified information, but only to the extent that the disclosure of such material would reveal the identity of a source who furnished information to the Government under an express promise that the identity of the source would be held in confidence, or, prior to the effective date of this section, under an implied promise that the identity of the source would be held in confidence;

(6) testing or examination material used solely to determine individual qualifications for appointment or promotion in the Federal service the disclosure of which would compromise the objectivity or fairness of the testing or examination process; or

(7) evaluation material used to determine potential for promotion in the armed services, but only to the extent that the disclosure of such material would reveal the identity of a source who furnished information to the Government under an express promise that the identity of the source would be held in confidence, or, prior to the effective date of this section, under an implied promise that the identity of the source would be held in confidence. At the time rules are adopted under this subsection, the agency shall include in the statement required under section 553(c) of this title, the reasons why the system of records is to be exempted from a provision of this section.

(l) **Archival Records**.

(1) Each agency record which is accepted by the Archivist of the United States for storage, processing, and servicing in accordance with section 3103 of title 44 shall, for the purposes of this section, be considered to be maintained by the agency which deposited the record and shall be subject to the provisions of this section. The Archivist of the United States shall not disclose the record except to the agency which maintains the record, or under rules established by that agency which are not inconsistent with the provisions of this section.

(2) Each agency record pertaining to an identifiable individual which was transferred to the National Archives of the United States as a record which has sufficient historical or other value to warrant its continued preservation by the United States Government, prior to the effective date of this section, shall, for the purposes of this section, be considered to be maintained by the National Archives and shall not be subject to the provisions of this section, except that a statement generally describing such records (modeled after the requirements relating to records subject to subsections (e)(4)(A) through (G) of this section) shall be published in the Federal Register.

(3) Each agency record pertaining to an identifiable individual which is transferred to the National Archives of the United States as a record which has sufficient historical or other value to warrant its continued preservation by the United States Government, on or after the effective date of this section, shall, for the purposes of this section, be considered to be maintained by the National Archives and shall be exempt from the

requirements of this section except subsections (e)(4)(A) through (G) and (e)(9) of this section.

(m) **Government Contractors**.

(1) When an agency provides by a contract for the operation by or on behalf of the agency of a system of records to accomplish an agency function, the agency shall, consistent with its authority, cause the requirements of this section to be applied to such system. For purposes of subsection (i) of this section any such contractor and any employee of such contractor, if such contract is agreed to on or after the effective date of this section, shall be considered to be an employee of an agency.

(2) A consumer reporting agency to which a record is disclosed under section 3711(f) of title 31 shall not be considered a contractor for the purposes of this section.

(n) **Mailing Lists**. An individual's name and address may not be sold or rented by an agency unless such action is specifically authorized by law. This provision shall not be construed to require the withholding of names and addresses otherwise permitted to be made public.

(o) **Matching Agreements**.

(1) No record which is contained in a system of records may be disclosed to a recipient agency or non-Federal agency for use in a computer matching program except pursuant to a written agreement between the source agency and the recipient agency or non-Federal agency specifying—

(A) the purpose and legal authority for conducting the program;

(B) the justification for the program and the anticipated results, including a specific estimate of any savings;

(C) a description of the records that will be matched, including each data element that will be used, the approximate number of records that will be matched, and the projected starting and completion dates of the matching program;

(D) procedures for providing individualized notice at the time of application, and notice periodically thereafter as directed by the Data Integrity Board of such agency (subject to guidance provided by the Director of the Office of Management and Budget pursuant to subsection (v)), to—

(i) applicants for and recipients of financial assistance or payments under Federal benefit programs, and

(ii) applicants for and holders of positions as Federal personnel, that any information provided by such applicants, recipients, holders, and individuals may be subject to verification through matching programs;

(E) procedures for verifying information produced in such matching program as required by subsection (p);

(F) procedures for the retention and timely destruction of identifiable records created by a recipient agency or non-Federal agency in such matching program;

(G) procedures for ensuring the administrative, technical, and physical security of the records matched and the results of such programs;

(H) prohibitions on duplication and redisclosure of records provided by the source agency within or outside the recipient agency or the non-Federal agency, except where required by law or essential to the conduct of the matching program;

(I) procedures governing the use by a recipient agency or non-Federal agency of records provided in a matching program by a source agency, including procedures governing return of the records to the source agency or destruction of records used in such program;

(J) information on assessments that have been made on the accuracy of the records that will be used in such matching program; and

(K) that the Comptroller General may have access to all records of a recipient agency or a non-Federal agency that the Comptroller General deems necessary in order to monitor or verify compliance with the agreement.

(2)(A) A copy of each agreement entered into pursuant to paragraph (1) shall—

(i) be transmitted to the Committee on Governmental Affairs of the Senate and the Committee on Government Operations of the House of Representatives; and

(ii) be available upon request to the public.

(B) No such agreement shall be effective until 30 days after the date on which such a copy is transmitted pursuant to subparagraph (A)(i).

(C) Such an agreement shall remain in effect only for such period, not to exceed 18 months, as the Data Integrity Board of the agency determines is appropriate in light of the purposes, and length of time necessary for the conduct, of the matching program.

(D) Within 3 months prior to the expiration of such an agreement pursuant to subparagraph (C), the Data Integrity Board of the agency may, without additional review, renew the matching agreement for a current, ongoing matching program for not more than one additional year if—

(i) such program will be conducted without any change; and

(ii) each party to the agreement certifies to the Board in writing that the program has been conducted in compliance with the agreement.

(p) **Verification and Opportunity to Contest Findings**.

(1) In order to protect any individual whose records are used in a matching program, no recipient agency, non-Federal agency, or source agency may suspend, terminate, reduce, or make a final denial of any financial assistance or payment under a Federal benefit program to such individual, or take other adverse action against such individual, as a result of information produced by such matching program, until—

(A)(i) the agency has independently verified the information; or

(ii) the Data Integrity Board of the agency, or in the case of a non-Federal agency the Data Integrity Board of the source agency, determines in accordance with guidance issued by the Director of the Office of Management and Budget that—

(I) the information is limited to identification and amount of benefits paid by the source agency under a Federal benefit program; and

(II) there is a high degree of confidence that the information provided to the recipient agency is accurate;

(B) the individual receives a notice from the agency containing a statement of its findings and informing the individual of the opportunity to contest such findings; and

(C)(i) the expiration of any time period established for the program by statute or regulation for the individual to respond to that notice; or

(ii) in the case of a program for which no such period is established, the end of the 30-day period beginning on the date on which notice under subparagraph (B) is mailed or otherwise provided to the individual.

(2) Independent verification referred to in paragraph (1) requires investigation and confirmation of specific information relating to an individual that is used as a basis for an adverse action against the individual, including where applicable investigation and confirmation of—

(A) the amount of any asset or income involved;

(B) whether such individual actually has or had access to such asset or income for such individual's own use; and

(C) the period or periods when the individual actually had such asset or income.

(3) Notwithstanding paragraph (1), an agency may take any appropriate action otherwise prohibited by such paragraph if the agency determines that the public health or public safety may be adversely affected or significantly threatened during any notice period required by such paragraph.

(q) **Sanctions**.

(1) Notwithstanding any other provision of law, no source agency may disclose any record which is contained in a system of records to a recipient agency or non-Federal agency for a matching program if such source agency has reason to believe that the requirements of subsection (p), or any matching agreement entered into pursuant to subsection (o), or both, are not being met by such recipient agency.

(2) No source agency may renew a matching agreement unless—

(A) the recipient agency or non-Federal agency has certified that it has complied with the provisions of that agreement; and

(B) the source agency has no reason to believe that the certification is inaccurate.

(r) **Report on New Systems and Matching Programs**. Each agency that proposes to establish or make a significant change in a system of records or a matching program shall provide adequate advance notice of any such proposal (in duplicate) to the Committee on Government Operations of the House of Representatives, the Committee on Governmental Affairs of the Senate, and the Office of Management and Budget in order to permit an evaluation of the probable or potential effect of such proposal on the privacy or other rights of individuals.

(s) **Biennial Report**. The President shall biennially submit to the Speaker of the House of Representatives and the President pro tempore of the Senate a report—

(1) describing the actions of the Director of the Office of Management and Budget pursuant to section 6 of the Privacy Act of 1974 during the preceding 2 years;

(2) describing the exercise of individual rights of access and amendment under this section during such years;

(3) identifying changes in or additions to systems of records;

(4) containing such other information concerning administration of this section as may be necessary or useful to the Congress in reviewing the effectiveness of this section in carrying out the purposes of the Privacy Act of 1974.

(t) (1) **Effect of Other Laws**. No agency shall rely on any exemption contained in section 552 of this title to withhold from an individual any record which is otherwise accessible to such individual under the provisions of this section.

(2) No agency shall rely on any exemption in this section to withhold from an individual any record which is otherwise accessible to such individual under the provisions of section 552 of this title.

(u) **Data Integrity Boards**.

(1) Every agency conducting or participating in a matching program shall establish a Data Integrity Board to oversee and coordinate among the various components of such agency the agency's implementation of this section.

(2) Each Data Integrity Board shall consist of senior officials designated by the head of the agency, and shall include any senior official designated by the head of the agency as responsible for implementation of this section, and the inspector general of the agency, if any. The inspector general shall not serve as chairman of the Data Integrity Board.

(3) Each Data Integrity Board—

(A) shall review, approve, and maintain all written agreements for receipt or disclosure of agency records for matching programs to ensure compliance with subsection (o), and all relevant statutes, regulations, and guidelines;

(B) shall review all matching programs in which the agency has participated during the year, either as a source agency or recipient agency, determine compliance with applicable laws, regulations, guidelines, and agency agreements, and assess the costs and benefits of such programs;

(C) shall review all recurring matching programs in which the agency has participated during the year, either as a source agency or recipient agency, for continued justification for such disclosures;

(D) shall compile an annual report, which shall be submitted to the head of the agency and the Office of Management and Budget and made available to the public on request, describing the matching activities of the agency, including—

(i) matching programs in which the agency has participated as a source agency or recipient agency;

(ii) matching agreements proposed under subsection (o) that were disapproved by the Board;

(iii) any changes in membership or structure of the Board in the preceding year;

(iv) the reasons for any waiver of the requirement in paragraph (4) of this section for completion and submission of a cost-benefit analysis prior to the approval of a matching program;

(v) any violations of matching agreements that have been alleged or identified and any corrective action taken; and

(vi) any other information required by the Director of the Office of Management and Budget to be included in such report;

(E) shall serve as a clearinghouse for receiving and providing information on the accuracy, completeness, and reliability of records used in matching programs;

(F) shall provide interpretation and guidance to agency components and personnel on the requirements of this section for matching programs;

(G) shall review agency recordkeeping and disposal policies and practices for matching programs to assure compliance with this section; and

(H) may review and report on any agency matching activities that are not matching programs.

(4)(A) Except as provided in subparagraphs (B) and (C), a Data Integrity Board shall not approve any written agreement for a matching program unless the agency has completed and submitted to such Board a cost-benefit analysis of the proposed program and such analysis demonstrates that the program is likely to be cost effective.

(B) The Board may waive the requirements of subparagraph (A) of this paragraph if it determines in writing, in accordance with guidelines prescribed by the Director of the Office of Management and Budget, that a cost-benefit analysis is not required.

(C) A cost-benefit analysis shall not be required under subparagraph (A) prior to the initial approval of a written agreement for a matching program that is specifically required by statute. Any subsequent written agreement for such a program shall not be approved by the Data Integrity Board unless the agency has submitted a cost-benefit analysis of the program as conducted under the preceding approval of such agreement.

(5)(A) If a matching agreement is disapproved by a Data Integrity Board, any party to such agreement may appeal the disapproval to the Director of the Office of Management and Budget. Timely notice of the filing of such an appeal shall be provided by the Director of the Office of Management and Budget to the Committee on Governmental Affairs of the Senate and the Committee on Government Operations of the House of Representatives.

(B) The Director of the Office of Management and Budget may approve a matching agreement notwithstanding the disapproval of a Data Integrity Board if the Director determines that—

(i) the matching program will be consistent with all applicable legal, regulatory, and policy requirements;

(ii) there is adequate evidence that the matching agreement will be cost-effective; and

(iii) the matching program is in the public interest.

(C) The decision of the Director to approve a matching agreement shall not take effect until 30 days after it is reported to committees described in subparagraph (A).

(D) If the Data Integrity Board and the Director of the Office of Management and Budget disapprove a matching program proposed by the inspector general of an agency, the inspector general may report the disapproval to the head of the agency and to the Congress.

(6) In the reports required by paragraphs (3)(D), agency matching activities that are not matching programs may be reported on an aggregate basis, if and to the extent necessary to protect ongoing law enforcement or counterintelligence investigations.

(7) [Redesignated]

(v) **Office of Management and Budget Responsibilities**. The Director of the Office of Management and Budget shall—

(1) develop and, after notice and opportunity for public comment, prescribe guidelines and regulations for the use of agencies in implementing the provisions of this section; and

(2) provide continuing assistance to and oversight of the implementation of this section by agencies.

§ 552b. Open Meetings

(a) For purposes of this section—

(1) the term "agency" means any agency, as defined in section 552(e) of this title, headed by a collegial body composed of two or more individual members, a majority of whom are appointed to such position by the President with the advice and consent of the Senate, and any subdivision thereof authorized to act on behalf of the agency;

(2) the term "meeting" means the deliberations of at least the number of individual agency members required to take action on behalf of the agency where such deliberations determine or result in the joint conduct or disposition of official agency business, but does not include deliberations required or permitted by subsection (d) or (e); and

(3) the term "member" means an individual who belongs to a collegial body heading an agency.

(b) Members shall not jointly conduct or dispose of agency business other than in accordance with this section. Except as provided in subsection (c), every portion of every meeting of an agency shall be open to public observation.

(c) Except in a case where the agency finds that the public interest requires otherwise, the second sentence of subsection (b) shall not apply to any portion of an agency meeting, and the requirements of subsections (d) and (e) shall not apply to any information pertaining to such meeting otherwise required by this section to be disclosed to the public, where the agency properly determines that such portion or portions of its meeting or the disclosure of such information is likely to—

(1) disclose matters that are (A) specifically authorized under criteria established by an Executive order to be kept secret in the interests of national defense or foreign policy and (B) in fact properly classified pursuant to such Executive order;

(2) relate solely to the internal personnel rules and practices of an agency;

(3) disclose matters specifically exempted from disclosure by statute (other than section 552 of this title), provided that such statute (A) requires that the matters be withheld from the public in such a manner as to leave no discretion on the issue, or (B) establishes particular criteria for withholding or refers to particular types of matters to be withheld;

(4) disclose trade secrets and commercial or financial information obtained from a person and privileged or confidential;

(5) involve accusing any person of a crime, or formally censuring any person;

(6) disclose information of a personal nature where disclosure would constitute a clearly unwarranted invasion of personal privacy;

(7) disclose investigatory records compiled for law enforcement purposes, or information which if written would be contained in such records, but only to the extent that the production of such records or information would (A) interfere with enforcement proceedings, (B) deprive a person of a right to a fair trial or an impartial adjudication, (C) constitute an unwarranted invasion of personal privacy, (D) disclose the identity of a confidential source and, in the case of a record compiled by a criminal law enforcement authority in the course of a criminal investigation, or by an agency conducting a lawful national security intelligence investigation, confidential information furnished only by the confidential source, (E) disclose investigative techniques and procedures, or (F) endanger the life or physical safety of law enforcement personnel;

(8) disclose information contained in or related to examination, operating, or condition reports prepared by, on behalf of, or for the use of an agency responsible for the regulation or supervision of financial institutions;

(9) disclose information the premature disclosure of which would—

(A) in the case of an agency which regulates currencies, securities, commodities, or financial institutions, be likely to (i) lead to significant financial speculation in currencies, securities, or commodities, or (ii) significantly endanger the stability of any financial institution; or

(B) in the case of any agency, be likely to significantly frustrate implementation of a proposed agency action, except that subparagraph (B) shall not apply in any instance where the agency has already disclosed to the public the content or nature of its proposed action, or where the agency is required by law to make such disclosure on its own initiative prior to taking final agency action on such proposal; or

(10)   pecifically concern the agency's issuance of a subpena, or the agency's participation in a civil action or proceeding, an action in a foreign court or international tribunal, or an arbitration, or the initiation, conduct, or disposition by the agency of a particular case of formal agency adjudication pursuant to the procedures in section 554 of this title or otherwise involving a determination on the record after opportunity for a hearing.

(d) (1) Action under subsection (c) shall be taken only when a majority of the entire membership of the agency (as defined in subsection (a)(1)) votes to take such action. A separate vote of the agency members shall be taken with respect to each agency meeting a portion or portions of which are proposed to be closed to the public pursuant to subsection (c), or with respect to any information which is proposed to be withheld under subsection (c). A single vote may be taken with respect to a series of meetings, a portion or portions of which are proposed to be closed to the public, or with respect to any information concerning such series of meetings, so long as each meeting in such series involves the same particular matters and is scheduled to be held no more than thirty days after the initial meeting in such series. The vote of each agency member participating in such vote shall be recorded and no proxies shall be allowed.

(2) Whenever any person whose interests may be directly affected by a portion of a meeting requests that the agency close such portion to the public for any of the reasons referred to in paragraph (5), (6), or (7) of subsection (c), the agency, upon request of any one of its members, shall vote by recorded vote whether to close such meeting.

(3) Within one day of any vote taken pursuant to paragraph (1) or (2), the agency shall make publicly available a written copy of such vote reflecting the vote of each member on the question. If a portion of a meeting is to be closed to the public, the agency shall, within one day of the vote taken pursuant to paragraph (1) or (2) of this subsection, make publicly available a full written explanation of its action closing the portion together with a list of all persons expected to attend the meeting and their affiliation.

(4) Any agency, a majority of whose meetings may properly be closed to the public pursuant to paragraph (4), (8), (9)(A), or (10) of subsection (c), or any combination thereof, may provide by regulation for the closing of such meetings or portions thereof in the event that a majority of the members of the agency votes by recorded vote at the beginning of such meeting, or portion thereof, to close the exempt portion or portions of the meeting, and a copy of such vote, reflecting the vote of each member on the question, is made available to the public. The provisions of paragraphs (1), (2), and (3) of this subsection and subsection (e) shall not apply to any portion of a meeting to which such regulations apply: Provided, That the agency shall, except to the extent that such information

is exempt from disclosure under the provisions of subsection (c), provide the public with public announcement of the time, place, and subject matter of the meeting and of each portion thereof at the earliest practicable time.

(e) (1) In the case of each meeting, the agency shall make public announcement, at least one week before the meeting, of the time, place, and subject matter of the meeting, whether it is to be open or closed to the public, and the name and phone number of the official designated by the agency to respond to requests for information about the meeting. Such announcement shall be made unless a majority of the members of the agency determines by a recorded vote that agency business requires that such meeting be called at an earlier date, in which case the agency shall make public announcement of the time, place, and subject matter of such meeting, and whether open or closed to the public, at the earliest practicable time.

(2) The time or place of a meeting may be changed following the public announcement required by paragraph (1) only if the agency publicly announces such change at the earliest practicable time. The subject matter of a meeting, or the determination of the agency to open or close a meeting, or portion of a meeting, to the public, may be changed following the public announcement required by this subsection only if (A) a majority of the entire membership of the agency determines by a recorded vote that agency business so requires and that no earlier announcement of the change was possible, and (B) the agency publicly announces such change and the vote of each member upon such change at the earliest practicable time.

(3) Immediately following each public announcement required by this subsection, notice of the time, place, and subject matter of a meeting, whether the meeting is open or closed, any change in one of the preceding, and the name and phone number of the official designated by the agency to respond to requests for information about the meeting, shall also be submitted for publication in the Federal Register.

(f) (1) For every meeting closed pursuant to paragraphs (1) through (10) of subsection (c), the General Counsel or chief legal officer of the agency shall publicly certify that, in his or her opinion, the meeting may be closed to the public and shall state each relevant exemptive provision. A copy of such certification, together with a statement from the presiding officer of the meeting setting forth the time and place of the meeting, and the persons present, shall be retained by the agency. The agency shall maintain a complete transcript or electronic recording adequate to record fully the proceedings of each meeting, or portion of a meeting, closed to the public, except that in the case of a meeting, or portion of a meeting, closed to the public pursuant to paragraph (8), (9)(A), or (10) of subsection (c), the agency shall maintain either such a transcript or recording, or a set of minutes. Such minutes shall fully and clearly describe all matters discussed and shall provide a full and accurate summary of any actions taken, and the reasons therefor, including a description of each of the views expressed on any item and the record of any roll-call vote (reflecting the vote of each member on the question). All documents considered in connection with any action shall be identified in such minutes.

(2) The agency shall make promptly available to the public, in a place easily accessible to the public, the transcript, electronic recording, or minutes (as required by paragraph (1)) of the discussion of any item on the agenda, or of any item of the testimony of any witness received at the meeting, except for such item or items of such discussion or testimony as the agency determines to contain information which may be withheld under subsection (c). Copies of such transcript, or minutes, or a transcription of such recording disclosing the identity of each speaker, shall be furnished to any person at the actual cost of duplication or transcription. The agency shall maintain a complete verbatim copy of the transcript, a complete copy of the minutes, or a complete electronic recording of each meeting, or portion of a meeting, closed to the public, for a period of at least two years after such meeting, or until one year after the conclusion of any agency proceeding with respect to which the meeting or portion was held, whichever occurs later.

(g) Each agency subject to the requirements of this section shall, within 180 days after the date of enactment of this section, following consultation with the Office of the Chairman of the Administrative Conference of the United States and published notice in the Federal Register of at least thirty days and opportunity for written comment by any person, promulgate regulations to implement the requirements of subsections (b) through (f) of this section. Any person may bring a proceeding in the United States District Court for the District of Columbia to require an agency to promulgate such regulations if such agency has not promulgated such regulations within the time period specified herein. Subject to any limitations of time provided by law, any person may bring a proceeding in the United States Court of Appeals for the District of Columbia to set aside agency regulations issued pursuant to this subsection that are not in accord with the requirements of subsections (b) through (f) of this section and to require the promulgation of regulations that are in accord with such subsections.

(h) (1) The district courts of the United States shall have jurisdiction to enforce the requirements of subsections (b) through (f) of this section by declaratory judgment, injunctive relief, or other relief as may be appropriate. Such actions may be brought by any person against an agency prior to, or within sixty days after, the meeting out of which the violation of this section arises, except that if public announcement of such meeting is not initially provided by the agency in accordance with the requirements of this section, such action may be instituted pursuant to this section at any time prior to sixty days after any public announcement of such meeting. Such actions may be brought in the district court of the United States for the district in which the agency meeting is held or in which the agency in question has its headquarters, or in the District Court for the District of Columbia. In such actions a defendant shall serve his answer within thirty days after the service of the complaint. The burden is on the defendant to sustain his action. In deciding such cases the court may examine in camera any portion of the transcript, electronic recording, or minutes of a meeting closed to the public, and may take such additional evidence as it deems necessary. The court, having due regard for orderly administration and the public interest, as well as the interests of the parties, may grant such equitable relief as it deems appropriate, including granting an injunction against future violations of this section or ordering the agency to make available to the public such portion of the transcript, recording, or minutes of a meeting as is not authorized to be withheld under subsection (c) of this section.

(2) Any Federal court otherwise authorized by law to review agency action may, at the application of any person properly participating in the proceeding pursuant to other applicable law, inquire into violations by the agency of the requirements of this section and afford such relief as it deems appropriate. Nothing in this section authorizes any Federal court having jurisdiction solely on the basis of paragraph (1) to set aside, enjoin, or invalidate any agency action (other than an action to close a meeting or to withhold information under this section) taken or discussed at any agency meeting out of which the violation of this section arose.

(i)   The court may assess against any party reasonable attorney fees and other litigation costs reasonably incurred by any other party who substantially prevails in any action brought in accordance with the provisions of subsection (g) or (h) of this section, except that costs may be assessed against the plaintiff only where the court finds that the suit was initiated by the plaintiff primarily for frivolous or dilatory purposes. In the case of assessment of costs against an agency, the costs may be assessed by the court against the United States.

(j)   Each agency subject to the requirements of this section shall annually report to Congress regarding the following:

(1) The changes in the policies and procedures of the agency under this section that have occurred during the preceding 1-year period.

(2) A tabulation of the number of meetings held, the exemptions applied for to close meetings, and the days of public notice provided to close meetings.

(3) A brief description of litigation or formal complaints concerning the implementation of this section by the agency.

(4) A brief explanation of any changes in law that have affected the responsibilities of the agency under this section.

(k)   Nothing herein expands or limits the present rights of any person under section 552 of this title, except that the exemptions set forth in subsection (c) of this section shall govern in the case of any request made pursuant to section 552 to copy or inspect the transcripts, recordings, or minutes described in subsection (f) of this section. The requirements of chapter 33 of title 44, United States Code, shall not apply to the transcripts, recordings, and minutes described in subsection (f) of this section.

(l)   This section does not constitute authority to withhold any information from Congress, and does not authorize the closing of any agency meeting or portion thereof required by any other provision of law to be open.

(m) Nothing in this section authorizes any agency to withhold from any individual any record, including transcripts, recordings, or minutes required by this section, which is otherwise accessible to such individual under section 552a of this title.

§ 553.   Rule Making

(a)   This section applies, according to the provisions thereof, except to the extent that there is involved—

(1)   a military or foreign affairs function of the United States; or

(2)   a matter relating to agency management or personnel or to public property, loans, grants, benefits, or contracts.

(b)   General notice of proposed rule making shall be published in the Federal Register, unless persons subject thereto are named and either personally served or otherwise have actual notice thereof in accordance with law. The notice shall include—

(1)   a statement of the time, place, and nature of public rule making proceedings;

(2)   reference to the legal authority under which the rule is proposed; and

(3)   either the terms or substance of the proposed rule or a description of the subjects and issues involved. Except when notice or hearing is required by statute, this subsection does not apply—

(A)   to interpretative rules, general statements of policy, or rules of agency organization, procedure, or practice; or

(B)   when the agency for good cause finds (and incorporates the finding and a brief statement of reasons therefor in the rules issued) that notice and public procedure thereon are impracticable, unnecessary, or contrary to the public interest.

(c)   After notice required by this section, the agency shall give interested persons an opportunity to participate in the rule making through submission of written data, views, or arguments with or without opportunity for oral presentation. After consideration of the relevant matter presented, the agency shall incorporate in the rules adopted a concise general statement of their basis and purpose. When rules are required by statute to be made on the record after opportunity for an agency hearing, sections 556 and 557 of this title apply instead of this subsection.

(d)   The required publication or service of a substantive rule shall be made not less than 30 days before its effective date, except—

(1) a substantive rule which grants or recognizes an exemption or relieves a restriction;

(2) interpretative rules and statements of policy; or

(3) as otherwise provided by the agency for good cause found and published with the rule.

(e) Each agency shall give an interested person the right to petition for the issuance, amendment, or repeal of a rule.

§ 554. Adjudications

(a) This section applies, according to the provisions thereof, in every case of adjudication required by statute to be determined on the record after opportunity for an agency hearing, except to the extent that there is involved—

(1) a matter subject to a subsequent trial of the law and the facts de novo in a court;

(2) the selection or tenure of an employee, except an administrative law judge appointed under section 3105 of this title;

(3) proceedings in which decisions rest solely on inspections, tests, or elections;

(4) the conduct of military or foreign affairs functions;

(5) cases in which an agency is acting as an agent for a court; or

(6) the certification of worker representatives.

(b) Persons entitled to notice of an agency hearing shall be timely informed of—

(1) the time, place, and nature of the hearing;

(2) the legal authority and jurisdiction under which the hearing is to be held; and

(3) the matters of fact and law asserted. When private persons are the moving parties, other parties to the proceeding shall give prompt notice of issues controverted in fact or law; and in other instances agencies may by rule require responsive pleading. In fixing the time and place for hearings, due regard shall be had for the convenience and necessity of the parties or their representatives.

(c) The agency shall give all interested parties opportunity for—

(1) the submission and consideration of facts, arguments, offers of settlement, or proposals of adjustment when time, the nature of the proceeding, and the public interest permit; and

(2) to the extent that the parties are unable so to determine a controversy by consent, hearing and decision on notice and in accordance with sections 556 and 557 of this title.

(d) The employee who presides at the reception of evidence pursuant to section 556 of this title shall make the recommended decision or initial decision required by section 557 of this title, unless he becomes unavailable to the agency. Except to the extent required for the disposition of ex parte matters as authorized by law, such an employee may not—

(1) consult a person or party on a fact in issue, unless on notice and opportunity for all parties to participate; or

(2) be responsible to or subject to the supervision or direction of an employee or agent engaged in the performance of investigative or prosecuting functions for an agency. An employee or agent engaged in the performance of investigative or prosecuting functions for an agency in a case may not, in that or a factually related case, participate or advise in the decision, recommended decision, or agency review pursuant to section 557 of this title, except as witness or counsel in public proceedings. This subsection does not apply—

(A) in determining applications for initial licenses;

(B) to proceedings involving the validity or application of rates, facilities, or practices of public utilities or carriers; or

(C) to the agency or a member or members of the body comprising the agency.

(e)   The agency, with like effect as in the case of other orders, and in its sound discretion, may issue a declaratory order to terminate a controversy or remove uncertainty.

§ 555.   Ancillary Matters

(a)   This section applies, according to the provisions thereof, except as otherwise provided by this subchapter.

(b)   A person compelled to appear in person before an agency or representative thereof is entitled to be accompanied, represented, and advised by counsel or, if permitted by the agency, by other qualified representative. A party is entitled to appear in person or by or with counsel or other duly qualified representative in an agency proceeding. So far as the orderly conduct of public business permits, an interested person may appear before an agency or its responsible employees for the presentation, adjustment, or determination of an issue, request, or controversy in a proceeding, whether interlocutory, summary, or otherwise, or in connection with an agency function. With due regard for the convenience and necessity of the parties or their representatives and within a reasonable time, each agency shall proceed to conclude a matter presented to it. This subsection does not grant or deny a person who is not a lawyer the right to appear for or represent others before an agency or in an agency proceeding.

(c)   Process, requirement of a report, inspection, or other investigative act or demand may not be issued, made, or enforced except as authorized by law. A person compelled to submit data or evidence is entitled to retain or, on payment of lawfully prescribed costs, procure a copy or transcript thereof, except that in a nonpublic investigatory proceeding the witness may for good cause be limited to inspection of the official transcript of his testimony.

(d) Agency subpenas authorized by law shall be issued to a party on request and, when required by rules of procedure, on a statement or showing of general relevance and reasonable scope of the evidence sought. On contest, the court shall sustain the subpena or similar process or demand to the extent that it is found to be in accordance with law. In a proceeding for enforcement, the court shall issue an order requiring the appearance of the witness or the production of the evidence or data within a reasonable time under penalty of punishment for contempt in case of contumacious failure to comply.

(e) Prompt notice shall be given of the denial in whole or in part of a written application, petition, or other request of an interested person made in connection with any agency proceeding. Except in affirming a prior denial or when the denial is self-explanatory, the notice shall be accompanied by a brief statement of the grounds for denial.

§ 556. Hearings; Presiding Employees; Powers and Duties; Burden of Proof; Evidence; Record as Basis of Decision

(a) This section applies, according to the provisions thereof, to hearings required by section 553 or 554 of this title to be conducted in accordance with this section.

(b) There shall preside at the taking of evidence—

(1) the agency;

(2) one or more members of the body which comprises the agency; or

(3) one or more administrative law judges appointed under section 3105 of this title. This subchapter does not supersede the conduct of specified classes of proceedings, in whole or in part, by or before boards or other employees specially provided for by or designated under statute. The functions of presiding employees and of employees participating in decisions in accordance with section 557 of this title shall be conducted in an impartial manner. A presiding or participating employee may at any time disqualify himself. On the filing in good faith of a timely and sufficient affidavit of personal bias or other disqualification of a presiding or participating employee, the agency shall determine the matter as a part of the record and decision in the case.

(c) Subject to published rules of the agency and within its powers, employees presiding at hearings may—

(1) administer oaths and affirmations;

(2) issue subpenas authorized by law;

(3) rule on offers of proof and receive relevant evidence;

(4) take depositions or have depositions taken when the ends of justice would be served;

(5) regulate the course of the hearing;

(6) hold conferences for the settlement or simplification of the issues by consent of the parties or by the use of alternative means of dispute resolution as provided in subchapter IV of this chapter;

(7) inform the parties as to the availability of one or more alternative means of dispute resolution, and encourage use of such methods;

(8) require the attendance at any conference held pursuant to paragraph (6) of at least one representative of each party who has authority to negotiate concerning resolution of issues in controversy;

(9) dispose of procedural requests or similar matters;

(10) make or recommend decisions in accordance with section 557 of this title; and

(11) take other action authorized by agency rule consistent with this subchapter.

(d) Except as otherwise provided by statute, the proponent of a rule or order has the burden of proof. Any oral or documentary evidence may be received, but the agency as a matter of policy shall provide for the exclusion of irrelevant, immaterial, or unduly repetitious evidence. A sanction may not be imposed or rule or order issued except on consideration of the whole record or those parts thereof cited by a party and supported by and in accordance with the reliable, probative, and substantial evidence. The agency may, to the extent consistent with the interests of justice and the policy of the underlying statutes administered by the agency, consider a violation of section 557(d) of this title sufficient grounds for a decision adverse to a party who has knowingly committed such violation or knowingly caused such violation to occur. A party is entitled to present his case or defense by oral or documentary evidence, to submit rebuttal evidence, and to conduct such cross-examination as may be required for a full and true disclosure of the facts. In rule making or determining claims for money or benefits or applications for initial licenses an agency may, when a party will not be prejudiced thereby, adopt procedures for the submission of all or part of the evidence in written form.

(e) The transcript of testimony and exhibits, together with all papers and requests filed in the proceeding, constitutes the exclusive record for decision in accordance with section 557 of this title and, on payment of lawfully prescribed costs, shall be made available to the parties. When an agency decision rests on official notice of a material fact not appearing in the evidence in the record, a party is entitled, on timely request, to an opportunity to show the contrary.

§ 557. Initial Decisions; Conclusiveness; Review by Agency; Submissions by Parties; Contents of Decisions; Record

(a) This section applies, according to the provisions thereof, when a hearing is required to be conducted in accordance with section 556 of this title.

(b) When the agency did not preside at the reception of the evidence, the presiding employee or, in cases not subject to section 554 (d) of this title, an employee qualified to preside at hearings pursuant to section 556 of this title, shall initially decide the case unless the agency requires, either in specific cases or by general rule, the entire record to be certified to it for decision. When the presiding employee makes an initial decision, that decision then becomes the decision of the agency without further proceedings unless there is an appeal to, or review on motion of, the agency within time provided by rule. On appeal from or review of the initial decision, the agency has all the powers which it would have in making the initial decision except as it may limit the issues on notice or by rule. When the agency makes the decision without having presided at the reception of the evidence, the presiding employee or an employee qualified to preside at hearings pursuant to section 556 of this title shall first recommend a decision, except that in rule making or determining applications for initial licenses—

(1) instead thereof the agency may issue a tentative decision or one of its responsible employees may recommend a decision; or

(2) this procedure may be omitted in a case in which the agency finds on the record that due and timely execution of its functions imperatively and unavoidably so requires.

(c) Before a recommended, initial, or tentative decision, or a decision on agency review of the decision of subordinate employees, the parties are entitled to a reasonable opportunity to submit for the consideration of the employees participating in the decisions—

(1) proposed findings and conclusions; or

(2) exceptions to the decisions or recommended decisions of subordinate employees or to tentative agency decisions; and

(3) supporting reasons for the exceptions or proposed findings or conclusions. The record shall show the ruling on each finding, conclusion, or exception presented. All decisions, including initial, recommended, and tentative decisions, are a part of the record and shall include a statement of—

(A) findings and conclusions, and the reasons or basis therefor, on all the material issues of fact, law, or discretion presented on the record; and

(B) the appropriate rule, order, sanction, relief, or denial thereof.

(d) (1) In any agency proceeding which is subject to subsection (a) of this section, except to the extent required for the disposition of ex parte matters as authorized by law—

(A) no interested person outside the agency shall make or knowingly cause to be made to any member of the body comprising the agency, administrative law judge, or other employee who is or may reasonably be expected to be involved in the decisional process of the proceeding, an ex parte communication relevant to the merits of the proceeding;

(B) no member of the body comprising the agency, administrative law judge, or other employee who is or may reasonably be expected to be involved in the decisional process of the proceeding, shall make or knowingly cause to be made to any interested person outside the agency an ex parte communication relevant to the merits of the proceeding;

(C) a member of the body comprising the agency, administrative law judge, or other employee who is or may reasonably be expected to be involved in the decisional process of such proceeding who receives, or who makes or knowingly causes to be made, a communication prohibited by this subsection shall place on the public record of the proceeding:

(i) all such written communications;

(ii) memoranda stating the substance of all such oral communications; and

(iii) all written responses, and memoranda stating the substance of all oral responses, to the materials described in clauses (i) and (ii) of this subparagraph;

(D) upon receipt of a communication knowingly made or knowingly caused to be made by a party in violation of this subsection, the agency, administrative law judge, or other employee presiding at the hearing may, to the extent consistent with the interests of justice and the policy of the underlying statutes, require the party to show cause why his claim or interest in the proceeding should not be dismissed, denied, disregarded, or otherwise adversely affected on account of such violation; and

(E) the prohibitions of this subsection shall apply beginning at such time as the agency may designate, but in no case shall they begin to apply later than the time at which a proceeding is noticed for hearing unless the person responsible for the communication has knowledge that it will be noticed, in which case the prohibitions shall apply beginning at the time of his acquisition of such knowledge.

(2) This subsection does not constitute authority to withhold information from Congress.

§ 558. Imposition of Sanctions; Determination of Applications for Licenses; Suspension, Revocation, and Expiration of Licenses

(a) This section applies, according to the provisions thereof, to the exercise of a power or authority.

(b) A sanction may not be imposed or a substantive rule or order issued except within jurisdiction delegated to the agency and as authorized by law.

(c) When application is made for a license required by law, the agency, with due regard for the rights and privileges of all the interested parties or adversely affected persons and within a reasonable time, shall set and complete proceedings required to be conducted in accordance with sections 556 and 557 of this title or other proceedings required by law and shall make its decision. Except in cases of willfulness or those in which public health, interest, or safety requires otherwise, the withdrawal, suspension, revocation, or annulment of a license is lawful only if, before the institution of agency proceedings therefore, the licensee has been given—

(1) notice by the agency in writing of the facts or conduct which may warrant the action; and

(2) opportunity to demonstrate or achieve compliance with all lawful requirements. When the licensee has made timely and sufficient application for a renewal or a new license in accordance with agency rules, a license with reference to an activity of a continuing nature does not expire until the application has been finally determined by the agency.

§ 559.   Effect on Other Laws; Effect of Subsequent Statute

This subchapter, chapter 7, and sections 1305, 3105, 3344, 4301 (2)(E), 5372, and 7521 of this title, and the provisions of section 5335(a)(B) of this title that relate to administrative law judges, do not limit or repeal additional requirements imposed by statute or otherwise recognized by law. Except as otherwise required by law, requirements or privileges relating to evidence or procedure apply equally to agencies and persons. Each agency is granted the authority necessary to comply with the requirements of this subchapter through the issuance of rules or otherwise. Subsequent statute may not be held to supersede or modify this subchapter, chapter 7, sections 1305, 3105, 3344 , 4301(2)(E), 5372, or 7521 of this title, or the provisions of section 5335(a)(B) of this title that relate to administrative law judges, except to the extent that it does so expressly.

SUBCHAPTER 3: Negotiated Rule Making Procedure
(sections 561 to 570) (omitted)

SUBCHAPTER 4: Alternative Means of Dispute Resolution
(sections 571 to 584) (omitted)

CHAPTER 6
Analysis of Regulatory Functions
(sections 601-612) (omitted)

CHAPTER 7
Judicial Review

Sec.
701.   Application; Definitions.
702.   Right of Review.
703.   Form and Venue of Proceeding.

704.   Actions Reviewable.

705.   Relief Pending Review.

706.   Scope of Review.

§ 701. Application; Definitions

(a) This chapter applies, according to the provisions thereof, except to the extent that—

(1) statutes preclude judicial review; or

(2) agency action is committed to agency discretion by law.

(b) For the purpose of this chapter—

(1) "agency" means each authority of the Government of the United States, whether or not it is within or subject to review by another agency, but does not include—

(A) the Congress;

(B) the courts of the United States;

(C) the governments of the territories or possessions of the United States;

(D) the government of the District of Columbia;

(E) agencies composed of representatives of the parties or of representatives of organizations of the parties to the disputes determined by them;

(F) courts martial and military commissions;

(G) military authority exercised in the field in time of war or in occupied territory; or

(H) functions conferred by sections 1738, 1739, 1743, and 1744 of title 12; chapter 2 of title 41; or sections 1622, 1884, 1891-1902, and former section 1641(b)(2), of title 50, appendix; and

(2) "person", "rule", "order", "license", "sanction", "relief", and "agency action" have the meanings given them by section 551 of this title.

§ 702. Right of Review

A person suffering legal wrong because of agency action, or adversely affected or aggrieved by agency action within the meaning of a relevant statute, is entitled to judicial review thereof. An action in a court of the United States seeking relief other than money damages and stating a claim that an agency or an officer or employee thereof acted or failed to act in an official capacity or under color of legal authority shall not be dismissed nor relief therein be denied on the ground that it is against the United States or that the United States is an indispensable party. The United States may be named as a defendant in any such action, and a judgment or decree may be entered against the United States: *Provided,* That any mandatory or injunctive decree shall specify the Federal officer or officers (by name or by title), and their successors in office, personally responsible for compliance. Nothing herein (1) affects other limitations on judicial review or the power or duty of the court to dismiss any action or deny relief on any other appropriate legal or equitable ground; or (2) confers authority to grant relief if any other statute that grants consent to suit expressly or impliedly forbids the relief which is sought.

§ 703. Form and Venue of Proceeding

The form of proceeding for judicial review is the special statutory review proceeding relevant to the subject matter in a court specified by statute or, in the absence or inadequacy thereof, any applicable form of legal action, including actions for declaratory judgments or writs of prohibitory or mandatory injunction or habeas corpus, in a court of competent jurisdiction. If no special statutory review proceeding is applicable, the action for judicial review may be brought against the United States, the agency by its official title, or the appropriate officer. Except to the extent that prior, adequate, and exclusive opportunity for judicial review is provided by law, agency action is subject to judicial review in civil or criminal proceedings for judicial enforcement.

§ 704. Actions Reviewable

Agency action made reviewable by statute and final agency action for which there is no other adequate remedy in a court are subject to judicial review. A preliminary, procedural, or intermediate agency action or ruling not directly reviewable is subject to review on the review of the final agency action. Except as otherwise expressly required by statute, agency action otherwise final is final for the purposes of this section whether or not there has been presented or determined an application for a declaratory order, for any form of reconsideration, or, unless the agency otherwise requires by rule and provides that the action meanwhile is inoperative, for an appeal to superior agency authority.

§ 705. Relief Pending Review

When an agency finds that justice so requires, it may postpone the effective date of action taken by it, pending judicial review. On such conditions as may be required and to the extent necessary to prevent irreparable injury, the reviewing court, including the court to which a case may be taken on appeal from or on application for certiorari or other writ to a reviewing court, may issue all necessary and appropriate process to postpone the effective date of an agency action or to preserve status or rights pending conclusion of the review proceedings.

§ 706. Scope of Review

To the extent necessary to decision and when presented, the reviewing court shall decide all relevant questions of law, interpret constitutional and statutory provisions, and determine the meaning or applicability of the terms of an agency action. The reviewing court shall—

(1) compel agency action unlawfully withheld or unreasonably delayed; and

(2) hold unlawful and set aside agency action, findings, and conclusions found to be—

(A) arbitrary, capricious, an abuse of discretion, or otherwise not in accordance with law;

(B) contrary to constitutional right, power, privilege, or immunity;

(C) in excess of statutory jurisdiction, authority, or limitations, or short of statutory right;

(D) without observance of procedure required by law;

(E) unsupported by substantial evidence in a case subject to sections 556 and 557 of this title or otherwise reviewed on the record of an agency hearing provided by statute; or

(F) unwarranted by the facts to the extent that the facts are subject to trial de novo by the reviewing court. In making the foregoing determinations, the court shall review the whole record or those parts of it cited by a party, and due account shall be taken of the rule of prejudicial error.

CHAPTER 8
Congressional Review of Agency Rule Making
(Sections 801 to 808) (omitted)

Provisions Relating to Administrative Law Judges
(Sections 1215, 1305, 3105, 3344, 3502, 4301, 5335, 5372, 7521, and 7532) (omitted)

Appendix C

The Constitution of the United States of America[a]

We the People of the United States, in Order to form a more perfect Union, establish Justice, insure domestic Tranquility, provide for the common defence, promote the general Welfare, and secure the Blessings of Liberty to ourselves and our Posterity, do ordain and establish this Constitution for the United States of America.

Article I

Section 1. All legislative Powers herein granted shall be vested in a Congress of the United States, which shall consist of a Senate and House of Representatives.

Section 2. The House of Representatives shall be composed of Members chosen every second Year by the People of the several States, and the Electors in each State shall have the Qualifications requisite for Electors of the most numerous Branch of the State Legislature.

No Person shall be a Representative who shall not have attained to the Age of twenty five Years, and been seven Years a Citizen of the United States, and who shall not, when elected, be an Inhabitant of that State in which he shall be chosen.

Representatives and direct Taxes shall be apportioned among the several States which may be included within this Union, according to their respective Numbers, *which shall be determined by adding to the whole Number of free Persons, including those bound to Service for a Term of Years, and excluding Indians not taxed, three fifths of all other Persons.*[1] The actual Enumeration shall be made within three Years after the first Meeting of the Congress of the United States, and within every subsequent Term of ten

---

[a] Italics are used to indicate provisions that have been modified by subsequent amendments.

[1] See Amendment XIV.

Years, in such Manner as they shall by Law direct. The Number of Representatives shall not exceed one for every thirty Thousand, but each State shall have at Least one Representative; and until such enumeration shall be made, the State of New Hampshire shall be entitled to chuse three, Massachusetts eight, Rhode Island and Providence Plantations one, Connecticut five, New York six, New Jersey four, Pennsylvania eight, Delaware one, Maryland six, Virginia ten, North Carolina five, South Carolina five and Georgia three.

When vacancies happen in the Representation from any State, the Executive Authority thereof shall issue Writs of Election to fill such Vacancies.

The House of Representatives shall chuse their Speaker and other Officers; and shall have the sole Power of Impeachment.

Section 3. The Senate of the United States shall be composed of two Senators from each State, *chosen by the Legislature thereof,*[2] for six Years; and each Senator shall have one Vote.

Immediately after they shall be assembled in Consequence of the first Election, they shall be divided as equally as may be into three Classes. The Seats of the Senators of the first Class shall be vacated at the Expiration of the second Year, of the second Class at the Expiration of the fourth Year, and of the third Class at the Expiration of the sixth Year, so that one third may be chosen every second Year; *and if Vacancies happen by Resignation, or otherwise, during the Recess of the Legislature of any State, the Executive thereof may make temporary Appointments until the next Meeting of the Legislature, which shall then fill such Vacancies.*[3]

No person shall be a Senator who shall not have attained to the Age of thirty Years, and been nine Years a Citizen of the United States, and who shall not, when elected, be an Inhabitant of that State for which he shall be chosen.

The Vice-President of the United States shall be President of the Senate, but shall have no Vote, unless they be equally divided.

The Senate shall chuse their other Officers, and also a President pro tempore, in the absence of the Vice-President, or when he shall exercise the Office of President of the United States.

The Senate shall have the sole Power to try all Impeachments. When sitting for that Purpose, they shall be on Oath or Affirmation. When the President of the United States is tried, the Chief Justice shall preside: And no Person shall be convicted without the Concurrence of two thirds of the Members present.

Judgment in Cases of Impeachment shall not extend further than to removal from Office, and disqualification to hold and enjoy any Office of honor, Trust or Profit under the United States: but the Party convicted shall

---

[2] See Amendment XVII.

[3] Ibid.

nevertheless be liable and subject to Indictment, Trial, Judgment and Punishment, according to Law.

Section 4. The Times, Places and Manner of holding Elections for Senators and Representatives, shall be prescribed in each State by the Legislature thereof; but the Congress may at any time by Law make or alter such Regulations, except as to the Place of Chusing Senators.

The Congress shall assemble at least once in every Year, and such Meeting shall be on the first Monday in December, unless they shall by Law appoint a different Day.[4]

Section 5. Each House shall be the Judge of the Elections, Returns and Qualifications of its own Members, and a Majority of each shall constitute a Quorum to do Business; but a smaller number may adjourn from day to day, and may be authorized to compel the Attendance of absent Members, in such Manner, and under such Penalties as each House may provide.

Each House may determine the Rules of its Proceedings, punish its Members for disorderly Behavior, and, with the Concurrence of two thirds, expel a Member.

Each House shall keep a Journal of its Proceedings, and from time to time publish the same, excepting such Parts as may in their Judgment require Secrecy; and the Yeas and Nays of the Members of either House on any question shall, at the Desire of one fifth of those Present, be entered on the Journal.

Neither House, during the Session of Congress, shall, without the Consent of the other, adjourn for more than three days, nor to any other Place than that in which the two Houses shall be sitting.

Section 6. The Senators and Representatives shall receive a Compensation for their Services, to be ascertained by Law, and paid out of the Treasury of the United States. They shall in all Cases, except Treason, Felony and Breach of the Peace, be privileged from Arrest during their Attendance at the Session of their respective Houses, and in going to and returning from the same; and for any Speech or Debate in either House, they shall not be questioned in any other Place.

No Senator or Representative shall, during the Time for which he was elected, be appointed to any civil Office under the Authority of the United States which shall have been created, or the Emoluments whereof shall have been increased during such time; and no Person holding any Office under the United States, shall be a Member of either House during his Continuance in Office.

Section 7. All bills for raising Revenue shall originate in the House of Representatives; but the Senate may propose or concur with Amendments as on other Bills.

---

[4] See Amendment XX.

Every Bill which shall have passed the House of Representatives and the Senate, shall, before it become a Law, be presented to the President of the United States; If he approve he shall sign it, but if not he shall return it, with his Objections to that House in which it shall have originated, who shall enter the Objections at large on their Journal, and proceed to reconsider it. If after such Reconsideration two thirds of that House shall agree to pass the Bill, it shall be sent, together with the Objections, to the other House, by which it shall likewise be reconsidered, and if approved by two thirds of that House, it shall become a Law. But in all such Cases the Votes of both Houses shall be determined by Yeas and Nays, and the Names of the Persons voting for and against the Bill shall be entered on the Journal of each House respectively. If any Bill shall not be returned by the President within ten Days (Sundays excepted) after it shall have been presented to him, the Same shall be a Law, in like Manner as if he had signed it, unless the Congress by their Adjournment prevent its Return, in which Case it shall not be a Law.

Every Order, Resolution, or Vote to which the Concurrence of the Senate and House of Representatives may be necessary (except on a question of Adjournment) shall be presented to the President of the United States; and before the Same shall take Effect, shall be approved by him, or being disapproved by him, shall be repassed by two thirds of the Senate and House of Representatives, according to the Rules and Limitations prescribed in the Case of a Bill.

Section 8. The Congress shall have Power to lay and collect Taxes, Duties, Imposts and Excises, to pay the Debts and provide for the common Defence and general Welfare of the United States; but all Duties, Imposts and Excises shall be uniform throughout the United States;

To borrow money on the credit of the United States;

To regulate Commerce with foreign Nations, and among the several States, and with the Indian Tribes;

To establish an uniform Rule of Naturalization, and uniform Laws on the subject of Bankruptcies throughout the United States;

To coin Money, regulate the Value thereof, and of foreign Coin, and fix the Standard of Weights and Measures;

To provide for the Punishment of counterfeiting the Securities and current Coin of the United States;

To establish Post Offices and Post Roads;

To promote the Progress of Science and useful Arts, by securing for limited Times to Authors and Inventors the exclusive Right to their respective Writings and Discoveries;

To constitute Tribunals inferior to the supreme Court;

To define and punish Piracies and Felonies committed on the high Seas, and Offenses against the Law of Nations;

To declare War, grant Letters of Marque and Reprisal, and make Rules concerning Captures on Land and Water;

To raise and support Armies, but no Appropriation of Money to that Use shall be for a longer Term than two Years;

To provide and maintain a Navy;

To make Rules for the Government and Regulation of the land and naval Forces;

To provide for calling forth the Militia to execute the Laws of the Union, suppress Insurrections and repel Invasions;

To provide for organizing, arming, and disciplining the Militia, and for governing such Part of them as may be employed in the Service of the United States, reserving to the States respectively, the Appointment of the Officers, and the Authority of training the Militia according to the discipline prescribed by Congress;

To exercise exclusive Legislation in all Cases whatsoever, over such District (not exceeding ten Miles square) as may, by Cession of particular States, and the acceptance of Congress, become the Seat of the Government of the United States, and to exercise like Authority over all Places purchased by the Consent of the Legislature of the State in which the Same shall be, for the Erection of Forts, Magazines, Arsenals, dock-Yards, and other needful Buildings; And

To make all Laws which shall be necessary and proper for carrying into Execution the foregoing Powers, and all other Powers vested by this Constitution in the Government of the United States, or in any Department or Officer thereof.

Section 9. The Migration or Importation of such Persons as any of the States now existing shall think proper to admit, shall not be prohibited by the Congress prior to the Year one thousand eight hundred and eight, but a tax or duty may be imposed on such Importation, not exceeding ten dollars for each Person.

The privilege of the Writ of Habeas Corpus shall not be suspended, unless when in Cases of Rebellion or Invasion the public Safety may require it.

No Bill of Attainder or ex post facto Law shall be passed.

No capitation, or other direct, Tax shall be laid, unless in Proportion to the Census or Enumeration herein before directed to be taken.

No Tax or Duty shall be laid on Articles exported from any State.

No Preference shall be given by any Regulation of Commerce or Revenue to the Ports of one State over those of another: nor shall Vessels bound to, or from, one State, be obliged to enter, clear, or pay Duties in another.

No Money shall be drawn from the Treasury, but in Consequence of Appropriations made by Law; and a regular Statement and Account of the Receipts and Expenditures of all public Money shall be published from time to time.

No Title of Nobility shall be granted by the United States: And no Person holding any Office of Profit or Trust under them, shall, without the Consent of the Congress, accept of any present, Emolument, Office, or Title, of any kind whatever, from any King, Prince or foreign State.

Section 10. No State shall enter into any Treaty, Alliance, or Confederation; grant Letters of Marque and Reprisal; coin Money; emit Bills of Credit; make any Thing but gold and silver Coin a Tender in Payment of Debts; pass any Bill of Attainder, ex post facto Law, or Law impairing the Obligation of Contracts, or grant any Title of Nobility.

No State shall, without the Consent of the Congress, lay any Imposts or Duties on Imports or Exports, except what may be absolutely necessary for executing its inspection Laws: and the net Produce of all Duties and Imposts, laid by any State on Imports or Exports, shall be for the Use of the Treasury of the United States; and all such Laws shall be subject to the Revision and Control of the Congress.

No State shall, without the Consent of Congress, lay any duty of Tonnage, keep Troops, or Ships of War in time of Peace, enter into any Agreement or Compact with another State, or with a foreign Power, or engage in War, unless actually invaded, or in such imminent Danger as will not admit of delay.

Article II

Section 1. The executive Power shall be vested in a President of the United States of America. He shall hold his Office during the Term of four Years, and, together with the Vice-President chosen for the same Term, be elected, as follows:

Each State shall appoint, in such Manner as the Legislature thereof may direct, a Number of Electors, equal to the whole Number of Senators and Representatives to which the State may be entitled in the Congress: but no Senator or Representative, or Person holding an Office of Trust or Profit under the United States, shall be appointed an Elector.

The Electors shall meet in their respective States, and vote by Ballot for two persons, of whom one at least shall not lie an Inhabitant of the same State with themselves. And they shall make a List of all the Persons voted for, and of the Number of Votes for each; which List they shall sign and certify, and transmit sealed to the Seat of the Government of the United States, directed to the President of the Senate. The President of the Senate shall, in the Presence of the Senate and House of Representatives, open all the Certificates, and the Votes shall then be counted. The Person having the greatest Number of Votes shall be the President, if such Number be a Majority of the whole Number of Electors appointed; and if there be more than one who have such Majority, and have an equal Number of Votes, then the House of Representatives shall immediately chuse by Ballot one of them for Presi-

dent; and if no Person have a Majority, then from the five highest on the List the said House shall in like Manner chuse the President. But in chusing the President, the Votes shall be taken by States, the Representation from each State having one Vote; a quorum for this Purpose shall consist of a Member or Members from two thirds of the States, and a Majority of all the States shall be necessary to a Choice. In every Case, after the Choice of the President, the Person having the greatest Number of Votes of the Electors shall be the Vice-President. But if there should remain two or more who have equal Votes, the Senate shall chuse from them by Ballot the Vice-President.[5]

The Congress may determine the Time of chusing the Electors, and the Day on which they shall give their Votes; which Day shall be the same throughout the United States.

No person except a natural born Citizen, or a Citizen of the United States, at the time of the Adoption of this Constitution, shall be eligible to the Office of President; neither shall any Person be eligible to that Office who shall not have attained to the Age of thirty-five Years, and been fourteen Years a Resident within the United States.

In Case of the Removal of the President from Office, or of his Death, Resignation, or Inability to discharge the Powers and Duties of the said Office, the same shall devolve on the Vice-President, and the Congress may by Law provide for the Case of Removal, Death, Resignation or Inability, both of the President and Vice-President, declaring what Officer shall then act as President, and such Officer shall act accordingly, until the Disability be removed, or a President shall be elected.

The President shall, at stated Times, receive for his Services, a Compensation, which shall neither be increased nor diminished during the Period for which he shall have been elected, and he shall not receive within that Period any other Emolument from the United States, or any of them.

Before he enter on the Execution of his Office, he shall take the following Oath or Affirmation:—"I do solemnly swear (or affirm) that I will faithfully execute the Office of President of the United States, and will to the best of my Ability, preserve, protect and defend the Constitution of the United States."

Section 2. The President shall be Commander in Chief of the Army and Navy of the United States, and of the Militia of the several States, when called into the actual Service of the United States; he may require the Opinion, in writing, of the principal Officer in each of the executive Departments, upon any subject relating to the Duties of their respective Offices, and he shall have Power to Grant Reprieves and Pardons for Offenses against the United States, except in Cases of Impeachment.

He shall have Power, by and with the Advice and Consent of the Senate, to make Treaties, provided two thirds of the Senators present concur; and he shall nominate, and by and with the Advice and Consent of the Senate,

---

[5] See Amendment XII.

shall appoint Ambassadors, other public Ministers and Consuls, Judges of the supreme Court, and all other Officers of the United States, whose Appointments are not herein otherwise provided for, and which shall be established by Law: but the Congress may by Law vest the Appointment of such inferior Officers, as they think proper, in the President alone, in the Courts of Law, or in the Heads of Departments.

The President shall have Power to fill up all Vacancies that may happen during the Recess of the Senate, by granting Commissions which shall expire at the End of their next Session.

Section 3. He shall from time to time give to the Congress Information of the State of the Union, and recommend to their Consideration such Measures as he shall judge necessary and expedient; he may, on extraordinary Occasions, convene both Houses, or either of them, and in Case of Disagreement between them, with Respect to the Time of Adjournment, he may adjourn them to such Time as he shall think proper; he shall receive Ambassadors and other public Ministers; he shall take Care that the Laws be faithfully executed, and shall Commission all the Officers of the United States.

Section 4. The President, Vice-President and all civil Officers of the United States, shall be removed from Office on Impeachment for, and Conviction of, Treason, Bribery, or other high Crimes and Misdemeanors.

Article III

Section 1. The judicial Power of the United States, shall be vested in one supreme Court, and in such inferior Courts as the Congress may from time to time ordain and establish. The Judges, both of the supreme and inferior Courts, shall hold their Offices during good Behavior, and shall, at stated Times, receive for their Services a Compensation which shall not be diminished during their Continuance in Office.

Section 2. The judicial Power shall extend to all Cases, in Law and Equity, arising under this Constitution, the Laws of the United States, and Treaties made, or which shall be made, under their Authority;—to all Cases affecting Ambassadors, other public Ministers and Consuls;—to all Cases of admiralty and maritime Jurisdiction;—to Controversies to which the United States shall be a Party;—to Controversies between two or more States;—*between a State and Citizens of another State;*[6]—between Citizens of different States;—between Citizens of the same State claiming Lands under Grants of different States, *and between a State, or the Citizens thereof, and foreign States, Citizens or Subjects.*[7]

In all Cases affecting Ambassadors, other public Ministers and Consuls, and those in which a State shall be Party, the supreme Court shall have original Jurisdiction. In all the other Cases before mentioned, the supreme

---

[6] See Amendment XI.

[7] Ibid.

Court shall have appellate Jurisdiction, both as to Law and Fact, with such Exceptions, and under such Regulations as the Congress shall make.

Trial of all Crimes, except in Cases of Impeachment, shall be by Jury; and such Trial shall be held in the State where the said Crimes shall have been committed; but when not committed within any State, the Trial shall be at such Place or Places as the Congress may by Law have directed.

Section 3. Treason against the United States, shall consist only in levying War against them, or in adhering to their Enemies, giving them Aid and Comfort. No Person shall be convicted of Treason unless on the Testimony of two Witnesses to the same overt Act, or on Confession in open Court.

The Congress shall have power to declare the Punishment of Treason, but no Attainder of Treason shall work Corruption of Blood, or Forfeiture except during the Life of the Person attainted.

Article IV

Section 1. Full Faith and Credit shall be given in each State to the public Acts, Records, and judicial Proceedings of every other State. And the Congress may by general Laws prescribe the Manner in which such Acts, Records and Proceedings shall be proved, and the Effect thereof.

Section 2. The Citizens of each State shall be entitled to all Privileges and Immunities of Citizens in the several States.

A Person charged in any State with Treason, Felony, or other Crime, who shall flee from Justice, and be found in another State, shall on demand of the executive Authority of the State from which he fled, be delivered up, to be removed to the State having Jurisdiction of the Crime.

No Person held to Service or Labour in one State, under the Laws thereof, escaping into another, shall, in Consequence of any Law or Regulation therein, be discharged from such Service or Labour, But shall be delivered up on Claim of the Party to whom such Service or Labour may be due.[8]

Section 3. New States may be admitted by the Congress into this Union; but no new States shall be formed or erected within the Jurisdiction of any other State; nor any State be formed by the Junction of two or more States, or parts of States, without the Consent of the Legislatures of the States concerned as well as of the Congress.

The Congress shall have Power to dispose of and make all needful Rules and Regulations respecting the Territory or other Property belonging to the United States; and nothing in this Constitution shall be so construed as to Prejudice any Claims of the United States, or of any particular State.

Section 4. The United States shall guarantee to every State in this Union a Republican Form of Government, and shall protect each of them

---

[8] See Amendment XIII.

against Invasion; and on Application of the Legislature, or of the Executive (when the Legislature cannot be convened) against domestic Violence.

Article V

The Congress, whenever two thirds of both Houses shall deem it necessary, shall propose Amendments to this Constitution, or, on the Application of the Legislatures of two thirds of the several States, shall call a Convention for proposing Amendments, which, in either Case, shall be valid to all Intents and Purposes, as part of this Constitution, when ratified by the Legislatures of three fourths of the several States, or by Conventions in three fourths thereof, as the one or the other Mode of Ratification may be proposed by the Congress; Provided that no Amendment which may be made prior to the Year One thousand eight hundred and eight shall in any Manner affect the first and fourth Clauses in the Ninth Section of the first Article; and that no State, without its Consent, shall be deprived of its equal Suffrage in the Senate.

Article VI

All Debts contracted and Engagements entered into, before the Adoption of this Constitution, shall be as valid against the United States under this Constitution, as under the Confederation.

This Constitution, and the Laws of the United States which shall be made in Pursuance thereof; and all Treaties made, or which shall be made, under the Authority of the United States, shall be the supreme Law of the Land; and the Judges in every State shall be bound thereby, any Thing in the Constitution or Laws of any State to the Contrary notwithstanding.

The Senators and Representatives before mentioned, and the Members of the several State Legislatures, and all executive and judicial Officers, both of the United States and of the several States, shall be bound by Oath or Affirmation, to support this Constitution; but no religious Test shall ever be required as a Qualification to any Office or public Trust under the United States.

Article VII

The Ratification of the Conventions of nine States, shall be sufficient for the Establishment of this Constitution between the States so ratifying the Same.

Done in Convention by the Unanimous Consent of the States present the Seventeenth Day of September in the Year of our Lord one thousand seven hundred and Eighty seven and of the Independence of the United States of America the Twelfth. In Witness whereof We have hereunto subscribed our Names.

*   *   *

Articles in addition to, and amendment of, the Constitution of the United States of America, proposed by Congress, and ratified by the several States, pursuant to the Fifth Article of the original Constitution.

Amendment I[9]

Congress shall make no law respecting an establishment of religion, or prohibiting the free exercise thereof; or abridging the freedom of speech, or of the press; or the right of the people peaceably to assemble, and to petition the Government for a redress of grievances.

Amendment II

A well regulated Militia, being necessary to the security of a free State, the right of the people to keep and bear Arms, shall not be infringed.

Amendment III

No Soldier shall, in time of peace be quartered in any house, without the consent of the Owner, nor in time of war, but in a manner to be prescribed by law.

Amendment IV

The right of the people to be secure in their persons, houses, papers, and effects, against unreasonable searches and seizures, shall not be violated, and no Warrants shall issue, but upon probable cause, supported by Oath or affirmation, and particularly describing the place to be searched, and the persons or things to be seized.

Amendment V

No person shall be held to answer for a capital, or otherwise infamous crime, unless on a presentment or indictment of a Grand Jury, except in cases arising in the land or naval forces, or in the Militia, when in actual service in time of War or public danger; nor shall any person be subject for the same offense to be twice put in jeopardy of life or limb; nor shall be compelled in any criminal case to be a witness against himself, nor be deprived of life, liberty, or property, without due process of law; nor shall private property be taken for public use, without just compensation.

Amendment VI

In all criminal prosecutions, the accused shall enjoy the right to a speedy and public trial, by an impartial jury of the State and district wherein the crime shall have been committed, which district shall have been previously

---

[9] Ratification of the first ten amendments was completed December 15, 1791.

ascertained by law, and to be informed of the nature and cause of the accusation; to be confronted with the witnesses against him; to have compulsory process for obtaining witnesses in his favor, and to have the Assistance of Counsel for his defence.

Amendment VII

In Suits at common law, where the value in controversy shall exceed twenty dollars, the right of trial by jury shall be preserved, and no fact tried by a jury, shall be otherwise re-examined in any Court of the United States, than according to the rules of the common law.

Amendment VIII

Excessive bail shall not be required, nor excessive fines imposed, nor cruel and unusual punishments inflicted.

Amendment IX

The enumeration in the Constitution, of certain rights, shall not be construed to deny or disparage others retained by the people.

Amendment X

The powers not delegated to the United States by the Constitution, nor prohibited by it to the States, are reserved to the States respectively, or to the people.

Amendment XI [1798]

The Judicial power of the United States shall not be construed to extend to any suit in law or equity, commenced or prosecuted against one of the United States by Citizens of another State, or by Citizens or Subjects of any Foreign State.

Amendment XII [1804]

The Electors shall meet in their respective states, and vote by ballot for President and Vice-President, one of whom, at least, shall not be an inhabitant of the same state with themselves; they shall name in their ballots the person voted for as President, and in distinct ballots the person voted for as Vice-President, and they shall make distinct lists of all persons voted for as President, and of all persons voted for as Vice-President and of the number of votes for each, which lists they shall sign and certify, and transmit sealed to the seat of the government of the United States, directed to the President of the Senate;—The President of the Senate shall, in the presence of the Senate and House of Representatives, open all the certificates and the votes shall then be counted;—The person having the greatest Number of votes for President, shall be the President, if such number be a majority of the whole number of Electors appointed; and if no person have such majority, then from the persons having the highest numbers not exceeding three on the list of those voted for as President, the House of Representatives shall choose immediately, by ballot, the President. But in choosing the President, the votes shall be taken by states, the representation from each state having one vote; a quorum for this purpose shall consist of a member or members from two-thirds of the states, and a majority of all the states shall be necessary to a choice. And if the House of Representatives shall not choose a President whenever the right of choice shall devolve upon them, *before the fourth day of March next following*,[10] then the Vice-President shall act as President, as in the case of the death or other constitutional disability of the President.—The person having the greatest number of votes as Vice-President, shall be the Vice-President, if such number be a majority of the whole number of Electors appointed, and if no person have a majority, then from the two highest numbers on the list, the Senate shall choose the Vice-President; a quorum for the purpose shall consist of two-thirds of the whole number of Senators, and a majority of the whole number shall be necessary to a choice. But no person constitutionally ineligible to the office of President shall be eligible to that of Vice-President of the United States.

Amendment XIII [1865]

Section 1. Neither slavery nor involuntary servitude, except as a punishment for crime whereof the party shall have been duly convicted, shall exist within the United States, or any place subject to their jurisdiction.

Section 2. Congress shall have power to enforce this article by appropriate legislation.

Amendment XIV [1868]

Section 1. All persons born or naturalized in the United States, and subject to the jurisdiction thereof, are citizens of the United States and of the State wherein they reside. No State shall make or enforce any law which shall abridge the privileges or immunities of citizens of the United States; nor shall any State deprive any person of life, liberty, or property, without due process of law; nor deny to any person within its jurisdiction the equal protection of the laws.

Section 2. Representatives shall be apportioned among the several States according to their respective numbers, counting the whole number of persons in each State, excluding Indians not taxed. But when the right to vote at any election for the choice of electors for President and Vice-President of the United States, Representatives in Congress, the Executive and Judicial officers of a State, or the members of the Legislature thereof, is denied to any of the male inhabitants of such State, being twenty-one years of age, and citizens of the United States, or in any way abridged, except for participation in rebellion, or other crime, the basis of representation therein

---

[10] See Amendment XX.

shall be reduced in the proportion which the number of such male citizens shall bear to the whole number of male citizens twenty-one years of age in such State.

Section 3. No person shall be a Senator or Representative in Congress, or elector of President and Vice-President, or hold any office, civil or military, under the United States, or under any State, who, having previously taken an oath, as a member of Congress, or as an officer of the United States, or as a member of any State legislature, or as an executive or judicial officer of any State, to support the Constitution of the United States, shall have engaged in insurrection or rebellion against the same, or given aid or comfort to the enemies thereof. But Congress may by a vote of two-thirds of each House, remove such disability.

Section 4. The validity of the public debt of the United States, authorized by law, including debts incurred for payment of pensions and bounties for services in suppressing insurrection or rebellion, shall not be questioned. But neither the United States nor any State shall assume or pay any debt or obligation incurred in aid of insurrection or rebellion against the United States, or any claim for the loss or emancipation of any slave; but all such debts, obligations and claims shall be held illegal and void.

Section 5. The Congress shall have power to enforce, by appropriate legislation, the provisions of this article.

Amendment XV [1870]

Section 1. The right of citizens of the United States to vote shall not be denied or abridged by the United States or by any State on account of race, color, or previous condition of servitude.

Section 2. The Congress shall have power to enforce this article by appropriate legislation.

Amendment XVI [1913]

The Congress shall have power to lay and collect taxes on incomes, from whatever source derived, without apportionment among the several States, and without regard to any census or enumeration.

Amendment XVII [1913]

The Senate of the United States shall be composed of two Senators from each State, elected by the people thereof, for six years; and each Senator shall have one vote. The electors in each State shall have the qualifications requisite for electors of the most numerous branch of the State legislatures.

When vacancies happen in the representation of any State in the Senate, the executive authority of such State shall issue writs of election to fill such vacancies: Provided, That the legislature of any State may empower the executive thereof to make temporary appointments until the people fill the vacancies by election as the legislature may direct.

This amendment shall not be so construed as to affect the election or term of any Senator chosen before it becomes valid as part of the Constitution.

Amendment XVIII [1919]

Section 1. *After one year from the ratification of this article the manufacture, sale, or transportation of intoxicating liquors within, the importation thereof into, or the exportation thereof from the United States and all territory subject to the jurisdiction thereof for beverage purposes is hereby prohibited.*

Section 2. *The Congress and the several States shall have concurrent power to enforce this article by appropriate legislation.*

Section 3. *This article shall be inoperative unless it shall have been ratified as an amendment to the Constitution by the legislatures of the several States, as provided in the Constitution, within seven years from the date of the submission hereof to the States by the Congress.*[11]

Amendment XIX [1920]

The right of citizens of the United States to vote shall not be denied or abridged by the United States or by any State on account of sex.

Congress shall have power to enforce this article by appropriate legislation.

Amendment XX [1933]

Section 1. The terms of the President and Vice-President shall end at noon on the 20th day of January, and the terms of Senators and Representatives at noon on the 3d day of January, of the years in which such terms would have ended if this article had not been ratified; and the terms of their successors shall then begin.

Section 2. The Congress shall assemble at least once in every year, and such meeting shall begin at noon on the 3d day of January, unless they shall by law appoint a different day.

Section 3. If, at the time fixed for the beginning of the term of the President, the President elect shall have died, the Vice-President elect shall become President. If a President shall not have been chosen before the time fixed for the beginning of his term, or if the President elect shall have failed to qualify, then the Vice-President elect shall act as President until a President shall have qualified; and the Congress may by law provide for the case wherein neither a President elect nor a Vice-President elect shall have qualified, declaring who shall then act as President, or the manner in which one who is to act shall be selected, and such person shall act accordingly until a President or Vice-President shall have qualified.

---

[11] Repealed by Amendment XXI.

Section 4. The Congress may by law provide for the case of the death of any of the persons from whom the House of Representatives may choose a President whenever the right of choice shall have devolved upon them, and for the case of the death of any of the persons from whom the Senate may choose a Vice-President whenever the right of choice shall have devolved upon them.

Section 5. Sections 1 and 2 shall take effect on the 15th day of October following the ratification of this article.

Section 6. This article shall be inoperative unless it shall have been ratified as an amendment to the Constitution by the legislatures of three-fourths of the several States within seven years from the date of its submission.

Amendment XXI [1933]

Section 1. The eighteenth article of amendment to the Constitution of the United States is hereby repealed.

Section 2. The transportation or importation into any State, Territory, or possession of the United States for delivery or use therein of intoxicating liquors, in violation of the laws thereof, is hereby prohibited.

Section 3. The article shall be inoperative unless it shall have been ratified as an amendment to the Constitution by conventions in the several States, as provided in the Constitution, within seven years from the date of the submission hereof to the States by the Congress.

Amendment XXII [1951]

Section 1. No person shall be elected to the office of the President more than twice, and no person who has held the office of President, or acted as President, for more than two years of a term to which some other person was elected President shall be elected to the office of the President more than once. But this Article shall not apply to any person holding the office of President, when this Article was proposed by the Congress, and shall not prevent any person who may be holding the office of President, or acting as President, during the term within which this Article becomes operative from holding the office of President or acting as President during the remainder of such term.

Section 2. This article shall be inoperative unless it shall have been ratified as an amendment to the Constitution by the legislatures of three-fourths of the several States within seven years from the date of its submission to the States by the Congress.

Amendment XXIII [1961]

Section 1. The District constituting the seat of Government of the United States shall appoint in such manner as the Congress may direct: A number of electors of President and Vice-President equal to the whole number of Senators and Representatives in Congress to which the District would be entitled if it were a State, but in no event more than the least populous State; they shall be in addition to those appointed by the States, but they shall be considered, for the purposes of the election of President and Vice-President, to be electors appointed by a State; and they shall meet in the District and perform such duties as provided by the twelfth article of amendment.

Section 2. The Congress shall have power to enforce this article by appropriate legislation.

Amendment XXIV [1964]

Section 1. The right of citizens of the United States to vote in any primary or other election for President or Vice-President, for electors for President or Vice-President, or for Senator or Representative in Congress, shall not be denied or abridged by the United States or any State by reason of failure to pay any poll tax or other tax.

Section 2. The Congress shall have power to enforce this article by appropriate legislation.

Amendment XXV [1967]

Section 1. In case of the removal of the President from office or of his death or resignation, the Vice-President shall become President.

Section 2. Whenever there is a vacancy in the office of the Vice-President, the President shall nominate a Vice-President who shall take office upon confirmation by a majority vote of both Houses of Congress.

3. Whenever the President transmits to the President pro tempore of the Senate and the Speaker of the House of Representatives his written declaration that he is unable to discharge the powers and duties of his office, and until he transmits to them a written declaration to the contrary, such powers and duties shall be discharged by the Vice-President as Acting President.

4. Whenever the Vice-President and a majority of either the principal officers of the executive departments or of such other body as Congress may by law provide, transmit to the President pro tempore of the Senate and the Speaker of the House of Representatives their written declaration that the President is unable to discharge the powers and duties of his office, the Vice-President shall immediately assume the powers and duties of the office as Acting President.

Thereafter, when the President transmits to the President pro tempore of the Senate and the Speaker of the House of Representatives his written declaration that no inability exists, he shall resume the powers and duties of his office unless the Vice-President and a majority of either the principal officers of the executive department or of such other body as Congress may by law provide, transmit within four days to the President pro tempore of the Senate and the Speaker of the House of Representatives their written declaration that the President is unable to discharge the powers and duties of his office. Thereupon Congress shall decide the issue, assembling within forty eight hours for that purpose if not in session. If the Congress, within twenty one days after receipt of the latter written declaration, or, if Congress is not in session, within twenty one days after Congress is required to assemble, determines by two thirds vote of both Houses that the President is unable to discharge the powers and duties of his office, the Vice-President shall continue to discharge the same as Acting President; otherwise, the President shall resume the powers and duties of his office.

Amendment XXVI [1971]

Section 1. The right of citizens of the United States, who are eighteen years of age or older, to vote shall not be denied or abridged by the United States or by any State on account of age.

Section 2. The Congress shall have power to enforce this article by appropriate legislation.

Amendment XXVII [1992]

No law, varying the compensation for the services of the Senators and Representatives, shall take effect, until an election of Representatives shall have intervened.

Index

adjudication, 8, 119–20, 173–74, 176–77, 200–3;
    and policy making, 195
administrative law:
    aspects, 10, 12, 43;
    vs. criminal law, 120;
    history, 3–4, 22–25, 44–48
Administrative Procedure Act (APA), 6, 12;
    history, 25–27, 29, 34, 273–74;
    and judicial review, 77, 80–81, 220;
    role of, 29–30, 32–33, 37–39, 41–43;
    and rules, 147–49, 153
asset forfeiture, 184–85

Brennan, William J., 82, 125, 202, 219
bubble concept, 114–15, 165–66
Burger, Warren, 55, 57, 65–66, 69, 71
Bush, George W., 145–46, 162, 170, 265

Clinton, Bill, 35, 71, 103, 162, 169, 265, 273
Code of Federal Regulations (CFR), 145–46, 154
Congress, role of , 34–35, 167–69, 170
court cases, analysis and citation, 16–19

Davis, Kenneth Culp, 4, 27 ,47, 53, 79, 86, 94, 166–67, 218
discretion, 9, 120, 205–6, 218–19

Environmental Protection Agency (EPA), 3, 61, 114, 165–66
estoppel, 207–8, 212, 218, 234
executive privilege, 261, 272–73

Federal Register (FR), 145–46, 148, 154, 206, 208
Federal Tort Claims Act (FTCA), 30, 34, 219, 235, 240–43, 255, 258–60, 273
Federal Trade Commission v. American Tobacco Co., 124
Fiorina, 34
Frankfurter, Felix, 23, 45–46, 78, 208
Freedom of Information Act (FOIA), 34, 261–62, 265–66, 273–74
Freund, Ernst, 23, 45, 219–20

General Accounting Office (GAO), 36, 70, 169
Goodnow, Frank, 23, 44
government, structure of, 40–42, 51–54, 56–57, 69–70

Gramm-Rudman-Hollings. *See* Balanced Budget and Emergency Deficit Control Act

Holmes, Oliver Wendell, 174, 234

Immigration and Naturalization Service (INS), 145–46, 155
Interstate Commerce Commission (ICC), 21, 32, 54

Jaffe, Louis, 47, 78, 80, 86, 104
judicial review, 7–8, 77–80, 82, 86, 114; threshold questions, 93–95, 98, 102–4

Legislative Reorganization Act, 28, 30, 32, 34
legislative veto, 65, 69
liability. *See* torts
Line-Item Veto Act, 71, 103

Marshall, Thurgood, 125, 137, 202

National Labor Relations Board (NLRB), 3–4, 24, 94, 195, 200, 202

Occupational Safety and Health Administration (OSHA), 5, 40, 55–56, 170
Office of Management and Budget (OMB), 35–36, 70–71, 169–71
ombudsmen, 228–29

Pierce, Richard J., Jr., 5–6, 47, 102–3, 114, 194, 218
President's Committee on Administrative Management (PCAM), 26, 30–31, 33, 37
Privacy Act, 261, 266–67

Reagan, Ronald, 35, 162, 265
Regulating Business by Independent Commission, 27
regulations. *See* rules
Rehnquist, William, 16, 55–58, 61, 125, 137, 142, 152, 169
Roosevelt, Franklin, 23–24, 26, 28, 30–31, 46
rule making, 119, 152–57, 162–67; vs. adjudication, 147–48, 172–73, 195, 200; and Congress, 167–68; and the courts, 172; presidential oversight, 171; types of, 155
rules, 8, 145, 147; types of, 148–49

Scalia, Antonin, 16, 48, 61, 109, 159, 242
Schwartz, Bernard, 27, 47–48, 86
Second Treatise on Civil Government, 56
Securities and Exchange Commission (SEC), 4, 24
stationary source. *See* bubble concept
subpoena power, 121, 136, 138
sunshine acts, 271–72

torts, 233–35, 238–45, 250–51, 255–60

Walter-Logan bill, 26, 32
warrants, 136, 138